Henry Davis Minot

The Land-Birds and Game-Birds of New England

With Descriptions of the Birds, their Nests and Eggs, their Habits and Notes

THE

LAND-BIRDS AND GAME-BIRDS

OF

NEW ENGLAND

WITH

DESCRIPTIONS OF THE BIRDS, THEIR NESTS AND EGGS,
THEIR HABITS AND NOTES.

WITH ILLUSTRATIONS.

BY

H. D. MINOT.

"To him who in the love of Nature holds
"Communion with her visible forms, she speaks
"A various language;"
   BRYANT'S THANATOPSIS.

SALEM, MASS.
NATURALISTS' AGENCY.
BOSTON: ESTES & LAURIAT.
1877.

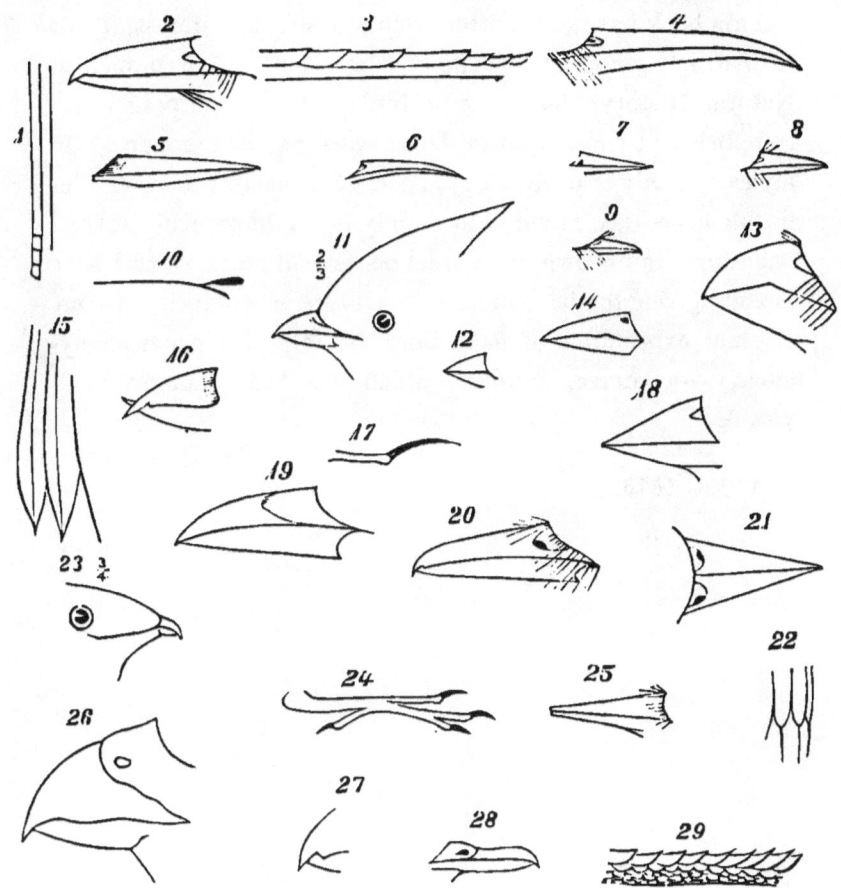

1. Booted tarsus of a Robin. 2. Bill of a Robin. 3. Scutellate tarsus of the Brown Thrush. 4. Bill of the Brown Thrush. 5. Bill of a nuthatch. 6. Bill of a creeper. 7. Bill of a warbler; genus *Helminthophaga*; 8, *Dendrœca*; 9. *Myiodioctes*. 10. Wing-feather of the Cedar-bird, with horny appendage. 11. Head of a Cedar-bird, with crest raised. 12. Bill of the Goldfinch. 13. Bill of the Rose-breasted Grosbeak. 14. Bill of the Sharp-tailed Finch. 15. Tail-feathers of the same bird. 16. Bill of a crossbill. 17. Hind-toe and claw of the Snow Bunting. 18. Bill of the Red-winged Blackbird. 19. Bill of the Canada Jay. 20. Bill of the Great Crested Flycatcher; (21.) as seen from above. 22. "Mucronate" tail-feathers of the Chimney Swift. 23. Head of the Chimney Swift. 24. "Syndactyle" foot of the Kingfisher. 25. Bill of the Downy Woodpecker. 26. Raptorial bill (genus *Accipiter*). 27. Tip of bill, genus *Falco*. 28. Bill of a pigeon. 29. Tarsus of a pigeon.

This book has been written from a desire to interest, if not to instruct, young people in that most attractive branch of Natural History, the study of birds. If this purpose is accomplished, I trust that its deficiencies may be pardoned. In my early study of ornithology, I felt great need of some similar book; hence my attempt to supply it. I have made several quotations in my own name from occasional notes which I have already given to the public. This is in accordance with my original expectation of publishing the following pages anonymously — a course, however, which has been thought inadvisable.

H. D. Minot.

Nov. 1st, 1876.

CONTENTS.

	PAGE.
Preface,	vii
Introduction,	1
§ A. Ornithology and Oölogy,	1
§ § B–G. Collecting Eggs,	4
§ H. Packing Eggs,	7
§ I. Blowing Eggs,	8
§ J. Cleaning and Mending Eggs,	11
§ K. Arrangement of Eggs,	11
§ L. Cabinet,	12
§ M. Nesting,	13
§ N. Birds' Homes,	14
§ O. Laying of Eggs,	15
§ P. Desertion,	16
§ Q. Exigencies,	17
§ R. Advice,	17
§ S. The Study of Birds,	18
§ T. Details of Structure; Terms of Description,	19
§ U. Measurements,	21
§ V, W. Classification; Scientific Names,	21
Land-birds and Game-birds of New England,	25
Chapter I. Order *Passeres*,	27
§ 1. Thrushes (*Turdidæ*),	28
§ 2. Bluebirds (*Saxicolidæ*),	50
§ 3. Sylvias (*Sylviidæ*),	53
§ 4. Titmice (*Paridæ*),	58
§ 5. Nuthatches (*Sittidæ*),	63
§ 6. Creepers (*Certhiidæ*),	68
§ 7. Wrens (*Troglodytidæ*),	70
§ 8. Wagtails (*Motacillidæ*),	79
§ 9. Warblers (*Sylvicolidæ*),	80
§ 10. Tanagers (*Tanagridæ*),	133
§ 11. Waxwings (*Ampelidæ*),	137
§ 12. Swallows (*Hirundinidæ*),	140

(v)

Chapter I. § 13. Vireos (*Vireonidæ*), . . . 151
§ 14. Shrikes (*Laniidæ*), ... 161
§ 15. Finches (*Fringillidæ*), . . . 166
§ 16. Larks (*Alaudidæ*), ... 237
§ 17. Starlings (*Icteridæ*), . . . 240
§ 18. Crows and jays (*Corvidæ*), . . 262
§ 19. Flycatchers (*Tyrannidæ*), . . 272

Chapter II. Order *Picariæ*, ... 293
§ 20. Goatsuckers (*Caprimulgidæ*), . . 294
§ 21. Swifts (*Cypselidæ*), ... 299
§ 22. Hummingbirds (*Trochilidæ*), . . 301
§ 23. Kingfishers (*Alcedinidæ*), . . 305
§ 24. Cuckoos (*Cuculidæ*), . . . 307
§ 25. Woodpeckers (*Picidæ*), . . . 311

Chapter III. Order *Raptores*, ... 326
§ 26. Owls (*Strigidæ*), ... 327
§ 27. Hawks and eagles (*Falconidæ*), . 345
§ 28. American vultures (*Cathartidæ*), . 375

Chapter IV. Order *Columbæ*, ... 377
§ 29. Pigeons and doves (*Columbidæ*), . 377

Chapter V. The Game-birds, ... 386
§ 30. Grouse (*Tetraonidæ*), . . . 386
§ 31. Partridges (*Perdicidæ*), . . . 393
§ 32. Snipe, etc. (*Scolopacidæ*), . . 399

Appendix, ... 413
   A. Ornithological Calendar for E. Massachusetts, 413
   B. Distribution of the Birds of New England, . 419
   C. A Key to the Eggs of Massachusetts, . . 423
   D. A Key to the Land-birds of New England, . 430
   E. Colorations peculiar to Young Birds, . . 439
        Or to Mature Birds in the Winter-season, . 439
   F. Additions and Corrections, ... 443
   G. Abstract of the Game-laws of Massachusetts, 444

Indices. 445
  Index to English Names (with references), . . 445
  Index to Scientific Names (with authorities and accent), 454

PREFACE.

This volume has been written to fill a place hitherto vacant in ornithological literature. The works of Wilson,[1] Audubon,[2] and Nuttall,[3] are costly, and rarely offered for sale, having been in a great measure superseded by modern authors. The recent and most complete work on American Ornithology,[4] that of Messrs. Baird, Brewer, and Ridgway, is also costly. Mr. Samuels' book on the "Birds of New England and Adjacent States"[5] has been thought too expensive to be within the reach of all, and more or less inaccurate and incomplete. Dr. Coues' admirable "Key to North American Birds,"[6] which is probably the best book of reference for collectors, and students of *inanimate birds*, treats merely of structure, classification, and specific descriptions. The same author's "Field Ornithology,"[7] and Mr. Maynard's "Naturalist's Guide,"[8] have also been

---

[1] "American Ornithology." Wilson. 9 vols. Philadelphia, 1814. Brought down by Ord to 1827. Also 4 volumes by Bonaparte, of the Birds not given by Wilson. Philadelphia, 1833.

[2] a. "Ornithological Biography." Audubon. 1838. b. Enlarged to "Birds of America" in 1844.

[3] "A Manual of the Ornithology of the United States and Canada." Nuttall. 1832. 1840.

[4] "North American Birds." Baird, Brewer, and Ridgway. Little, Brown, & Co., Boston, 1874.

[5] "Birds," or "Ornithology and Oölogy," "of New England (and Adjacent States)." E. A. Samuels. 1867.

[6] "Key to North American Birds," with a list of fossil birds. Coues. Naturalists' Agency, Salem, Mass.

[7] "Field Ornithology," with "a Check List of North American Birds."* Coues. Naturalists' Agency, Salem, Mass.

*The check-list has been published separately. The older Smithsonian list may be obtained from the Naturalist's Agency, Salem, Mass. To the above-mentioned books of reference may be added various local catalogues, and the first volume, lately published, of "Life-histories of the Birds of Eastern Pennsylvania, by Thomas G. Gentry."

[8] "The Naturalist's Guide," "with a complete catalogue of the birds of Eastern Massachusetts," and notes relative to their migrations, etc. C. J. Maynard. Fields, Osgood, & Co., Boston, 1870.

written for collectors, being chiefly manuals of taxidermy. The former, so far as it extends, is the fuller of the two. The author of this ornithological biography has endeavored to make it inexpensive, trustworthy, original, and not a compilation. He is aware that it is incomplete, treating only of the land-birds and game-birds, which are, of all, however, the most accessible to a majority of persons, the most numerous, and certainly the most generally interesting. He hopes, however, that should this volume be favorably received, some naturalist will undertake the biography of the wading and swimming birds, which he himself is incapable of doing, not having had opportunities to make sufficient observations. This volume may be found further incomplete, and he hopes therefore that criticisms and corrections will be freely made, that into a second edition, should there be one, he may incorporate additional facts. That he might not be, or seem guilty of plagiarism, he has written his biographies before reading those of others, and has afterwards consulted Wilson, etc., for such interesting facts as were unmentioned by himself. These borrowed statements, or passages quoted for their intrinsic value, have been invariably attributed to their authors, or placed in quotation-marks.[*] Sometimes, however, in spite of these precautions, he has employed much the same words as other writers, in describing the same facts. The biographies of the game-birds have been contributed by a friend, except those of the Canada and Pinnated Grouse.

The author has endeavored to mention in detail the ordinary or minor notes of various birds, since these are often more satisfactorily characteristic than musical notes, which are usually heard during a limited portion of the year. He has, moreover, endeavored, when possible, to convey an idea of several songs

---

[*] In the case of a few rare birds, the author has satisfied himself with corroborating the statements of others, instead of making statements based entirely upon his own authority and experience. He has not hesitated, however, to state *very general facts*, which he cannot personally attest, such as that vultures feed chiefly on carrion, etc. These cases are principally confined to remarks on distribution and habitat.

through the medium of words, but he has generally been obliged to employ other means, since it is difficult to do the former satisfactorily. It is probable that, were a dozen persons asked to express verbally any music of this kind, they would each employ different syllables. Many birds have two or three easily distinguishable combinations of musical sounds, or in different districts of the country have songs which are very distinct. The notes of many warblers, particularly those occurring in Massachusetts as migrants only, need to be learned and studied more than those of any other group of our *avifauna*. The author does not pretend to have treated these completely or satisfactorily, the less so that he has lost several memoranda. The warblers sing, however, during their migrations in spring, particularly in the early morning, more than many naturalists suppose. Mr. Allen, in the preface to his "Notes on Some of the Rarer Birds of Massachusetts," makes the following admirable and instructive remarks on the variation in birds' songs, distributions, etc.

"Only by knowing thoroughly the fauna of a locality can the subsequent changes in it, induced by its becoming more densely settled, or by other causes, be traced. As is well known, the mammalian and bird faunæ of all the older settled parts of the United States are vastly different from what they were two hundred years ago. These changes consist mainly in the great decrease in numbers of the representatives of all the larger species, not a few of which are already extirpated where they were formerly common; a few of the smaller species of both classes have doubtless increased in numbers. Two causes operate unfavorably upon the larger ones; the disforesting of the country and the sporting propensities of the people, everything large enough to be shot, whether useful or otherwise, being considered as legitimate game."

"Many of the water-fowl that are now only transient visitors, as the Canada Goose, the several species of Merganser, Teals, Black Duck and Mallard, undoubtedly once bred in this state, as did also the Wild Turkey and the Prairie Hen."

"In comparatively recent times, geologically speaking, probably other causes, as climatic, have been operating to effect a gradual northward migration, in certain species at least. These changes are of great interest, not only generally, but in a scientific point of view, and we shall be able to trace them and their causes only by comparing, from time to time, exhaustive faunal records of the same localities.

"In a district so little diversified as that portion of Massachusetts lying east of the Connecticut River, it is perhaps a little unexpected that marked discrepancies should occur in the observations made at adjoining localities by equally competent naturalists, in respect to the relative abundance of certain species. As every experienced observer must have noticed that the birds of passage, as many of the Warblers especially, vary greatly in numbers in different years, and in the time occupied by them in passing a given locality, it is less surprising that at different points they should vary in abundance the same year. Among the birds that regularly breed in the district in question, there are some that are not equally common at all points."

"Birds, as probably other animals, are not quite so invariable in their habits as has been commonly supposed, nor in the precise character of their notes and songs, or the situation and materials of which they compose their nests. Hence one should not rashly question the accounts given by usually reliable authorities, because in particular instances they do not accord with their own observations. Neither should differences in habits, in song, etc., be taken as infallible evidence of a difference of species."

"How universally the Chipping Sparrow (*Spizella socialis*) breeds in trees, and generally at an elevation of several feet, is well known, but several authentic instances of this bird's nesting on the ground have come to my knowledge, one of which I myself discovered. Variations of this character in other species are of occasional occurrence, examples of which have doubtless been met with by every experienced collector.

"The materials which birds select in the construction of their nests are well known to vary in different localities; the greater care exhibited by some species to secure a soft warm lining at the north that are much less precautious in this respect at the south, is already a recorded fact. Aside from this, the abundance of certain available materials occurring at only particular localities gives a marked character to the nests there built, which serves to distinguish them from those from other points. Some of the Thrushes, for instance, make use of a peculiar kind of moss at some localities that elsewhere, from its absence, are compelled to substitute for it fine grass or dry leaves. At Ipswich, on Cape Cod, and perhaps generally in the immediate vicinity of the sea, the Purple Grackles (*Quiscalus versicolor*) and Red-winged Blackbirds (*Agelœus phœniceus*), and in fact numerous other species, in building their nests often use little else than dry eel-grass or 'sea-wrack,' which results in nest-structures widely different in appearance from those of their relatives residing in the interior. Every egg-collector is aware of the wide variations eggs of the same set may present, not only in the markings and in the tint of the ground color, but in size and form, and especially how wide these differences sometimes are in eggs of different birds of the same species. Also how different the behavior of the bird is when its nest is approached, in some cases the parents appearing almost utterly regardless of their own safety in their anxiety for their eggs or helpless young, while other parents of the same species quietly witness the robbing of their nest at a safe distance, and evince no extraordinary emotion. Those who have witnessed this, and have also watched the behavior of birds when undisturbed in their quiet retreats, will grant, I think, the same diversity of disposition and temperament to obtain among birds that is seen in man himself.

"In respect to the songs of birds, who that has attentively listened to the singing of different Robins, Wood Thrushes or Purple Finches, has not detected great differences in the vocal powers of rival songsters of the same species? Different individuals of some species, especially among the Warblers, sing so differently that the expert field ornithologist is often puzzled to recognize them; especially is this so in the Black and White Creeper (*Mniotilta varia*) and the Black-throated Green Warbler (*Dendrœca virens*). But the strangest example of this sort I have noticed I think was the case of an Oriole (*Icterus Baltimore*) that I heard at Ipswich last season. So different were its notes from the common notes of the Baltimore that I failed entirely to refer them to that bird till I saw its author."

"Aside from such unusual variations as this, which we may consider as accidental, birds of unquestionably the same species, as the Crow, the Blue Jay, the Towhe[10] and others, at remote localities, as New England, Florida, Iowa, etc., often possess either general differences in their notes and song, easily recognizable, or certain notes at one of these localities never heard at the others, or an absence of some that are elsewhere familiar. This is perhaps not a strange fact, since it is now so well known that birds of the same species present certain well marked variations in size according to the latitude and elevation above the sea of the locality at which they were born, and that they vary considerably, though doubtless within a certain range, in many structural points at one and the same locality. In other words, since it is known that all the different individuals of a species are not exactly alike, as though all were cast in the same die, as some naturalists appear to have believed.

"Certain irregularities in the breeding range of birds have also come to light. It is perhaps not remarkable that a pair of birds of species that regularly breed in northern New England should now and then pass the summer and rear their young in the southern part, as has been the case in certain known instances in the Snow Bird (*Junco hyemalis*), the Pine Finch (*Chrysomitris pinus*), and the White-throated Sparrow (*Zonotrichia albicollis*); but it is otherwise with the Snow Bunting (*Plectrophanes nivalis*), which rarely breeds south of Labrador, of which there is a single well authenticated instance

---

[10] It is to be remarked that a variety of this bird has recently been found in Florida.

of its breeding near Springfield. The casual visits of northern birds in winter, which we may suppose sometimes results from their being driven south by want of food or the severity of the season, are also less remarkable, it appears to me, than the occurrence here of southern species, as of the two Egrets, the Little Blue Heron (*Florida Cærulea*) the Gallinules and other aquatic species, which never, so far as known (with one exception perhaps), breed so far north. In the latter case they are generally young birds that reach us towards fall in their chance wanderings.

"It may here be added that the cause of the migration of our birds still offers an interesting field for investigation. Observers are of late noting that in the case of some northern species that reach us only occasionally in their winter migrations, young birds only are at first seen, but if the migration continues the older birds appear at a later date. But sometimes young birds only are seen. This frequently happens in the case of the Pine Grosbeak (*Pinicola eneucleator*). The cause of their visits is not always, it is evident, severe weather; the last named species appearing sometimes in November,—weeks before severe cold sets in — while at other times it is not seen at all during some of our severest winters. The probable cause is more frequently, doubtless, a short supply of food, as last winter was remarkable in this state for its mildness and for the great number of northern birds that then visited us. It has repeatedly been observed that on their first arrival these unusual visitors are generally very lean, but that they soon fatten; an argument in favor of the theory that their migration was compelled by a scarcity of food.

"Probably fewer birds are actually permanently resident at a given locality than is commonly supposed, for species seen the whole year at the same locality, as the Blue Jay, the Titmouse, the Brown Creeper, and the Hairy and Downy Woodpecker, etc., in Massachusetts, are represented, not by the same, but by different sets of individuals, those seen here in summer being not those seen in winter, the species migrating north and south, *en masse*, with the change of season. We are generally cognizant of a migration in a given species only when the great "bird wave" sweeps entirely past us either to the north or south. Some species, however, seem actually fixed at all seasons, and are really essentially non-migratory, as the Spruce Partridge, and Quail (*Ortyx Virginianus*) are in New England. But only a small proportion, doubtless, of the so-called non-migratory birds at any given locality are really so.*

"In connection with this topic of migration, the fact that some of the young or immature individuals of our marine birds, as the Herring Gull (*Larus argentatus*) and other species of that family, and several of the Tringæ, linger on our coast during summer, while the adult all retire northward, is one of some interest. Mature and strong birds only, in species that breed far to the north, evidently seek very high latitudes. Birds of the first year also appear to roam less widely than the older. In different species of the Gull family it is generally only the mature birds that in winter are seen far out at sea, though in the same latitudes the young may be numerous along the coast. All observant collectors are well aware of the fact that those birds that first reach us in the spring, of whatever species, are generally not only very appreciably larger, but brighter plumaged and in every way evidently more perfect birds than those that arrive later; and that in those species that go entirely to the north of us there is a much larger proportion of paler colored and immature birds, especially among the *Sylvicolidæ*, or warblers, towards the close of the migrating season than earlier. Hence the presence here of a few individuals in summer of species that usually go farther north is not always sufficient evidence that the species breeds with us." [11]

Good illustrations are of great assistance to young students, teaching them, better than words, characteristic details of

---

* "In respect to the proof whereon this proposition rests, see my remarks on this point in the Memoirs of the Boston Society of Natural History, Vol. i, Pt. iv, p. 488 (foot note)."

[11] Several passages or sentences have, for convenience, been omitted in this extract.

structure, and the general differences of appearance in the birds of various families or groups. The illustrations of this volume are woodcuts in outline, the only satisfactory form, not greatly increasing its cost, of which the author has bethought himself. He has drawn most of the figures from nature — he hopes with accuracy, though, since the scales vary, and (when fractional) are only approximate, they do not satisfactorily represent the relative size of the birds figured.[12] The outlines of the Chickadee, Night "Hawk," and Golden-winged Woodpecker, have been copied from Wilson's pictures; those of the Winter Wren were suggested by a picture in Dr. Coues' "Key to North American Birds." The details of structure have all been drawn from nature by the author, though several hints have been taken from the latter volume. The outlines of birds very well known, or nearly related to others figured, have been omitted. It may be here remarked that in the figure of the Traill's Flycatcher the tail is broader and more rounded than is observable in the living bird when at rest. In some other figures, the notch of the bill is indistinct.

This volume contains several facts, never before published, so far as the author knows, except a few, which have appeared in magazines or pamphlets. It also possesses new features, which will, it is hoped, facilitate the acquisition of a thorough knowledge of our birds, though it contains no more scientific details than necessary. The classification, with slight changes in sequence, is that used by Professor Baird and Dr. Coues. The introduction (which is divided into sections, marked by letters) relates chiefly to the formation of a collection of eggs, containing, however, a section on structural details, and another on classification. Each of the succeeding chapters treats of an ornithological *order*, though the last treats of the game-birds. Each chapter is divided into sections, which are *continuously* numbered throughout (in Arabic figures), and which mark the various *families* (subfamilies being otherwise indi-

---

[12] These have not been drawn so as to exhibit the longest primary, spurious feathers, *scutellæ*, or the like, unless in the plate.

cated). The *genera* of each section are marked by Roman numerals, and the *species* belonging to them by capital letters in parenthesis. The biography of each species is divided into four parts :— (a) a description of the mature birds (but not of the young, for which see the Appendix E) ; (b) a description of their nest and eggs ; (c) a description of their habits, and (d) of their notes. In the first part, various minute details are frequently omitted, which it has been thought unnecessary to introduce. In spelling the English names of birds, the following system has been here adopted. *Specific names* are begun with capital letters to distinguish them from similar names of groups (e. g. the Crow Blackbirds) ; when they are composed partly of a family-name, such as "thrush," that name is never compounded with another (e. g. Wood Thrush) ; when they are compounds of "bird," that word is united by a hyphen to a noun immediately preceding, but not to an adjective, except in cases to the contrary, established by long usage (e. g. Cat-bird, Blue Bird, but Swamp Blackbird).

Finally, that this book may prove useful to students, interesting to lovers of nature, and acceptable to the public, is the hope and wish of its

1876. AUTHOR.

INTRODUCTION.

§ A. Ornithology is the science of birds, and oölogy that of eggs, or, in a common but limited sense, that of birds' eggs. The two are intimately connected, and often form a joint study, one embracing the other. They are useful, because, when properly pursued, they cultivate observation and a love of nature, and necessitate healthful exercise. "Ornithology," says an enthusiastic but anonymous writer, "has two departments, which are more or less incompatible, namely : Natural History, and Science, or the study of animate birds, and of those inanimate. The former, especially as opposed to an extreme of the latter, I recommend to all young students as the higher and better pursuit of the two. I further advise them, when not shooting at targets or legitimate game, never to fire a gun. My own experience has proved that, when science is so far advanced as at present, one can obtain an accurate knowledge of our birds, and a good collection of their eggs, by following the above rule, and having proper books of reference, or a like resource. Egg-collecting can be conducted under humane principles. A parent-bird should never be shot, except in cases of extreme necessity, it being often preferable even then to snare the female by placing a slip-noose of horse-hair around the inner edge of her nest and attaching it to some neighboring object. I myself, from as near a standpoint as possible, and often aided by an opera-glass, observe, if I can, the female when actually *upon* her nest, since other birds may be about it, and may even make complaints from sympathy, or because their own nests are near by.[1] Should she fly too soon, I either return after a few moments' absence or concealment (as I often do in preference to doing mischief by keeping her too long from her nest), or I follow her with my eye, endeavoring not to lose sight of her nor to confuse her with any other species, and note, so far as possible, all her markings, which, until I became an expert, I always noted down on the spot, to compare with full descriptions at home. Practice enables one to recognize many birds, particularly the larger ones, at a glance, and to note readily the most characteristic markings; but there is no objection to shooting hawks, which are less easily identified otherwise than smaller species. There are some persons who are too inaccurate to follow this method, and with such, or with those personally unknown to you, it is well never to exchange. Males are generally more easily identified than females, and frequently sit upon their nests, though most often appearing when their mates are disturbed. Confusion may easily arise from two varieties of one species, but both forms rarely occur in the same district, and, according to a strict definition of the word "variety," can never normally do so. The only varieties (not belonging to original types) which occur in New England among land-birds, are the Gray-cheeked Thrush, the Bronzed Blackbird,[2] and the Red-naped Woodpecker, of which the first-named has been sometimes ranked as a species, and

---

[1] It may be added that Cow-birds never lay their eggs but in the nests of other birds. See § 17, III.

[2] "This bird is thought to build in holes, while the Crow Blackbird does not."

at least has not been known to breed in the eastern United States.[3]

"Bird-collecting, on the other hand, unavoidably leads to more or less cruelty, in many cases to absolute barbarity, and is at present carried to an alarming excess. Slaughter by hundreds should be permitted among only a few eminent and competent naturalists, such as Messrs. Allen and Coues. Otherwise, it becomes an outrage upon nature, a positive injury to science, and a mere source of self-gratification. Young collectors, who are not to become scientists, should form their collections for the sake of beauty in nature, and might well be satisfied with two good specimens, well-mounted, of each kind, namely: the mature male and female. In the case of a scientific collection this would be wholly inadmissible, and collectors should certainly shoot any specimen of a kind never before taken in that district where they may chance to meet it, or those birds which they find in a country new to themselves, or perhaps to all ornithologists. Otherwise, may I venture to ask what new facts one can make known from owning the skins of several hundred unfortunate robins? All our rarer birds, or those of market-value, are in danger of being altogether exterminated, through a foolish sense of glory on man's part, or through his reckless destruction of other than human life. It is also to be regretted that so many birds are shot, before laying their eggs, owing to the condition of their plumage and their abundance, during or immediately after their spring migrations. Nature's resources should be drawn upon only in cases of necessity, or in contribution to the advancement of mankind. Violation of nature, as of the natural

---

[3] See farther § 13, I, D and E, for the very slight distinction between the Warbling and Philadelphia Vireo.

laws, must entail misery, and finally cause us bitterly to regret our present thoughtlessness and inhumanity; errors which will probably continue until stricter and efficient laws, consequently more general and simple laws are passed."

The above remarks may need modification, but they express a spirit worthy of serious reflection.

§ B.[4] In forming a collection of eggs the chief requisites are:—

(1) Boxes of various size. Those of a cylindrical shape and made of tin are the best, as they take up least room in the pocket, and are easily slipped in and out. A box, which cannot be carried in the pocket, is comparatively worthless.

(2) A supply of cotton-wool, a cheap material and the most satisfactory for packing on account of its elasticity.

(3) A cabinet.

(4) A knife to cut small branches or the like.

To these may be added climbing-irons, egg-drills, blow-pipes, etc., though not *absolutely* necessary.

§ C. In winter, or as spring approaches, study the descriptions of various birds, nests, eggs, and the nature of the localities as well as the position in which the latter are usually found. Find in advance suitable spots for the search of any desired nest, especially if you do not live in the country.

§ D. If in your rambles you should see a nest (not an old one), approach it carefully to see the bird; this being generally indispensable, as eggs are often to be identified through the parent only. If the female, who usually sits upon the nest much

---

. [4] The following remarks are addressed to the inexperienced only.

INTRODUCTION.   5

oftener than the male, flies too soon, retire and return in a few minutes. Adopt the same plan for a bird, whom you have flushed from the ground, and do not at once recognize. If you fail to find the nest (granted that there be one there, and that the bird was not merely feeding[5]), on returning, note the exact spot from which she rises. If you think to recognize her, make yourself positive of facts. If not, note with the utmost accuracy her size, markings, and the shape of the bill, and identify her as soon as possible.[6] To determine her size, remember that the Humming bird is about $3\frac{1}{4}$ inches long, the Song Sparrow or Snow-bird 6 or more, the Robin about $9\frac{1}{2}$, and the Crow nearly 20. Also observe the comparative length of her tail.

§ E. If you have an opportunity, study the works of Wilson and Audubon. The former's figures are very life-like, and their coloring generally true, though often too high-toned or otherwise incorrect. It is still more worth your while to examine the collection of the Boston Society of Natural History.[7] If this is inaccessible to you, another is probably more worthy of your attention than descriptions, or even accurate paintings.

§ F. A nest containing sound eggs, but without the parent-birds, generally indicates that all the eggs have not been laid, or that the parents are temporarily absent. Should you find

---

[5] Many birds, when frightened from their nests on the ground, feign lameness or the like.

[6] Shooting the parents when collecting *for yourself* is optional. See quoted remarks in § A.

[7] The building of this Society is on Berkeley street (near Boylston) in Boston. It is at present open to the public on Wednesdays and Saturdays from 10 A. M. to 5 P. M. The birds of New England are not separated from those belonging to other parts of the world.

an incomplete nest, you must judge for yourself how soon it will be finished. A pair of our smaller birds, in the latter part of May or in June, ordinarily spend from five to ten days in building one, and sometimes end their work sufficiently in advance to allow the female vacation for a day or even two. Earlier in the season, other birds are generally occupied two or three weeks. Woodpeckers are very uncertain in this respect, and it is often difficult to decide when their nests should be broken into to obtain the eggs, unless one can watch them closely at their work (carried on chiefly in the morning) and observe the final cessation of chips. The creepers, nuthatches, Chickadees, and certain wrens customarily lay their eggs in deserted woodpeckers' holes or other cavities, which they line with warm materials, though the Chickadees occasionally excavate for themselves with great and long-continued labor.

After the first egg has been laid, one is generally added on each succeeding day (apparently most often in the morning) until the complement is made,[a] before which time the nest should not be visited, except in cases of necessity. Most birds lay four or five eggs (occasionally three or six) in a set, commonly fewer in that of a second brood than before. Many wrens, titmice, and kingfishers often lay more; the former even ten, or very rarely twelve. Gallinaceous birds are also prolific, and two or three hen-birds are said sometimes to lay in the same nest. Humming-birds, eagles, and pigeons, usually lay two eggs in a set, as do also old birds of other species, particularly among the hawks and owls. Many sea-birds have only one. If a nest be found with the same number of eggs for two

---

[a] To this law the chief exceptions are the birds of prey, and the cuckoos, but among the smaller land-birds the *average rate* of laying is one a day. Thus among different species the time for laying four eggs varies from three to even seven days, generally being four.

or three days, the proper inference generally is that no more will be laid. If the egg of a Cow-bird (§ 17, III) be discovered, it should be taken home, or destroyed (at a distance from the nest), unless observations are to be made upon the young when hatched.

§ G. A method of finding nests, which may often be practised with success, is that of "tracking" birds, when seen with food for their mates or material for building. It is generally a wearisome and patience-exhausting process, and frequently causes disappointment. It may often be facilitated by the scattering of feathers, horse-hairs, string, cotton-wool, straw, etc., in places where they will attract the attention of the architects, in whose work you are interested. The nests of woodpeckers may often be found, by tracing to their source the loud rapping of the builders, or by observing on the ground the chips, which are usually fresh (unless, as is rarely the case, the excavation be made in an unsound tree).

§ II. When you take eggs, pack them at once, bearing in mind that the smaller ones are very delicate, and even the larger ones easily broken.[9] If they are of the former class, having taken from the box most of the cotton-wool, leave a layer on the bottom, in which make a slight depression with the finger, and lay the first egg. The following rules should be observed:—(1) An egg must not come in contact with another, with the bottom, sides, or cover of the box. (2) The cotton-wool must be tightly packed. To pack it loosely is a

---

[9] Much danger will be obviated by blowing the eggs first, when practicable. If fresh eggs are allowed to grow cold, or to remain long unblown the contents are less easily removed. The reverse is said to be the case, when eggs containing embryos are left unblown for two or even three days. See § I and *note*.

mistake frequently made, and attended by consequent accidents. (With larger eggs less care is required, and those of hawks or owls may often be carried safely in a handkerchief.) When all the eggs have been safely stowed away, the box should be put in the pocket in such a way that they shall not be violently jarred, when a fence is clambered over, or the body otherwise ungently moved. A small nest, if either rare or curious, should be taken with any small branches, to which it may be attached, and brought home in a suitable box or basket, and not squeezed in the hand or pocket; a bulky one may be safely carried in the hands. A nest on the ground must be taken up with peculiar care, as it may otherwise fall apart, and should afterwards, if necessary, be stitched together. Nests, to be properly preserved, must be placed in some receptacle, where they will be free from dust, and, if composed of woolly materials or of feathers, constantly supplied with benzine or crystallized camphor, to prevent the ravages of moths.

Eggs, to be sent by mail or express, should not be packed so tightly as for ordinary transportation, and may be first surrounded by tissue-paper. "Single eggs," says Dr. Coues, "may be safely mailed to any distance in auger-holes bored in wood." Boxes may be sent by mail at a trifling cost, when not sealed. Tin boxes, such as are used for tobacco, with tightly fitting covers, are the best.

§ I. On reaching home, the eggs must not be left in places where they are likely to be broken or lost, but at once blown and placed in your cabinet. The following are directions for blowing an egg in the old-fashioned way, which possesses two or three advantages over the modern process (among others, that of not requiring expense, to many persons an important consideration) :—

Holding the egg lightly between the thumb and forefinger of the left hand, with a sharp pin in the right hand, make a small hole at or near the smaller end, and at the greater, or on the same side, a large one in accordance with the size of the egg, which is next placed between the thumb and forefinger of the right hand. Then place your mouth at the smaller hole and breathe out gently but steadily, and the contents, if fresh, run out at the other. Be sure that none are left, and even remove, if possible, the lining of the shell, though no risk should be run of breaking the latter. When any difficulty occurs, shake the egg, or give a quick puff if safe to do so; otherwise, inject a little water from the mouth. In certain cases, shaking is even preferable to blowing. During the process of incubation, the contents of an egg thicken, and the young is gradually formed, until the blowing finally becomes impossible. When the egg is not fresh, enlarge the larger hole (but never the other), and blow persistently and patiently, taking care that the yolk or young does not, by suddenly slipping out, allow the egg to collapse between your fingers, or break it by being forced through too narrow an exit. If the contents are too thick to blow easily, they should be carefully cut off with small scissors, whenever protruding beyond the shell. If it is impossible to blow the egg, enlarge the holes so as to allow the gas to escape freely, but surround them with camphor-gum or the like, as otherwise the odor is extremely disgusting and the egg, after losing its original colors, gradually drops to pieces. I have seen eggs successfully preserved in this manner, decomposition being quickened by the occasional injection of water.

The modern and very general manner of blowing eggs

necessitates the use of several instruments; the blow-pipe and egg-drill,[10] which are the most important, the syringe, forceps, dissecting-scissors, etc. To follow this method, drill with a light twirling motion a small hole on one side of the egg, remove from the opening the inner membrane, which often (as in the larger of *two* holes) interferes with further action, and insert the blow-pipe. Then breathe gently, not forcibly, and the contents, if fresh, will flow out about the pipe, but, if not, a little water should be injected, and the egg gently shaken. Should there be further difficulty, inject warm water, put the egg in a dark, warm place, with the hole turned upward, and at the end of a few hours, after shaking it, remove as much as possible of the yolk, etc., which must finally be altogether disposed of, particularly in the case of white eggs. Then inject more water, and again leave it. Young may be cut up by slender scissors, having delicate blades at an angle with their handles, and removed by a fine wire, slightly hooked, or by small forceps. Fresh eggs, if not too large, may be "blown" or rather sucked by means of a suction-tube with a bulb. Specimens, when thoroughly rinsed and ready for the cabinet, should be placed on blotting paper to dry (with the opening turned downward), where not exposed to a strong light. Carbonate of soda is said to render a hardened yolk soluble in water, but it must not come in contact with the outer shell. There are various other details, too numerous to mention, connected with the blowing of eggs by instruments, such as gumming a series of very thin paper-wafers about an opening made in a delicate shell, such as that of a very small specimen, of one cracked, or of one nearly hatched.[11]

---

[10] These may be obtained at the Naturalist's Agency, Salem, Mass. The present address is Mr. S. E. Cassino.

[11] Several ideas expressed in the preceding paragraph, have been borrowed from various articles on this same subject.

Note.— Take care in making a hole not to injure any markings; and, when blowing, place beneath a pail or basin containing a few inches of water to catch the egg, should it slip. An egg when full is very easily broken, but when blown may often be dropped without injury on to a carpet or the like. One with the contents entirely removed floats in water with only about a third or less of the shell beneath the level of the surface. A thin-shelled egg may be held to the light to ensure emptiness.

§ J. Eggs may be cleaned with a soft, wet rag, dipped in tooth-powder, or by the careful use of an ink-eraser (with a flat, pointed, steel blade), though the latter may injure the surface. Certain eggs (but none of those described in this volume) are calcareous, and their chalky shells cannot be safely cleaned. Others, however, have a certain "bloom," like that of a grape, which can be washed off.

To mend an egg, if broken into bits of manageable size, take one a little smaller and of no value, wet it, or coat it with a very delicate varnish, and place on it the bits of shell in their proper positions, so that they shall fit together. For large eggs, a mould of putty, if carefully shaped, may be used instead. Cracks may be brushed with collodion. The common method of glueing bits together with mucilage and thin paper is often clumsy or dangerous, and, even if successful, generally ruins the fair appearance of any specimen.

§ K. Place your eggs, when blown, promptly in your cabinet, and have some means of identifying them afterwards. Labels should be altogether avoided, as they greatly mar the beauty of a collection, and any writing on the shell should be condensed and placed on the under side, where it will be inconspicuous (or near the "drill-hole," if there be one). There are various methods of marking, but whichever be followed should be uniformly observed. Perhaps the best is to write[12] on each egg a number of the Smithsonian or Dr. Coues' Checklist (followed by S. or C. to indicate which); for instance on a Wood Thrush's egg either 148 S. or 3 C. To this may be added another number, referring to your note-book, which should be a blank-book, with long but wide pages ruled by lines forming several columns of suitable width. In these columns (with proper headings) should be written first the number of reference, and then the name of the bird, its number on the check-lists; the number of eggs originally in the nest, by whom collected or from whom obtained, the place and date of collection; also, when desirable, remarks as to the size, incubation, or peculiarities of the eggs, the position and structure of the nest. It is often well to avoid mention of the place where the eggs of hawks, herons, etc., were found, as these birds frequently build conspicuous nests in restricted localities, to which, if not too much disturbed, they return year after year. Secrecy is often as desirable for an ornithologist as for a sportsman. Eggs should be arranged in the proper sequence of families, etc., and those of each species should be kept distinct from others. All of one kind may be grouped together, or duplicates may be separated from better and representative specimens.

§ L. A *cabinet* may be strictly a cabinet, consisting of pigeon-holes or shelves, and screwed to the wall, or a box, a

---

[12] Purple ink will be found to flow more freely than ordinary black ink. Figures should be fine and made with care. They may be written on a bit of paper gummed over the "drill-hole," though it is better to write on the shell itself, unless too delicate, or unless the egg be very small.

long and rather flat one being the best, or a chest of drawers, which is the most convenient. The latter may be fitted with a series of small, shallow trays, made of paper or paste-board, though these diminish the attractiveness of a collection, and are more or less dangerous. I have found a rather deep layer of fine sea-sand, such as may be obtained at almost every grocer's store, much more satisfactory, since it forms a pleasing background for the eggs, which can be fixed in it firmly, and is always exempt from moths or other insects: fine saw-dust is the best substitute.

All cabinets should be dark when closed, as many eggs fade when exposed to the light, particularly those which are blue or green.

§ M. Having now followed the eggs from the time when the mother was scared from her nest, until they were placed in a cabinet, I shall return to speak of the difficulty in frightening certain birds when incubating, chiefly the hawks. Individuals, rather than species, vary in this respect, though the smaller are undoubtedly more often timid than others. One hawk glides silently from her nest as you approach; another flies when you rap the tree energetically with a stick; whereas a third remains until the crackling of branches, as you ascend, causes her to seek safety in flight. Hawks, moreover, are often obliged to leave the nest, after the eggs are laid, if their mates either die or fail to supply them with sufficient food. As about ninety per cent. or more of the nests found in a large "hawkery" are old, except a few nests belonging to crows and squirrels, and as hawks and owls, moreover, often inhabit such, not always rebuilding them, one naturally is doubtful about climbing far, on finding a large nest of sticks, which is likely to contain eggs only once out of ten times. A hawk cannot often be seen when sitting on her nest, and the only signs, which rarely deceive, are the small feathers, which usually cling to the nest, or to a branch near it. Dead leaves inside of a nest indicate further emptiness, or occupation by squirrels, who usually, in building, heap together hay, straw, and pine-needles, or the like. In the absence of all the above-mentioned signs, judgment is required, but no further rules can be safely laid down. It may be remarked that smaller birds are also often brave or even bold in protecting their nests.

In climbing, never leave one hold before testing and securing another; remember that pine-limbs are less to be trusted than those of hard-wood trees; place your feet, if possible, next to the trunk, and, if inclined to dizziness, do not look down. Gloves, old clothes, a soft hat (and climbing-irons, when convenient) form the necessary outfit, as large eggs may be safely brought down in a cloth cap, grasped firmly by the teeth. Never take one egg from a set in a hawk's nest, if you wish for the rest, as these latter will often disappear mysteriously before your return. None of the hawks (*i.e. Falconidæ*), with the exception of the Ospreys and eagles, show a disposition to attack. These latter have been known to inflict dangerous wounds, and at the same time are, I believe, the only species generally occupying the same nest year after year, with the exception of the Duck Hawk (?) and Sparrow Hawk. I do not recall many other birds who do so, with the marked exception of the swallows and Pewees, who sometimes rebuild their old homes.

§ N. All birds have an affection for some haunt, whither, if left undisturbed, they return every spring. These haunts are often extensive, enabling them to change their residence annually, until they are finally driven away. Cat-birds frequently return every year to the same thicket, and I have known the Red-eyed Vireo to build his nest in the same tree where it was built and robbed the year before. Likewise Pewees very often choose successively two or three building-sites very close to one another. The less familiar species are not so attached to particular spots, but generally build their nests each summer in the same tract of land (a tree-warbler in the same woods, etc.). Hawks (and occasionally even crows) become attached to a certain grove or pine-wood, and build near the same place several years in succession, sometimes though repeatedly robbed. Woodpeckers (who always lay their eggs in holes) do not usually, so far as my observations have extended, occupy the same holes twice, but leave them to be used by Chickadees, or other birds. Feelings of attachment are much stronger in some species than in others, being often nearly extinct. They are more marked in civilized districts, where there is less range of country than in other parts of the State. Many birds forsake their haunts, if disturbed, but apparently return sometimes after a long absence. The evidence of identical birds returning to the same spot is very strong, particularly in the case of individuals peculiarly marked.

§ O. There are not many birds, who, in a temperate climate, do not habitually raise a second brood; and there are probably very few, who do not do so, if the first is broken up or destroyed. They rarely raise the second in the same nest as the first, but generally build another (often hurriedly) near the site of the former, particularly if that has been disturbed or removed. The principal exceptions to this latter statement are the Pewees, swallows, and those birds who lay their eggs in holes. The second set of eggs usually appears from four to six weeks after the first, if that has not met with serious mishaps; otherwise, sooner. If a hawk's nest be robbed,[13] the parents commonly repair an old nest near by, often hastily lining it with evergreen or the like, and at the end of about a fortnight two or three eggs are laid. The Sharp-shinned Hawks, Kingfishers, Golden-winged Woodpeckers, and very probably other species, are said to continue sometimes for several days to lay eggs almost daily, after the first sets have been taken, though continually robbed. Smaller birds have been known to build a second, and even a third nest, within a few feet of the previous ones, when these were removed.

They have also been known to cover the eggs of a Cow-bird, by building a second story, or even a third, which became their own nursery. Such cases are, however, exceptional, and lead me to speak of desertion.

§ P. Birds differ widely in respect to desertion, the woodpeckers, especially the Golden-winged, being in case of disturbance uncertain in their movements. The latter often leave forever the excavation, on which they are at work, if they imagine that they are watched, though occasionally regardless of those passing by. If their eggs be disturbed, they sometimes "desert," and at other times the female continues to lay eggs in the manner already described. She often deepens her nest, and lays a second set. A general rule is that birds will not desert their nests (if not injured) when one egg is taken from three or four, two from five or six, and three from more than six. Never handle a nest or eggs, not to be at once

---

[13] Unless that of a Marsh (or Sparrow?) Hawk.

taken; the bird does not perceive your "touch," as many persons suppose, but one's hand very often so disturbs the nest, and the exact position of the eggs, that the intrusion becomes very marked. As a rule, a nest should never be visited from the time of its discovery until all the eggs are laid, and an egg should never be taken except from a complete set.

§ Q. Should you find a nest of value, when you have not a box, mark the spot by observing some conspicuous landmark, unless it be necessary to take the nest at once. Otherwise, carry large eggs, and those taken from a hole or a frail nest, wrapped in a handkerchief, and carry small eggs in their nests, placed upright, with a handkerchief tied tightly over the whole. Packing in either case is desirable, soft, clean moss being generally the best material to be found in the woods.

When a hole is enlarged with a hatchet or knife in order to reach any eggs, the parent almost invariably "deserts," and it is therefore necessary to break it open at the proper time, since all or no eggs should be taken from such a nest. In at least one of the cases before cited, relating to the Pigeon Woodpeckers, the hole was large enough to allow the insertion of the hand and fore-arm. This species, however, as has already been remarked, frequently deepens the hole to lay again; so do other woodpeckers.

§ R. Health, energetic perseverance, honesty, experience, and moderation, are the necessary qualities or cardinal virtues of a wise and successful collector. It is for young oölogists an excellent rule, which has, however, many exceptions, never to take more than one egg from a nest, nor to have more than two or three of one species, except when (very) rare, peculiarly marked, or suitable for an advantageous exchange.

If inexperienced, do not make exchanges with another inexperienced person, who may unintentionally cheat you, or with one unknown to you, who may purposely cheat you. Remember that eggs often vary greatly in value in different parts of the country, and do not accept any price-list as a basis for exchange. Endeavor by energy to arrive at approximate completion, have some definite object in view, such as a cabinet comprising all the eggs of Massachusetts, and do not unwisely form a miscellaneous collection everywhere incomplete.

§ S. To know the notes of all our birds is a great assistance in finding their nests, and in finding, distinguishing, or studying the birds themselves, who sing chiefly on or soon after their arrival from the South, during their migrations, and the mating-season in spring, or early summer. It is best to study their music at sunrise, or in the early morning (particularly in the case of species migrating), and also at evening. Even families may (to a limited extent) be classified by their notes. To study birds, in relation to their habits or notes, walk in their haunts, continually pausing to catch the slightest sound, which, if not recognized, should be traced to its source, or to allow the birds to gather about or approach you. If necessary, follow them silently and persistently, but remember that stealthiness sometimes alarms them more than an open approach. If several species be together, do not be misled by the confusion of their songs, and do not hastily attribute the note of one kind to another bird immediately near. Both squirrels and "chipmonks" frequently produce notes, which might excusably distract the attention of an unpractised ornithologist. By looking up, especially on very clear days, you may often see hawks, or other birds, flying over silently.

An opera-glass, if a sufficiently strong magnifier, or occasionally a telescope, will be found very useful, as it enables one to recognize a bird without disturbing it, and to distinguish colors, when the object is distant, or at a great height among branches. It is more difficult to distinguish colors just before or after sunset than at other times of the day, particularly if they be exposed to the sunlight. That hour should therefore be avoided.

§ T. Of anatomy and details of structure I shall not here speak at length, since they are not referred to in this volume more often than convenience requires.[14] The *bill* consists of two *mandibles*, the line between which is called the *gape* or often the *commissure*. The true *cere*, which belongs only to the parrots and birds of prey, is a thick skin which covers the upper mandible at its base, and in which are the nostrils, though often concealed by feathers.

The principal wing-feathers are the *primaries*, which (with perhaps exceptions) are always nine or ten, except in flightless birds, and which form the end or "point" of the wing. They are the long outer feathers, of which the shafts (if the wing be spread) are more or less parallel, forming an evident angle with those of the adjoining secondaries. A so-called "*spurious*" *primary* is usually the first or outermost, when very much shorter than the rest. (It differs from the "bastard wing" or "spurious quills" in being a single feather and beneath the second primary.) The "*shoulder*" of the wing is the "*bend*" near its connection with the body. The tail is *even* or *square*, *rounded* or *forked*, as viewed when half-closed; if slightly forked, *emarginate*, if very deeply

---

[14] The reader is referred for a full treatise to the introduction of Dr. Coues' "Key to N. A. Birds."

forked, *forficate*. A *cuneate* tail is the exact opposite to one forficate.

The *tarsus*, often called the "leg," extends from the base of the toes to the first joint above, and in a majority of birds is unfeathered. If without scales in front (unless near the bottom) it is "*booted*," or if with scales, *scutellate*. (If covered with very small scales which do not overlap one another, it is *reticulate;* or it may be *granulated* as in the Fish Hawk.)

The following is a vocabulary of several other descriptive terms. *Auriculars* (or *ear-patch*), the feathers behind, but a little below the level of the eye. *Circumocular*, about the eye. *Crown*, top of the head (usually above the eye). *Eye-patch*, a tract of color enclosing the eye. *Eye-stripe*, a line running *through* the eye (so to speak). *Interscapulars*, feathers on the back between the wing-shoulders, or between the head and rump. *Iris*, (pl. *irides*), a colored circle enclosing the pupil of the eye. *Lore*, the feathers about the base of the bill, or between the bill and the eye. *Maxillary line*, one running backward from the gape, and bordering the throat. *Median line*, one dividing the crown. *Nape* (or *nuchal* patch), the hind-head (properly above the *cervix*, or hind-neck). *Superciliary line*, a stripe immediately above the eye. *Vermiculation*, very fine "waves." ♂ signifies *the male*, ♀ *the female;* = signifies "equal to," > "more than," and < "less than." "Inch" or "inches" is abbreviated to *in.*, and decimal numbers (written with a dot before) generally indicate hundredths of an inch.

Except where there are indications to the contrary, the "upper parts" generally include the upper surface of the wings and tail, though the "under parts" frequently refer to the body only. The "crown" includes the forehead (or even the nape). The "rump" (or lower back) often includes the upper tail-coverts, the "belly" the under tail-coverts, etc. The "sides" invariably refer to those of the breast and belly.

§ U. Measurements of both birds and eggs are made in straight lines between two points. To measure the length of a bird, lay it on its back, and make the tip of the bill (so far as reasonable), and the end of the longest tail-feather, touch the ruler or paper on which they are laid; then measure the distance between these points. Measure (with compasses) the *tarsus* in front, and the bill from the tip of the upper mandible to the feathers actually or apparently belonging to the forehead.[15] The "depth" of a bill is its vertical width near the base, when closed. Eggs may be measured by dividers, or by a ruler with a slide. For accurate measurements a ruler marked decimally (or even with hundredths) is best. $\frac{1}{16}$ of an inch equals about ·06.

§ V. Birds form a *class* of the Animal Kingdom. They are composed of three (or more?) distinct *subclasses;* the *Aves Aëreæ*, *Insessores*, or typical "perchers;" the *Aves Terrestres*, *Cursores*, or gallinaceous birds and "waders;" and the *Aves Aquaticæ*, *Natatores*, or "swimmers." These are grouped into several *orders* (such as the *Raptores* or "birds of prey"), which are divided into *families* (as the *Raptores* into *Strigidæ*, *Falconidæ*, etc., or the hawks, including eagles, the owls, and vultures). The *orders* are sometimes more primarily divided into *suborders*, and *families* into *subfamilies*. Thus the *Passeres* consist of the *Oscines* or singing passerines, and the

---

[15] There are other methods of making this measurement.

Clamatores or non-singers;[16] likewise the *Turdidæ* consists of the *Turdinæ*, or typical thrushes, who have a "booted" tarsus, and the *Miminæ*, or mocking-thrushes, who do not possess this feature. Combinations of less important distinctions in structural detail characterize the *genera;* and therefore birds belonging to the same *genus* have exactly the same structure. The difference between *species* is marked by coloration, and often size. To illustrate the foregoing, take as a subject the common Song Sparrow. He belongs to the *Insessorian* group, the order of *Passeres*, and the suborder *Oscines*. His family is that of the *Fringillidæ*, or finches, and his genus *Melospiza*. His specific name is *melodia*, but there is also a variety, *M. fallax*. "Extremely similar; wings and tails slightly longer; paler, grayer; the streaks not so obviously blackish in the centre. Whole of the Rocky Mountains and Great Basin; scarcely distinguishable." (Coues.)

§ W. The classification of birds (or other objects in nature) necessarily entails certain absurdities, being more or less artificial. The method of modern classification is that of descending from the higher to the lower groups, but sequence is too often insisted on among groups, which diverge (so to speak) from a common centre. The division of families, genera, etc., is more or less arbitrary, a certain degree of difference being necessary to separate them, whereas minor (or fractional) differences cause intermediate groups. Let $\times$ represent the degree of dissimilarity between two *genera;* then $\frac{\times}{n}$ represents the difference between two *subgenera* (of the same genus); $1 + \frac{\times}{n}$ between subfamilies, $2 \times$ between families, $2 + \frac{\times}{n}$ be-

---

[16] A rather technical distinction.

tween suborders, and 3 × between orders. Forms in nature are everywhere so delicately blended that theoretically it is almost impossible to "draw any lines." A *species* (even though exhibiting much individual variation) is constituted by all those birds, who, since the present organization of birds has existed, might be the descendants of a single pair.

[The phenomena of *albinism* and *melanism* can here be only briefly referred to. In the latter, which is very rare, birds are abnormally dark or black. In albinism, which is not uncommon, birds are partially or wholly abnormally white (or even yellow); sometimes they are partly bleached. Such conditions of plumage need cause confusion only among birds of the same *genus*, and rarely then, being seldom complete.] There are often *varieties*, geographical races, or forms rendered appreciably distinct by the effects of climate, etc. By a strict definition of the term, *varieties* must have different distributions (at least during the breeding-season), though accidental stragglers may occur far from their usual *habitat*. A specific *type* is usually the variety first named. *Hybrids*, or "crosses," are the joint offspring of two species, but they do not often occur among birds in a natural state.

A bird's *scientific name* consists of a generic (subgeneric) and specific, or also subspecific, title, e. g., *Turdus* (*Hylocichla*) *Swainsoni*, Var. *Aliciæ*, or simply *Turdus Aliciæ*.[17] Family-names end in *idæ*, those of subfamilies in *inæ*. Scientific names are usually begun with a capital, are italicized, and, when following English names, put in parenthesis. Specific names, however, are ordinarily spelt without a capital, unless derived from proper names. It is best to form *no* Latin

---

[17] *Turdus Aliciæ* is often ranked as a species.

Genitives in *ii*, a single one being more correct. (See Messrs. Allen and Greenough's "Latin Grammar," Part 1, § 10, 4, b.)

NOTE.— Many still existing scientific names are unworthy of retention, but they have not been altered in this volume on account of the established rule of priority, which necessitates, however, many incongruities. The authorities for these names are given in the second index. Great care has been bestowed upon the orthography of English names, since great latitude exists in this respect, no system being yet established. Certain rules have here been followed, with the exceptions produced by general or the best usage.

LAND-BIRDS AND GAME-BIRDS

OF

NEW ENGLAND.

Aves, or *birds*, form a *class* of the Animal Kingdom, and have, in their classification, been primarily divided by eminent ornithologists into three *subclasses* (lately dispensed with, however, in "North American Birds"): *Aves Aëreæ* or *Insessores* (aërial birds or "perchers"), *Aves Terrestres* or *Cursores* (terrestrial birds or "runners"), and *Aves Aquaticæ* or *Natatores* (aquatic birds or "swimmers"). The general rule of division is this: hind-toe[1] on a level with the other toes, "perchers"; hind-toe not insistent[1] and feet not fully webbed, "runners"; hind-toe elevated,[1] but feet fully webbed, "swimmers." This rule is applicable only to typical forms, with which other forms are ranked through evident affinity. It is to be remarked that, in a great measure, æsthetic or intuitive perception is the best means of determining position. By modern classification birds are arranged on the descending method, by which the highest and most refined types occupy the highest position. Thus, the *Cursores* include those birds who scratch for their food (turkeys, grouse, etc.), and the waders (such as snipe, plover, herons, rails, etc.). These two suborders (*Gallinæ* and *Grallatores*) represent[2] (in the approximate proportion of one to four) about two-elevenths of

---

[1] In certain cases wanting, or apparently wanting.
[2] In number of species (according to Coues' list).

North American birds. The *Natatores* include various sea-birds, the swans, geese, ducks, terns, gulls, pelicans, petrels, and cormorants, and form about one-fourth of our fauna. The *Insessores* include all the typical land-birds, 377 of the 635 North American species admitted in Dr. Coues check-list, and more than one-half of about 300 species, known to have occurred in Massachusetts. In this volume I have, with the exception of the game-birds, treated the typical land-birds only. The *Insessores* contain five orders, described in the following chapters.

CHAPTER I.

FIRST ORDER. PASSERES.

These birds "are the typical *Insessores*, as such representing the highest grade of development, and the most complex organization, of the class. Their high physical irritability is coördinate with the rapidity of their respiration and circulation; they consume the most oxygen, and live the fastest, of all birds."[1] All our forms, at least, are characterized as follows: bill without a cere, or a soft basal membrane; front-toes never only two, or united throughout (*i. e.* two of them), hind toe never wanting; tail-feathers twelve. This group may be characterized, *as a whole*, as the only order of birds, of which all the species invariably build a nest in which to lay their eggs. Among the birds breeding in Massachusetts there is no exception to this rule, except the parasitic Cow-bird.

"*Passeres*, corresponding to the Insessores proper of most ornithologists, and comprising the great majority of birds, are divisible into two groups, commonly called suborders, mainly according to the structure of the lower larynx. In one, this organ is a complex muscular vocal apparatus; in the other the singing parts are less developed, rudimentary, or wanting. In the first, likewise, the tarsus is *normally* covered on either side with two entire horny plates, that meet behind in a sharp ridge; in the other, these plates are subdivided, or otherwise differently arranged. This latter is about the only *external* feature that can be pointed out as of extensive applicability; and even this does not always hold good. For example, among our birds, the larks (*Alaudidæ*), held to be Oscine, and certainly to be called songsters, have the tarsus perfectly scutellate behind."[1]

The *Oscines*, or singing *Passeres*, technically considered the

---

[1] Dr. Coues; "Key to North American Birds."

only musical birds, form about one-third of our ornithological fauna, and in Massachusetts are represented by eighteen families.

The *Clamatores*, or non-singing *Passeres*, are represented by the flycatchers (§ 19).

§ 1. The **Turdidæ**, or *thrushes*, now considered the highest group among birds, and ranked accordingly, are $6\frac{1}{2}-12$ inches long. Bill not conical (which term in ornithology necessitates rather straight outlines, and a depth approaching the length) but at least twice as long as high; with the upper mandible usually hooked and slightly notched; also bristled and with open nostrils (pl. 1, fig. 2). Average length of the tarsus about 1·15 inch; middle toe nearly or quite equal; other toes considerably shorter, and approximately equal. Primaries ten, the first being more or less spurious. Tail never forked, but often rounded, and of *twelve feathers* as in all our other oscine birds. The *Saxicolidæ* (§ 2) and *Sylviidæ* (§ 3) differ but little in structure or plumage: their coloration is, however, very much brighter, and their tails (at least in the genera *Sialia* and *Regulus*) are more or less forked. Our bluebirds are, moreover, seven inches long or less, and our "sylvias" all less than five.

The typical groups of these three families (including the subfamilies *Turdinæ* and *Regulinæ*) are characterized by *booted tarsi* (pl. 1, fig. 1). The other subfamilies, *Miminæ* and *Polioptilinæ* (the mocking-thrushes and gnatcatchers), have *scutellate tarsi* (pl. 1, fig. 3), and rather long, rounded tails. I am inclined to think that the *Harporhynchi* (Gen. III) are entitled to the rank of a subfamily. Their bills are unnotched, unhooked, and frequently curved (pl. 1, fig. 4). Their eggs, moreover, are markedly different from those of all other thrushes. The common Blue Bird may be considered a representative of the *Saxicolidæ*, while the *Sylviidæ* are closely related to the titmice and warblers. The Wood Thrush and Catbird are good types of their respective groups, though several thrushes nest upon the ground, or have spotted eggs.

The subfamilies of the thrushes are:
TURDINÆ, Genus *Turdus*, I.
(Highly musical). Subgenus *Hylocichla* (A–E.[2] fig. 1).
(Moderately musical). Subgenus *Planesticus* (F).

MIMINÆ, Genera II and III.

I. TURDUS
(A) MUSTELINUS. *Wood Thrush.* " *Song Thrush.*"
(A common summer-resident in Massachusetts.)

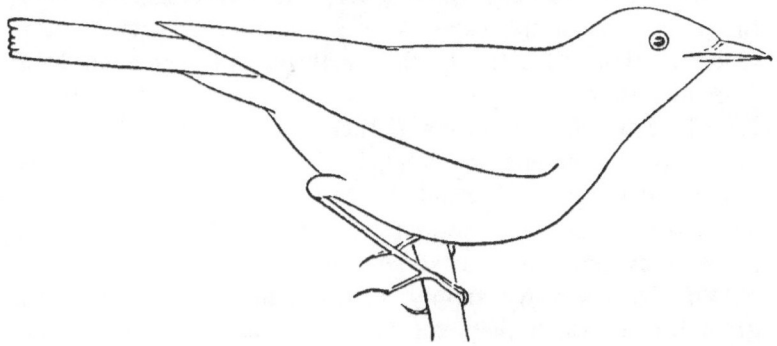

Fig. 1. Wood Thrush (⅟₂).

(*a*). About eight inches long. *Above*, soft but bright reddish-brown (or "tawny"), gradually *becoming soft* "*olive-dusky*" on *the rump, tail, and* end of the *wings*. Beneath, white, with a very slight buff tinge upon the breast; spotted on the breast and sides with dark brown (or "dusky").

(*b*). The nest sometimes closely resembles that of the Robin, but it is often composed outwardly of moss and even twigs, though subject to considerable variation in composition and structure. It is built, never very far from the ground, in a bush or tree, in the woods (especially those of low growth), and often in a swampy place. The eggs of each set are four

---

[2] The wood thrushes. The robins (F) are well-known; (G) has been separated from them, and placed in subgenus *Hesperocichla*.

or five, and like those of the Robin, but smaller, measuring 1·10—1·00×·70 of an inch. Those of the first set are usually laid near Boston in the last week of May—those of the second, if any, in the early part of July.

(c). The Wood Thrushes probably represent the highest type among birds; excelling all others, except their immediate relatives, in details of structure, in the quiet beauty of their coloration, and in the refinement of their habits; and they are certainly to be ranked among the finest singers of the world.

Though possessed of comparatively little power of flight, yet the Wood Thrushes, like most other birds, migrate very far (more than a thousand miles),—about the tenth of May reaching Massachusetts, to the northward of which, in New England, they rarely go. But they are common in southern New England from the time of their arrival until that of their departure in September or October; during the summer-months inhabiting groves and woods of various kinds, oftenest, perhaps, those which are swampy or of low growth. In such places they build their nest and rear their young, and there obtain the necessary supply of insect-food, either from the ground, over which they can run with some rapidity, or from the bushes and trees, among which they move with such leisure and dignified grace as would become a prince. The most conspicuous feature in the Natural History of these birds is the apparent modesty and the actual love of privacy or solitude, which they generally, though not invariably possess. These lend a charm to the study of their habits and their music, but they also cause difficulty in acquiring an intimacy with them,— a difficulty, however, which can be overcome. Though the Wood Thrushes are so fond of individuality and retirement, that they are never properly gregarious, and that they prefer retreats in woodland, where they are unlikely to be disturbed, to all other suitable haunts, yet they often build their nests in quite conspicuous places, and frequent the immediate neighborhood of man. Nor are they then more shy than under other circumstances,—in fact, the female is generally prompted by instinctive motherliness to sit as bravely on her nest, when built upon a roadside, as when in a swamp of alders. The Wood Thrushes usually sing from a high branch, whereas they find their food on or near the ground; but, wherever they are, they generally preserve, except when running, a rather erect attitude, observable also in the Robin and the other (typical) thrushes. If I have forgotten to speak of other habits, let the reader go to the haunts already described, or to cool woods on the banks of some rapid-running brook, and there learn them.

(*d*). In the cool of the morning, or at evening, from the time when the sun sets until dusk becomes dark, the Wood Thrush, having mounted to a perch so high that his outbursts of heavenly music shall not be confined to earth or lost in the surrounding shrubbery, pours out such a melody, that he seems at every utterance " to be endeavoring to recall his very soul, that fled to heaven on the winged notes of his last liquid melody." At other times of the day, if it is cloudy, or if he is in dark, cool woods, he sings while he is busied in providing for himself or his family, and as he moves through the bushes. This song is rarely one continuous strain, but consists of many detached variations, a series of liquid, metallic, rich, powerful, and expressive notes, which are so exquisite that the all-absorbed and unobtrusive musician seldom if ever fails to charm whoever hears him. Yet, it ought to be remembered that, though some Wood Thrushes can produce such music as perhaps no other birds can rival, others of them are greatly inferior to their fellows.

The ordinary notes of the Wood Thrush are a mellow *chirp*, more metallic and less melancholy in tone than that of the Wilson's Thrush, a *chuck* (sometimes combined with it), and a simple *chip*, such as belongs to a large majority of all the birds described in this volume.

All, who wish to have an insight into the charms, which attend the study of animated birds, should observe the Wood Thrush in his native haunts, and faithfully attend the delightful concerts, which he so often repeats in the cooler hours of the day, in June, July, and even August.

(B) FUCESCENS. *Wilson's Thrush. Tawny Thrush. Common Thrush.* "*Cheeury.*" "*Veery.*" ("*Nightingale.*")

(In Massachusetts the most common of the wood thrushes, A–E.)

(*a*). 7–7½ inches long. Above, soft, bright reddish-brown (or "tawny"). Beneath, white; breast strongly tinged with fulvous (or a pinkish brown), and, together with the sides of the throat, sparsely—sometimes almost imperceptibly—streaked with small dusky spots.

(*b*). The nest is usually placed on the ground, and rarely in a bush or low tree. It is generally composed of grasses and dead leaves, to which grape-vine bark is sometimes added, and it is often lined with finer grasses and roots, or even horse-hairs. I have commonly, but not always, found it in tussocks of grass or hillocks of moss, in swamps or near them. The eggs average $.85 \times .60$ of an inch, and are *light* blue, green-tinted. In Massachusetts, the first annual set (of four or five) generally appears in the last week of May, or the first of June; a second set (of three or four) is sometimes laid in July.

(*c*). The Wilson's Thrushes are in Massachusetts the most common of the so-called "wood thrushes," but in northern New England are rare, being generally much less common than the Hermit or Swainson's Thrush in New Hampshire and Maine. They reach the neighborhood of Boston, in their annual spring-migrations, almost invariably on or about the eighth day of May, and very often before pear-trees have blossomed,— a fact which I mention, because the blossoming of those trees has frequently been spoken of as coincident with the arrival of these birds from their winter-homes in the South. Their first appearance is in those haunts where they pass the summer; and in the swamps three or four sometimes collect and engage in the quarrels entailed by courtship, previous to mating. The Wilson's Thrushes, though not so fond of solitude as the Wood Thrush, are rather shy, and yet they often wander in quest of food to the orchard, garden, and the immediate neighborhood of man or his dwellings. They prefer, however, to remain in the swamps and the adjacent woods, during a great part of the day. They can run over the ground with rapidity, but in the woods they usually poke about quietly among the pine-needles and dead leaves, where they can find the insects on which they feed, and in the swamps walk over the decayed vegetation, which has become matted on the ground, or has accumulated on the stagnant pools of water. When disturbed, while thus busied, they generally fly to a bush near the spot, and sit there quite motionless, occasionally uttering their chirp, until it seems to them safe to return to their interrupted occupation. They also obtain much of their food from trees, and are particularly fond of pine-groves, where they may often be seen, generally on the broader-backed limbs. They seem, when perching, to prefer these to the smaller branches, as they also do a post to a fence-rail, apparently liking a broad surface to stand upon rather than one which they must grasp. They are rarely seen far from the ground, and seldom protract their flight for more than a hundred yards, except occasionally when conveying food to their young from a comparatively remote orchard, garden, or swamp.

They deserve to be regarded on a cultivated estate not only as sources of pleasure, but also as extremely useful. Mr. Samuels, in an article on the Robin in his book entitled "Birds of New England and Adjacent States," says: "In fact, the Thrushes seem designed by nature to rid the surface of the soil of noxious insects not often pursued by most other birds. The warblers capture the insects that prey on the foliage of the trees; the flycatchers seize these insects as they fly from the trees; the swallows capture those which have escaped all these; the woodpeckers destroy them when in the larva state in the wood; the wrens, nuthatches, titmice and creepers, eat the eggs and young that live on and beneath the bark; but the thrushes subsist on those that destroy the vegetation on the surface of the earth."[3]

---

[3] Many thrushes obtain much of their food from trees; the Swainson's Thrushes most of it. Many sparrows feed as thrushes do.

(*d*). The voice of the Wilson's Thrushes is not so fine as that of the Wood Thrush, and, when heard from a near standpoint, sounds peculiarly muffled, though, when heard at a greater distance, it becomes mellow and much clearer. From the first of June until the time of their departure (the first of September) draws near, one may often hear in the day-time the simple song of these birds, "*cheéury, cheéury, cheéury,*"[4] which they give utterance to, generally from some bough in the pine-groves, or the other woods which they frequent. It is in the summer-evenings that this song is somewhat prolonged, becoming "more glorious"; and the male, when his mate is on her nest, sometimes repeats it at night, whence he is among the birds, upon whom the epithet "Nightingale" has been bestowed.

The ordinary note of the "Veeries" is a characteristic and peculiar *chirp*, a liquid sound, often uttered in a seemingly petulant and melancholy tone; besides which they often give utterance to *chips, chicks,* "lisps" like those of the Cedar-bird, and a harsh "grating" sound, much like that of other birds and peculiar to the mating-season.

The two thrushes already described are summer-residents in Massachusetts. The other (typical) thrushes, whom I am about to describe, only pass through this State, spending their summers in a more northern climate.

(C) PALLASI. *Hermit Thrush.* "*Swamp Thrush.*" "*Swamp Robin.*"

(Common near Boston in April and October.)

(*a*). About seven inches long. *Above, soft dusky-olive, becoming rufous on the rump and tail.* Under parts white; breast buff-tinged and darkly spotted; sides olive-shaded.

(*b*). The nest of the Hermit Thrush, which has rarely been found in Massachusetts, is placed almost invariably upon the

---

[4] This chant, which is not unlike some of the Wood Thrush's music, consists of three or four triplets on a descending scale, in each triplet the first note being the highest.

ground, occasionally in swamps, but more often on sunny, sloping, and shrubby banks near them. It is much like that of the Wilson's Thrush (B), though usually rather larger, coarser, and more loosely constructed. The Hermit Thrushes often lay two sets of three or four eggs, one in the first week of June, and one about a month later. Their eggs are very much like those of the "Veeries" (B), but are larger, averaging $.90 \times .65$ of an inch. They are light greenish blue, *never* spotted.

(c). In the woods about Boston (and of course in other woods), whether swampy or dry, and also along the wooded roadsides, from the middle of April until the first of May, one may see a great number of Hermit Thrushes. During their stay here, these birds, often in pairs, and sometimes in small parties (a fact, which shows that their name is not altogether an appropriate one), spend their time, for the most part in silence, busied among the dead leaves and underbrush, occasionally resting on a low perch, and rarely flying far when disturbed. They are quiet birds, and, though often easily approached, prefer those places where they are not likely to be intruded upon. On leaving this State in the spring, they pass on to northern New England and to Canada, where they spend the summer and rear their young, being in some localities the most common thrushes. In October, they return to Massachusetts in the course of their journey to their winter-homes in the South, and a few linger until November is well advanced.[5] During their sojourn here in autumn, they frequent the ground much less than in spring, and feed largely on various kinds of berries, many of which they find in swamps.

These birds are to be associated with October, when the roads, hardened by frost, are neither muddy nor dusty, when the paths through the woods are strewn with the soft fallen

---

[5] Mr. Maynard, writing of the Hermit Thrush in the "Naturalist's Guide," says that he has "taken it in Coos County, New Hampshire, on October 31st, although the ground was covered with snow, six inches deep at the time; also in Oxford County, Maine, as late as November 6th." He adds that "a few undoubtedly breed here."

leaves, which rustle pleasantly beneath one's feet, when the clear, cold, exhilarating weather is well adapted to exercise, when the maples are in the utmost splendor of their brilliant coloring, and finally when the hills, covered with the oaks of low growth, where once forests stood, glow with the rich crimson, which at last becomes a dull brown, showing winter to be near at hand.

(*d*). The Hérmit Thrushes very rarely sing except in the summer-season, and generally, while with us, their only notes are a mellow *chirp*, a loud *chuck*, rarely uttered (especially in spring?), and a single low whistle, which seems to come from a more distant point than that which the bird occupies. When frightened from their nests they often utter a very characteristic dissyllabic note, expressive of their sorrow. Their song is strikingly fine, and recalls the melody of the Wood Thrush to one familiar with that melody, though lacking the power and full music of the latter, being, as Mr. Burroughs has said, silvery rather than golden. It usually begins with a few low, rich notes, which are followed by the higher and more ringing ones.

Though the Hermit Thrushes bear a strong general resemblance to the two other " wood thrushes," whom an inexperienced observer is likely to see in any part of this State (A and B), yet they are rarely seen in the company of those birds, preceding them in the spring-migrations, and returning to the South later. They sometimes are found during their annual journeys in company with the Gray-cheeked or Swainson's Thrush, but the former is rare, and seldom has any reddish-brown tinting on the upper parts, and the latter has both rather distinct habits and notes. Let the young student, who wishes to distinguish several closely allied species, *mark the points of difference*, and not the similar characteristics of each, and let him avoid employing only one means of distinction, such as coloration.

(D) SWAINSONI. *Swainson's Thrush. Olive-backed Thrush.* "*Swamp Robin*"?

(A rather rare migrant through Massachusetts.)

(*a*). 7–7½ inches long. Above, soft, dusky olive (occasionally with a reddish-brown tinge). Sides of the head buff, and breast strongly tinged with the same color. The latter and the sides of the throat, thickly spotted with dusky. *Eye-ring buff.*

(*b*). The nest is a rather bulky structure, usually composed of twigs, mosses, grasses, leaves, etc., with no mud, and sometimes lined with the coal-black hairs of a certain moss. It is placed in a spruce, low tree, or perhaps a bush, from three to ten feet above the ground. It is often built beside a road or wood-path. The first set, of three or four eggs, is usually laid in the first, or perhaps more often the second week of June; the second set is laid four or five weeks later. The eggs are much like those of the Scarlet Tanager, being about $.95 \times .70$ of an inch, and light blue, olive-tinged, either finely marked with indistinct brown, or coarsely spotted (with a few fine markings beside), chiefly at the great end, with obscure lilac, and two shades of brown.

(*c*). Though the Swainson's Thrushes are by no means very common migrants through Eastern Massachusetts, yet a vigilant and energetic ornithologist can hardly fail to meet with them in the spring. Groves of tall hemlocks are among the places, where, about the middle of May, I have seen these birds, not on the ground, but among the branches of the trees, from which they occasionally dart into the air and catch insects in the manner of flycatchers. I have also met them in swampy roads, or even in orchards, and have observed them on the ground, often moving quite rapidly, or pausing in a rather erect attitude. Probably, it is partly because of their usual shyness while migrating, partly because they often frequent the higher branches, and partly because two of their ordinary notes are very much like those of the Snow-birds (of whom a few linger in May), that they are often considered rarer than they are. Before June all the Olive-backed Thrushes pass beyond the limits of this State, and of these many spend the summer in northern Vermont or New Hampshire, and in Maine, some of them revisiting the neighborhood of Boston about the first of October, when the wonderful instinct of migration prompts them to return to Florida or still further to the South. In a certain township among the White Mountains I have studied the habits of these birds, who there inhabit various kinds of woodland, particularly those which have swamps or brooks in them, but keep nearer the ground, and exhibit much less shyness in those wild woods than they habitually do, when traveling.

In autumn, however, they are much less shy and active than they are in spring; and, during the fall-migrations, they may be found in woods and copses. There they pick up food from the ground and the lower branches of bushes or trees, since at that season there are few winged insects, of a size acceptable to them, to be caught in the air, and since before the severer frosts of autumn have come, and before the Hermit Thrushes are abundant, a large supply of food suitable to them can be found among the dead leaves, many of which have then already fallen.

To resume the remarks just interrupted,— in the woods of the White Mountains, they sing almost throughout the summer, and often throughout the day, for the old forests of New Hampshire are always cool and shady. They more often sing, however, in the early morning, or at sunset, as does the Wood Thrush, and, like that bird, they frequently perch on a high and prominent bough when about to sing. They usually stay on their nests rather more boldly than the Hermit Thrushes are wont to do, and watch over their young, when they have left the nest, with great care, showing as warm an interest in their offspring, as I have ever seen displayed in birds.

(*d*). The ordinary note of the Swainson's Thrushes, especially when in their summer-homes, is an attractive one, exactly resembling the word "whit" brusquely whistled in a tolerably low tone, and very quickly. Their song-notes exhibit less variation than those of any of their immediate relations, being all nearly on the same pitch, and reminding one forcibly of the less brilliant singers among the Wood Thrushes, and bearing more resemblance to the notes of that bird than to those of any other. Though, as I have said, less varied than those of the other "wood thrushes," they are sweet, clear, and liquid, and possess great charm.

The other notes of the Olive-backed Thrushes, are a *chuck* of alarm, a feeble *tsip* quite uncharacteristic, and a cry of *chick*, *chick-a-sit*, etc., like that of the Snow-bird, to which I have heard them give utterance in spring, when chasing one another through the branches, or when slightly alarmed. They have also a feebly whistled *peep*, heard chiefly in autumn.

The "New Hampshire Thrushes," though they correspond to the Wood Thrush of Massachusetts, are yet inferior to that bird. How then would they be ranked by Buffon, who wrote of the latter, says Wilson, "that the Song Thrush of Europe had, at some time after the creation, rambled round by the Northern ocean, and made its way to America; that advancing to the south it had there (of consequence) become degenerated by change of food and climate, so that its cry is now harsh and unpleasant, 'as are the cries of all birds that live in wild countries inhabited by savages.'"?

(E) ALICIÆ. *Gray-cheeked Thrush.* *Alice's Thrush.* *Arctic Thrush.*

(In New England a rare migrant.)

(*a*). 7½-8 inches long. Above soft, subdued olive-green. Sides of the head gray. Beneath white, with little or no buff; breast and sides of the throat spotted with dark brown. It is said that specimens of this species grade inseparably into others of *Swainsoni* (*D*). But distinctions are not to be based wholly on coloration.

(*b*). The Gray-cheeked Thrushes build their nests in Arctic countries, most often on the ground. The only egg of this species in my collection is like that of the Swainson's Thrush, but more thickly and minutely marked. (See *D*, *b*.)

(*c*). The Gray-cheeked Thrush is thought by some ornithologists not to be a valid species, but, if not a species distinct from the Swainson's Thrush, it is a very distinct variety or geographical race.⁶ It differs from that bird, slightly in coloration, and markedly as to distribution, habits (song), and notes.

The Arctic Thrushes are the rarest of those who migrate through Massachusetts, particularly that part which borders upon the sea, since they generally prefer a more inland route to the North than this State affords. I have occasionally seen them in the latter part of April or in May, but they are shy and very timid, so that it is difficult to approach them closely, as, when startled, they fly about restlessly. Perhaps, on this account, they have escaped general observation. They are eminently terrestrial birds, and spend nearly all their time on the ground, picking up their food among the fallen leaves in such places as the Hermit Thrush frequents; often preferring, however, dry land and solitary spots, where they run but little risk of being disturbed. They stand rather more erectly than the "Swamp Robins" so called (*T. Pallasi*), but it must be remembered that erectness of bearing is a general characteristic of all "wood thrushes." They pass the summer in the Arctic region, and, on their return to the South, pass through the neighborhood of Boston about the first of October, but are then extremely rare, since "in the fall-migrations they follow for the most part a route far from the sea-shore."

(*d*). Their ordinary note is a single low, and perhaps to some ears rather melancholy whistle — "whéu." As to their other notes I am uncertain, and I have never heard their song, but Dr. Brewer, in "North American Birds," says that it is totally different "from that of all our other Wood Thrushes. It most resembles the song of *T. Pallasi*, but differs from it in being its exact inverse, for whereas the latter begins with its lowest and proceeds on an ascending scale, the former begins with its highest, and concludes with its lowest note. The song of the *T. Swainsoni* on the other hand, exhibits much less variation in the scale, all the notes being of nearly the same altitude."

---

⁶ If a variety, Swainson's Thrush is the other variety, and the Olive-backed Thrush the species including both.

(F) MIGRATORIUS. (*American*) *Robin.*
(An extremely common summer-resident in Massachusetts, where a few pass the winter.)

(*a*). 9-10 inches long. Above, dark (olive) gray; head and tail almost black, both with white spots. Breast of a peculiar ruddy red or orange-brown, in pale specimens merely dun-colored. Chin, under tail-coverts, etc., white, more or less black-streaked. Bill generally yellow.

(*b*). The Robins build their nests in bushes, vines, the larger garden-shrubs, or most often in trees; evergreens, particularly pines and spruces, being preferred to all others. Where these latter are wanting, they often build their nests in orchard-trees, or in those which shade the streets; occasionally, however, placing them about some building. The nest is "saddled" to a bough or placed in a fork, from three to fifty feet above the ground, and is a very firm though rather rude structure, consisting chiefly of mud, and of dry grass or its equivalent.

The eggs of each set are four or five, delicate greenish blue, and about $1.15 \times .80$ of an inch. I have found freshly laid eggs of this species from May first until the twentieth of July; two or even three broods being usually raised, if the parents are undisturbed.

(*c*). The Robins are undoubtedly in summer the most abundant of all the birds in Massachusetts, and to most country-residents in this State are probably the most familiar; but in northern New England they are much less common than in most other parts of the eastern states. Dr. Brewer, however, has written that "in the valleys amongst the White Mountains, where snow covers the ground from October to June, and where the cold reaches the freezing-point of mercury, flocks of Robins remain during the entire winter, attracted by the abundance of berries." A few certainly spend the winter about us, in the swamps, and also in cedar-woods; for, though these latter contain but few berries, or none, yet the thick foliage of many of the trees affords safe shelter from heavy storms of snow, when protection is so much needed. Though I have seen companies of Robins in February, it is not usually until the early part of March that they come from the South; on their arrival, collecting in flocks and feeding on barberries, small fruits of the same kind, and such other suitable food as they can find. They retire, at this season, a few minutes before the hour of sunset, generally passing the night in spruces; and, in the early morning, arising before the sun, they generally betake themselves to the southern slope of some hill, where the snow has melted, thus offering to them the comfort of a little bare ground, and there they pass the day.

It is very wonderful that birds employed in active exercise throughout the day, perhaps a bright one, when the heat of the sun is strong, can pass the night in sleep and inactivity, when but little shielded from the bitterness of the weather in March, that month, which in New England is with ghastly inappropriateness called the first month of spring. It is also wonderful that, whereas in midwinter most birds sleep fourteen or fifteen hours out of twenty-four, and pass only nine or ten in exercise, in the latter part of June, when the longest days of the year occur, they require little more than half that amount of rest to counterbalance the fatigue of at least sixteen hours' labor. I have known Robins to awake and to begin their daily duties before half-past three o'clock in the morning, and to be still moving about after eight in the evening; at that season of the year, moreover, when the male must provide for his young as well as for himself. In the case of many birds, either the male or the female sits on the nest, whilst the other forages, but I have known instances in which the male never sat on his nest, so that all the active duties in the care of his family devolved upon him.

The Robins continue to come from the South until the first of April, and during the greater part of that month are inclined to be gregarious, but they finally separate, and many begin to build; many waiting, however, until May, or even June. As is well known, in the cultivated parts of the country they do not often retire to the woods (except in winter), preferring to remain in open lands, in the neighborhood of man, and about cultivated estates, and are so little wild as to inhabit Boston Common and other equally frequented places. In the country, they pass the summer in villages and such other haunts as I have described, gathering into flocks in the latter part of August, and journeying to warmer climates in September or October. Robins are in some parts of the State so plentiful, that in May sixty of their nests, containing eggs, were found in an area of fifteen acres. Had Massachusetts then been populated by these thrushes in that proportion of parent-birds to an acre, it would have contained nearly 40,000,000 of them, whereas I suppose that it actually contained less than 1,000,000.

To those who consider Robins either useless or injurious to man the following remarks on the nature of their food may be of interest. In winter and in the early part of spring, they feed chiefly upon berries, such as those of the barberry, poisonous "ivy," etc., but as soon as the frost is expelled from the ground, they begin their attacks upon the earthworms, and constantly renew them throughout the summer and in September, wherever earthworms are abundant. One may often see Robins gathered on a lawn, particularly after hard showers, eagerly engaged in unearthing their prey, now running along so quickly that it is almost impossible to detect the motion of their feet (which, in fact, is not hopping, but walking), now stopping, and, having cocked their heads to one side that their ears may be near the ground, listening intently, then passing on, or perhaps stopping, and with two or three vigorous strokes of their bills, pulling out the worms, which are soon disposed of. When they fail to secure their prey, after a few bold "digs," they generally move on and do not make any further attempt to obtain it. They make extensive raids upon cherries " and strawberries," *when ripe*, and feed upon ripe pears and apples, especially in autumn, generally meddling with these latter fruits when fallen to the ground, and not when on the trees. In return for these robberies, they destroy innumerable "cut-worms" and other injurious creatures of the same kind, and confer, in this way, great benefits upon farmers and fruit-growers, for they are *much* more dependent upon the flesh of insects than upon other food. I think that there is no doubt that between fifty and a hundred Robins eat a million worms and injurious caterpillars, if not more, during their annual sojourn in the neighborhood of Boston. Professor Treadwell has recorded the instance of a young Robin in confinement, who ate in twelve hours 140 *per cent.* of his own weight, and consumed fourteen feet of earthworms.

The Robins possess greater powers of flight than do the other thrushes, and can fly far and rapidly, often moving through the air at a considerable height above the ground, particularly when migrating. They have a habit of jerking their tail, which the "wood thrushes" do not possess, and which is particularly noticeable when they utter their notes of alarm. They are not brave, with individual exceptions, but are easily frightened, particularly when sitting on their nests, and yet they are by no means shy, and frequent familiarly the neighborhood of man.

(*d*). The Robins have besides their song, and a very faint whistle like the Cedar-bird's lisp, but one note, which is constantly varied, usually being in the winter, early spring, and fall, more dreary than in the summer, when it is sometimes merely a *chirp*, though at other times it is uttered in a tone of excitement or vehemence and rapidly repeated. The cry of the young is somewhat harsher than that of the mature birds, who are very pleasant singers, and often warble a cheerful, energetic song, consisting of a few monotonous notes, which are repeated with some little variation, chiefly in the morning and at dusk, in spring or summer.

It is to be hoped that eventually the American people will become as fond of the American Robins, as the English are of their smaller "Robin Red-breasts," whose name our Pilgrim Fathers bestowed upon the Thrushes of this country, now so common and familiar to us.

(G) NÆVIUS. *Varied Thrush. Oregon Robin.*

(One specimen of this bird, whose proper *habitat* is the Pacific Slope, has been taken at Ipswich, Mass., in December.)

(*a*). 9–10 inches long; slate-color. Beneath, orange-brown. Band across the breast, black. Under tail-coverts, white. ♀ duller.

(*b*). The eggs of this species measure about 1·15 × ·80 of an inch, and are greenish blue, darkly spotted.

(*c*). Its habits are presumably much like those of our Robin.

(*d*). "From this bird it may be readily distinguished by the difference of its notes, which are louder, sharper, and delivered with greater rapidity." Dr. Cooper "describes the song as consisting of five or six notes in a minor key, and in a scale regularly descending."

II. MIMUS

(A) POLYGOTTUS. *Mocking Bird.*

(A very rare, or almost accidental summer-visitor to southern New England.)

(*a*). 9–10 inches long. Above, rather light ashy gray. Beneath, white. Wings and tail dark, with conspicuous white patches.

(*b*). The nest is built near the ground, often in a conspicuous situation. Audubon describes it as "coarsely constructed on the outside, being there composed of dried sticks of briars, withered leaves of trees, and grasses, mixed with wool. Internally it is finished with fibrous roots disposed in a circular form, but carelessly arranged." An egg before me measures 1·00 × ·75 of an inch, and is of a very light dull blue, rather coarsely spotted with lilac and rather faint purplish or reddish umber.

(*c*). So many Mocking Birds have recently been captured in New England and Massachusetts itself, that they cannot longer be well considered escaped cage-birds. They must therefore be ranked here as very rare summer-residents. Since, however, their presence is almost exceptional, since their habits are much like those of the common Cat-bird, since their powers of mimicry and song are well-known, and finally, since I am personally unacquainted with their natural mode of life, I have thought it best not to attempt their biography in this volume. For an enthusiastic and splendid description, I refer my readers to the second volume of Wilson's Ornithology.

(B) CAROLINENSIS. *Cat-bird.*
(A common summer-resident.)

(*a*). 8½–9 inches long. Slate-colored. Crown and tail, black. Under tail-coverts, chestnut-red.

(*b*). The nest of the Cat-bird, which in Massachusetts is usually finished in the last week of May, is generally placed in a bush, thicket, or briar, and is composed outwardly of sticks (and sometimes one or two rags intermixed), being lined with strips of bark from the grape-vine or cedar, dead leaves, rootlets, and other things of the same sort. The eggs of each set are 3–5, usually four, of a fine dark green, bluish-tinted, and measure about ·95 × ·70 of an inch. Two broods are sometimes raised in the summer.

(*c*). The Cat-birds are in summer very common in the old "Bay State," and are familiar to many of its inhabitants, usually appearing in their haunts here in the first week of May, some returning to the South in September, others waiting until the middle of October. Though very numerous in the cultivated districts of Massachusetts, they are rather rare in the northern parts of New England; and yet " they have been met with in Arctic countries," as have Robins also. They for the most part prefer the neighborhood of man and of cultivated soil, though one may often find their nests in wild spots, far from any house, since they roam over all the open country. Though never properly gregarious, individuals do the work of a host in destroying injurious insects; eating the caterpillars, which they find in orchards, shrubbery, bushes, and thickets, and feeding upon " cut-worms," which they obtain in ploughed lands. This fare they vary by occasionally catching winged insects, as they fly through the air, but more often by eating berries of various kinds, chiefly such as grow in swamps.

From the nature of their usual employment, they rarely have occasion to perch very far above the ground, or to take other than short flights, since they pass most of their time in shrubbery,—when frightened, generally taking refuge in a thicket, or a clump of bushes, so as to be effectually lost to sight. Though not habitually bold, they are often brave in resenting intrusions on their nests, giving a " warm " reception to cats, driving away or killing snakes, and occasionally flying at man. Two things are easily observable in the habits of these thrushes, namely: When on the ground, they can move about with agility, and when perched, they often flirt their tails, or, when singing, depress them in a peculiar manner, which renders their attitude rather ludicrous. In autumn, before their departure, the Cat-birds become rather reserved and shy, and I have sometimes been able to detect their presence only by occasionally hearing their characteristic cry, or seeing them fly into " scrub " or other shrubbery, with their broad tails expanded to their fullest extent, as they crossed some road or path and dove into a thicket beyond. Their habits in the fall of the year illustrate the fact, that in spring most birds can easily be detected, if even carelessly sought for at the proper season, because of their song, their comparatively little shyness, and those bright tints, which, in the case of many birds, are exchanged for duller tints, when the summer either is over or draws near to its end; whereas in autumn, on the other hand, many birds quietly, and in silence seldom broken, continue to spend their days about us, and to migrate through those places where they were conspicuous in spring, escaping our observation through their greater shyness and retirement. There are two other partial explanations of the actually and apparently greater abundance of certain birds, when passing to the *North* through Eastern Massachusetts than when returning,—which are, that in the autumnal migrations many species for the most part choose a more inland route, and that in spring, the warblers, for instance, are prompted to their long journeys by a sudden outburst or a gradual approach of genuine warmth, such as gives life to the insects on which they feed; whereas in fall, unless startled by a sudden visitation of cold, they gradually leave their summer-homes, and by degrees straggle (if I may use the expression) to their winter-haunts.[7]

(*d*). The song of the Cat-birds, which is very much like that of the Brown Thrush, is in some respects a striking one, for the tone and accent are very marked; and, though some of the notes are rather harsh or uncouth, others are very mellow. This song is not a definite or limited one, but is repeated for several minutes together, from the time of their arrival until the summer is nearly over, especially at evening; but it is not unfrequently marred or interrupted by the mimicry of others' notes, for, though the Cat-birds do not possess the wonderful powers of the Mocking Birds, yet they are clever mimics, imitating Quail, Pewees, Least Flycatchers, and even hens, with great exactness. I have been more than once deluded by these musicians into the belief that I distinctly heard birds, whose presence I justly but little expected in the places, where I have thus been momentarily deceived. The Cat-birds have a mellow *chuck*, a chattered alarm-note, which I am inclined to think that they seldom use, and a familiar harsh cry, which resembles the " mew " of a cat, whence their common name, and also, probably, that instinctive but irrational antipathy, which many boys entertain for this bird.

III. HARPORHYNCHUS

(A) RUFUS. *Brown Thrush*. "*Song Thrush*." "*Thrasher*." "*Mavis*."

(A common summer-resident in southern New England.)

(*a*). About eleven inches long. Above, bright reddish-brown; below, white (or tinged), streaked with dark brown, but throat unmarked. Wings with white bars. Tail very long.

(*b*). The nest is placed in a bush (occasionally in a tree, such as the cedar) or on the ground; never far from it. When placed in a bush, sticks are generally used in its construction; in all situations the nest being usually composed, wholly or

---

[7] It is hoped that the author will be excused for these digressive remarks by those persons who are well acquainted with the facts mentioned.

partly, of strips of cedar-bark and the like, together with dead leaves and similar substances. The eggs are dirty white, covered with very numerous and minute *light* brown markings, and average 1·05 × ·80 of an inch, or more. One specimen is slightly tinged with green. In Eastern Massachusetts, two sets of these eggs (containing four or five) are laid every year, the first of which commonly appears in the last week of May, though sometimes exceptionally in the second week.

(c). Not only do the notes of the Brown Thrush bear a strong resemblance to those of the Cat-bird, but their habits also correspond closely to those of that bird. The "Song Thrushes" reach the neighborhood of Boston, more often in the first than in the second week of May, or perhaps most often in the last week of April, and are common summer-residents throughout southern New England, many not withdrawing until October. They are rare, however, in Northern Vermont, New Hampshire, and Maine. Though on their arrival one may often see them on cultivated estates and near houses, yet they almost invariably, so far as I know, pass their summers in that species of shrubbery known as "scrub," or in low cedar-woods, where underbrush abounds, and are much less familiar toward man than are their relations the Cat-birds. They feed upon berries, caterpillars, wasps, or beetles, and, while engaged in procuring them, may often be seen moving from bush to bush, with a characteristic flight, and with their long tails so outspread as to be very conspicuous. When they perch, the "Thrashers" flirt or depress their tails in the manner of the last species, to whom I have already referred; and they likewise are very bold in the defence of their nest, often hissing with the vehemence of a pugnacious goose. They frequently have refused to leave their nests on my approach, unless to fly at me in a way, which used to frighten me heartily, when young. They are so brave and at the same time so unsociable as rarely or never to congregate, either for the sake of mutual protection or of companionship. They may be seen, however, in pairs, rustling loudly among the dead leaves, or hopping along the ground with remarkable agility. I have called them "brave," and yet, when their young are reared, they resume their natural shyness, avoid man, and on his approach disappear in the surrounding shrubbery; but the instinct of motherhood can inspire bravery in those habitually timid, when emergencies occur which require courage.

(*d*). The loud *chuck* of the Brown Thrushes, their indescribable note of alarm or displeasure, and their song are all, as has been intimated, much like those of the Cat-bird. Their song is very pleasing, being loud, emphatic, and wonderfully varied; so much so that it is sometimes well-nigh impossible to believe that one bird can produce such widely different notes, but, though called "mockers," the "Thrashers" never mimic other creatures, so far as I have observed. Often, if interrupted, when singing, they softly repeat the syllables "tu-whit, tu-whit," and immediately resume their song. In May, at evening, I have often listened to them, when, having chosen a high perch, they have sung sweetly and loudly; and it was when thinking of such singing that Wilson wrote: "The human being, who, amidst such scenes, and in such seasons of rural serenity and delight, can pass them with cold indifference, and even contempt, I sincerely pity; for abject must that heart be, and callous those feelings, and depraved that taste, which neither the charms of nature, nor the melody of innocence, nor the voice of devotion of gratitude or devotion reach."

§ 2. **Saxicolidæ.** Stone-chats and bluebirds. (See §1.)
I. SIALIA
(A) SIALIS. (*Eastern*) *Blue Bird.*
(Very common in Massachusetts during the warmer half of the year.)

(*a*). $6\frac{1}{2}$-7 inches long. Above, bright blue (in females, immature specimens, and specimens in winter-plumage, often interrupted by dull-colored patches). Belly white; other under parts bright, ruddy brown or chestnut. ♀ usually much duller or paler than ♂.

(*b*). The nest is generally placed in the hole of a tree or post, or in a bird-box. The eggs, which measure about ·85 ×

·62 of an inch, are *light* blue (very rarely white). Two sets of 4-6 are usually laid each year in this State, of which the first commonly appears about the first of May.

(c). The familiar Blue Birds are the first birds to come from their winter-homes to the Eastern States; for they reach the neighborhood of Boston, invariably no later than March, and sometimes in February. They have once reached it, according to Dr. Brewer, on the twenty-eighth day of January, though never known to pass the winter here. In summer they are very common and generally well-known throughout southern New England, though comparatively rare to the northward, as in the case with many other of our common birds. Whilst migrating, they usually fly very high, and one may often be apprised of their coming, before seeing them, by hearing their warbled note, which they frequently utter when on wing. By the middle of March they become quite common, and may be seen in small companies, perched on telegraph-wires, or ridgepoles of barns, on fences or trees, occasionally calling to one another, or moving from place to place. Cheerless as the season then is, they contrive to exist, though naturally insectivorous, until warmer weather causes an abundance of insects; and they even mate during the cold weather, with which spring is inaugurated in this part of the world. In April, they gather various warm materials, and build their nests by placing them in a bird-box, or at the bottom of a hole in some tree; and in these nests their eggs are laid about the first of May, when but few other of our birds have begun incubation. The haunts of the Blue Birds are well-known, and few naturalists can pass through farms, orchards, gardens, or fields, or travel over roads through cultivated lands and villages, without associating with them these companions of every student of nature. The Blue Birds are not only pleasant friends, but are also useful laborers in behalf of agriculturists, as is proved by the nature of their food, and the manner in which they obtain it. Though in the early spring, and more so in fall, various berries afford them nourishment, yet in May, and throughout the summer, they feed quite exclusively upon insects, chiefly upon beetles, many of which are injurious. As they often rear two or even three broods of young during their annual sojourn in Massachusetts, they necessarily destroy an incalculable number of pests (at the rate of between fifty and a hundred thousand to a pair in four months). So soon as the young of the first brood are old enough to leave the nest, the female soon begins again to lay, while the male takes charge of the young, teaching them how to catch their prey. He may often be seen to perch in some open spot, and, flying into the air (much in the manner of flycatchers), to seize some passing insect, or, pausing with rapidly quivering wings, to snap up some grasshopper or beetle from the grass, immediately returning to his perch. Though the Blue Birds have been known to take long flights, when traveling, yet they rarely fly far at other times, and, though when journeying they move through the air at a considerable height, at other times they usually remain rather near the ground, but they never, as a rule, stand on it, except occasionally when collecting bits of straw or the like, with which to build their nests. In autumn they gather in small flocks, and in October generally depart from this State, though a few linger until November.

(d). The only song of the Blue Birds is a repetition of a " sadly-pleasing " but cheerful warble of two or three notes, *tinged* (so to speak) by a mournful tone. This they often give utterance to when on wing, as well as when perched. In autumn, and when with their young, their usual note is a single sad whistle, but they occasionally use a peculiar chatter as a call-note to their young, whose notes differ from those of their parents.

I shall here close my account of these birds, deservedly popular as forerunners of spring, companions of man, and cheerful, beneficial laborers, by quoting a few lines from one of Alexander Wilson's poems.

In Autumn

" The Blue-bird, forsaken, yet true to his home,
" Still lingers, and looks for a milder to-morrow,
" Till forc'd by the horrors of winter to roam,
" He sings his adieu in a lone note of sorrow.

> "While spring's lovely season, serene, dewy, warm,
> "The green face of earth, and the pure blue of heav'n,
> "Or love's native music have influence to charm,
> "Or sympathy's glow to our feelings is ᵃ giv'n.
>
> "Still dear to each bosom the Blue-bird shall be;
> "His voice, like the thrillings of hope, is a treasure;
> "For, thro' bleakest storms if a calm he but see,
> "He comes to remind us of sunshine and pleasure!"

NOTE. The European Stone-chat or "Wheat-ear" (*Saxicola œnanthe*) occurs in Northern North America as a wanderer, and is included by Dr. Coues in his "List of the Birds of New England." In his "Key" he describes it as follows (the length being 5–6 inches?) : " Adult : — ashy gray ; forehead, superciliary line and under parts white, latter often brownish-tinted ; upper tail coverts white, wings and tail black, latter with most of the feathers white for half their length ; line from nostril to eye, and broad band on side of head, black ; bill and feet, black ; *young* everywhere cinnamon-brown, paler below ; * * * * * * ."

§ 3. Sylviidæ. (See § 1.)

I. REGULUS

(A) CALENDULUS. *Ruby-crowned* "*Wren.*" *Ruby-crowned* "*Kinglet.*"[9]

(Common in Massachusetts in April and October.)

(*a*). 4–4½ inches long. Above, greenish olive ; below, white, impure and yellow-tinged. Wings with two white bars, and (like the tail) with light edgings. Eye-ring, impure white. Crown in mature specimens with a *scarlet patch*, wanting in immature birds (and females?[10]) ; moreover, in some specimens, small and orange-colored.

(*b*). I believe that there is no record of the nest and eggs

---

[a] In the original "are," evidently through inadvertance.
[9] These birds have been called "Kinglets" from their scientific name (*Regulus*), meaning "little king."
[10] I have seen in spring pairs of these birds, highly colored, and apparently fully matured, of whom the males had a brilliant *carmine* patch, and the females no patch at all, or none evident.

having ever been discovered. They are probably like those of allied British species, and of the Golden-crowned "Wren" (B, b).

(c). The little Ruby-crowned "Wrens," almost the smallest of North American birds, with the exception of the humming-birds, habitually pass the summer in the countries, which lie to the northward of New England.[11] They reach the neighborhood of Boston, when traveling from the North, in the first or second week of October, and are quite common throughout that month, a few lingering until the middle of November, and still fewer occasionally passing the winter here. In autumn, regardless of the cold frosts, they always seem to be happily employed, either in pairs or singly, in ransacking trees in woods or orchards and elsewhere, for the small insects and eggs, which lie concealed beneath the bark, and in its crevices. They can but rarely be detected here in winter, since they commonly spend that season in the indefinite "South." In spring they generally return to us about the middle of April, and are very common until the middle of May or earlier, when they totally disappear. They may be found in orchards or woodland, and about cultivated estates, everywhere leading the same busy, restless life, which they never for a moment forsake, while daylight lasts. They may be seen now clinging to some cluster of opening leaves or budding flowers, perhaps head downwards, now hopping to a neighboring twig, now flying into the air to dexterously seize a passing insect, then calling to their mates if they be near, or uttering their sweet and joyous song. Though not gregarious, they are of a sociable disposition toward other birds, and in fall often associate with Chickadees, nuthatches, creepers, "Gold-crests," and Downy Woodpeckers, and in spring with various migrating warblers, if there be any to join, whose habits are at all like

---

[11] Wilson, however, says: "From the circumstance of having found them here in summer, I am persuaded that they occasionally breed in Pennsylvania." Mr. Charles C. Abbott, in speaking of their breeding in New Jersey, says that "at least we have as evidence of this their presence in June, and also that of their young in August."

their own. They are not usually shy or suspicious, but are so engrossed in their important occupations that they are easily approached, and are not disturbed, when closely watched. They have but little time to think of danger, and continue their career of constant activity (interrupted only by darkness and incubation), apparently regarding all living things as creatures innocent as they themselves.

(d). In autumn and winter their only note is a feeble lisp. In spring, besides occasionally uttering an indescribable querulous sound, and a harsh " grating " note, which belongs exclusively to that season, the Ruby-crowned " Wrens " sing extremely well, and louder than such small birds seem capable of singing. Their song commonly begins with a few clear whistles, followed by a short, very sweet, and complicated warble, and ending with notes like the syllables *tú-we-we, tú-we-we, tú-we-we*. These latter are often repeated separately, as if the birds had no time for the prelude, or are sometimes merely prefaced by a few rather shrill notes with a rising inflection.

It is astonishing, under existing circumstances, that neither nest nor egg of the Ruby-crowned " Wrens " has been discovered, or at least described. It is probable, and on their account it is to be hoped, that they may long continue to rear their young in happiness and peace, undisturbed by naturalists, in the immense forests of the North.

(B) SATRAPA. *Golden-crowned " Wren." Golden-crowned " Kinglet." " Gold-crest."*

(Moderately common from October until April or May.)

(a). Like *calendulus* (A), except on the head. Crown with a yellow patch (enclosing in ♂ a scarlet one), bordered in front and on the sides by a continuous black line.

(b). The nest of these birds has never, so far as I know, been discovered by any naturalist, previously to this year (1875). Wilson, indeed, thinking that the English " goldcrest " was identical with ours, which is not the case, quoted a description of the nest and eggs of that bird from Dr.

Latham.[12] I therefore have the honor of recording the discovery of the nest of the Golden-crowned "Wren," which I made this summer, on the sixteenth day of July, in a forest of the White Mountains, which consisted chiefly of evergreens and white birches. Having several times observed the bird there, I at last detected them in the act of conveying food to their young, and soon tracked them to their nest. This hung four feet above the ground, from a spreading hemlock-bough, to the twigs of which it was firmly fastened; it was globular, with an entrance in the upper part, and was composed of hanging moss, ornamented with bits of dead leaves, and lined chiefly with feathers. It contained six young birds, but much to my regret no eggs.

(c). The Golden-crowned "Wrens" come to Massachusetts from their summer-homes in the latter part of October or in November, and, though a majority of them move on to the South, many pass the winter here, and continue their residence in this State until April or even the second week of May. During the winter they are for the most part gregarious, and may often be seen in small flocks, moving about among trees; more often among those (such as birches) which spring up beside wood-paths than those growing elsewhere. But they also visit cultivated lands and orchards, generally avoiding evergreens (so far as I have observed), probably, because they do not readily find among them, in cold weather, the small insects and their eggs, which infest the bark of other trees, and upon which they chiefly depend for food.[13] I have always found them more abundant on the edges of lanes through our woods than in other places, and there one may watch them scrambling about from twig to twig and from tree to tree, so busily engaged as to almost ignore one's immediate presence. They are not quite so restless as the Ruby-crowned "Wrens," but are equally so-

---

[12] "American Ornithology," Vol. I, p. 127.

[13] The nuthatches, creepers, and titmice, all affect the pines in winter, and therefore I am at a loss to explain the apparent dislike of these birds to those trees in that season. About the fact I do not think myself mistaken. They share the Chickadee's partiality for white birches.

ciable, and often join the merry Chickadees and their followers, in pursuit of their common prey. In spring, when the cold of winter has become somewhat modified, they are rather less social, roam more freely, and finally move northward, their place being immediately supplied by others, who have been living in a warmer climate. These possess habits more nearly akin to the habits of the Ruby-crowned "Wrens" than those of their predecessors, and frequently catch insects in the air, or obtain them by fluttering before some opening cluster of leaves, while so doing, causing their wings to quiver rapidly, "and often exposing the golden feathers of their head, which are opened and shut with great adroitness," which they also more frequently do when skipping about from bough to bough. Many pass the summer in Northern Maine, and in certain parts of the White Mountains, but none breed in a more southern country, unless in New Jersey, as Dr. Abbott thinks is the case. They are "quite common at Umbagog in June;" "and judging from the condition of female specimens taken, lay their eggs about June 1st." Messrs. Maynard and Brewster "found several pairs in the thick hemlock woods, that evidently had nests in the immediate vicinity."

(d). Beyond an occasional weak note, or a cry of *tsee-tsee-tsee*, the Golden-crowned "Wrens" are usually silent, whilst staying in their winter-homes, except on the approach or arrival of spring, when they sometimes give utterance to a twittered warble, which resembles the weaker song-notes of the Chickadees. In their summer-homes they have a song, which Mr. Maynard has described as "a series of low, shrill chirps, terminating in a lisping warble;" and, when with their young, they twitter constantly, as do also many other birds.

Note.—Cuvier's "Kinglet" (*Regulus Cuvieri*) is a source of conjecture to all modern ornithologists. It was obtained by Audubon near the banks of the Schuylkill River, in June, 1812. Only one specimen was taken, which differed from *satrapa* in having the crown-patch entirely vermilion and two black stripes on each side of the head. I have suspicions of having seen this species in New England, but they are too vague to render the supposed circumstance probable.

II. POLIOPTILA

(A) CÆRULEA. *Blue-gray Gnatcatcher.*

(A very rare or exceptional summer-resident in New England.)

(*a*). 4–4½ inches long. "Clear ashy blue, bluer on head; forehead, and line over eye, black (wanting in ♀): outer tail feather white." Bill, feet, and rest of the tail, black. Under parts (bluish) white.

(*b*). "The nest is placed on a tree, from ten to fifty feet above the ground, and is cup-shaped, firm, but small and neat." An egg in my collection measures ·60 × ·48 of an inch, and is *pale* greenish blue, dotted with reddish-brown and a little obscure lilac.

(*c*) (*d*). The Blue-gray Gnatcatchers are said to have wandered to Massachusetts, but their usual *habitat* is further to the southward. They are insectivorous, and dart "about from one part of the tree to another with hanging wings and erected tail, making a feeble chirping, *tsee*, *tsee*, no louder than a mouse." (Wilson.) They generally hunt "on the highest branches." Mr. Burroughs says of this bird in "Wake-Robin:" "Its song is a lisping, chattering, incoherent warble, now faintly reminding one of the goldfinch, now of a miniature cat-bird, then of a tiny yellow-hammer, having much variety, but no unity, and little cadence." He previously remarks, in his charming sketches, that "in form and manner it seems almost a duplicate of the cat-bird, on a small scale. It mews like a young kitten, erects its tail, flirts, droops its wings, goes through a variety of motions when disturbed by your presence, and in many ways recalls its dusky prototype."

§ 4. The **Paridæ,** or *titmice*, together with the two next families, the nuthatches and creepers, form a natural, plainly colored group, and might appropriately be called "tree-gleaners." They all lead an active life, scrambling about among trees in search of insects and their eggs, but never flying far, though partially migrant. The chickadees not unfrequently alight on the ground, and often hang head downwards, but they never habitually cling to the trunk. The creepers, on the other hand, climb much like woodpeckers, confining themselves to the trunks or larger upright limbs, and never touch the earth; while the nuthatches in their habits are intermediate between the two. As regards music, however, the chickadees are intermediate, for the nuthatches are wholly unmusical, while the creepers have a warbled song. They all, however, agree in building a nest in some cavity, usually the hole of a tree, and in laying small, white, spotted eggs, but the titmice are the most prolific, laying in one set always more than five eggs, and sometimes more than ten. They are all unsuspicious and sociable, though, in Massachusetts, only the chickadees are strictly gregarious. The three families are all partially characterized as follows: length less than seven inches; bill neither hooked nor notched; tarsi scutellate; toes not completely cleft; primaries ten, the first short or spurious; tail-feathers twelve. In the *Paridæ* the bill is short, stout, pointed, and with convex outlines, the nostrils are concealed, the tarsus is "longer than the middle toe and claw," the tail is long, and about equal to the wings. In the *Sittidæ* the nostrils are likewise concealed, but the bill is long, rather slender, acute, and with a convex outline beneath only; the tail is short (pl. 1, fig. 5). In the *Certhiidæ* the bill is slender and decurved, the nostrils are exposed, and the tail-feathers are stiff and pointed (pl. 1, fig. 6). All the creepers and titmice of North America belong to the typical groups or subfamilies, *Certhiinæ* and *Parinæ*.

I. PARUS

(A) ATRICAPILLUS. *Black-capped Titmouse. Chickadee.*

(Common in Massachusetts throughout the year, but much less abundant in summer than in the other seasons.)

(*a*). 5-5½ inches long. (Tail and wings 2½.) Above, ashy, variously tinted. Beneath, white, in winter often tinted with "rusty" or buff. *Crown, nape, and throat black; intervening space* (nearly) *white.*

(*b*). The Chickadees either select a natural cavity or a deserted woodpecker's home, or with great labor excavate a hole for themselves, in a post or a tree. They rarely select a sound tree, but much prefer a decayed one, particularly a white birch, in which from one to thirty feet above the ground, on the side (or often on the top of a trunk, if a broken one), they make an excavation, from three inches to a foot deep, with a narrow entrance, if possible. At the bottom they place warm and soft materials, such as hairs, moss, feathers, and wool; and the female, usually in the last week of May (near Boston), lays six or sometimes more eggs — often again laying, later in the season. The eggs average ·63 × ·50 of an inch; and are white, either spotted with reddish-brown, or finely freckled with a rather paler shade, which approaches flesh-color.

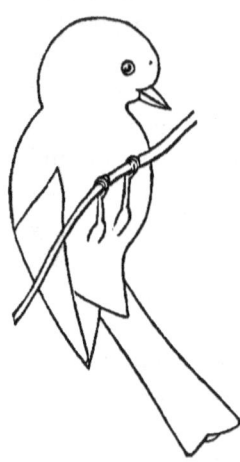

Fig. 2. Chickadee (½).

(c). The Chickadees are so abundantly distributed, or well represented by closely allied species, throughout the greater part of North America, that probably to a majority of its inhabitants they are, on the whole, more familiar than any other birds. They are common residents in all the New England States, but in many parts of Massachusetts are much less common in summer than in winter, when many have come from the North. At the beginning of every new year, they may be found in abundance in the neighborhood of Boston, more often in small flocks than otherwise. One may then watch them closely, for they are not shy, as they move about among the higher branches, and the lower branches, or even on the ground, where they peck at fallen cones, or at such refuse as can afford them any nourishment. When on the trees, their motions are characterized by constant energy; and the better to obtain their minute prey (small insects and eggs, such as infest bark) they assume many peculiar attitudes, to maintain which great (comparative) muscular strength is required — such attitudes as hanging by the claws, or clinging to cones with the head downwards. They are so merry, genial, and sociable, that their society is sought for, as it were, by other birds, such as creepers, nuthatches, Downy Woodpeckers and "kinglets," whose habits are much like their own, and who frequently join them in their pleasant rambles and active scrambles. They roam wherever there are trees, be they near houses, or in the depths of the forests, in valleys or on hill-sides;[14] but evergreens, particularly pines, and white birches, are their favorites. They never take other than short flights, and often, as Wilson says, "traverse the woods in regular progression from tree to tree," in this manner traveling several miles every day. They are very unsuspicious, and allow one to approach closely, so that by remaining motionless I have often induced them to surround my person. Mr. Samuels mentions an instance of one perching on the toe of his boot as he sat in the woods; and a young man of Northern New Hampshire once told me that they were so tame in cold weather as to feed from his hand, but his friends were possibly young and inexperienced birds, or at least were probably those who had passed the summer in some country uninhabited by man.

In regard to the manner in which the hardy little Titmice pass the night, I have some interesting information to offer for the perusal of my readers and I shall here quote from my ornithological diary. "February 10th. This afternoon, just before sunset, I noticed two Chickadees, feeding on the ground, and pecking at a bone, to which a remnant of meat was attached. After saving one of them from a cat, who was stealing towards and was about to catch them, I remained there fifteen minutes. They scarcely left the ground during that time, except to take a low perch, until half-past five, when one flew away over the house-top and disappeared. The other continued to hop about on the ground; and then, without any intimation of his purpose, abruptly flew to the piazza, whither I followed him. He took possession of a Pewee's nest, which

---

[14] Among the White Mountains to an elevation of 4,000 feet (?)

stood upon the top of a corner-pillar, adjoining the house, and, having stared at me for a moment, *tucked his head under his wing*,[15] and apparently leaned against the wall. I think that he went to sleep almost immediately, for, on my stepping from the piazza, he started (as if from sleep) and turned to look at me; but he soon composed himself once more to his slumbers." "Feb. 12th, 1875. I found my friend, the Chickadee, fast asleep to-day at 5.35 P. M." "Feb. 18th. I have continued to find the Chickadee retiring to rest in the nest on the piazza. Another retires as regularly at sunset, and sleeps in a hole of a white birch, evidently once a Chickadee's nest, perhaps his own." "March 13th. At five minutes after six this morning a Chickadee suddenly uttered his '*chick-a-dee-dee-dee*' from a pine, and then for five minutes repeated his whistle of *pe-wee*. Two companions then came, and the small flock, thus formed, moved off."

In spring the Titmice gradually disperse, many to seek more northern homes, and some, after mating, to prepare homes for their offspring here. In summer they are shyer than in winter and often retire to secluded spots to rear their young, for whom they exhibit a tender affection, which sometimes prompts them, if robbed of their eggs, to follow boldly the intruder, uttering plaintive cries and whistles, which almost force one to repent of having disturbed the peace of such loving parents. In autumn, when family-cares are over, the Chickadees gather in companies and resume a merry life.

(*d*). They have a great variety of simple or quaint notes, all of which seem to be expressive of perpetual happiness, for many of them are constantly repeated throughout the year, and none are restricted to one season. Besides their well-known chant "*chick-a-dee-dee-dee-dee*," which has given them their name, they have an exquisite whistle of two notes (nearly represented by high G and F, upon the piano), which is very

---

[15] I have here emphasized this fact, because I have lately read, where I do not now remember, that it was "a ridiculous supposition that wild birds ever put their bills under their wings when sleeping."!

sweet and clear, and various minor but equally expressive notes (among them a simple *tsip*), as well as certain guttural cries, one of which sounds like a rapid utterance of the French phrase "tout de suite," and is indicative, as it were, of the restless disposition of these birds.

The Chickadees are universal favorites, and no birds have a better right to be than these social and happy pygmies. I have invariably found them to be very amiable, rarely disputing one with another, but Wilson considered them quarrelsome, and speaks of having followed one, the singularity of whose notes surprised him. Having shot it, he found its skull fractured (as he supposed by a companion) but afterwards healed. One passed the winter in my neighborhood whose chant may be tolerably well expressed by the syllables " *chick-a-pu-pu-pu*," the latter notes being somewhat like those of a Canary-bird, but there is no reason to believe that his cranium was cracked.

(B) HUDSONICUS. *Hudsonian Chickadee. Hudson Bay Chickadee.*

(*a*). About five inches long. "Pale olive-brown; crown similar, but browner; below on sides, and behind, pale chestnut." "Chin and throat brownish-black."

(*c*). The Hudson Bay Titmice pass the summer in Arctic countries (and in north-eastern Maine?) usually penetrating northern New England in cold weather only. Their habits resemble those of the common Chickadees. "Mr. Brewster took a single specimen at Concord, Massachusetts, on October 29th, 1870," the only recorded instance of their capture in this State.

(*d*). Their song-note is harsher and "more quickly given" than that of our Chickadees.[16]

§ 5. **Sittinæ.** Nuthatches. (See § 4.)

I. SITTA

(A) CAROLINENSIS. *White-breasted Nuthatch. White-bellied Nuthatch.*

---

[16] Maynard.

(Common here, in spring and autumn, in certain localities. In Massachusetts a few pass the summer, and a few the winter.)

(*a*). About six inches long. Above, ashy blue. Outer tail-feathers, black with white patches. Wings marked with the same colors. Under tail-coverts tinged with "rusty." Other under parts and sides of the head (even above the eyes), white. *Crown and nape, black* (in young and ♀ s, impure, restricted, or wanting).

(*b*). The nest and eggs correspond closely to those of the chickadee (§ 4, I, *A*, *b*), but the latter are larger, averaging ·80 × ·60 of an inch, and are rather coarsely spotted with (reddish-)brown and purplish. Four or five are said to constitute the usual set, but at what time they are laid in Massachusetts I am uncertain.

(*c*). The White-bellied Nuthatches are abundant in but a few parts of New England. In Eastern Massachusetts they are less rare in spring and autumn than in the other seasons; but only a few breed or pass the winter here. As it seems to be advisable to quote from Wilson a full description of some bird's habits, to show the usual style of that author, I shall here repeat his remarks about these birds. After describing their appearance, their non-identity with the European Nuthatch, and their nest and eggs, he writes as follows:—

"The male is extremely attentive to the female while sitting, supplying her regularly with sustenance, stopping frequently at the mouth of the hole, calling and offering her what he has brought, in the most endearing manner. Sometimes he seems to stop merely to enquire how she is, and to lighten the tedious moments with his soothing chatter. He seldom rambles far from the spot, and when danger appears, regardless of his own safety, he flies instantly to alarm her. When both are feeding on the trunk of the same tree, or of adjoining ones, he is perpetually calling on her; and from the momentary pause he makes it is plain that he feels pleased to hear her reply.

"The White-breasted Nuthatch is common almost every where in the woods of North America; and may be known at a distance by the notes *quank, quank*, frequently repeated, as he moves upward and down, in spiral circles, around the body and larger branches of the tree, probing behind the thin scaly bark of the white oak, and shelling off considerable pieces of it in his search after spiders, ants, insects and their larvæ. He rests and roosts with his head downwards; and appears to possess a degree of curiosity not common in many birds; frequently descending, very silently, within a few feet of the root of the tree where you happen to stand, stopping, head downward, stretching out his neck in a horizontal position, as if to reconnoitre your appearance, and after several minutes of silent observation, wheeling around, he again mounts, with fresh activity, piping his unisons as before. Strongly attached to his native forests he seldom forsakes them; and amidst the rigors of the severest winter weather, his note is still heard in the bleak and leafless woods, and among the howling branches. Sometimes the rain, freezing as it falls, encloses every twig, and even the trunk of the tree, in a hard transparent coat or shell of ice. On these occasions I have observed his anxiety and dissatisfaction, at being with difficulty able to make his way along the smooth surface; at these times generally abandoning the trees, gleaning about the stables, around the house, mixing among the fowls, entering the barn, and examining the beams and rafters, and every place where he may pick up a subsistence.

"The name Nuthatch has been bestowed on this family of birds from their supposed practice of breaking nuts by repeated hatchings, or hammerings with their bills. Soft shelled nuts, such as chestnuts, chinkapins, and hazel nuts, they may probably be able to demolish, though I have never yet seen them so engaged; but it must be rather in search of maggots that sometimes breed there, than for the kernel. It is, however, said that they lay up a large store of nuts for winter; but as I have never either found any of their magazines, or seen them collecting them, I am inclined to doubt the fact. From the great numbers I have opened at all seasons of the year, I have every reason to believe that ants, bugs, small seeds, insects and their larvæ, form their chief subsistence, such matters alone being uniformly found in their stomachs. Neither can I see what necessity they could have to circumambulate the trunks of trees with such indefatigable and restless diligence, while bushels of nuts lay scattered round their roots. As to the circumstance mentioned by Dr. Plott, of the European Nuthatch 'putting its bill into a crack in the bough of a tree, and making such a violent sound, as if it was rending assunder,' this, if true, would be sufficient to distinguish it from the species we have just been describing, which possesses no such faculty. The female differs little from the male in color, chiefly in the black being less deep on the head and wings."

To the above extract I have only to add that it should be remembered that Wilson wrote this account in Pennsylvania, in the first years of this century, and that further knowledge of this bird's habits may be obtained by studying those of the Red-bellied Nuthatch, who leads a very similar life.

(d). The note of the White-bellied Nuthatch is monotonous, unmusical, and yet striking; it differs from that of the next species in usually being pitched on a somewhat lower key. There is also another note, properly distinct, which is rather more subdued, though shriller. This scarcely differs in tone from the ordinary cry of the Red-bellied Nuthatch. Both sounds are sure to attract the attention of a person who may hear them for the first time, and to remain firmly fixed in his memory.

(B) CANADENSIS. *Red-bellied Nuthatch.*

(In Eastern Massachusetts, common in October, and less so in winter and spring.)

(a). 4½–5 inches long. Above, bright ashy or leaden blue. Outer tail-feathers black, white-spotted. Beneath, (pale) rusty-colored, except on the chin, which is white. In ♂ crown, and broad stripe through the eye, black. Intermediate space (and forehead), white. In ♀ no black cap, and eye-stripe dusky.

(b). The eggs are exactly like those of the Chickadee (§ 4, I, A); and moreover the nest is in many respects like the nest of that bird, though sometimes placed in a horizontal limb of a decayed tree, a situation in which I have never found the home of a titmouse. In northern New England the female lays about June first, and occasionally again in July.

(c). The Red-bellied Nuthatches habitually spend the summer in the woods and forests of northern New England and other rather cold countries, though a few may occasionally breed in this State, particularly in the western and well-wooded portions. They appear in Massachusetts about the first of October, and I have invariably found them quite common during that month in the neighborhood of Boston. Many retire to the South in November; and those who pass the winter here may easily escape observation, for they are generally silent, often frequent the large tracts of woods which are but little penetrated by man in midwinter, and not unfrequently almost lose their individuality, so to speak, by joining troops of Chickadees. They are by no means rare in April or the early part of May, when many pass through in their annual spring-migrations. As I have intimated, they are so sociable as to associate somewhat with other birds, but they are not often gregarious in Massachusetts, and usually are seen singly or in pairs, and not in flocks, as they are further north. They are more fond of pines than other trees, feeding upon their seeds, as well as on the insects about them, and among them are to be found, busied in almost every conceivable attitude, sometimes moving up and down the trunk, as often with the head pointing downward as upward, and at other times scrambling about the branches or the cones. They are not confined, however, to trees, for they sometimes climb about fences or old buildings, and occasionally descend to the ground, where they pick up fallen seeds. In comparing this species with the White-breasted, Wilson says that "its voice is sharper, and its motions much quicker than those of the other, being so rapid, restless and small, as to make it a difficult point to shoot one of them. When the two species are in the woods together, they are easily distinguished by their voices, the note of the least being nearly an octave sharper than that of its companion, and repeated more hurriedly."

(d). The only note of the Red-bellied Nuthatch is an unmusical sound, like the word "ank," which, says Mr. Maynard, is repeated more deliberately and less querulously in the breeding-season than at other times; a fact, which I also have noticed. It is, however, varied considerably in pitch at all times of the year.

§ 6. Certhiidæ. Creepers. (See § 4.)

I. CERTHIA

(A) FAMILIARIS.[17] *Brown Creeper.*

(In Eastern Massachusetts very rare in summer, but common in winter.)

(a). About 5½ inches long. Bill slender and decurved; tail-feathers rigid and acuminate (as in other *Certhiinæ*). Below, white. Tail unmarked. Other upper parts curiously and finely marked with several browns and whitish.

(b). Wilson says that "the Brown Creeper builds his nest in the hollow trunk or branch of a tree, where the tree has been shivered, or a limb broken off, or where squirrels or Woodpeckers have wrought out an entrance, for nature has not provided him with the means of excavating one for himself." Mr. Gregg (in a Catalogue of the Birds of Chemung County, New York) says that "the nest of this species is built of dry twigs attached to the sides of some perpendicular object;" and that he "discovered one on the attic of a deserted log house; the nest rested upon the inner projection of the gable clapboard, and was cemented together with a gummy or gelatinous substance." The only nest that I have found in the neighborhood of Boston was a few feet from the ground, placed in the cavity formed by the rending of a tree by lightning. The eggs, which were fresh on the twentieth day of May, were grayish-white, speckled with reddish-brown, chiefly at the larger end, and measured about ·60 × ·50 of an inch. A nest, containing young, found in a New Hampshire forest, was much like one found " in a large elm in Court Square, Springfield,

---

[17] Once called *Americana* and "American Creeper."

about ten feet from the ground, and built behind a strip of thick bark, that projected in such a way, as to leave a protected cavity behind it." Dr. Brewer has described the eggs as "nearly oval in shape, with a grayish-white ground, sparingly sprinkled with small, fine, red and reddish-brown spots. They measure ·55 × ·43 of an inch."

(c). In Eastern Massachusetts the Brown Creepers are in winter common, less so, however, than in March, April, and October, when migrating from South to North or *vice versa;* on the milder winter-days they may often be seen, as in spring and fall, about open woodland, near houses, and " even in village streets ;" whereas during the colder weather they frequent thicker and more sheltered woods. Only a very few pass the summer in this State, a much larger number inhabiting the extensive forests of northern New England, during that season.

Like the titmice and nuthatches (with whom they often associate, not being themselves gregarious), they are habitually among trees; but, unlike those birds, they rarely if ever descend to the ground, and never hang with the head downwards. They are constantly in pursuit of insects; hunting for them somewhat in the manner of woodpeckers, by clinging to the trunk or larger branches of the trees, on which they have alighted, propping themselves with their stiff tail-feathers, and moving about as securely as on a flat surface. Their progress is generally systematic, for they usually alight near the foot of the tree, and climb up toward the top; but they are often induced, perhaps by a lack of insects, to desert one tree for another, before they have examined it thoroughly. Moreover, they often ascend in spirals, particularly on the trunks of the pine, one of their favorite trees, and thus confuse the observer, as they are soon lost to sight. Often, when I have awaited their appearance on one side, they have flown off to a neighboring tree, or, when I have run round to their side, they have climbed round to mine. But they are not shy, and it is not difficult, when aided by even a very little experience, to " keep track " of their movements, and to watch their motions.

(d). The ordinary notes of the Brown Creepers are a feeble lisp, a *chip* which they generally repeat when flying, and a peculiar cry of *cree-cree-cree-cree*, which is much less often heard than the others. Their indescribable song is a very pleasant one, being somewhat like the far finer music of the Winter Wren, and is varied, some of the notes being loud and sweet, while others are much feebler and less full in tone. It is repeated both in spring and summer, but never, I think, before March.

The Creepers are harmless birds, and as well as their allies, the titmice and nuthatches, should be considered extremely useful, since they help largely to preserve our trees and to protect forest-growth. While men continue unwisely to destroy large woods in this State, thus exposing others and leaving no provision for the future, these birds will be more and more needed to remove those prominent causes of vegetable decay, injurious insects. Therefore they should be preserved.

§ 7. The **Troglodytidæ,** or *wrens*, form a distinct group, though quite closely allied to several families.. They are insectivorous, and pass their time near the ground. Though not climbers, they are eminently creepers. They are migratory but not gregarious. They are for the most part (possibly in all cases) musical. They lay several or many eggs in one set; these are small, white, reddish, or brown, and generally finely marked. The *Troglodytes* inhabit shrubbery or woodland, and build their nest in some cavity, such as the hole of a tree; but the *Cistothori* frequent marshes or meadows, and build a globular nest, which is suspended among the reeds, or in the grass. The *Troglodytidæ* are characterized as follows: colors plain; general size less than six inches (though in one North American species eight); bill rather long and slender, unbristled and unnotched; nostrils exposed, but overhung by a scale; tarsi scutellate; toes partly united; primaries ten, but the first very short; tail-feathers not acuminate (fig. 3).

The *Motacillidæ* (§ 8) are in New England represented by one species only (belonging to the subfamily *Anthinæ*). They possess the following features: average length, about six inches (?); bill slender, somewhat notched, scarcely bristled, but above "slightly concave at base;" nostrils exposed; tarsus scutellate; " hind toe considerably longer than the middle one;" primaries nine. The wagtails are virtually terrestrial warblers, closely allied to the *Seiuri*.

It may be observed that our land-birds, as at present arranged, form a series, which may be artificially classified by food. Thus the higher *Oscines* are chiefly insectivorous, the shrikes partly insectivorous, but otherwise carnivorous, while the subsequent families are chiefly granivorous. The *Clamatores* and *Picariæ*, the *Raptores*, and the *Columbæ*, form a very similar sequence, the pigeons being, so to speak, vegetarians.

I. TROGLODYTES

(A) HYEMALIS.[18]   *Winter Wren.   Wood Wren.*

(Quite common in Massachusetts, during the migrations, in April and October.)

Fig. 3. Winter Wren.

(*a*). About four inches long. Tail rather short. Essentially like the next species in coloration; but superciliary line,

---

[18] This species has been placed by Baird in this genus (subgenus *Anorthura*), by other authors in the genus *Anorthura*, with the specific name *hyemalis* or *troglodytes*. Prof. Baird has recently called it a variety of the European *T. parvulus*. I have here called it the Wood Wren, because Audubon's so-called "Wood Wren" (*T. Americanus*) is now known to be the same as the House Wren (*T. ædon*), and because the Winter Wrens inhabit woods, almost exclusively, whereas our other wrens do not. The name is therefore extremely appropriate. For the Great Carolina Wren (*Thryothorus Ludovicianus*) see a note at the end of this biography.

and (generally) markings on the wing, whitish. Habits very different.

(*b*). "Five eggs, not quite fresh, which I took from a nest in the White Mountains on the 23rd of July (probably those of a second set), were pure crystal-white, thinly and minutely speckled with bright reddish-brown, and averaging about ·70 × ·55 of an inch. The nest, thickly lined with feathers of the Ruffed Grouse, was in a low moss-covered stump, about a foot high, in a dark swampy forest, filled with tangled piles of fallen trees and branches. The entrance to the nest, on one side, was very narrow, its diameter being less than an inch, and was covered with an overhanging bit of moss, which the bird was obliged to push up on going in." (H. D. Minot.) Dr. Brewer describes other eggs as measuring ·65×·48 of an inch, and "spotted with a bright reddish-brown and a few pale markings of purplish-slate, on a pure white ground." The nest containing these eggs, which were six in number, "was built in an occupied log-hut, among the fir-leaves and mosses in a crevice between the logs." It was found by Mr. William F. Hall "at Camp Sebois, in the central eastern portion of Maine."

(*c*). The Winter Wrens are not very common in this State, and are generally seen here only in April and October, when migrating. They spend their summers in the most northern parts of New England and the cold countries beyond, and their winters to the southward of Massachusetts.[19] They are so little social as to generally travel singly, and to avoid the neighborhood of man, usually frequenting, when journeying, woods, or roadsides bordered by them, though I have also seen them in woodpiles near houses or barns. In such places they busy themselves about the piles of brush and logs; when frightened often taking refuge in stone walls, if any be near, where, on account of their small size and great activity, they are as much at home as squirrels. When they have once taken to such a retreat, it is impossible to keep sight of them for any great length of time. Wilson says that in winter they are

---

[19] I have heard of but few instances of their being seen in this State in winter.

"quite at home, even in the yards, gardens, and outhouses of the city,"[20] and also speaks of their singing while in Pennsylvania.

I have several times seen them in the forests of the White Mountains, both in valleys and on hill-sides,— in those grand, dark, and cool forests, which have been left undisturbed by man for years, if not forever, where the ground is covered with fallen trees, with logs piled upon one another and covered with rich moss, and where the damp soil, unparched by the sun, in summer gives birth to innumerable ferns, of great variety and extraordinary beauty. In such spots, their natural haunts, the Wood Wrens seemed to be less shy than they commonly are during their migrations (which is not the case with most birds), and I have there often watched them, creeping agilely about with their long legs and constantly "ducking" their bodies in their peculiar manner, or singing from the top of some brush-heap or some pile of tangled limbs.

(d). When traveling they are silent, but they have an exquisite song, which I have often heard in their summer-homes. It is one which cannot fail to attract the attention of an observant person, though it may lead to a long search for the musician, before he is found. It is very lively and hurried, and the notes seem to tumble over one another in the energy with which they are poured out. They are full of power, though many are shrill, and are garnished with many a gay trill; in some passages reminding one of the Canary-bird's song, though infinitely finer. Their tone and spirit are wonderful and alone render them quite characteristic. Dr. Brewer speaks of the "querulous note" of these birds, which I do not remember to have ever heard.

One of the prettiest little scenes that I have ever seen in nature was partly enacted by a Winter Wren, who, in nimbly scrambling about a stone wall, nearly ran into a "chipmonk," basking in the sun on the top of it. The surprise and pertness

---

[20] Wilson wrote these words nearly seventy years ago, when Philadelphia was a city of about 80,000 inhabitants.

of both creatures, at this unexpected meeting, were very ludicrous and yet very charming.

NOTE.— *Thryothorus Ludovicianus.* Great Carolina Wren. (Said to have occurred in Connecticut.)

(*a*). Nearly six inches long. Above, reddish-brown; beneath, chiefly tawny. Superciliary stripe, white or buffy. Wings, tail (and under tail-coverts?), black-barred. Wings often somewhat white-spotted.

(*b*). "The nest is composed of various warm materials, placed in a cavity, such as the hole of a tree, or some hole in a building." An egg in my collection measures about ·75 × ·55 of an inch, and is dull white, spotted somewhat coarsely with obscure lilac and several rather quiet browns, which are chiefly collected at the crown.

(*c*). "The Great Carolina Wrens (*Thryothorus Ludovicianus*), so far as I know, have not previously been reported as visitors to Massachusetts, but there are at present two apparently passing the summer in a small wooded swamp near Boston. It is believed that they have arrived since the fourth of July, soon after which my attention was attracted by their loud notes, which I immediately recognized through their general likeness to the notes of other wrens, and the descriptions of Wilson and Audubon. It is further believed that they are now building or have recently built their nest, the female being rarely seen, though the male often visits the shrubbery about the house. Though unwilling that they should be shot, I have no doubt as to their identity, partly on account of their music, which I have never before heard, though familiar with our birds. Moreover the description of the birds which I wrote on the spot, where I first obtained a good view of the male, corresponds in every important particular to the descriptions given by standard authors. To facilitate the detection of these birds elsewhere in Massachusetts, I offer a slight sketch of their habits and notes, as just observed.

"The Carolina Wrens, being shy, are not easily studied, for, on man's approach, they often discontinue their song, and hide themselves in the surrounding shrubbery, or in a neighboring wall. They sometimes betray their presence, however, by their quarrelsome disposition, and their noisy anger at the supposed intrusion of other birds. They remain near the ground, flying a little way with a rather loud fluttering, actively hopping from twig to twig somewhat impetuously, and with the tail often cocked in the air, or pausing to sing, when they assume a more upright posture, accompanied by a depression of the tail.

"Their notes, except their chatter, which is much like that of the House Wren, are generally loud, musical whistles, which exhibit great variation. Sometimes they form a series of triplets, all of which may individually be on a descending or an ascending scale; sometimes they resemble the word *chirrup*, the first syllable being much dwelt upon, and at other times may be well represented by the syllables we'-u, we'-u, we'-u, we'-u. This music is often delivered with volubility, but it is always characterized, apart from any similar notes to be heard near Boston, by a remarkable clearness or openness. Such is the biography of the Carolina Wrens in Massachusetts."

"H. D. Minot."
"*July* 15*th*, 1876."

To this account it may be added that the Carolina Wrens are not always shy, that they are ventriloquists, and that they possess a greater variety of sweet musical notes than has been indicated in the foregoing account. It is now believed, after further observations, that they arrived before July, and chose for their home a drier and sunnier place than the above-mentioned swamp, to which, however, they have frequently wandered, at least the male.

(B) ÆDON. *House Wren.*

(A very common summer-resident in southern New England, though locally distributed.)

(*a*). $4\frac{1}{2}$–$5\frac{1}{2}$ inches long. Above, rather dark *wren*-brown. Below, light creamy or grayish brown (rarely rusty-brown). Everywhere finely "waved" with darker brown, but not conspicuously on the crown. Coloration variable. Superciliary line sometimes whitish. Tail $1\frac{1}{2}$-2 inches long.

(*b*). The nest, generally a heap of twigs lined with warmer materials, is usually built in a bird-box, or in a hole of a post or tree; but it is also often built in very extraordinary situations, such as the sleeve of a coat (Wilson), a clay pot, a disused spout, or other equally odd place. The eggs of each set are six to nine; like those of the Long-billed Marsh Wren (II, B, b), but much lighter and more reddish; they average about $.60 \times .48$ of an inch. In Eastern Massachusetts two sets are occasionally laid in the summer, one usually appearing in the first week of June.

(*c*). The House Wrens, though rare in the northern part of New England, and so locally distributed in the southern portion as never to be seen in certain parts of it, are yet common in Massachusetts, Rhode Island, and Connecticut, and even very abundant in some parts of these States. They usually reach the neighborhood of Boston in the first week of May, and leave it in September, when the frost has rendered it difficult for them to obtain their ordinary food, which consists entirely of spiders, other insects, and their eggs. The House Wrens frequent exclusively cultivated grounds, and the immediate neighborhood of man, so much so as to be " very numerous in the gardens of Cambridge," and other like cities. They are so fearless as to have built in occupied houses, and so impertinent and quarrelsome as sometimes to seize upon the nests of other birds for their own convenience, regardless of rights of property or ownership, and they invariably drive away from their own homes other wrens who may have intruded. They are, moreover, so brave as to often attack cats, generally with success. When not engaged in quarrels or robbery, in building or incubation, they are busy in hunting for insects, particularly spiders, in shrubbery, gardens, and orchards; and they do not ramble about in the gloomy recesses of wood-piles as the Winter Wrens do. But in winter, when far away from their summer homes, and yet enjoying warm weather, their habits are different from those with which we are here familiar. Mr. Allen, in speaking of their habits in Florida, in winter, says that they keep " so closely concealed that it is difficult to shoot" them "except when on the wing.[21] Both this and the Carolina wren are exceedingly quick in their movements, and if they are watching the collector when he is about to shoot at them, they are pretty sure to dodge the charge; although he finds the bushes and foliage where the bird sat riddled by the shot, he usually searches in vain for the specimen he is sure he ought to have killed. When approached in old grassy fields or pine openings, they will allow one to almost tread on them before attempting to get away, and then, instead of taking to wing, often seek to escape by running off like a mouse beneath the grass. The term "house" wren, usually applied to this bird, is decidedly a misnomer, since it frequents the fields, the thickets, and even the forest, as much as the vicinity of houses. In the wilds of Florida, where human habitations are few, there is nothing whatever in its habits to suggest this name."

Other instances might be cited to show how very injudiciously names have often been bestowed upon birds, more so than in the present case, with which there is but little fault to find. Particularly should be condemned the practice of naming species after the place where they were first captured, for the title may afterwards become utterly inappropriate.

(*d*). The House Wrens have a chirp not unlike that of an insect, a peculiar chatter, and a charming song, which cannot be satisfactorily described, as is the case with the music of most other birds. This song consists of a few loud and sprightly notes, followed by a loud and very characteristic trill, which is its most prominent feature. It may often be heard in the summer and in May.

II. CISTOTHORUS

(A) STELLARIS. *Short-billed Marsh Wren. Meadow Wren.*

(In New England, a rather rare summer-resident, found only in the warmer parts.)

(*a*). About 4½ inches long. Below, white. Breast and sides

---

[21] I have here taken the liberty of very slightly altering the text, without changing its meaning, that it might better accord with my own.

of a light warm brown. Wings and tail barred. Like *C. palustris* above, but streaked with white on the back, *nape, and rump.*

(*b*). The nest is essentially like that of the next species; but, no mud is used in its composition, it is generally placed in fresh-water marshes or meadows (being sometimes built in long grass), and the hole is usually on the under side. The eggs are generally six, sometimes more, very frail, white, and about ·55 × ·43 of an inch. The first and commonly the only set is laid, in Eastern Massachusetts, in the early part of June.

(*c*). I must confess to not being so very familiar with the Meadow Wrens as I should like to be before writing their Natural History, for in the southern parts of New England they are very generally rare, and in the northern parts are not to be found at all. They come to Eastern Massachusetts about the middle of May, and inhabit the fresh-water marshes and meadows, in certain localities, until the latter part of August, when they retire to the South. On their arrival, they busy themselves in building their peculiar nests, and it has been observed that they generally build several near together, every year, perhaps for the sake of protection. They are generally occupied in hunting for insects among reeds, rushes, or tall grass, but it is not easy to assure one's self of this fact, since they are shy, and, to use a sportsman's expression, "lie very close." They can also creep about and through the reeds as silently and actively as a mouse.

(*d*). The Meadow Wrens have a harsh unpleasant chatter, but also a simple and yet very pleasant song, which reminds one of the songs of certain sparrows, though often characterized by a peculiar wren-trill.

(B) PALUSTRIS.[22] *Marsh Wren. Long-billed Marsh Wren.* (Less common in Massachusetts than the preceding species.)

(*a*). 5–5½ inches long. Above, brown. Below, white; sides shaded with brown. Tail dusky-barred. Wings and under

---

[22] By some authors placed in the genus *Telmatodytes* (considered by Baird a subgenus).

tail-coverts slightly marked. Interscapulars and crown, quite or nearly black; the former white-streaked. Superciliary line, white.

(*b*). The nest is suspended among the reeds or long grass, or is built in a bush in marshes. It "is formed outwardly of wet rushes mixed with mud, well intertwisted, and fashioned into the form of a cocoa nut. A small hole is left two-thirds up, for entrance, the upper edge of which projects * * *. The inside is lined with fine soft grass, and sometimes feathers; * * *." (Wilson.) The eggs are usually six, and are laid in early June. They are light (reddish?) chocolate-brown, so finely marked with a darker shade, as to appear, from a distance, uniformly dark, and average about ·58 × ·45 of an inch.

(*c*). The Marsh Wrens are not to be found in northern New England, and in Massachusetts are even less common than the Meadow Wrens, to whom they are very closely allied in their habits. They frequent a few of both the salt-water and fresh-water marshes in this State, from the middle of May until the latter part of August. They spend their time in procuring the insects, on which they habitually feed, from the reeds and grasses, among which they move with great agility. Being rather less shy than the Short-billed Marsh Wrens, they can more often be seen, frequently in their favorite attitude, with their tail cocked in the air.

(*d*). They have a harsh chatter, if it can properly be so called, a peculiar sound; but, I have never heard them sing, nor have I ever heard a well-authenticated case of another person doing so.

There are, I regret to say, no pretty traditional tales to be told about our wrens, nor is there any hereditary affection for them, such as is felt for "Jenny Wren" in England.

§ 8. **Motacillidæ.** Wagtails. (See § 7.)

I. ANTHUS

(A) LUDOVICIANUS. *Brown Lark.* "*Titlark.*" "*Pipit.*" "*Wagtail.*"

(A common migrant, in spring and autumn, along the coast of New England.)

(*a*). About 6¼ inches long. Above, pure dark brown ("olive-shaded"?), slightly streaked. Under-parts and superciliary line, light buffy-brown. Breast and sides dusky-streaked. Tail dark; outer tail-feathers partly white.

(*b*). The Titlarks breed chiefly in Arctic countries, and never in New England.

(*c*). They pass through Massachusetts in spring and autumn, when traveling to and from their summer-homes, and are then common on the sea-shore, "in the Fresh Pond marshes of Cambridge," and sometimes in old fields. They usually collect in loose flocks, and feed on seeds and insects, which they pick up on the ground, where they can run with ease and rapidity. They have a singular habit of jerking their tails, which is very noticeable. When disturbed, they generally fly away to quite a distance and high in the air, resuming their labors, if they may be so called, when they alight. They retire in summer to breed in Labrador and other cold countries, where they are said to sing.

(*d*). When with us their only note is a feeble one, a simple chirp, which is often repeated.

§ 9. The **Sylvicolidæ**, or *American warblers*, form a group, which may perhaps be best defined negatively. By the omission, however, of the *Icterinæ* (or chats), who probably should be ranked as a family intermediate between the warblers and tanagers, their characteristics may be considered the following. Length, 4-6½ inches; bill twice as long as high; commissure entirely straight or slightly curved, unless interrupted by a terminal notch; nostrils exposed; tarsus scutellate; "hind toe shorter than the middle;" primaries nine (fig. 4). It is doubtful how many subfamilies there should be, but the following well-defined groups exist.

Seiurinæ, or *lark-warblers* (I). Bill notched, scarcely bristled. Birds streaked beneath. Tail not marked or forked.

Geothlypinæ, or *thicket-warblers* (II, III). Bill notched, scarcely bristled. Birds wholly unstreaked. Tail not marked or forked. In Geothlypis, the *wings* are approximately *equal in length to the tail.*[23]

Helminthophaginæ, or *worm-eating warblers* (IV, V, VI). *Bill acute, unbristled, and unnotched* [23] (pl. 1, fig. 7).

Mniotiltinæ, or *creeping warblers* (VII, VIII). Bill scarcely bristled, and never (very) distinctly notched; hind-toe much longer than its claw. (Except in structure, however, the Parulæ and Mniotiltæ are widely different.)

Sylvicolinæ, or *wood-warblers* (IX, X). Bill notched, and with short bristles (pl. 1, fig. 8). Tail not unmarked, unless in *æstiva*, where it is slightly forked. In other cases white-blotched. *Perissoglossæ* are characterized by the tongue.

Setophaginæ, or *fly-catching warblers* (XI, XII). *Bill noticeably broader than high*, also *notched, usually hooked, and always with long bristles* [23] (pl. 1, fig. 9).

This last group is ranked as a subfamily, the others being united by Dr. Coues as *Sylvicolinæ*, though Prof. Baird further sets apart the *Geothlypinæ*. (For remarks on *Icterinæ*, see §10.) The warblers are, no doubt, to many persons the most charming of our birds. They are eminently peaceful, and prettily colored, brightly, sometimes brilliantly. Musically, however, they are generally surpassed by the thrushes, vireos, and finches. They are insectivorous, migratory, and in some cases gregarious, except in summer. Among their nests are some of the neatest and prettiest specimens of bird-architecture. The eggs are, for the most part, four or five, white, spotted with brown and lilac.

I. SEIURUS

(A) NOVEBORACENSIS. *Water "Thrush." Water "Wagtail."*

(Common, perhaps locally so, during their migrations through Massachusetts, where, however, a few breed.)

(a). 5½–6 inches long. Dark brown above (tinged with olive). Superciliary line and under parts white, *tinged* with

---

[23] Characteristics underscored do not belong to other warblers.

yellow. Throat and breast thickly spotted with very dark brown. "Feet dark."

(b). The nest is usually built on or near the ground, in a swamp or at least the neighborhood of water. The eggs of each set are usually four, average ·85 × ·67 of an inch, though variable in size, and in coloration closely resemble those of the Golden-crowned "Thrush" (C, b). A nest, which I found near Boston, contained fresh eggs in the first week of June.

(c). The Water "Thrushes" are to be found in northern New England as summer-residents, but, though a very few pass the summer in Massachusetts, they are common in this State, or at least parts of it, only during their migrations — in the third and fourth weeks of May, and the first or second of September. While in the neighborhood of Boston, they remain near streams and bodies of water or in wet woodland, and pick up the little insects, and other things upon which they feed, almost exclusively from the ground, often wading, however, in shallow water. When sojourning here, they are not very shy, and it is easy to approach them so as to watch their peculiar motions, which recall those of the sandpiper, and are yet partially characterized by a constant jerking of the tail — a habit which belongs to several other common birds, such as the Pewee, who depresses the tail, however, instead of jerking it upwards. The Water "Thrushes" are, on the other hand, very shy in their delightful summer-homes, and would almost escape notice, but for their very charming song. As it is, they are rarely seen, for they are very nimble on the ground, and on man's approach leave their paddling in the mountain-brooks, and their pleasant labors on the banks, to hide in thickets or underbrush. Imagine a forest, which man has never invaded, and through it flowing a cool, clear stream, whose course is broken by the rocks, round which it bends, or over which it falls into some foaming pool, and you will know the haunts of these birds; imagine music, which can hardly be excelled, and you can faintly realize the charms of such places, if you do not already know them.

(d). "The Water 'Thrushes' song is loud, clear, and exquisitely sweet, and begins with a burst of melody, which becomes softer and more delicate until the last note dies away, lost in the ripple of the stream, above which the birds are generally perched. It is probably sometimes repeated at night, as is the song of the Wood 'Wagtail,' and how enchanted should I be to hear it in the coolness of the woods and stillness of the night." It may quite often be heard in spring, during the migrations and the season of courtship, as well as the ordinary note of these birds, a sharp *chick*, which usually expresses alarm.. As I have heard it, however, it is a simple song, merely characterized by unusual loudness and clearness. It is greatly to be regretted that not more persons are familiar with the pleasing music of the Water "Thrushes," whose love of retirement has unfortunately allowed few others than naturalists to know them.

(B) LUDOVICIANUS. *Large-billed Water " Thrush." Water Warbler.*

(So far as I know, the only instances known of this bird coming to Massachusetts and northern New England, are those recorded by Mr. Allen, who shot one "April 28, 1869, on Mount Tom," and by Mr. Irving Frost, who shot another " at Norway, Maine, in May, 1865.")

(*a*). About six inches long. Like the last species, but below buffy, chiefly behind, with fewer and less prominent streaks (none on the throat), and with " legs pale."

(*b*). The nest and eggs are like those of the common Water Thrush, but the latter are a little larger, averaging ·90 × ·70 of an inch.

(*c*). The Large-billed Water Thrushes have a very different *habitat* from their immediate relations, and very rarely occur in New England. They are closely allied to the Water Wagtails in habits; like those birds, frequenting woodland and the neighborhood of water, and being addicted to wading and to jerking their tails.

(*d*). Their ordinary note is probably the same *chuck*, but their song is said to be more glorious than that of the other species, which I have just described. It begins with loud, clear, and ringing notes, and ends with the softer notes, which die away almost imperceptibly. It was this song that Wilson described as having heard the Water Thrush utter in the vast cane-brakes of the South, where these birds find a home during a part of the year.

(C) AUROCAPILLUS. *Golden-crowned " Thrush." " Oven-bird." " Wagtail."*
(In Massachusetts a common summer-resident.)

(*a*). 6-6½ inches long. Olive above. Below white. Breast and sides (darkly or) black-streaked. *Crown orange, bordered by black stripes.* (Details omitted.)

(*b*). The nest is placed on the ground, in the woods. It is usually lined with hairs, and is generally but not invariably roofed. The eggs of each set — only one being commonly laid in Massachusetts, and that about June first, or perhaps earlier — are usually four, averaging between ·90 × ·70 and ·80 × ·62 of an inch. They are subject to considerable variation, but are generally (creamy) white, with *either* minute lilac markings about the crown, *or* markings of reddish-brown and faint lilac scattered (not very thickly) chiefly in blotches, either all over the egg, or only about the greater end.

(*c*). The birds, of whom I am about to write, are variously called Golden-crowned "Thrushes," having formerly been classed with the thrushes[24] (and their crown being dull orange), "Oven-birds," because of the usual construction of their nests, and "Wagtails," because of their habit of flirting their tails, by which name I shall refer to them. They are common summer-residents throughout New England ; much less so, however, in the northern parts, though known to breed in Arctic countries. They generally reach Massachusetts in the first week of May and leave it in September, sometimes lingering almost until October, quite unobserved, because of their rarely broken silence at that season. They frequent woodland of

---

[24] Mr. Maynard adheres to this arrangement.

various kinds, but pine-groves are perhaps their favorite haunts. In such places they are usually to be seen on the ground, walking about quietly, silently, and with an amusing deliberateness, and picking up their food from among the fallen leaves; but they betake themselves to trees (rather than to bushes), when frightened, when engaged in their pretended or real quarrels during courtship, or when they wish to utter their peculiar chant. They are endowed with strong parental affection, and, when the nest is approached, both male and female exhibit great concern, or the latter, if disturbed whilst sitting on her nest, feigns lameness, as many other ground-nesting birds do, and flutters nimbly away, until, having led the unwary pursuer to a distance, she "takes to wing."

(d). The Wagtails' loud monotony — *wee-chée, wee-chée, wee-chée, wee-chée, wee-chée, wee-chée, wee-chée, wee-chée, wee-chée,*— which is repeated rapidly with a steadily increasing volume, is heard, at intervals, throughout the day. Their ordinary notes are a *chuck* of alarm, and a sharp *chick*, employed chiefly during the period of mating. At night I have often heard the male sing very sweetly, his chatter being followed by a low musical warble, such as I have rarely heard him utter during the day, except sometimes at dusk. He generally pours out this music while descending through the air from a height to which he has just mounted; but these performances are almost exclusively confined to the season when his mate is sitting on her eggs or young.

The Wagtails are much oftener heard than seen, the more so that they are never gregarious; but the oddity of their familiar chant, the quaintness of their habits, and their strong conjugal and parental affection, must ever endear them to the appreciative naturalist.

II. GEOTHLYPIS

(A) TRICHAS. *Maryland "Yellow-throat." Black-masked Ground Warbler.*

(A common summer-resident throughout New England.)

(a). About five inches long. ♂ olive-green above. Forehead, and a broad bar through the eye, black, bordered above by grayish. Belly white. Other under parts, yellow. ♀ with no black or grayish. More olive above. Head browner. Beneath, white, yellow less and paler.

(b). The nest is usually placed on the ground—almost invariably beside a brook or in a swamp—but occasionally in a thicket or briar. It is composed of (leaves) fine grasses, etc., is often lined with hairs, and is sometimes roofed. The eggs average ·70 × ·55 of an inch, and are white, sometimes with no markings, but commonly with a few reddish-brown blotches about the greater end, or with a ring about the crown of *fine* reddish-brown and lilac markings, or with numerous spots and blotches of the same colors distributed over the entire surface. They vary greatly in coloration, but the ground-color is always (?) white, and is not usually *much* marked. In all parts of New England two sets of these eggs are laid annually, as a rule, in Massachusetts the first generally appearing in the last week of May.

(c). The "Maryland Yellow-throats" are probably (on an average, throughout New England) the most abundant of our warblers in summer, and in certain parts of Maine and New Hampshire are nearly the most common birds. They come to Massachusetts, from their southern winter-homes, in the first or second week of May, and do not altogether leave it before October. On their arrival, before retiring to the places where they build their nests, they spend much of their time in trees, often those on cultivated estates; but, later in the season, they betake themselves to swamps, thickets, and bushes along the roadsides, and are then seen chiefly on or near the ground. They constantly move their tails, both when on the ground, and when hopping from twig to twig, for they rarely take other than short flights. In their haunts, which cannot be well defined or enumerated, they are ever busy, when not interrupted, in catching the insects and caterpillars, upon which they feed; and yet, though not shy, they are continually watchful, and mindful of intruders.

(d). Besides a sharp *chuck*, which is loud enough to attract the attention of every passer-by, a simple *chick*, less often heard, and a chatter, much finer and less harsh than that of the Cat-bird, the "Maryland Yellow-throats" have a characteristic set of notes, which resemble the syllables *wée-chee-chee*, repeated several times, with a marked emphasis on the *wee*. This is varied to *wée-chee-chée-wee*, which is repeated in the same manner, and again to a song, which is not unlike that of the Yellow Warbler, though sufficiently distinct.

The "Maryland Yellow-throats" are among our most beneficial birds, and cannot in any way do injury to man or his property. Whoever is unfamiliar with them can easily make their acquaintance, and a charming acquaintance it will prove to be. In a certain place, where I took many walks, these birds seemed to be traveling companions, whenever I followed the highways, so constantly did I see them along the roadsides.

(B) PHILADELPHIA. *Mourning Warbler.*

(Quite common (locally) in certain parts of northern New England as a summer-resident, but a very rare migrant through Massachusetts, where none pass the summer, so far as I know.)

(*a*). Five inches or more long. Olive above. Beneath, bright yellow. Head, warm (ashy-) gray. Throat black, often waved with gray.

(*b*). The eggs and nest correspond closely to those of the Maryland Yellow-throat in every respect, but the former, so far as I know, are never either plain white or coarsely marked.

(*c*). The Mourning Warblers are among the birds who are extremely rare in Massachusetts, even during the migrations, though they breed quite commonly in certain parts of northern New England, and also in places much further to the southward. During their occasional brief sojourn in this State, in the latter part of May, and still more rarely in September, they usually frequent the haunts of the Maryland Yellow-throats, but are also sometimes seen examining the foliage of tall trees (up the trunks of which, for a little way, I have strong reason to believe that they sometimes scramble). I invariably see in spring a few pairs in the "scrub," especially where swampy. In their summer-homes they inhabit copses and thickets in open spots, finding their food in piles of brush, on the ground, etc., never, however, jerking their tails in the manner of their relations.

(*d*). The Mourning Warblers have a sharp chirp, a feeble *tsip*, and a warbled, liquid song (likened to that of the House Wren, Water Thrush, and Maryland Yellow-throat), which is generally delivered from a high perch.

III. OPORORNIS

(A) AGILIS.[25] *Connecticut Warbler.*

(A migrant in New England. Extremely rare in spring, and generally rare in autumn, though more than a hundred specimens were taken at Cambridge in two years, when these birds were extraordinarily abundant in fall.)

(*a*). About 5¼ inches long. Above, olive-green, becoming ashy-tinted on the head. Eye-ring whitish. Throat (and upper breast), ashy or brownish. Other under parts, yellow. Crown, olive in autumn.

(*b*). I believe that the nest and eggs of these birds have never been discovered by any ornithologist.

(*c*). The Connecticut Warblers have hitherto, with two remarkable exceptions, been very rare migrants through Massachusetts; but they may become more common hereafter. I have seen them but once in spring (then only an individual on the tenth of May), and but a few times in September. The following observations were made at the Fresh Pond Marshes of Cambridge, in the autumns of 1870 and 1871, and illustrate the habits of these birds.

"Mr. Henshaw found them almost constantly engaged in seeking their food on the ground. When startled they would fly up to the nearest bush, upon which they would sit perfectly

---

[25] The Kentucky Warbler (*O. formosus*) may stray to New England, though I know no instance of its so doing. It has been known to breed in Eastern New York.

motionless, in a manner closely resembling the Thrushes. If not further disturbed they immediately returned to the ground, * * *. If greatly startled they took a long flight among the bushes, and could rarely be found again."

(*d*). I have heard them utter only *tsips* and *chirps* whilst in their usual haunts, namely, swampy thickets, and shrubbery near them. I have never heard their song, nor read any description of it.

IV. HELMITHERUS

(A) VERMIVORUS. *Worm-eating Warbler.*[26]

(Though found in Maine, this species very rarely comes so far to the north-eastern part of the United States as to reach New England.)

(*a*). About 5½ inches long. Greenish-olive above. Head and under parts, buff. The head is marked with two dark stripes bordering the crown, and two running from the eyes to the back.

(*b*). The nest is placed on or near the ground. The eggs are described as averaging about ·70 × ·55 of an inch, and being pure white, minutely spotted with reddish-brown, chiefly at the larger end, where lilac is intermixed.

(*c*). The Worm-eating Warblers so seldom come to this State, that, I regret to say, I have never seen them here. The various accounts of their habits and notes which I have read are more or less conflicting and unsatisfactory; but from them I have gathered that the Worm-eating Warblers inhabit both woodland and shrubbery, and usually feed on caterpillars and spiders, which they find on the ground, or "among the dead leaves of a broken branch," being very nimble in securing their prey. They are never gregarious, but, even during their migrations, travel alone or in pairs, sometimes, however, with their young in autumn.

(*d*). Their notes are "a feeble chirp," a "complaining call"

---

[26] The closely allied Swainson's Warbler (*H. Swainsoni*) has been erroneously reported from Massachusetts.

of "*tsee-dee-dee*," and a song which has been variously described, but which, from all accounts, does not seem to be a very pleasing one.

I regret that I am obliged to write brief, and on that account less interesting biographies (if I may so far flatter myself) of some of the warblers, about whom, because of their general rarity here, I know little and cannot obtain much information.

V. PROTONOTARIA

(A) CITRÆA. *Prothonotary Warbler.*

(So far as I know, there is but one authentic instance of this bird being captured in New England — then at Calais, Maine, on October 30th!).

(*a*). About 5½ inches long. Golden-yellow. Back olivaceous. Rump, light ashy-blue; wings and tail darker. Tail-feathers marked with white.

(*b*). Dr. Brewer speaks of three nests. One of these "was built within a Woodpecker's hole in a stump of a tree, not more than three feet high;" another "was built within a brace-hole in a mill;" and a third "in a hollow snag, about five feet from the ground, in the river bottom." The eggs average ·68 × ·55 of an inch, and are cream-white with lilac, purplish-brown (and black) markings.

(*c*). The Prothonotary Warbler have little or no right to be included in the list of the birds of Massachusetts, and I have never seen them here (unless perhaps once a pair, at dark in October). They prefer the borders of streams, and neighborhood of water, to drier ground, and swampy thickets to the woods and forests. Otherwise their habits are essentially like those of the Worm-eating Warbler, and other allied species.

(*d*). Their ordinary note is said to be like the feeble *tsip* of the White-throated Sparrow, but of more characteristic notes I know nothing. The "Prothonotaries" strongly resemble the Blue-winged Yellow Warblers, who are much more likely to occur in southern New England, and therefore should an inexperienced student meet either in his rambles through this State, let him carefully note which it is.

VI. HELMINTHOPHAGA

(A) PINUS. *Blue-winged Yellow Warbler.*
(No one, I believe, has reported the presence of this bird in New England, except Mr. Samuels.)

(*a*). About five inches long. Like the Prothonotary Warbler; but rump (like the back) olive, wing-bars and tail-blotches white (or nearly so), and eye-stripe, or lore, black.

(*b*). The nest is placed on the ground, in wooded land. The eggs average about ·70 × ·55 of an inch, and are white, with a few reddish-brown spots about the greater end.

(*c*). The Blue-winged Yellow Warblers, being foreigners to New England, I can only describe through others. Wilson says of this species that it "haunts thickets and shrubberies, searching the branches for insects; is fond of visiting gardens, orchards, and willow trees, of gleaning among blossoms, and currant bushes; and is frequently found in very sequestered woods, where it generally builds its nest." Mr. Samuels, whose account has been rejected by some ornithologists, says: "In 1857, in the month of May, about the 12th or 15th, I found a small flock in a swamp in Dedham, Mass. They were actively employed in catching flying insects, and were so little mistrustful, that they permitted me to approach quite near, and observe their motions. I noticed nothing peculiar in them; but they had all the activity and industry of the true arboreal Warblers."

(*d*). Dr. Brewer says that "in regard to the song of this bird, Mr. Trippe states that its notes are very forcible and characteristic. He describes them as a rapid chirrup resembling *chuuchich, k'-a-re-r' r' r' r' r'* (!). According to Mr. Ridgway they are wonderfully like the lisping chirrup of the *Coturniculus Passerinus*" (or Yellow-winged Sparrow).

(B) CHRYSOPTERA. *Golden-winged Warbler.*
(A rather uncommon, or even rare, summer-resident in Massachusetts.)

(*a*). About five inches long. Above, slaty-blue. Whole crown and broad wing-bars, rich yellow. Below, white. Throat, and stripe through eye, black. Tail-feathers white-blotched. ♀ with less pure colors than ♂.

(*b*). The nest is placed on the ground, in woodland, generally near swamps, and is variously lined. Four eggs taken by me from a nest found near Boston average about $.68 \times .55$ of an inch, and are white, marked, chiefly at the great end, with reddish-brown. They were taken on the 8th of June and correspond with those found by Mr. Maynard on June 12th, 1869.

(*c*). The Golden-winged Warblers have at last been recognized as summer-residents in Massachusetts of no very great rarity, and are not so largely migrant through this State, as was once supposed, for indeed it probably forms nearly their most northern limit. They reach the neighborhood of Boston about the 10th of May, and do not retire to the South until September. During the summer they inhabit woodland, particularly that which is swampy, but soon after their arrival I have several times met them among the trees on cultivated estates, where I have noticed, contrary to the observations of some other persons, that they remain chiefly on or near the ground (not infrequently, however, among the higher branches), and rarely catch insects on the wing. On the contrary, they often recall the titmice. They have a habit, observable in their relations, of occasionally hopping from the ground to snap an insect from the foliage above.

(*d*). Their notes are a *tsip*, a louder *chip*, and a sharp alarm-note. They also have a brief and rather unattractive song of four or five peculiar syllables, uttered in a characteristic, rather harsh tone, and resembling *dsee-dsee-dsee-dsee*.

BB. LEUCOBRONCHIALIS. *White-throated* (*Golden-winged*) *Warbler*.

The following is an extract from the "Quarterly Bulletin of the Nuttall Ornithological Club," for April, 1876 (Vol. I, No. 1).

"*Description of a New Species of Helminthophaga; by William
  "Brewster. Helminthophaga leucobronchialis. Pl.* 1.

" Adult male: summer plumage. Crown, bright yellow,

slightly tinged with olive on the occiput. Greater and middle wing-coverts, yellow, not so bright as the crown. Superciliary line, cheeks, throat and entire under parts; silky-white, with a slight tinge of pale yellow on the breast. Dorsal surface —exclusive of nape which is clear ashy—washed with yellow, as are also the outer margins of the secondaries. A narrow line of clear black passes from the base of the upper mandible, through and to a short distance behind the eye, interrupted however by the lower eyelid, which is distinctly white. No traces of black upon the cheeks or throat, even upon raising the feathers. Bill black. Feet, dark brown. Dimensions— length, 5·19; extent, 7·88; wing, 2·45; tarsus, ·71; tail, 1·86; culmen, ·53.

"It will be seen from the above description that this bird resembles most closely the Golden-winged Warbler (*Helminthophaga chrysoptera*.)

"The entire absence of black or ashy on the cheeks and throat, the peculiar character of the superciliary line, and the white lower eyelid, present however differences not to be reconciled with any known seasonal or accidental variation of that species. The restricted line of black through the eye gives the head a remarkable similarity to that of *Helminthophaga pinus*, but the semblance goes no farther.

"The specimen above described was shot by the writer in Newtonville, Mass., May 18, 1870. It was in full song when taken and was flitting about in a thicket of birches near a swampy piece of oak and maple woods. As nearly as can be remembered it did not differ much in either voice or actions from *H. chrysoptera*. The first notice of this specimen appeared in the 'American Sportsman,' vol. v, p. 33. * * * *

"As previously remarked the differences in coloration in the present bird from any of its allies are so great, and of such a nature, as to render any theory of accidental variation exceedingly unlikely, while hybrids—at least among the smaller species of undomesticated birds — are of such shadowy and problematical existence that their probable bearing upon the present case is hardly worthy of consideration."

* * * * * * * * * *

(C) RUFICAPILLA. *Nashville Warbler.*
(Quite common as a migrant through this State, where a very few regularly breed.)

(*a*). About 4½ inches long. Above, dull olive. Beneath, yellow. *Back of head, slate.* Crown more or less marked with chestnut-red. In ♀, head-markings indistinct, and crown patch often wanting.

(*b*). The nest is placed on the ground, either in some open part of the woods, or amongst the shrubbery of some southerly-facing bank. It is commonly composed of dead leaves, strips of thin bark, grasses, etc., and is often lined with hairs. The eggs of each set are four, averaging about ·63 × ·50 of an inch, and are here laid about the first of June. The eggs are white, and vary between the extremes of being finely and thickly marked about the crown with lilac, and being thinly and coarsely blotched at the greater end with reddish-brown; these markings being sometimes combined.

(*c*). The Nashville Warblers are summer-residents throughout New England, but they are apparently more numerous in the northern than in the southern portions. In Massachusetts they are rare during summer, but are common at the time of their migrations, which here occur about the middle of May[27] and of September. In spring and autumn, whilst traveling, they habitually frequent lightly-timbered woodland, and somewhat, also, shrubbery about houses, but where they are resident in summer they chiefly affect dry scrub-land, often that which is partially wooded. Their constant activity and industry, combined with their general adherence, while traveling, to the higher branches of the pines, chestnuts, oaks, and maples, which they usually prefer to other trees, often renders it difficult to detect their presence, even when quite abundant. They travel singly or in pairs and remain long in one tree or cluster, not being easily frightened. The two great difficulties in studying the habits of our warblers, are the almost nonde-

---

[27] I have seen them from the 5th until the 20th.

script coloration of some species in autumn, and the fact that many kinds, even in spring, can only be identified by most naturalists upon a close examination, to obtain which it is necessary to shoot the birds, when of course their habits can no longer be studied. It is for these reasons that it is important to know the minor notes of various species, for by these one can often easily distinguish two species otherwise closely alike, especially if such notes are associated with other more marked characteristics. Thus one can in this way always distinguish "Yellow-rumps" at a great distance, for though their ordinary "chuck" is very much like that of the "Black-polls" (who are here in autumn at the same time), yet their manner of flight is different.

(*d*). The ordinary notes of the Nashville Warblers are a simple *chip*, a loud *chink*, and a peculiar alarm-note (?) entirely characteristic, which is hardly, I think, as Wilson says, much like "the breaking of small dry twigs, or the striking of small pebbles of different sizes smartly against each other for six or seven times," though it may be recognized by that description. It is "loud enough," as that author says, "to be heard at the distance of thirty or forty yards."

Their song is simple but pretty, more resembling that of the common Summer Yellow-bird (*D. æstiva*) or Chestnut-sided Warbler than that of any other species. It may be represented by the syllables *wee'-see-wee'-see, wit'-a-wit'-a-wit'*.

(D) CELATA. *Orange-crowned Warbler.*

(This species was reported from Maine by Audubon, and a specimen was shot by Mr. Allen at Springfield on the fifteenth of May, 1863.)

(*a*). Essentially like the Nashville Warbler (C); but with the slate of the latter wanting, the chestnut supplied by orange-brown, and the yellow green-tinged.

(*b*). Nest and eggs probably like those of the last species.

(*c*). The Orange-crowned Warblers are unknown to me personally, but probably there is little or no difference between their habits and those of the Nashville Warblers, to whom they are very closely related. They probably frequent open woodland and orchards, and display a like agility in capturing their prey among the higher branches.

(*d*). Their song Dr. Gambel "describes as commencing in a low, sweet trill, and ending in *tshe-up*." "Their usual note is a sharp chip."

Dr. Brewer, thinks that Audubon's account of this bird is incorrect, but whether that is the case or not I do not know.

Bonaparte, in his continuation of Wilson's Ornithology, says: "During winter, the Orange-crowned Warbler is one of the most common birds in the neighbourhood of St. Augustin, Florida, almost exclusively frequenting the orange trees. Their manners resemble those of the kindred species, though they have a remarkable habit of constantly inflecting the tail like the Pewee. The note consists of a chuck, and a faint squeak, but little louder than that of a mouse."

(E) PEREGRINA. *Tennessee Warbler.*

(A very rare migrant through Massachusetts, though a summer-resident in northern New England.)

(*a*). About 4¾ inches long. Above, yellow-tinted olive-green, with modifications. Superciliary line and under parts, white (or yellowish). ♀ duller above. (See synopsis, p. 81.)

(*b*). The nest and eggs are essentially like those of the Nashville Warbler, though the eggs vary, and exhibit certain peculiar forms, and though the nest is "often placed in woods."

(*c*). The Tennessee Warblers are extremely rare in Eastern Massachusetts, and are nowhere common in New England, except in a few northern localities, such as Lake Umbagog, where they are summer-residents. They journey through this State in the latter part of May, and again about the middle of September. I have met them here twice in open woodland; Mr. Maynard shot four males, on apple-trees in Newtonville, between the 18th and 24th of May, 1869; a pair were shot by Mr. William Brewster, near Mt. Auburn on high oak trees; and Mr. Allen has "taken it repeatedly at Springfield, where he has always esteemed it rare." Audubon considered these birds active, and also expert fly-catchers, and speaks of their mellow *tweet*, uttered when they are on wing, or when fluttering before clusters of leaves. Wilson has written of the first specimen that he obtained that "it was hunting nimbly among the young leaves, and like all the rest of the family of Worm-eaters, seemed to partake a good deal of the habits of the Titmouse."

(d). "Its notes were few and weak." "Its song bears a resemblance to that of *H. ruficapilla*, only the notes of the first part are more divided, and the latter part is shriller. The male, while singing, is generally perched on some high dead branch. In this habit it resembles the *H. ruficapilla* and *H. chrysoptera*." (Maynard.) "Its notes resemble the low, subdued whistle of the common summer Yellow-bird." (Boardman.)

VII. MNIOTILTA

(A) VARIA. *Black and White* "*Creeper.*"

(A common summer-resident in southern New England, though rarer further to the northward.)

(a). Five or more inches long. Belly white. Otherwise black. Wings barred, tail spotted, and other parts streaked, with white. But ♀ white beneath (obsoletely) streaked on the sides. (Details omitted.)

(b). The nest is built in woods and groves, and is placed on the ground (*rarely*, in the hole of a tree). The eggs average ·65 × ·55 of an inch; are elliptical; and are white (cream-tinted), covered with small and rather dark brown blotches and spots, chiefly at the great end, or evenly sprinkled with small light reddish-brown markings. One set of four or five is here laid in the last week of May (sometimes earlier or later),, and occasionally a second when the season is more advanced.

(c). The Black and White "Creepers" are very common summer-residents throughout southern New England, though rare in the more northern portions, where in many large tracts even of wooded land they are not to be found at all. They reach Eastern Massachusetts, sometimes as early as the last week of April, sometimes not until the second week of May, and remain here until September, during a part of which month migrants of this species continue to pass through from the North on their way to the South. The warblers generally inhabit woodland of various kinds, but occasionally visit orchards and like places near the habitations of man, toward whom they exhibit no shyness, and also seek their food among the bushes of the " scrub," where they find the caterpillars, small insects, and insect-eggs, upon which they habitually feed. They differ from all our other warblers in their method of obtaining their food, which is to a certain extent entirely distinctive, though much like that of the true creepers (*Certhiidæ*), from whom they principally differ in being much less systematic in their researches, and in occasionally busying themselves upon the ground. They pass most of their time in scrambling about the trunks and larger limbs of trees, rarely perching, and also in running over old fences, such as contain rotten and moss-grown or lichen-covered wood. While thus engaged, they almost invariably keep their head pointed toward the direction in which they are moving. They rarely take other than short flights, when not traveling, but after remaining for a moment on the trunk of one tree, seldom longer, fly to a neighboring one. They are never strictly gregarious, but they possess such conjugal and parental affection that they are often seen in pairs (or family-groups). When the female is frightened from her nest on the ground, which is often partially concealed, she usually feigns lameness, and flutters away with trailing wings and tail, in the hope of distracting the intruder. (Dr. Coues speaks of these birds building in the holes of trees, which, says Dr. Brewer, " is probably an error, or, if ever known to occur, an entirely exceptional case." I have found two of their nests near Boston thus situated, of which the first was in a pine-grove in the cavity of a tree rent by lightning, and about five feet from the ground, and the other on the top of a low birch stump, which stood in a grove of white oaks. These facts show how erratic birds frequently are in changing their habits, and how much corroborative testimony is needed to establish a single fact in Natural History.)

(d). The Black and White "Creepers" have a very great variety of notes, and perhaps utter more distinct sounds, exclusive of song, than any other of our birds, though it is very possible that other warblers, with whom I am less familiar, possess the same power. The notes of the so-called "Creepers" are a weak but pure *tsip*, a harsher *tsip*, much like that of the Chestnut-sided Warbler, a loud *chick*, which sometimes becomes a *chink*, an alarm-note, *chick-a-chick*, *chick-chick*, a chant, if it can properly be so-called, of *tsee-tsee-tsee-tsee*, which is uttered in another tone so as to sound more like *chee-chee-chee-chee*, and their rather feeble and unmusical refrain of *wee-sée, wee-sée, wee-sée, wee-sée, wee-sée*. To the last and most frequently repeated chant a few sweet and musical notes are generally added in May and June, and these combined form their only song.

There are hardly any birds more familiar to the ornithologist in the woods than the Black and White "Creepers," since they are common, are free from shyness, and usually remain near the ground, with their boldly marked plumage in conspicuous contrast with the bark of the white oaks and chestnuts, to which they so often turn their attention. They are eminently useful, and few creatures do more good in protecting the growth and life of our forest-trees, and the trees of woodland freshly sprung up to supply the place of a former growth.

VIII. PARULA

(A) AMERICANA. *Blue Yellow-backed Warbler.* "*Blue Yellow-back.*"

(A summer-resident in northern New England, and usually a common migrant through Massachusetts, where a very few breed.)

(a). About 4½ inches long. Above, blue, ashy-tinted, with a yellowish patch on the back. Lore black. *Throat and part of the breast, yellow, with a rich, dark brownish patch.* Upper throat immaculate. Other under parts, wing-bars, and tail-spots, white. ♀ rather duller, with less distinct markings.

(Details omitted.)

(*b*). The nest is globular, with an entrance on the side, and is composed principally of hanging mosses. It is usually placed in the woods, twenty or more feet from the ground, at the end of a bough of some hard-wood tree or evergreen. It usually contains four or five freshly laid eggs in early June, which average about ·62 × ·48 of an inch, and are white (or cream-tinted) with spots and confluent blotches of reddish-brown and lilac, chiefly about the crown.

(*c*). The "Blue Yellow-backs" are summer-residents through-

Fig. 4. Blue Yellow-backed Warbler (½).

out the eastern United States, more commonly in Northern Maine and New Hampshire than in Massachusetts, where only a few breed, chiefly, probably, in the valleys of the Connecticut and Nashua Rivers. Near Boston they are extremely rare in summer, but are generally common in the second and third weeks of May and September, during their migrations, being, however, sometimes rare, and sometimes extremely abundant. I can in no way, I believe, better describe their habits than by detailing the observations which I made upon them this spring (1875), when they were very numerous in my immediate neighborhood. They came on the eleventh of May, and did not wholly disappear until the twenty-second of that month, after which I saw none, except a few in autumn. They chiefly frequented the budding maples, the orchard-trees, and the shrubs and bushes which were just pushing forth their young leaves; sometimes alone, more often in pairs, and less commonly in small parties of three and four. They constantly skipped from twig to twig, much as a Chickadee does, often turning their heads in peculiar attitudes so as to reach the crannies behind the buds, and occasionally even hanging head downwards, the better to effect their purposes through their constant activity. They would often take short flights into the air in order to seize some passing insect, and then would immediately return to their former avocations, usually on the same tree. A great charm in the disposition of these pretty and graceful little birds was their entire fearlessness of man, which was so absolute, that I many times was within two or three feet of them, even when I was not motionless. The "Blue Yellow-backs," whilst migrating, may also be found in the more open and lightly timbered woodland, but seldom among the pines. In their summer-homes they inhabit both the evergreens and hard-wood trees, wherever grouped in abundance, and very generally prefer the higher branches, where they build their nests (for they never, so far as I know, descend to the ground). These nests are beautiful objects, and very admirable architectural works, which distinguish their builders from all the other members, at least the American members, of their large family, the warblers; for though nearly all of them build neat and pretty nests, none ever construct nests so striking in appearance as these, which are globular, with an entrance on one side. They are often suspended from the bough of a hemlock, and are usually composed of rather long Spanish moss, which is a very pretty material for nest-building. Wonderful must that instinct be which enables the little warblers to weave the long threads together with security and compactness, and finally to arrange them in the desired form that the globular shape may be so nearly perfected. From cases of which I have known, I have strong reason to believe that these nests in Massachusetts are sometimes, perhaps accidentally, not entirely rounded, but are left largely uncovered, which I at one time supposed to be due to the warmer climate, but I have since learned that specimens from the Southern States are like those from Maine, and perfect in shape.

(*d*). The ordinary notes of the "Blue Yellow-backs" are a *tship*, a *chick*, often loud, a cry of *chick-a-chick-chick*, and occasionally a trill, which approaches a chatter. Their song, which I have often heard in May, as well as June, though rather weak and unmusical, is yet quite loud, more so, I think, than some other authors have represented. It begins with a trill of rising inflection and marked accent, which is followed either by twitters, or by notes which remind me of those of the "Black-throated Greens," or by still others like them. In this song I have sometimes recognized a peculiar hoarse tone, which seemed to characterize it strongly.

IX. PERISSOGLOSSA

(A) TIGRINA. *Cape May Warbler.*

(In Massachusetts generally extremely rare, especially in autumn. In summer, "common at Umbagog," Maine.)

(*a*). 5-5½ inches long. Above, yellowish-olive; back dark-streaked. Crown dark. Lores black. Beneath, bright yellow. Breast and sides black-streaked. Throat strongly tinged with the bright orange-brown of the ear-coverts. Rump yellow. Wing-bars and tail-spots, white; former often fused.

(*b*). A nest found in the neighborhood of Boston, closely resembled that of the Yellow Bird (§ X, A) in every respect. The five eggs, which were fresh in the first week of June, also were like those of that species, and probably unlike the usual form, described by Dr. Brewer as measuring " ·70 × ·55 of an inch," and having "a pinkish-white ground, blotched with purple and brown of various shades and tints. They are disposed chiefly about the larger end, usually in a ring."

(*c*). The Cape May Warblers are very rare in Massachusetts, more so, however, during some years than during others, and are so very seldom to be seen near Boston that I have very little information to offer to my readers in regard to their habits. Mr. Maynard has never seen them in the eastern part of this

State, where, however, some were shot from (blossoming?) apple-trees by Dr. Bryant, but he found them common at Umbagog, Maine, where they spent their time in the tops of the taller evergreens. In northern New England they are summer-residents, but in the southern parts can hardly be considered as other than very rare migrants. I have occasionally seen them in May, but only once in September, which is partly due to their frequenting so much the higher branches, where they are not easily detected.

X. DENDRŒCA

(A) ÆSTIVA. (*Summer*) *Yellow Bird*.[28] (*Blue-eyed*) *Yellow Warbler*. *Golden Warbler*.

(In southern New England a very common summer-resident.)

(*a*). About five inches long. Yellow with modifications. Breast, and even the back, streaked (often indistinctly) with orange-brown. *Tail-feathers not blotched with white as in all other Dendrœcæ.*

(*b*). I shall describe the nest at length, as it is essentially like those of several other species. It is composed outwardly of very fine grasses, interwoven with woolly or cottony materials, which form a substantial wall. This is often covered with caterpillar's silk, and is lined with wool, down from plants (particularly a dun-colored kind), horse-hairs, and rarely feathers. Nuttall aptly calls this structure "neat and durable." It is to be found on cultivated grounds and in gardens, as well as in pastures and swamps, though even a different situation is sometimes chosen; it is generally placed in a low bush, such as the barberry or currant-bush, but occasionally in the branches of a shade-tree at a considerable height above the ground.

The eggs average ·67 × ·50 of an inch, and are usually *either* grayish-white, green-tinted, with spots and blotches of lilac (which is often obscure) and various browns chiefly about the larger end, *or* (more rarely) white, with lilac (obscured) and sandy or yellowish-brown markings grouped principally about

---

[28] The Goldfinch (*Chrysomitris tristris*, § 15, IV, A), is also called the Yellow Bird.

the crown. The above colorations are the extremes, between which there are various intermediate forms. It is remarkable that the eggs, though so variable, are very generally characteristic of the birds, and unlike those of other warblers. In Eastern Massachusetts four or five eggs are laid about the first of June, but no second brood is raised unless some accident befalls the first.

(c). The Yellow Birds are the most common and familiar of all our warblers; and who is there that does not, or who ought not to know these beneficial and charming little birds, who are so pleasantly associated with the arrival here of actual spring, since generally in the first week of May they come from the South? Throughout the summer they are to be found about us, but when autumn comes they leave us, and generally, before the first week of September has passed away, they have gone. Yet they are very hardy, and stray to the Arctic shores, though hardly anywhere common to the northward of Massachusetts, where they are, in most parts of the State, abundant. They inhabit pasture-land and cultivated grounds, being not infrequently seen near houses, and never retiring to the woods. They are not sufficiently social to gather in flocks, but, on the contrary, though of a pleasant-tempered and affectionate disposition, seem always to be absorbed in the search of insects, through our orchard-trees, shade-trees, and shrubbery. They never seek for these insects on the ground, or in the higher tree-tops, and rarely seize them in the air, but whilst pursuing them continually move among the lower branches, occasionally taking short flights from one place to another.

(d). The Yellow Bird's song is simple, yet very pleasing, and one does not become tired of it, though repeated often, as it has several variations. It nearly resembles the syllables *weé-chee-weé-chee-weé-i-u*, but is like the song of several other warblers. The loud *chirp* of the Yellow Birds is often heard from the branches, among which they are busy, and often is repeated plaintively, when their nest is disturbed.

Though probably less familiar toward man than many people suppose, the Yellow Birds do not repel his advances, and certainly greatly benefit him by their constant industry in destroying insects, particularly small caterpillars and cankerworms, of which they are very fond.

(B) DISCOLOR. *Prairie Warbler.*
(In Eastern Massachusetts, a summer-resident of no great rarity.)

(*a*). About 4½ inches long. Olive above, with brick-red spots on the back. Under parts, bright yellow. A peculiar mark on the side of the head, and side-streaks on the throat and breast, black. (Details omitted.)

(*b*). The nest of the Prairie Warbler differs from that of the Yellow Bird (A) in being usually lined thickly with horsehairs (whereas the other is often lined with a dun-colored plant-down), and in being almost invariably semi-pensile. It is usually placed within a few feet of the ground, in a bush or low tree, in a rocky pasture or the "scrub." The eggs average ·65 × ·52 of an inch, and are pure white, generally either with delicate lilac (and a few inconspicuous light brown) markings, which form a ring about the crown (such being those which I have found near Boston), or with lilac, purplish, and umber-brown markings. Near Boston one set of three or four eggs is laid in the first week of June.

(*c*). The Prairie Warblers are among the smallest and most retired of their family. They are summer-residents in the eastern United States so far to the northward as Massachusetts, in which State they are rather rare in the western part, but quite common in some other portions. In certain localities near Boston they are quite abundant from the second or third week of May until the latter part of August. They frequent almost exclusively rocky pasture-lands and the "scrub," and I have but once seen or heard them elsewhere, in that case having heard their song in some shrubbery on a cultivated estate, far from their usual haunts. Though perhaps, as Wilson remarks, easily approached and not shy, yet they almost invariably shun the neighborhood of man, and live quite solitarily in pairs among the pastures where they build their nests. There, when household duties do not interfere, they are busied, not with such marked activity as some other warblers, from dawn until evening, in searching among the branches of low bushes and saplings for the small caterpillars and insects upon which they feed. They do not usually make any demonstrations if their nest is examined, but remain quietly in the neighborhood of it until they can safely return. They do not attempt to lead off the intruder by feigning lameness, as many other warblers do, especially those who habitually build their nests on or very near the ground.

(d). Their song cannot fail to attract the attention of every person who hears it, and who takes an interest in birds. Its notes, resembling the syllables *zee-zee-zee-zee-zee-zee-zee*, are uttered in a very peculiar tone, and each note is a little higher and louder than the preceding. The birds, on uttering it, frequently depress their tail. The ordinary note of the often silent Prairie Warblers is a *chirr*.

(C) PENNSYLVANICA. *Chestnut-sided Warbler.*
(In southern New England, a common summer-resident.)

(a). About 5¼ inches long. Back, light ashy-yellow, black-streaked. Under parts, white. Wing-bars the same, generally forming one patch. Crown, yellow, bordered by white. Lore, continuously with a line through the eye and one down to a *chestnut-red patch on the side of the breast*, black.

(b). The nest is usually coarser than that of the Yellow Bird (A), and contains fewer woolly materials. It is often composed outwardly of narrow strips of thin bark or dried grasses, mixed with a few bits of plant-down, and inwardly of very fine straw, which is lined with hairs. Such is the description of two nests before me. The nests are commonly placed from two to eight feet above the ground in a low bush, shrub, or sapling, and are either built in a fork or otherwise secured (but are never pensile). The situations generally chosen are the "scrub-lands," or open woods in low grounds which contain bushes, vines, etc. Near Boston they are usually finished, and contain four or five fresh eggs, about the first of June. The eggs average ·68 × ·50 of an inch, and are generally white with purplish- or reddish-brown spots and blotches, which are sometimes confluent. These markings are either scattered over the egg, more thickly at the larger end than the other, or are grouped in a ring about the crown. An egg of this species in my collection is buff (darker than that of the Wood Pewee) with a few lilac markings, but I have seen no others like it.

(c). The Chestnut-sided Warblers are summer-residents throughout New England, but are much more abundant in the southern parts than further to the northward. They reach the neighborhood of Boston in the second week of May, and pass the entire summer here. They are never gregarious, but usually they are particularly common at the time of their spring-migrations, when they frequent considerably the shrubbery and trees of cultivated estates, before retiring to their summer-haunts. Their habits at this time have often reminded me of those of the "Yellow-rumps," for they are often much in the air, taking flights from one place to another at quite a height from the ground, that is, from thirty to sixty feet above it. At other times they glean quietly among the foliage of the maples, and other budding trees, generally among the lower branches. Occasionally they perform a rapid and graceful movement through the air to seize some passing insect, or stand like a flycatcher to watch the flies and gnats, which they now and then secure by darting after them. They never seek their food upon the ground, so far as I know, and only descend to it when picking up materials for their nests. Their haunts in summer are chiefly pasture-lands, "scrub," and open, moist woodlands, such as contain oaks, chestnuts, and maples, and an undergrowth of bushes, vines, and saplings. I have never met these birds in thick or dark woods, and have but once seen their nest placed in an evergreen, it being in that instance in a low spruce by a brookside. It is to be remembered, however, that in different sections of the country birds show preference for different kinds of land, and often vary their habits to an extent that is surprising, and even confusing. Finally come those variations in coloration, caused by climate, which have caused so much discussion as to species and varieties. All this shows that properly one man ought not to write the Natural History of other than a small tract of country, and that, before the habits of our birds can be thoroughly known, it will be necessary to station competent naturalists, who can devote their whole time to making observations and accurately noting them, at various points in the regions of the different *faunæ*, all of whom shall work under a system and a superintendence. This plan is not at present a feasible one, but the advantages of it would be numerous, for the flights of birds (particularly should ornithologists be stationed near meteorological observation-posts) could be foretold with considerable accuracy to sportsmen and other ornithologists, who are already, however, by far too destructive.

(*d*). The ordinary notes of the Chestnut-sided Warbler are a soft *tsip*, a louder and harsher *tsip*, uttered in a peculiar tone, and much like that of the Black and White "Creeper," and a rather loud *chip*. Mr. Samuels speaks of their having "at times, a rattling cry something like the alarm-note of the Maryland Yellow-throat." Their song is attractive and musical, though containing but a few simple notes. One variation resembles the syllables *wée-see-wée-see-wée-see* (each of which is higher than the preceding, except the sixth, which is lower than the fifth). The other common variation is almost exactly like the song of the little Yellow Bird (A), and consequently like that of various other warblers.

(D) CASTANEA. *Bay-breasted Warbler.* (*Autumnal Warbler?*)

(Through Eastern Massachusetts a rare migrant.)

(*a*). About $5\frac{1}{2}$ inches long. Back, light ashy-yellow, black-streaked. Under parts, white. Wing-bars white, (generally) forming one patch. Forehead and sides of head, black. Crown, throat, and breast, chestnut (or deep chestnut-red). Belly and ear-patch usually buff-tinged, but sometimes white. ♀ with paler chestnut than the ♂.

(*b*). The nest is rather coarsely built, and is placed in the bough of an evergreen (usually the hemlock) from ten to twenty feet above the ground. Four or five eggs (in one case reported by Mr. Maynard, six) are laid in Northern New Hampshire and Maine in the second week of June. These eggs average ·68×·50 of an inch, and are bluish-green, with markings of brown and lilac, generally gathered in a ring about the crown.

(c). The Bay-breasted Warblers are among the many species who appear in Massachusetts as migrants only, and who pass the summer in a colder climate.[29] They are, as a rule, very rare throughout the State in spring, and in autumn are never seen here. Mr. Allen, however, in speaking of this species, says that " in the Connecticut valley it is generally more or less common and sometimes very abundant."

The Bay-breasted Warblers arrive here, after leaving their winter-homes in the South, in the third or fourth week of May, and frequent the woods and trees in open lands. I have generally seen them among budding maples, which like willows possess great attractions for the migrant warblers, but I have also seen them among pines. They are extremely active, and busily seek for their food among the branches, occasionally fluttering before the clusters of foliage, but they are not very shy, and usually permit a near approach.

They are rare among the White Mountains, but Mr. Maynard speaks of them as being " most abundant of the *Sylvicolidæ* at Umbagog," and adds that " these birds are found in all the wooded sections of this region where they frequent the tops of tall trees." He thinks that they are " confined during the breeding season to the region just north of the White Mountains range," and makes the following interesting remarks on their travels. " This species," says he, " together with *Geothlypis philadelphia* and *Helminthophaga peregrina*, seems to pursue a very eccentric course during the migrations. Avoiding the eastern and middle States, the majority pass along the

---

[29] I have since learned that specimens have been taken here in both June and July.

borders of the Great Lakes, through Ohio, southern Illinois (Ridgway), down the Mississippi Valley, across into Texas and so on into Mexico and Central America where they winter. Returning in spring they (at least *D. castanea*) pursue a more southern route, keeping along the coast as far as the New England States, where they ascend the Connecticut Valley, generally avoiding eastern Massachusetts."

(*d*). " The first part of the song is like that of the Black-poll Warbler, but it has a terminal warble similar to that of the Redstart to which it bears a striking resemblance, with the exception that it is given with less energy." The Bay-breasted Warblers are usually silent during their migrations.

NOTE.—The above quotations from Mr. Maynard are from his pamphlet, entitled "A Catalogue of the Birds of Coos Co., N. H., and Oxford Co., Me., with Annotations, etc."

(E) STRIATA. *"Black-poll" Warbler. Autumnal Warbler (?).*

(Common migrants through Massachusetts both in spring and autumn.)

(*a*). About 5½ inches long. ♂. Back streaked with olivaceous (-ash?) and black. *Crown down to the eyes black*. Sides of the head and under parts, white. Sides of the breast marked with black streaks which crowd into a fine chain running to the bill. Wing-bars and tail-blotches, white. ♀. Dusky olive-green above, black-streaked. Under parts not (usually) pure white, or very markedly streaked.

(*b*). The nest is essentially like that of the "Black-throated Green," though coarser. It is usually placed near the ground, in an evergreen, and always in the thick woods. It has never been found in Massachusetts, but in northern New England it is generally finished in the latter part of June. The eggs of each set, usually four, average about $\cdot 68 \times \cdot 50$ of an inch, and are commonly (grayish-?) white with spots and blotches of purplish and different browns. The blotches predominate, and are scattered over the whole egg. Other forms occur.

(*c*). The Black-poll Warblers are usually among the most common migrants through this State to northern New England

and the countries beyond; but, like other migrants, they vary greatly in abundance from year to year in certain places, and are occasionally quite rare in spring near Boston. They usually make their appearance here late in the season, and though I have seen them in the middle of May, they generally do not arrive before the last week of that month, and then remain here, or continue to pass by, throughout the first few days of June. They at that time frequent evergreen and hard-wood trees indifferently, hunting for insects among both the lower and higher branches, and occasionally seizing them in the air. They are less gregarious than in the fall of the year, and one often sees pairs or individuals, much more often than when they are returning, probably because at the time of their spring migrations they are mated for the summer. But a very small proportion of them pass the summer in Northern New Hampshire, a larger number being then resident in Northern Maine and the majority in Canada and Labrador. They affect exclusively the woods and forests which contain a great many evergreens, and rarely visit the lightly timbered and more open woodland. They return to Eastern Massachusetts in the last week of September, and are commonly plentiful during a greater part of October. They often frequent pines in preference to all other trees, generally remain among the upper branches or in the very tree-tops, and spend most of their time in snapping up passing insects, which they sometimes take an opportunity to do, whilst moving from one tree to another.

(*d*). The "Black-polls" have soft and loud *chips*, an unmusical trill, shorter than that of the "Chipper," and three or four notes, suggestive of knocking pebbles together. Their song is monotonous, weak, and unmusical. It resembles the syllables *tsi-tsi-tsi-tsi-tsi*, repeated in a nearly unvarying tone.

[EE. *Autumnal Warbler*. (See Appendix E, family *Sylvicolidæ*.)

I do not propose to occupy much space in discussing the question:—are the Autumnal Warblers mentioned by Wilson, Audubon, and Nuttall, the young of "Black-poll" or of the

Bay-breasted Warblers? I have only "Wilson's Ornithology" at hand, and unfortunately no specimen of the bird in question. But the weight of evidence seems to show that the bird as colored and described by Wilson represents the young of the latter; and yet is it not possible that he may have accidentally obtained a young Bay-breasted Warbler from among a company of "Black-polls"?[30] Coues admits that the young of the two species are so much alike as often to be indistinguishable. It is certain that the small warblers seen here in October, which resemble the Autumnal Warblers, are young "Black-polls," as is indicated by the fact of their abundance and by their habits. Mr. Maynard states it as a positive fact.

Their note is a feeble Cedar-bird-like *lisp;* but Wilson speaks of the males warbling in autumn "low, but very sweet notes," which perhaps is a mistake. (See D, *d,* E, *d.*)]

(F) BLACKBURNIÆ. *Blackburnian Warbler. Hemlock Warbler.*

(Generally not a common migrant through Massachusetts, where this species occasionally breeds.)

(*a*). About 4½ inches long. ♂ dark above. Wing-patch, white. Head, *throat, and breast, brilliant orange,* with a border to the crown and a broad stripe through the eye black. Sides black-streaked, and belly nearly white. ♀ essentially like ♀ *striata* (E) above. Superciliary line, throat and breast, yellow. Otherwise like ♂.

(*b*). A nest of this species, containing young, which I found in Northern New Hampshire, was placed about twenty feet from the ground in a pine. Another, which I was so fortunate as to find in a thick hemlock-wood near Boston, was also about twenty feet above the ground. It contained three young and a yet unhatched egg, which measures ·65×·50, and resembles the egg of the Chestnut-sided Warbler (D), being white, with lilac and principally reddish-brown markings, grouped at the

---

[30] The legs in Wilson's picture are, however, colored like those of the "Black-poll," and not like those of the "Bay-breast."

larger end. Mr. Maynard thought that the "Blackburnians" built in the highest branches of the spruces and hemlocks, and such is very probably their custom.

(c). The male Blackburnian Warblers are the handsomest of all their large family, for the combination of delicacy and brilliancy in the orange of their throat is unsurpassed. It is a curious fact that they are apparently much more numerous than the females during the migrations, which is the case with several other birds. This phenomenon has never been satisfactorily explained, and cannot be accounted for merely by the superior gaiety of the male's coloration. It has also been observed that when traveling the males of many birds precede the females, and that in winter they occasionally remain in somewhat colder climates.[31]

The Blackburnian Warblers usually reach Eastern Massachusetts about the tenth of May, though I have seen them as early as the twenty-first of April, when I observed a pair feeding upon ivy-berries, the insects upon which they generally feed not then being common. They are usually rather rare here, and make but a brief stay among our woods and trees, showing a fondness for pines and other evergreens. I have seen as many as three males together, though they more often travel singly. They do not often catch insects in the air, but usually remain in trees at a moderate height. Mr. Allen, in his "Notes on Some of the Rarer Birds of Massachusetts," says that in "some seasons they are extremely abundant at some localities, and commonly are not rare, except in particular situations. Mr. Scott observes that for several weeks in May, in 1866, he could remain at a single place in the woods and shoot ten to twenty per hour." This statement has been severely but amusingly criticised: "several weeks must indicate at least three, and had he shot ten hours a day, as he well might have, he would in that time have shot *three thousand or more from a single place in the woods.*"

---

[31] The fact stated in relation to their wintering has not, I believe, been well determined.

An interesting anecdote, relative to these birds, has been communicated to me by a student in the Institute of Technology. On the eleventh of May, 1875, a male of this species fell stunned through the ventilator, on to the floor of the drawing room in the topmost story. He was finally placed on the sill of an open window, from which, when revived by the fresh air and sun, he afterward took flight. In summer the Blackburnian Warblers are common in northern New England, where they inhabit woodland, particularly evergreen-swamps, but in Massachusetts are extremely rare, or rather accidental.

(*d*). When together in family-parties, they twitter constantly. Their ordinary note is a *chip*, or weak syllables like those uttered by the Golden-crowned "Wrens," as *tsee-tsee* or *tsee-tsee-tsee*. Their song is not very musical, though simple and pleasing. As I have heard it in their summer-homes, it resembles the syllables *wee-seé-wee-seé-wee-seé* (*wee-seé-ick*). As heard in spring I may liken it to *weé-see-weé-see*, *tsee-tsee-tsee-tsee-tsee-tsee-tsee-tsee*. The latter syllables are on an ascending scale; the very last is shrill and fine.

(G) CÆRULEA. *Cærulean Warbler. Blue Warbler.*

(It is possible and probable that this species may occasionally stray to Massachusetts, but I know no instance of its having done so.)

(*a*). 4-4½ inches long. ♂ of an exquisite blue, black-streaked. Under parts white, with sides streaked. Wing-bars white. In the (unstreaked?) ♀ the blue is greenish, and the white yellowish. Superciliary line also yellowish.

(*b*). Audubon says: "The nest is placed in the forks of a low tree or bush, more frequently on a dog-wood tree. It is partly pensile, * * *. The fibres of vines and of the stalks of rank herbaceous plants, together with slender roots, compose the outer part, being arranged in a circular manner. The lining consists entirely of the dry fibres of the Spanish moss. The female lays four or five eggs, of a pure white colour, with a few reddish spots at the larger end."

(*c*). I have never seen the Cærulean Warblers, and I have

never known them to stray so far to the northward as Massachusetts, though, indeed, reported from Nova Scotia. They are said to prefer the deep woods, where they inhabit the tree-tops.

(*d*). Audubon speaks of their song as "extremely sweet and mellow," but Mr. Ridgway says that they possess "only the most feeble notes" (Dr. Brewer). This is one instance among many, and a simple one, of disagreement between two authorities (in this case, the former probably being the less trustworthy). I have seen no less than six wholly different descriptions of the song of one species, the name of which I do not now remember, none of which seemed to me reliable or satisfactory, and yet they were all written by men whom one would naturally regard as good authorities. Moreover, it was very evident that not more than one or two were descriptive of the same notes, though the bird in question had but one song. It is, therefore, certain that some of these authors attributed to this bird music that it never uttered. In most cases of the kind it is to be remembered that many birds have two songs, many variations of one song, or a simple unmusical chant, to which a terminal warble is added in May or June.

(II) CÆRULESCENS. *Black-throated Blue Warbler. Canada Warbler.*

(Generally not very common during their migrations through Massachusetts.)

(*a*). Five inches or more long. ♂, slaty-blue above, white beneath. Sides of head and whole throat, continuously jet-black. Wings and tail dark; the former with *a large white spot on the edge of the wing* (at the base of the primaries) and no bars. ♀, above dull olive-green, blue-tinged. Below, white or yellowish. Wing-spot characteristic but sometimes inconspicuous.

(*b*). The nest is probably always built near the ground, and most often in an evergreen. An egg found by Mr. Burroughs and described by Dr. Brewer is grayish white, "marked around the larger end with a wreath, chiefly of a bright umber-brown with lighter markings of reddish-brown and obscure purple. A few smaller dottings of the same are sparingly distributed over the rest of the egg. Its measurements are ·70 by ·50 of an inch."

(c). The Black-throated Blue Warblers are not only summer-residents in the more northern New England States, but also in Massachusetts, where, however, they are very rare as such, unless in the western and more mountainous portions. They reach the neighborhood of Boston in the third week of May, and are more common here from that date until the first of June than at any other period of the year. They return to the South in September, and I have seen them as late as the last day of that month. An instance has been reported of a pair passing the winter in Boston, which was a most extraordinary circumstance, since their usual *habitat* at that season is, I believe, beyond the United States. Birds, however, often wander, so far as direct evidence goes, more than a thousand miles from their usual homes, sometimes perhaps intentionally, but more often, probably, because forced to do so in search of food, or by adverse weather. It is generally difficult to understand their eccentric movements on land, whereas it is easy to understand why birds, who have ventured out to sea, should be compelled by winds to deviate from their course. When with us in spring, the "Black-throated Blues" are to be seen generally in pairs or singly, but occasionally in small companies of three or four, in which latter case quarrels frequently arise between the males. They are very dexterous in obtaining their insect-prey; sometimes seizing it in the air, with the skill of a true flycatcher, and at other times finding it among the branches of the various trees which they frequent. Now they twist their heads into seemingly painful postures, the better to search the crannies in the bark or blossoms, now spring from a twig to snap up an insect in the foliage above their heads, instantly returning, and now flutter before a cluster of opening leaves, with the grace of a hummingbird. Occasionally they descend to the ground, and are so very tame that once, when I was standing motionless, observing some warblers near me, one hopped between my feet to pick up some morsel of food. I have often been able to make close observations upon birds, by remaining entirely motionless and allowing them to gather about me, and thus have accurately learned their habits, without disturbing their happiness.

(*d*). The ordinary note of the "Black-throated Blues" is a simple *chip*, which is sometimes closely repeated, after the manner of the Chipping Sparrow. They have also a chatter, employed chiefly as a battle-cry, and a loud alarm-note, resembling the *chuck* of the Snow-bird. The males have an unmusical song, the tone of which resembles somewhat that of the Blue Yellow-back's song, or that of the Night Hawk's note, being peculiar, and rather harsh or guttural. It usually consists of three (rarely four) syllables, of which the last two are the highest in tone and the most emphatic, and sounds like "*zwee-zwee-zwee.*" It is sometimes varied and lengthened so as to resemble the syllables [*che-wée*] *che-wée* [*see*] *wée-see zwée*. It is characteristic in tone, and is wholly unlike the music of our other warblers, with the exception of one form of the song of the "Black-throated Green."

(I) VIRENS. *Black-throated Green Warbler.* "*Black-throated Green.*"

(In New England a common summer-resident, but "rather confined to certain districts.")

(*a*). About five inches long. ♂, olive-green above. Wings and tail dark, with white-edged feathers; former white-barred. *Whole side of head, rich yellow* (with occasional indistinct markings). Throat and breast, black. ♀ (and ♂ in autumn) with the black restricted or wanting. Other under parts, white or yellowish. Outer tail-feathers, largely white.

(*b*). The nest is *usually* placed in a pine, in a horizontal fork near the end of a bough, from twenty to fifty feet above the ground (but sometimes lower). It is finished in June, sometimes in the first week, sometimes not until the last. It is composed outwardly of narrow strips of thin bark, bits of twigs from vines, dried grasses, and such odds and ends as the birds have found convenient to employ, and inwardly of bits of wool, feathers, and plant-down, but it is generally lined with hairs and fine shreds of vegetable substance. It is usually small, neat, and very pretty. The eggs of each set are three or four, and average $.67 \times .55$ of an inch. They are commonly (creamy) white, with reddish or umber-brown, and *purplish* markings, grouped principally about the crown. These markings are for the most part either clear and delicate, or a little coarse and rather obscure; but the eggs are better characterized by their shape, being rather broad in proportion to their length.

(c). I owe much to the charming little "Black-throated Greens" for the pleasure which they have many times afforded me, but I know no means of requiting them, unless by writing their biography with peculiar care.

They are summer-residents throughout New England, but are particularly common in certain parts of Eastern Massachusetts. They prefer pines to all other trees, but in the regions of the Nashua and Connecticut Valleys, in the North, and whilst migrating, they are to be found in "mixed" woods, in the former cases especially those which contain other evergreens. They reach Boston (which now comprises tracts of genuine country) about the fifth of May, sometimes earlier, but rarely much later, and generally, for a day or two before the middle of that month, are very abundant, owing to the migrants bound for homes in a colder climate. After these passengers have disappeared, the "Black-throated Greens" here confine themselves almost exclusively to groves of pine or cedar, chiefly those in high land, and only occasionally stray to orchards or other places, though so tame as sometimes to visit vines growing on the piazza, where I have known them to build their nests. They remain here throughout the summer, and do not altogether disappear until the first week of October. They do not often catch insects in the air, except in spring, and rarely descend to the ground, except for the sake of taking a bath, which they do so prettily that an appreciative spectator cannot fail to enjoy it as much as the birds themselves. They find their food principally among the branches of the evergreens which they frequent, are constantly active whilst in search of it, and never rest in the manner of the Pine Warblers, who are much lazier. They generally remain in one spot for several minutes, and then fly to another at quite a distance, seldom staying long in one group of trees. Though active, they are not restless, as many of their kindred are, but rather are comparatively deliberate in their motions. There is to me a fascination in watching these birds, as they move among the tree-tops, and a charm in listening to their drowsy notes, which (without poetical exaggeration) seem to invite one, on a warm day, to lie down and slumber on the pine-needles that are strewn over the ground — though to persons too practically minded, the mosquitoes at that season permit no such repose.

(*d*). The ordinary notes of the "Black-throated Greens" are numerous, being a *tsip*, a *chick*, which is sometimes soft and sometimes loud, a *check*, a *chuck*, which is used chiefly as a note of alarm, and a sharp *chink*, which is generally indicative of distress. Their song has several variations, of which the two most often heard are *wée-see-wée-see-wée-see* (in which the middle notes are the highest) and *wēē-sēē-wée-see-sēē* (in which the second note is higher than the rest, the second couplet uttered in a lively way, and the other notes drawled out in a manner peculiar to this species). To these simple chants a few terminal notes are not infrequently added, which sometimes consist of a repetition, and, rarely, resemble those of the "Black-throated Blue's" music. These songs are very characteristic; and, if one has once heard them, he cannot often confound them with those of other birds.

The "Black-throated Greens" are, to me, with perhaps the exception of the Pine Warblers, the most attractive members of their family, on account, I think, of their pleasing, familiar, and oft-repeated songs, which are heard from the time of their arrival nearly throughout the summer, which form so fitting an accompaniment to the whisperings of the pines, and to which I am never weary of listening. Another reason, however, is that they show a fondness for the pines as great as my own, though, no doubt, from very different motives. The majesty of those trees, their gracefulness, their freshness throughout the year, their beauty in summer, when, after a hard shower, the light of the setting sun breaks upon them, their beauty in winter, when their branches are loaded, many to the ground, with snow, or when they are covered with glittering ice, their whisperings in the breezes of spring and summer, their sighing and whistling in the southern gales, and finally their odor, combine to render them the finest, I think, of all our forest trees.

(J) PINUS. *Pine Warbler.* (*Pine-tree Warbler.*) *Pine-creeping Warbler.* ("*Pine Creeper.*")

(A common summer-resident in the pine-tracts of Massachusetts.)

(*a*). 5½–6 inches long. Upper parts, olive. Belly and two wing-bars, white. Superciliary line, throat, and breast, bright yellow. ♀ duller, often with little yellow below. In both sexes "tail-blotches *confined to two outer pairs of tail feathers, large, oblique.*"

(*b*). The nest is usually to be found in the same situation, and is otherwise essentially like that of the "Black-throated Green" (I). Though generally finished in the last week of May it has been found in the earlier part of the month. The eggs of each set are usually four, and average ·67 × ·52 of an inch. They are white, with purplish and brown markings, or fine markings of three shades of brown, sprinkled chiefly at the "great end."

(*c*). The Pine Warblers have a very extensive breeding-range, and are probably to be found in summer throughout New England, in the pine-wooded districts. They are the first of their family to reach the Eastern States in spring, and I have seen them near Boston on the first of April. They usually, however, arrive here in the first or second week of that month, and return to the South in the latter part of September, occasionally lingering until the middle of October. Except in the summer-season, they are often more or less gregarious, and associate with the "Red-polls" (*D. palmarum*) and "Yellow-rumps." Moreover, in winter, spring, and fall, they find much of their food upon the ground, as do the other warblers that I have just mentioned, particularly the former. They derive their name of "Pine-creepers" from the fact that they occasionally cling to the trunks of trees, and that they can move along the horizontal limbs with ease and activity; but I have never known them to progress in the manner of the creepers or woodpeckers.

Their habits in summer do not differ very essentially from those of the "Black-throated Greens." At that season, and more particularly at the time of their migrations in April, they may be found in woods of various kinds, but they have a most marked preference for pine-woods and groves, from which they occasionally ramble to near orchards. They do not often catch insects in the air, but generally seek them among the higher branches; and it is often difficult to discover their whereabouts —the more so that seemingly they are capital ventriloquists. They have always seemed to me quiet and rather indolent, and remarkably attentive to their dress. I have sometimes seen them pause, for at least fifteen minutes, to smooth their feathers or to rest, every minute "drawling out" their sweet note quite mechanically. At other times they are very active, and it is then impossible to keep sight of them for any great length of time. As I have observed males, both in spring and summer, who apparently had neither mates nor nests, I think it quite certain that there are bachelors among birds.[32] The Pine Warblers are not only extremely useful in protecting our evergreens, but are also very charming, partly, no doubt, because there is a spice of "something" in their character which we cannot altogether sanction from a moral point of view.

(*d*). Their note is as deliciously drowsy as that of the "Black-throated Green," but is not so often repeated, though

---

[32] There is other evidence that such is undoubtedly the case. An interesting article on the subject has been written by Mr. Abbott of New Jersey.

heard both earlier and later in the year. It is apparently a delicately trilled whistle, but really a series of fine notes, as is proved by the fact that the birds open and shut their bills, whilst emitting the sound. It closely resembles one of the Snow-bird's whistles, and also the trill of the Swamp Sparrow. The Pine Warblers have also a *chip*, and a few weak notes, such as *chip-a-see*, and *we-chée-we-chée-we-chée*, which are not very expressive, and are not often heard.

(K) PALMARUM. "*Red-poll*" *Warbler*. *Palm Warbler*. "*Yellow Red-poll*."

(A common migrant through Massachusetts.)

(*a*). About five inches long. Dull olive above, (obsoletely) streaked. Crown, reddish-crimson (or "chestnut"). Beneath, yellow, inconspicuously streaked on the breast with bright reddish-brown. Tail-feathers with a few white blotches. (Details omitted.)

(*b*). The nest is said to be placed on the ground, usually in a swampy locality. The eggs of each set are four (?); average about ·70 × ·55 of an inch; and are (creamy) white, with purplish, faint lilac, and reddish-brown markings, chiefly at the larger end.

(*c*). The Yellow "Red-polls" pass the summer in the North, almost entirely beyond the limits of New England, and the winter in the South, and consequently appear in Massachusetts as migrants only. They are usually common near Boston in the latter part of April, and the first week of May, as well as in the latter part of September, and sometimes the earlier part of October. Their favorite haunts are swamps and their neighborhoods, but they also frequent "scrub," hedge-rows, ploughed lands, gardens, and orchards. They almost invariably gather in loose flocks, and often associate with other warblers, and with various sparrows. They are much more terrestrial in their habits than any of their immediate relations (*i. e.*, the *Dendrœcœ*) and always are on or not very far from the ground. They fly quite gracefully, and are nimble when on the ground or when moving from branch to branch in a bush or tree. Their most noticeable habit, and the one which best distinguishes them from the rest of their family, is that of flirting their tails. almost exactly as the common Pewee does. They do this particularly when on their perches, from which they often fly directly to the ground to seize some small insect or seed which they have spied in the grass, or perhaps on the bare earth, while perched above.

As I have mentioned the food of this species, perhaps it will not be amiss to speak of that of this large family in general, the warblers, and of their usefulness to man. Though certain kinds often eat seeds (generally those of the pine or of weeds), and others partake of small berries *in spring and autumn*, a majority feed exclusively upon insects. These insects include the smaller caterpillars, various small winged insects, in one case particularly those insects which infest the bark of trees, and which the nuthatches do so much to exterminate, and, more generally, those which frequent the foliage and blossoms, especially at the time of the spring-migrations. They often include, moreover, spiders, but rarely the beetles; in the destruction of the latter, larger birds being more efficacious. Thus, though many warblers are neutral in regard to the agricultural, and what are often considered the most important, interests of man, none, so far as I know, do him any injury, whereas many greatly benefit him in the preservation of our orchard-trees, our shade-trees, our evergreens, and even our shrubbery and garden-plants. Though not, I trust, altogether useless, the above remarks seem almost unnecessary, as very fortunately the warblers have never, I believe, been persecuted.

(*d*). The ordinary notes of the Yellow "Red-polls" are a *chip*, which sometimes is closely repeated several times, and a *chuck*, which is less loud than that of the Snow-birds, but much more mellow. They have also in spring a few expressive twitters, a few rather weak musical notes, and their true song-note, which is a whistled trill, less sweet and smooth than that of the Pine Warbler. It is possible that in their summer-homes these birds produce a fuller song, but I have no evidence of such being the case. I am, moreover, inclined to think that they never *sing* very agreeably.

(L) CORONATA. *Yellow-rumped Warbler.* " *Yellow-rump.*" " *Myrtle Bird.*" " *Willow Warbler.*"

(A very common migrant through Massachusetts.)

(*a*). About 5¼ inches long. ♂, in spring and summer, slaty; black-streaked. Wings browner, and concealing the rump, when closed. Throat and belly, white. *Crown, rump, and a patch on the side of the breast, bright yellow.* Wing-bars, etc., white. ♂, in fall and winter, and ♀ generally browner, with less pure colors. Young, brown above, and white below, with a few slender side-streaks sometimes extending across the breast; rump yellow. Various intermediate stages of coloration also exist.

(*b*). "The nest is usually placed in a bush, is constructed of various soft materials, and is lined with horse-hairs, down, or some other suitable material." Mr. Maynard speaks of nests found in Northern Maine in early June, all of which "contained four fresh eggs," as being built in low spruces about four feet from the ground, and constructed of hemlock twigs, lined with feathers. A nest which I found in Northern New Hampshire was somewhat different, but contained three eggs, which were white, marked with purplish and brown, and averaged ·68 × ·50 of an inch. Dr. Brewer describes others as measuring about ·75 × ·55 of an inch, and being white, or often bluish, "blotched and spotted with reddish-brown, purple, and darker shades of brown."

(*c*). The "Yellow-rumps" are among the most abundant of all the migrants who travel through Massachusetts, being always very common here at times between the twentieth of April and the last of May, and again in the latter part of September and in October. They pass the summer principally in Labrador and Canada, and also to a certain extent in the White Mountain Region, and Northern Maine; but I know no well authenticated instance of their so doing in this State. I have, however, known them to pass the winter here, though usually at that season they inhabit the most southern United States and even warmer climates. I have several times, in December and January, found them near Boston, in swamps, where they were feeding upon the berries, and also among cedars.[33]

Whilst here in spring, they are to be found on the roadsides, in swamps, in pastures, in "scrub-land," and amongst the trees and shrubbery of cultivated estates, but rarely in woods, though in northern New England such are their summer-haunts. They generally move about in flocks, often very loose ones, inclusive of immature specimens in various stages of coloration. They prefer the orchard and hard-wood trees to the pines, and usually take their perch among the latter to look out for passing insects. They more generally frequent the higher than the lower branches, and from these fly to snap up insects in the air, usually at some distance, afterwards often alighting in another tree. At other times, unlike the flycatchers, they glean among the branches and look for insects among the foliage and blossoms. In autumn their habits are essentially the same, except that they are more upon the ground, feed more upon berries, sometimes those of house-vines, and show a greater liking for hedge-rows and like places, where they often associate with the "Yellow Red-polls" or with the sparrows. They may generally be distinguished at a distance by their habit of being much in the air, and of taking long flights (as compared with those of other warblers) at quite a height above the ground.

(*d*). The "Yellow-rumps" have a soft *chip*, and a loud *check* or *chuck* (which sometimes is softened to *chup*). I have often heard them sing in May, throughout the day, much like the Purple Finch, but without the richness, fulness, continuity, or melodiousness of that bird's music, especially if heard from a near standpoint. This song is often varied, and sometimes has reminded me of certain of the "Maryland Yellow-throats'"

---

[33] Mr. Charles C. Abbott states that they pass the winter in New Jersey.

notes. In October I have once or twice heard the "Yellow-rumps" utter a warble, which was soft, sweet, and very rich.

(M) MACULOSA. *Black and Yellow Warbler.* "*Magnolia Warbler.*"

(A rather rare migrant through Massachusetts.)

(*a*). About five inches long. Dark above. *Rump, yellow. Crown ashy* (-blue?). Forehead and a broad bar through the eye, black. Under parts yellow; breast black-streaked. *Wing-patch,* etc., *white.* ♀, with head-markings and streaks less distinct.

(*b*). The nest is usually built in a low spruce, often near a path through the woods, three or four feet from the ground, and is finished in the first week of June. (A second is sometimes built about the first of July.) It is composed outwardly of pine-needles, hemlock-twigs, or the like, and is lined with horse-hairs or the black fibres of a certain moss. The eggs average ·63 × ·50 of an inch, and are white with lilac and brown, or umber-brown, markings, often forming a ring about the crown. Some eggs of this species which I found in Northern New Hampshire are clouded at the larger end with obscure lilac and three shades of a beautiful, bright, but peculiar brown.

(*c*). The Black and Yellow Warblers are perhaps, with the exception of the Blackburnian Warblers, the handsomest of their family, and therefore it is to be regretted that they are in Massachusetts only for a short time in the latter part of May, being even then not common. They arrive here about the middle or twentieth of that month, and linger for a few days, but, after having passed the summer in the woods of Canada, Northern New Hampshire, and Maine, return to the South by an inland route, avoiding this State, or at least the eastern part of it. Whilst here, they frequent woods, trees, and shrubbery of various kinds, particularly spruces, generally in pairs or singly. They do not exhibit so many traits of the flycatchers as several other warblers do, but usually catch insects in the air, only as they move from one tree to another.

They generally alight among the lower branches, to which chiefly they confine themselves, and among which, as well as about the blossoms, they industriously search for insects and their eggs.

(*d*). The song of the Black and Yellow Warblers is sweet and musical. It is sometimes rather soft, vividly recalling the song of the Yellow Bird (and allied songs), and less so that of the "Yellow-rump," being to a certain extent like both. At other times, it is louder, and again like that of the Yellow Bird (*D. æstiva*), with additional musical notes. The ordinary notes of these birds are a *tsip*, a cry of *tsip-tsip-tsip*, a soft and loud *chip*, a *chick* or *chink* like that of the Rose-breasted Grosbeak, and an *ank*, which recalls the similar note of the "Golden Robin." Unfortunately of all these numerous sounds not one is distinctively characteristic of these warblers, who are somewhat shy; but fortunately, on the other hand, bright colors cannot always be concealed.

This species is the last of the twelve *Dendrœcœ*, who invariably visit Massachusetts every year, and five of whom commonly breed here. The birds of this genus (*Dendrœca*) are in many ways the most charming members of the feathered creation, being prettily and brightly colored, and extremely graceful and dexterous in their motions. Their songs, though never very striking or brilliant, are simple, pleasing, and musical, and their nests and eggs are models of beauty. In addition to these charms, these birds are extremely useful, and do much to protect our trees and shrubs from the injuries of caterpillars and the numerous winged insects that infest them.

XI. MYIODIOCTES

(A) CANADENSIS. *Canada "Flycatcher." Canada Flycatching Warbler.*

(A summer-resident in northern New England, but rare in Massachusetts, except as a migrant.)

(*a*). 5-5¼ inches long. In general appearance like the Black and Yellow Warbler (X, M), but with no white on the wings and tail. ♂, ashy-blue above of a curious tint, and bright yellow beneath. Crown almost streaked with black. Superciliary line, yellow. Throat bordered by a black line, from the bottom of which black streaks (often wholly inconspicuous) run down the breast. ♀, with the blue impure and black restricted.

(*b*). The nest is usually placed on the ground, in swampy woodland. In Eastern Massachusetts four or five eggs are laid about the first of June. These eggs average ·68 × ·50 of an inch, and are white, generally clouded delicately at the larger end with brown and lilac.

(*c*). The Canada "Flycatchers" are common summer-residents in the woods of northern New England, but in Massachusetts, though their nests have been found, for instance, at Lynn, they are rare except as migrants. They arrive at Boston on the twentieth of May, or even later, and I have observed them here traveling as late as the fifth of June. During their visits, which are individually brief, they frequent woodland, often that which is swampy, though also dry pines, and the shrubbery in or near it. Occasionally they venture to gardens and shrubbery near houses, but they are naturally fond of retired or even secluded spots. They journey singly or in pairs, and are never gregarious, nor often very numerous in any one place. Among the White Mountains they frequent those forests where the undergrowth of ferns and living plants, and the entanglement of moss-covered logs and stumps, are both so rich.

The Canada Warblers are very active, occasionally alighting on the ground, and almost invariably keeping near it, and move among the shrubbery from one low branch to another, continually catching insects in the air. They occasionally run over fences or walls with great ease, and, in fact, in all their motions exhibit grace and agility. They are not very shy, and suffer a near approach to inquisitive persons. When, however, their nest is approached, they become vigilant and anxious, particularly the males, who plainly show their distress. These latter, in such cases, often fly about among the branches above one's head at quite a distance from the ground, emitting their notes of complaint, but at other times, mindful of household cares, continue to collect insects among the bushes and lower limbs of the surrounding trees. I remember watching one, who in fifteen minutes, during my presence, collected as many moths and caterpillars, continually uttering his loud *chuck*, and yet I could not find his nest, so well did he avoid indicating its immediate whereabouts. I have known Cat-birds, in a like way, to sing even whilst holding in their bills a worm, or perhaps material for their nests, though it certainly seems a difficult performance.

(*d*). The Canada "Flycatchers" have a very sweet and agreeable song, which unfortunately, is not often to be heard here. It is simple, like those of the other warblers, but is rather more pleasing than those of the Yellow Bird or Redstart, which it usually resembles. Their ordinary notes are a soft and loud *chip*, and a *chuck*, which is almost exactly like that of the Maryland "Yellow-throat."

(B) PUSILLUS.[34] *Green Black-capped* (*Flycatching Warbler* or) "*Flycatcher.*" (*Wilson's*) "*Black-cap.*"
(A migrant through Eastern Massachusetts in spring.)

(*a*). Five inches long, or less. Olive above. Bright yellow beneath. Crown, black; but in ♀ obscure, or simply olive. Forehead, yellow.

(*b*). The nest is built in a bush or shrub, and near the ground. The eggs average $.63 \times .48$ of an inch, and are white, marked with reddish-brown at the larger end.

(*c*). Dr. Brewer says that the "Wilson's Black-cap is found throughout the United States from ocean to ocean, and as far north as Alaska and the Arctic shores, where, however, it is not common." I know no instance of these birds passing the

---

[34] The Hooded Warbler (*M. mitratus*) never, so far as I know, strays to Massachusetts or any part of New England, though vaguely reported to do so. I have, therefore, omitted it. Description :—5 or more inches long. Olive above, and bright yellow beneath. Tail-feathers with a few white blotches. *Male* with head black, except on the sides and forehead, which are golden-yellow. The Small-headed Flycatcher (*Muscicapa minuta*) is an entirely apocryphal species.

summer so far to the southward as New England, though they may occasionally do so. They are quite common in Eastern Massachusetts between the tenth and the last of May, but I have never seen them at other times of the year. They frequent singly, or in pairs, woods, thickets, and the neighborhood of streams and water. They usually, but not always, remain near the ground among the bushes and shrubbery, often snapping up insects in the air, and even seeming to turn summersaults. They are constantly active, and are among the busiest of our transient visitors.

(d). Their song is much like an extension of the Redstart's notes, and not unlike the song of the common Yellow Bird (*D. æstiva*), though rather less pretty. They have also a *chip* (a *chuck?*) and some harsh notes, resembling the syllables *zee-zee-zee-zee*, of which the latter are the lower in tone.

XII. SETOPHAGA

(A) RUTICILLA. *Redstart.*

(In a greater part of New England a common summer-resident.)

(a). About $5\frac{1}{4}$ inches long. ♂, lustrous black. Sides of the breast, patches on the wing, and basal half of the tail-feathers, except the middle pair, flame-color, or in some places nearly vermilion. Belly, white. ♀, greenish above, and white beneath. Vermilion of the male simply yellowish. Wings and tail elsewhere dark (the latter from below seeming almost black-tipped, but otherwise yellowish). The female is rather a nondescript in appearance.

(b). The nest is placed in a fork, sometimes next to the trunk, in a low tree or shrub, from five to twenty feet above the ground. It is composed of thin strips of bark, dried grasses, caterpillar's silk and other soft materials, and is sometimes lined with horse-hairs. The four or five eggs of each set usually average ·65 × ·50 of an inch, and are white, with purple or lilac, and brown (not very dark), scattered quite thickly at the larger end and thinly at the other. They can generally be easily distinguished.

(c). The Redstarts are familiar to all the ornithologists of New England, though much less common in many northern and western localities than in other parts, where they are the most common of the woodland-warblers. They are summer-residents throughout the north-eastern United States, but they pass the winter in a warmer climate. They reach Massachusetts between the fifth and tenth of May, and leave it in the early part of September, but, except in spring, when I have seen three or four together on their arrival, I have never observed them to be at all gregarious. They frequent woods and groves of various sorts, but generally avoid isolated trees and shrubbery. Occasionally, however, they approach the ground,[35] though they usually remain at some distance from it, often at a great height. During their residence here, they never wander far, and never take other than very short flights. They are, however, continually catching small flies, gnats, and mosquitoes in the air. They also search for them among the branches, in the manner of the vireos, and their handsome tail, outspread, then shows to great advantage. They are more wonderfully active and dexterous than most other warblers, renowned as they all are for their industry and skill.

The male Redstarts, inclusive of the young in various stages, who, for a long time, much resemble the females, are more abundant than those of the opposite sex, and consequently they often have occasion in May to quarrel for the possession of the females, though otherwise peaceful. Though easily caused to desert their nests, they possess great conjugal and parental affection, as do nearly all the more highly organized birds. Inclination to desertion varies with individuals more than with species, but is widely different among the several families and orders.

(d). The song of the Redstarts is simple and pleasing, but constantly varied. Sometimes it is merely a rather shrill *che-wée-o* or *che-wée-o-wée-o*, at other times it is *che-wée-see-wée-see-*

---

[35] I have since observed that the female obtains much of the food for her young from the ground.

wée, or a soft *wée-see-wée-see-wée*, much like the song of the Yellow Bird (*D. æstiva*), and again a series or repetition of a few gentle notes, which form an indefinite song.

The Redstarts have also a soft *chip*, which is often repeated in the manner of the Snow-bird, a loud *chip*, a *chick*, and a few minor notes of no importance.

This species is the last of our numerous warblers (unless the chats), and I regret having already finished the biographies of these useful and charming birds.

XIII. ICTERIA

(A) VIRENS. *Yellow-breasted Chat. Chat.*

(In New England of rare occurrence, and in the three southern States only.)

(*a*). Seven inches long. Above, bright olive-green. Throat and breast, rich yellow. Belly, and superciliary line, white. Lore, black.

(*b*). The nest is composed of leaves, grasses, strips of bark, etc., and is placed in a thicket, bush, or briar. The eggs average about $1 \cdot \times \cdot 80$ of an inch, and are white, sometimes with reddish-brown and obscure lilac spots sprinkled over the surface (often more thickly about the crown), and sometimes with rather faint lilac blotches only (which are occasionally confined almost entirely to the smaller end), these being the two extremes of coloration.

(*c*). Of the remarkable Yellow-breasted Chats I shall here make but brief mention, since they have never fallen under my personal observation, and because of their very rare occurrence in New England. I have never seen them near Boston, and I know but two instances of their capture here. They reach Pennsylvania "about the first week in May," and inhabit "close thickets of hazel, brambles, vines and thick underwood." During the mating-season they perform the most extraordinary antics in the air, and often at night.

(*d*). While so doing, and at other times, they utter a great variety of extraordinary sounds, some of which are musical whistles, and others "like the barking of young puppies," "the mewing of a cat," or equally peculiar noises. Wilson, from whom I have already quoted, says that "all these are uttered with great vehemence, in such different keys, and with such peculiar modulations of voice, as sometimes to seem at a considerable distance and instantly as if just beside you; now on this hand, now on that." Wilson's biography of this bird is extremely interesting, but unfortunately too long for transcription.

§ 10. The **Tanagridæ,** or *tanagers*, form a brilliant group, intermediate between the finches and warblers (see fig. 5). They have nine primaries, and scutellate tarsi. All the North American species are characterized more or less plainly by a tooth in the middle of the commissure. The Scarlet Tanager may be considered a type. They have been called "dentirostral finches," but, on the other hand, are closely allied to the warblers through the chats.

The *Icteriinæ*, however, are distinguished by the following features from the tanagers and all other warblers, except *Geothlypes*. Wings about equal in length to the tail. They differ from *Geothlypes* in having an unnotched, unbristled bill, which is not more than twice as long as high, if as much; also in size, being larger than any of the true warblers. "They are represented in the United States, virtually by one species only."

The *Ampelidæ* (§ 11) are in New England represented only by the *Ampelinæ* or *waxwings*. This subfamily should, perhaps, stand near the *Clamatores* (to whom the *Corvidæ* bear no direct affinity), but their true position has not yet been determined. They are usually placed next to the swallows, whom they resemble in the scutellate tarsi, and in the bill, which is broad, and only about half as long as the commissure. (See § § T, U, of the Introduction.) They have, however, ten primaries, of which the first is spurious, and a notch in the bill. They are also crested, and in full plumage have curious waxlike appendages to certain quills, "and sometimes the tailfeathers" (pl. 1, figs. 10 and 11). They show an affinity to the flycatchers, in their eminent skill in fly-catching,[36] as occasionally displayed, and in their want of musical powers, for, though absurdly called "chatterers," they are notably silent birds. Moreover, "their tarsus is not strictly oscine." They are, however, gregarious. The common Cedar-bird may be taken as a type.

I. PYRANGA

(A) RUBRA. *Scarlet Tanager.*

(Though locally distributed, a generally common summer-resident in southern New England.)

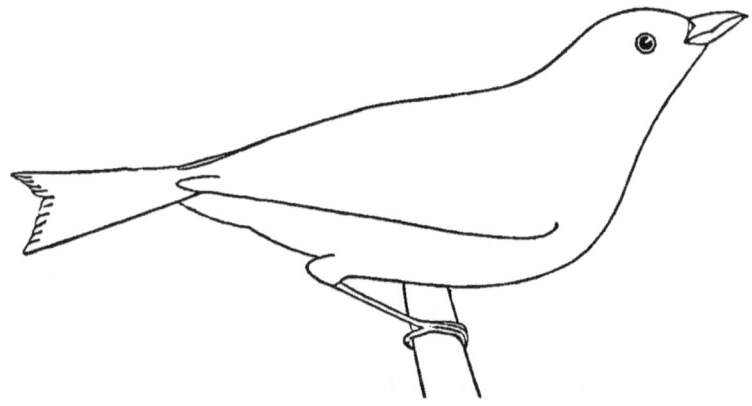

Fig. 5. Scarlet Tanager ($\frac{1}{2}$).

(*a*). About $7\frac{1}{2}$ inches long. ♂, scarlet; wings and tail black. ♀, olive-green above. Below, (greenish) yellow.

(*b*). The nest is loosely constructed of straws, twigs, etc., and is usually placed from ten to thirty feet above the ground, generally in an oak-wood, but sometimes in an orchard or other place and in evergreens. Three or four eggs are here laid about the first of June, averaging ·90×·65 of an inch

---

[36] It is to be remembered, however, that the birds of many families are very skilful in preying upon insects in the air, scarcely less so than the true flycatchers.

(though I have a specimen measuring 1·10×·70 of an inch). They are strongly like the eggs of the Swainson's Thrush (§1, I, D), being light greenish-blue, with usually rather faint (but sometimes thick and strong) markings of umber-brown, which is sometimes replaced by purplish.

(c). The gaudy Scarlet Tanagers are summer-residents throughout the eastern United States, but are rare in northern New England and Canada, beyond which they never (?) go. They reach Eastern Massachusetts in the second or third week of May, and leave it in September, but during their stay here are rather confined to localities. They frequent orchards, and groves of chestnuts, oaks, and nut-trees, often showing a preference for swampy woods if not too thick. They feed upon the larger winged insects, upon caterpillars, upon seeds and berries, and so never have occasion to be much on the ground. They often arrive in pairs, but at other times they appear in small parties of three or four, mating subsequently, after the males have fought the quarrels incident to the period of courtship. In the latter part of May they build their loosely constructed nests, and the females lay their eggs, the incubation of which occupies them about thirteen days, the usual period of incubation among a majority of the Insessorian birds. In this stage of their household duties, the wonderful wisdom everywhere displayed in nature is peculiarly noticeable. The brilliantly colored males carefully avoid the nest, and approach it, when necessary, with caution and stealth, fearful of betraying its presence; whereas the females, with their plain coloration assimilated to the surrounding foliage, sit upon it with safety, and care for their young. If, however, the nest is actually invaded or hostilely approached, the males show themselves, with their plumage in bold and rich contrast to the green leaves; and I have known them to carry off the eggs, how, I cannot positively say. I have known several instances of birds removing even their young, though in many cases it seemed almost impossible for them to do so. In the case of the Scarlet Tanagers, to which I have just referred, one could plainly see their eggs from the ground through the bottom of the nest, which was frailly composed of straw. During my ascent of the tree, without disturbing the branch in which the nest was placed, I observed the parents several times returning to the tree, and, upon my arrival at a point, from which I could look into the nest, I found it empty. A careful search disclosed no pieces of broken shell or traces of the yolk on the lower branches, or on the ground, directly below. The eggs were undoubtedly conveyed to a place of safety, but whether ever returned or successfully hatched, I do not know.

(*d*). The Scarlet Tanagers have an agreeable song or whistle, which reminds one of the Robin's music, or the finer and delicious music of the Rose-breasted Grosbeak, but it differs from both in having a certain harshness. Their ordinary note is a pensively uttered *chip-churr*, which is often introduced so as to interrupt their warble. Such other notes as they may have, I do not now recall.

(B) ÆSTIVA. *Summer Red Bird.*

(Of very rare occurrence in Massachusetts, being for the most part an inhabitant of the Southern States.)

(*a*). 7½–8 inches long. ♂, vermilion. ♀, like ♀ *rubra* (A), but duller, and with brownish rather than greenish shades (Coues).

(*b*). "The nest is usually built on one of the lower limbs of a post-oak, or in a pine sapling, at a height of from six to twenty feet above the ground."[37] The eggs average about ·90 × ·65 of an inch, and are of "a bright light shade of emerald-green, spotted, marbled, dotted and blotched with various shades of lilac, brownish-purple, and dark brown." (Dr. Brewer.)

(*c*). The Summer Red Birds have been taken in Massachusetts but a very few times, though they have wandered so far to the North as Nova Scotia. Wilson describes their habits as follows, and says of this species that "its manners * * * partake very much of those of the Flycatcher; for I have fre-

---

[37] This statement is made on the authority of the late Dr. Gerhardt.

quently observed both male and female, a little before sunset, in parts of the forest clear of underwood, darting after winged insects, and continuing thus engaged till it was almost dusk." "The food of these birds consists of various kinds of bugs, and large black beetles. In several instances I have found the stomach entirely filled with the broken remains of humble bees. During the season of whortle-berries they seem to subsist almost entirely on these berries; but in the early part of the season on insects of the above description."

(d). "The note of the male is a strong and sonorous whistle, resembling a loose trill or shake on the notes of a fife, frequently repeated; that of the female is rather a kind of chattering, approaching nearly to the *rapid* pronunciation of *chicky-tucky-tuck*, *chicky-tucky-tuck*, when she sees any person approaching the neighbourhood of her nest. She is, however, rarely seen, and usually mute, and scarcely to be distinguished from the color of the foliage at a distance."

Having never seen the Red Birds alive, I have no further remarks to make upon their habits.

§ 11. **Ampelidæ.** Waxwings. (See § 10.)[38]

I. AMPELIS

(A) CEDRORUM. *Cedar-bird. Cherry-bird. (Carolina) Waxwing.* " *Canada Robin.*"

(A common resident in New England, but nomadic and irregular in appearance.)

(a). 6-7 inches long. Of a peculiar warm brown (or creamy chocolate?). Chin, black. Forehead, and a broad stripe through the eye, continuously the same. Belly, yellow (or yellowish). Under tail-coverts, and some fine markings on the head, white (or whitish). Tail, yellow-tipped. Strange appendages, resembling bits of red sealing-wax, are found, often upon the wings, and sometimes upon the tail, of full-plumaged specimens.

---

[38] This family should more properly stand between the vireos and swallows as § 12.

(b). The nest is rather bulky, and is composed of fine grasses, weeds, roots, fibres, leaves, strips of bark, etc., being sometimes lined with finer grasses or hairs. It is usually placed in an orchard-tree or in a cedar, but sometimes in other situations — such as the tops of birches or pasture-trees, commonly from eight to twenty feet above the ground. Four or five eggs are laid in the latter part of June or in July. They average about $.80 \times .60$ of an inch; and are of a dirty bluish-white, with black and a few dark purplish spots.

(c). The Cedar-birds, to a certain extent, spend the winters in Eastern Massachusetts, but otherwise arrive from the South in the first or second week of March. They are found, in summer, throughout New England, and are in most places common during that season. Through winter they remain in flocks — usually in retired parts of the country — and feed upon berries until spring, when they venture into more open districts. At this time their demeanor is not such as to inspire cheerfulness to the person observing them, for they usually sit motionless upon the tops of bare trees, and there occasionally give utterance to their dreary whispers, until they fly away. They move through the air rapidly, steadily, and as if under military discipline, so unbroken are their ranks. They commonly disappear, like several other birds, at uncertain times of the year, and undoubtedly go to some place where their favorite food is abundant during the time that they are absent from one's own neighborhood. In May they usually become common, and appear in smaller companies in almost all parts of the open country. These flocks finally become divided into pairs, who build their nests when nearly all our other birds have hatched the eggs of their first or even second broods. The Cherry-birds, in summer, sometimes imitate the habits of the fly-catchers (to whom they are, perhaps, more closely allied than is now admitted), and I have seen them perform graceful evolutions in the air, in the manner of the King-birds. As their name indicates, they sometimes eat cherries, but much less often than is commonly supposed by certain farmers, who are but too ready to discharge their guns at these birds, in spite of their usefulness in destroying caterpillars.

Nuttall in speaking of the Cedar-birds says:—" an eye-witness assures me he has seen one among a row of these birds seated upon a branch dart after an insect, and offer it to his associate when caught, who very disinterestedly passed it to the next; and, each delicately declining the offer, the morsel has proceeded backwards and forwards before it was appropriated."

(*d*). The "wheezy" lisp of the Cedar-birds seems to be the only sound which they emit, throughout the year, and they often utter it when on wing. Dr. Brewer says of a young cage-bird that "besides its low lisping call, this bird had a regular faint attempt at a song of several low notes, uttered in so inaudible a tone that it would be almost inaudible at even a short distance."

The Cherry-birds are certainly handsome, particularly if their crest be raised, though they possess but little bright coloring; and there are probably few birds who find a readier sale at the country taxidermist's than these. In regard to their habits, they are perhaps uninteresting; but their manner of flight, when in parties, is nearly unsurpassed.

(B) GARRULUS. *Bohemian Waxwing. Northern Waxwing.*

(A Northern bird, of which, so far as I know, no specimen has ever been obtained in this State.)

(*a*). 7-8 inches long. Like (A), except as follows. Brown, partly orange-tinted. With white on the wings, but little on the head; and with no yellow on the belly. *Under tail-coverts, chestnut-red.*

(*b*). These birds never breed in the United States, or at least the southern portions. The eggs are described by Dr. Brewer as measuring about 1·00 × ·70, or less. They are of a color varying "from a light slate to a yellowish stone-color," and are much spotted, chiefly with some dark purplish shade. They are considered very rare.

(*c*). The Waxwings are of very rare occurrence in the eastern United States, being habitual residents of the North and West, but they have occasionally wandered so far to the southward as Massachusetts and even Connecticut. I have never seen them, but I suppose their habits to be in every way like those of the Cedar-birds. They are said to be shy and watchful, but very affectionate. Having forgotten to do so before, I may here remark that the Cedar-birds often show a fondness for some one tree, to which they persistently return, even if disturbed several times. One Sunday I remarked six in a bare maple, and, again passing the place on the following Sunday, I was surprised to observe them perched in the same tree, as if they had not moved for a week.

§ 12. The **Hirundinidæ**, or *swallows*, may be distinguished from all our other birds by the following combined features. Tail-feathers twelve; primaries nine; tarsi short and scutellate; bill broad, low, short, and with the culmen (or upper outline) only half as long as the gape, which extends to the longitude of the eye. They have remarkably long wings, conformably to their mode of life and "constant aërial activity." Most of our species have a highly metallic lustre (in certain parts), which, except in the martins, is similar in the two sexes. This feature is not, so far as I know, observable in any other family, unless among the ducks.

Our insessorian birds may, in regard to color, be classified as follows:

(1). Partly metallic; sexes alike. Certain swallows.

(2). Partly metallic; sexes unlike. Certain hummingbirds (*Troch.*).

(3). Partly metallic in male only. Certain pigeons.

(4). Lustrous or brightly colored; sexes alike. Crows, certain jays and warblers.

(5). Lustrous or brightly colored; sexes unlike; females duller, etc. Bluebirds, martins, certain warblers, finches, and starlings; also one flycatcher (S. W. of U. S. etc.) (and the Blue Crow?)

(6). No metallic tints; sexes much alike; male characterized by a color-patch, wanting or much restricted in the female. "Wrens" or kinglets, nuthatches, woodpeckers, certain warblers (and finches?).

(7). Male brightly, female plainly colored.[39] Tanagers; certain warblers, finches, and starlings.

[(8). Plainly colored;[39] with bright crown-patch in both sexes, certain flycatchers; with tail brightly tipped, the waxwings.]

(9). Plainly or dully colored.[39] Sexes alike. Thrushes, gnatcatchers, titmice, creepers, wrens, wagtails, vireos, shrikes, flycatchers, swifts, cuckoos, owls, most of the hawks, certain warblers, swallows, finches, starlings, jays, and pigeons.

(10). Plainly or dully colored.[39] Sexes unlike. ' Goatsuckers," kingfishers, harriers, and smaller falcons. Perhaps also certain finches, the Bobolink, and Blue Crow.

The swallows are preëminently insectivorous (perching less often than any other oscine birds), and consequently migratory. They are also preëminently social and consequently gregarious, at least very often. Most of them breed in communities or in colonies, to which they return each spring in greater numbers than before. These settlements, as I have once or twice observed among the Bank Swallows, are formed by a very few pairs, whose number is often slowly increased from year to year. It is probably in this manner that the Cliff Swallows have gradually become dispersed over eastern North America, where possibly they were once unknown. There are probably no birds whose past history would be more interesting than that of the swallows. No birds better or more curiously exhibit the modifying influence of civilization than these. Those kinds who formerly built on cliffs, or in the hollows of trees, now build their nests, almost exclusively in Massachusetts, in situations about the buildings of man. It is said by Dr. Coues, who quotes from Dr. Rufus Haymond, in "The American Naturalist," for June, 1876, that an instance of the Bank Swallow using an artificial nest, so to speak, has already occurred. Dr. Haymond says: "The White Water Valley

---

[39] Black and white, the various browns and grays, are eminently the plain colors. In this synopsis, however, grayish-blue, olive, olive-green, and even yellow, especially in connection with green, are often considered plain colors (chiefly in contrast).

Railway, in Brookville, Indiana, is built upon stone piers, and spans the hydraulic canal, some five or six feet above the water. While at the depot during the past summer I saw a bank swallow fly under the building with several blades of grass in her bill; and being curious to see what she would do with them, I watched her, and saw her carry them through a two-inch auger hole, which had been bored through a pine board. The spot was inaccessible, owing to the water; but I know from the droppings about the hole that this was her nest." It is almost needless to add that this species usually burrows in sand. The swallows lay four or five eggs, which are white, unmarked, or spotted with brown and purplish.

I. HIRUNDO
(A) HORREORUM. *Barn Swallow.*

(A very common summer-resident in most inhabited parts of New England.)

(*a*). About $4\frac{1}{2}$ inches long from bill to fork of the tail. Above, a dark lustrous steel-blue. An imperfect collar, the same. Under parts and forehead, chestnut-red. Belly and lower breast, paler. *Tail forficate.* Outer feathers much longer than the others (from $\frac{1}{2}$–2 inches), and all, except the middle pair, with a white spot.

(*b*). The nest is placed on the beams or rafters of a barn or similar building, and usually is finished here by the middle of May. A set of four or five eggs is then laid, and often another in June, or even the early part of July. The eggs average ·75 × ·55 of an inch, and are white, sprinkled tolerably thickly with purplish and brown.

(*c*). The Barn Swallows are to be found almost throughout New England. They reach the neighborhood of Boston generally in the last week of April, but sometimes earlier, and return to the South in the first week of September. They are usually very common in those places where they are found, since they are almost invariably more or less colonial. They are particularly abundant in old country-villages, and about farms, where most of the barns, on account of their liberal size, afford them, among cobwebbed rafters, plenty of suitable nesting-places. I shall sketch the habits of these birds by considering their manner of life, through the latter's various stages.

The Barn Swallows, when young, are constantly supplied with food by their parents, until they are able to take short flights from beam to beam in the barns. Later, they venture from these buildings, but are obliged to be at rest much of the time and still to be fed by their parents. As they become more accustomed to the exercise of their wings, they fly more boldly, procure much or all of their own food, and are by the first of September strong enough to bear the fatigue of their long migratory flights to the South. On their return in the spring, they are capable of remaining on wing through at least fifteen hours of the twenty-four. Their manner of flight is rapid and graceful, and so interesting as to well repay close attention. They rarely fly far near the ground, nor do they reach such a height as some other species. They prefer telegraph-wires to other perches, and on these long rows of them may often be seen; and in fact these wires seem almost to influence these birds in their choice of a summer-home.

It was formerly believed that the Barn Swallows, and others, passed the winter torpid in mud at the bottom of lakes, and in caves. Much astounding evidence has been produced to prove the correctness of this absurd theory, which is, however, too unnatural to long exist under the régime of modern science. Wilson is eloquent in his condemnation of this belief, and considers it too ridiculous to be worthy of serious refutation, which is, in fact, the case.

(d). The young Barn Swallows often utter a series of twitters, which resemble the laugh of a tickled child, and the older birds also have various twitters, some of which are sprightly and musical.

(e). I shall not describe at length the twitters and guttural cries of the various swallows, both because they are more easily learned than described, and because when described can hardly aid one in distinguishing the different species.

The Barn Swallows are so well known, that I have mentioned no details in their habits. Their colonizations, their constantly uttered notes, and their flights, are familiar to nearly all, and the latter have long since been made the theme of many an author.

II. PETROCHELIDON

(A) LUNIFRONS. *Cliff Swallow. Eave Swallow.* "*Republican.*"

(Locally very abundant in New England, but much less so, probably, than they will be ten years hence.)

(*a*). About five inches long. *Tail scarcely forked.* Upper parts, and a spot on the breast, steel-blue. *Rump*, sides of the head, and throat, *chestnut-red*. Breast, paler, belly, white. Forehead, brownish.

(*b*). The nest is generally somewhat bottle-shaped, is composed chiefly of a delicate mud-plaster, often intermixed with bits of straw, and is naturally brittle. It is placed under the outside eaves of barns or outhouses, and never (?) in Massachusetts on cliffs, as is usual in wilder parts of the country, in accordance with the original habits of these swallows. Several of these nests, sometimes as many as a hundred, are generally placed in a row. The eggs are essentially like those of the Barn Swallow (I, A, *b*), so much so as often to be indistinguishable, and are laid about the same time.

(*c*). The Cliff Swallows, who in many ways closely resemble the Barn Swallows, are resident in Eastern Massachusetts from the first week of May until September. They are very abundant in certain localities in New England; but, as they are eminently colonial, they are not to be found scattered through every township. They have essentially the same habits as the Barn Swallows, except that they alight much more frequently, often upon the ground to pick up mud for their nests. Their flight is not very noticeably different from that of their relatives, and their notes also bear much the same character, being, however, more like those of the White-bellied than those of the Barn Swallow. It is difficult, as well as almost unnecessary for me to describe these minor distinctions, and I shall therefore make no further mention of them.

The most interesting remarks to be made upon the Eave Swallows are those which relate to their immigration from the western United States to New England and other parts of the country. An accurate account of their movements within the last century could hardly fail to be interesting, but I doubt if a sufficient number of notes and dates can now be obtained to effect this purpose. Indeed, the history of the so-called " Republicans" would probably be far more interesting than an account of their habits could be (partly because the latter are well known, and the former is not); but I regret that I am unable to present it to the public. "When or where" the Cliff Swallows " first appeared in Massachusetts," says Dr. Brewer, "is not known. I first observed a large colony of them in Attleboro' in 1842. Its size indicated the existence of these birds in that place for several years. The same year they also appeared, apparently for the first time, in Boston, Hingham, and in other places in the neighborhood." The Eave Swallows are still increasing throughout the Eastern States, and are constantly making their appearance in places where they have not been observed before. An excellent place to study them, particularly for summer-tourists, is Mount Desert, where the birds were, and still are, I suppose, very abundant (at least at Bar Harbor). Their habits are easily learned, as they are constantly in the open air, and about the village-streets, where all, who wish to, may gaze upon them.

One agreeable trait in the character of the " Republicans" is their general amiability. In spite of their gregariousness and crowded dwellings, they never become confused, and rarely quarrel. Could a map be drawn indicating the position of their communities, all their colonies might well be named Philadelphia.

(*d*). See I, A, (*e*).

NOTE.—Bonaparte, in his continuation of "Wilson's Ornithology," says of the Cliff Swallow: "A very singular trait distinguishes the migrations of this bird. While the European or white variety of the human race is rapidly spreading over this continent, from its eastern borders to the remotest plains beyond the Mississippi, the Cliff Swallow advances from the extreme western regions, annually invading a new territory farther to the eastward, and induces us to conclude, that a few more summers will find it sporting in this immediate vicinity, and familiarly established along the Atlantic shores."

"Within ten or twelve years [date of writing, 1825], they have become familiar in different localities of Ohio, Kentucky, &c., whence they are extending very rapidly, and have recently appeared in the western part of New-York. In order to show the rapid progress of this little stranger, we quote the following passage from Mr. Clinton's interesting paper.

"The Fulvous Swallow 'first made its appearance at Winchell's tavern, on the high road, about five miles south of Whitehall, near Lake Champlain, and erected its nest under the eaves of an outhouse, where it was covered by the projection of a roof. This was in 1817, and in this year there was but one nest; the second year seven; the third twenty-eight; the fourth forty; and in 1822 there were seventy, and the number has since continued to increase.'

'It appeared in 1822 at Whitehall, on the fifth of June, and departed on the twenty-fifth of July, and these are the usual times of its arrival and disappearance.'"

Audubon states, but where I do not now remember, that the Cliff Swallows were somewhere found in New England on its first settlement at that place, many years ago.

III. TACHYCINETA

(A) BICOLOR. *White-breasted Swallow. White-bellied Swallow.*

(A common summer-resident nearly throughout New England.)

(*a*). About six inches long. Lustrous steel-green above. White beneath.

(*b*). The nest is usually built in a martin-box or other like receptacle, and, in Massachusetts, very rarely in the hole of a tree, as is not unfrequently the case in many other States. The eggs of each set are four or five, average ·75 × ·55 of an inch, and are white, unmarked. Two broods are generally raised.

(c). The White-bellied Swallows usually announce spring to the people of Boston and the vicinity in the first week of April; but after their arrival they are sometimes obliged, when discouraged by the cold, to retreat temporarily southward to a warmer latitude. As our ancestors long since discovered this fact in relation to their swallows, they have handed down to us the wise proverb that "one swallow does not make a summer." The White-bellied Swallows return to their winter-homes about the middle of September, when all the other swallows have gone (and I have seen them here as late as the twenty-third). They congregate "upon the salt marshes during the latter part of August and first of September, literally by millions; the air is so completely filled with them that it is almost impossible to discharge a gun without killing some" (Maynard). They may also be seen at that season perched in long lines on fences, ridge-poles, and wires, or slowly moving through the air at a considerable height, generally in large flocks, catching insects as they fly. In spring they travel more often singly, and fly rather indirectly but with great rapidity, no doubt occasionally deviating from their course to seize a passing gnat or fly.

In summer they are to be found in nearly all the cultivated districts of Massachusetts, and in many of the wild as well as other districts of more northern lands, where, in many places, they retain their primitive habit of nesting in hollow trees, which, says Mr. Maynard, they have also done lately at Ipswich, in this State. As, however, they are now rather dependent upon the nesting-places provided by man, they are perhaps as common in Boston and other cities as in the country, if not more so. They are less locally distributed than other species, and on this account are probably better known. They are, I think, quicker in their motions than the other swallows, and also differ from them in not being colonial, except in their primitive state, though several sometimes occupy apartments in the same box, and thus show the social spirit of their family. They often skim over fields, ponds, or rivers, with an exquisite grace, but at other times mount to a great height—so far as to be wellnigh lost to sight. They are less peaceable than the Barn Swallows, and often quarrel in the air at the period of mating; but this species is justly regarded, among all our birds, as one of man's most pleasing companions.

The White-bellied Swallows are fond of wandering, more so than their relatives, and often may be seen two or three miles from their homes, now flying across the valleys, now dashing above the hills, and now gliding over the water, as if actually on its surface. Embodiments of grace, activity, and power, they sweep through the air, and show us by their ever varied flight how many things have been created to give us pleasure from variety alone, as well as from intrinsic beauty.

(*d*). Their notes are rather more eccentric and guttural than those which I have already mentioned, but are equally full of animation.

IV. COTYLE

(A) RIPARIA. *Bank Swallow. Sand Martin.*

(Locally common throughout New England.)

(*a*). About five inches long. Upper parts, and a band across the breast, dull brown. Under parts, white.

(*b*). The nest is constructed of a few loose materials, and is placed at the bottom of burrows dug out by the birds. These excavations are from fifteen to twenty-four inches deep, and are made in sand-banks, usually those on the sea-shore or near other bodies of water, but sometimes those on the roadsides or in other situations. The eggs average ·68 × ·50 of an inch, and are white; being almost exactly like those of the White-bellied Swallow, though smaller. Two sets of four or five are generally laid in the course of the season, of which the first appears here in the latter part of May.

(*c*). The Bank Swallows are in New England the most plainly colored of their family, and the only ones who retain here their former habits of nesting. They migrate at the same time as the Cliff Swallows, but I have never observed them in company with those birds. They may be seen in their summer-haunts flying either over the surface of land and water, or at some height in the air, though rarely very far above the ground. They fly much like the other swallows, though perhaps less steadily and with less sailing, but they seldom wander far from the banks in which their nests are placed. They are found throughout New England, and much further to the northward, but are much confined to localities, both because of their disposition to colonize, and the necessity of their selecting a place where the earth is of a character suitable to their purposes.

Their choice of a summer-home is undoubtedly influenced very considerably by the nature of the soil, as it is impossible for them to burrow in all kinds of earth. Extremely interesting details may be learned through the study of their excavations, as these latter vary greatly in size, depth, and the angle at which they run, in accordance with the variation of the soil. The Bank Swallows invariably select a bank, the sand of which will not "cave in," and then burrow to a stratum where the pebbles, which might fall down upon their eggs or young, are not found. Their colonies sometimes increase from year to year with rapidity, and, if not disturbed, in the course of a few seasons consist of a large number of excavations.

How wonderful is that instinct which enables these swallows to find out the best places for their homes, and how wonderful their skill in making these secure! When a small party boldly advance to a country, hitherto unknown to them, who can define that sense which enables them to discover and select the most fitting bank for their purposes, or even the best part of it? What, indeed, prompts them to part from their fellows and to become pioneers in new settlements? Instinct can never be fully understood by man, nor its workings.

Wilson, speaking of the "Sand Martins," says:—"We have sometimes several days of cold rain and severe weather after their arrival in spring, from which they take refuge in their holes, clustering together for warmth, and have been frequently found at such times in almost a lifeless state with the cold, which circumstance has contributed to the belief that they lie torpid all winter in these recesses."

(*d*). The Bank Swallows are usually more silent than the other species, though one might not gather this impression from a flock; and their notes are less musical.

V. PROGNE

(A) PURPUREA.[40] *Purple Martin.* "*Black Martin.*" *Martin.* "*Cape Cod Swallow.*"

(The Martins, though formerly abundant, are now very generally rare in New England, being confined to a few tracts of country and to localities.)

(*a*). 7–8 inches long. " Lustrous blue-black; no purple anywhere. The ♀ and young are much duller above, and more or less white below, streaked with gray." (Coues.)

(*b*). The nest and eggs are essentially like those of the White-bellied Swallow (III) in every respect, except that the latter are larger than the eggs of that bird, averaging ·95 × ·70 of an inch.

(*c*). The Purple Martins reach Eastern Massachusetts on the first of May, or earlier, and leave it about the first of September. They are very locally distributed, and in many places are at present never seen. They are " very abundant upon Cape Cod," and are perhaps as common in Boston and other cities as in the country. They are allied in many ways to the White-bellied Swallows — particularly so in their habits. The latter, however, become more common every year; but the former have deserted many places, where they were once well known, though they are probably multiplying in their present homes.

"The Martin" says Wilson "differs from all the rest of our Swallows in the particular prey which he selects. Wasps,

---

[40] Various scientific names have been bestowed upon this bird, but the present seems to me the most satisfactory.

bees, large beetles, particularly those called by the boys *goldsmiths*, seem his favorite game. I have taken four of these large beetles from the stomach of a Purple Martin, each of which seemed entire and even unbruised."

"The flight of the Purple Martin unites in it all the swiftness, ease, rapidity of turning and gracefulness of motion of its tribe. Like the Swift of Europe, he sails much with little action of the wings. * * *."

(*d*). "His usual note *peuo peuo peuo*, is loud and musical; but it is frequently succeeded by others more low and guttural." To the above extract I have nothing of interest to add.

§ 13. The **Vireonidæ**, or *vireos* (sometimes called "greenlets"), possess the following features in common with the *Laniidæ*, or *shrikes* (§ 14), at least with our subfamily, *Laniinæ*.

Bill rather short and stout, distinctly notched and hooked, also well furnished with bristles; tarsus scutellate; primaries ten, but with the first in the *Vireonidæ* often spurious, or seemingly absent. (Fig. 6.)

The *Laniidæ* differ distinctly in being more than seven inches long, in having the "sides of the tarsi scutellate behind," and in having long, rounded tails. The bill, moreover, is large and stout (not so broad as high, and scarcely twice as long), while the feet are comparatively weak. The shrikes might well be called "raptorial passeres," being notorious for their boldness and mode of slaughter among others birds, etc. They are unsocial and unmusical, though perhaps mimics. Like the vireos, normally they are never seen on the ground, but they possess a much stronger flight than their small relatives. They build rather bulky nests in the woods, and lay eggs, rather coarsely marked, and never (?) with a pure white ground. The Butcher-bird is a type (fig. 7). The vireos, on the other hand, are small, insectivorous birds, allied in habits to many of the warblers. They frequent, for the most part, woodland, and are rarely if ever seen upon the ground. They usually flutter among the branches in search of their prey, though they occasionally snap it up in passing from tree to tree. They are not gregarious, but are extremely affectionate toward one another, and peaceable in their relations to other birds. They are very musical, and warble cheerfully, energetically, and often very sweetly. They build small, cup-shaped, pensile nests, which are rarely softly lined. The eggs are four or five, and pure white, with a few small spots near the larger end, of some shade of brown.

Our species have been divided into several subgenera, but I have here followed Dr. Coues in uniting them under one genus.

I. VIREO

(A) SOLITARIUS. *Solitary Vireo.* *Blue-headed Vireo.*

(Rather rare in Massachusetts, especially as a summer-resident.)

(*a*). About $5\frac{1}{2}$ inches long. Olive-green above, and white beneath. Head, bluish-ash; eye-ring, and line to bill, white. Sides olive-shaded. Wing- and tail-feathers white-edged, and wings white-barred.

(*b*). The nest of the Solitary Vireo is open and pensile, like those of the other vireos. It is placed, never far from the ground, in the fork of a horizontal branch, always in the woods, and sometimes in swampy ones. It is usually larger, and more loosely constructed of somewhat finer materials, than that of the "Red-eye" (*c*). One, now lying before me, is composed chiefly of thin strips of pliable bark, is lined with fine grasses and a very few roots, and is somewhat ornamented outwardly with plant-down, lichens, and bits of dead leaves. Audubon speaks of others as being lined with hairs, which I have never known to be the case. In Massachusetts, three or four eggs are laid in the first week in June. They average $\cdot 77 \times \cdot 58$ of an inch, and are pure white, with a very few minute and generally reddish-brown spots principally at the larger end.

(*c*). The Solitary Vireos are less well known than our other vireos, since they are more given to solitude, and never frequent the immediate neighborhood of man. In this respect they resemble the White-eyed Vireos, but are much less common here, for in the breeding-season the southern limit of their range is about the northern limit of the latter's range. They are common summer-residents throughout northern New England, inhabiting there the woods strictly, but as such are very rare in Massachusetts. Indeed, some ornithologists have expressed doubt as to their actually breeding here, but I have found their nest near Boston, and have seen, with the bird on it, a nest in the Nashua Valley (below Lancaster) which a companion found. I have heard of other instances, which establish the fact beyond doubt.

The Solitary Vireos are in Massachusetts to be found as migrants in the last week of April and again in September, but are not at either time abundant. They inhabit throughout the year both the dry and swampy woods of oaks, maples, and nut trees, avoiding the evergreens, and among the branches search for their insect-food. Though fond of retirement, they are not shy or timid, especially when moved by parental affection. I have known the females to stay on their nests until I could almost lay my hand upon them, and then to remain immediately about my person, often approaching within a foot of me, and constantly uttering their plaintive cries. These notes generally bring the males to the scene, who are, however, as is the case with many birds, less willing to expose themselves.

(*d*). The music of the Solitary Vireos is delicious, but is particularly agreeable in an otherwise still, and cool forest, being peculiarly harmonious with those two charms of Nature, woodland stillness and woodland coolness. Their song, like that of the Red-eyed Vireos, is a continuous warble, but is more musical, mellow, and tender, and is uttered in another tone. It is particularly sweet at the mating-season, which comes in the early part of May. These birds, who are unfortunately almost silent during their migrations, have a few low whistles also, and a querulous note (like the syllable *ank*), much like that of the "Red-eye," but yet distinct.

(B) FLAVIFRONS. *Yellow-throated Vireo.*

(Not a common summer-resident in Massachusetts, except locally.)

(*a*). Nearly six inches long. Olive-green above, becoming bluish-ash on the rump. Throat and breast, bright yellow; belly, white. Eye-ring, etc., yellow. Wings and tail generally dark; former with two white bars.

(*b*). The nest of this species is pensile, but rather larger and deeper than those of the other vireos, being between 3 and $3\frac{1}{4}$ inches wide, and nearly as deep. It is placed in the fork of a horizontal branch, from three to fifteen feet above the ground, as often in the orchard as in the woods, though I have found it in pines. It is composed of narrow strips of thin bark, such as that of the cedar or large vines, is lined with pine-needles or grasses, and is usually ornamented on the outside with caterpillar's silk and large pieces of lichen. The four eggs, which are generally laid here in the first week of June, average $\cdot 80 \times \cdot 60$ of an inch, and are white, with black and either purplish or brownish spots, which are sometimes, but not usually, quite numerous (about the crown).

(*c*). The Yellow-throated Vireos reach Eastern Massachusetts in the second week of May, and leave it in September. They are locally distributed through our State, and are rare in certain neighborhoods. They are (perhaps) our handsomest vireos, and certainly possess great charms as singers. They excel all their relations in architectural taste and skill, and construct a beautiful nest, ornamented outwardly with lichens, plant-down, and caterpillar's silk, but plainly or even roughly finished inside — thus differing from that of the hummingbird, which it otherwise resembles very much, except in being pensile. It is altogether one of the prettiest nests to be found among our specimens of bird-architecture. It is extremely interesting to watch it in the progress of its construction. The birds are occupied about a week in that process, beginning by firmly twining dry grasses around the twigs from which it is to be suspended, and always working downwards until the frame is completed. It is almost impossible, even on watching them closely, to tell exactly how they weave the grasses together, or how they attach many of their ornamentations. Wonderful is that innate skill which enables them, with their simply constructed bill alone, to fashion a home for themselves, of which man with his complicatedly organized fingers, and the aid of all his inventions, cannot (probably) make the like! It seems probable that instinct rather than any acquired skill insures perfection (and yet it is perhaps true that many birds have improved in architecture from generation to generation[41]). On the last day, the female is chiefly occupied in smoothing and shaping the nest by turning round and round inside, and then on the following day, or the next, begins to lay her eggs.

The Yellow-throated Vireos frequent the woods which are lightly timbered with oaks, chestnuts, and maples, or even pines, and also orchards. Among the branches of the trees in these places they are almost continually moving in search of caterpillars and other insect-food.

(*d*). Their song lacks the expression of the Solitary, the volubility of the Red-eyed, the quaintness of the White-eyed, and the tenderness of the Warbling Vireo's song, and yet, with all these wants, is very charming. It is difficult to describe it exactly, but it consists of two or three warbled notes on an ascending scale, and then, after a pause, others with a falling accent, all being repeated disjointedly in a characteristic voice. Their ordinary querulous note is distinct from that of the "Red-eye," being somewhat harsher, and is often rapidly repeated.

I may finally say of these birds whose biography I have just written, that they are useful to the farmer and agriculturist, and deserve on all accounts to be protected.

(C) OLIVACEUS. *Red-eyed Vireo.*

(A common summer-resident throughout New England.)

(*a*). About six inches long. Olive-green above (often of quite an indescribable shade), becoming ashy on the crown, which is bordered by a narrow black line. Superciliary line

---

[41] It is to be considered that such improvement as is here referred to arises from adaptation to circumstances rather than from efforts to realize an ideal.

white; eye-stripe dusky. Under parts, white; sides olive-shaded. Wings and tail, generally dusky. Iris red.

(b). The nest is hung from a fork, usually near the end of a limb, between four and twenty feet above the ground, in the woods, in a shade-tree, in an orchard-tree, or occasionally in a pine. It is small, and cup-shaped; but, though very serviceable, is rarely very neatly made. It is constructed of strips of thin bark, occasionally of that of the white birch, is lined almost invariably with pine-needles, where pines exist, and is sometimes ornamented, if I may say so, with chips, bits of newspaper or wasps' nests, and caterpillar's silk. It is finished here about the first of June; and in the first week of that month four or five eggs are laid. These eggs average $.83 \times .62$ of an inch, and are white, with a few brownish-black spots at the larger end. A second set is sometimes laid in July.

(c). When I announce that I am going to write about the habits of one of our most familiar birds and the most voluble songster that we possess, who all through the day, when nearly every other bird is quiet, prolongs his cheerful warble in almost every grove — sometimes even among the trees of our cities, though such haunts he usually avoids — many will know that I refer to the Red-eyed Vireo. These vireos may be found throughout New England, in the latter part, if not nearly the whole, of May, in the summer-months, and in September. They inhabit many kinds of woods, also groves, and clumps or rows of trees about houses, particularly those near wooded land.

They show more familiarity to man than the other species, except the Warbling Vireos, and are almost everywhere common and well-known. They rarely pursue insects in the air in the manner of the flycatchers, but seize them as they themselves flutter among the branches of the trees, in which they usually remain at no very great height from the ground. I have noticed that the males, while the females are upon their nests, generally select a spot at some distance from them, which they make their haunt and concert-grove. They have never struck me as very active insect-hunters, since they devote so much of their time to music. They evidently, however, never suffer from hunger, and they are certainly diligent in the care of their young. They are very affectionate toward one another, and are fond of returning to the same spot year after year. It is pleasant to observe this attachment to their summer-homes, and to know where to welcome them as old friends, when they return in the spring.

(d). Their song consists of a few notes, which are warbled again and again with little intermission or variety (and which are *sometimes* interrupted now and then by a low whistle). This music would be monotonous, were it not for its wonderful cheerfulness, energy, and animation, in these qualities resembling the Robin's song. The "Red-eyes" have also a *chip*, a chatter like a miniature of the Oriole's scold (and to be heard in the season of courtship), and a peculiarly characteristic querulous note, which, like others, cannot be described accurately, whence the advantage of studying birds through nature, and not through books.

The Red-eyed Vireos are deservedly popular on account of their cheerful disposition, and enlivening song, which is kept up (less steadily, however, in the latter part of the season) from the time of their arrival until they leave us for the South, when the autumnal frosts become too severe, and the weather too cold, to admit of a sufficiency of the insect-food upon which they depend.

(D) GILVUS. *Warbling Vireo.*

(A common summer-resident in Massachusetts, but very much less abundant than the "Red-eye.")

(a). About five inches long. Above, a dull olive-green, which approaches mouse-color. Crown, ashy-tinged. Rump, brighter; wings darker and browner; and sides of the head paler. Superciliary line, dull white. Under parts, white — *distinctly* shaded on the sides (but feebly on the breast) with the color of the back, or light olive-green.

(b). The nest is usually placed at a considerable height above the ground (from twenty to sixty feet), and rarely elsewhere than in an elm, poplar, or button-wood tree. It is always pensile, but Audubon speaks of one fastened to the trunk of a tree, in which situation I have never found it, so far as I remember. The eggs of the Warbling Vireo are white, with a few "reddish-black" or brown spots at the larger end, and average about ·77×·58 of an inch. A set of four or five is laid near Boston in the first week of June.

(c). The Warbling Vireos reach Eastern Massachusetts in the second week of May, and leave it in the same week of September. They are common in many parts of our State, and I have seen them in Northern New Hampshire, but in

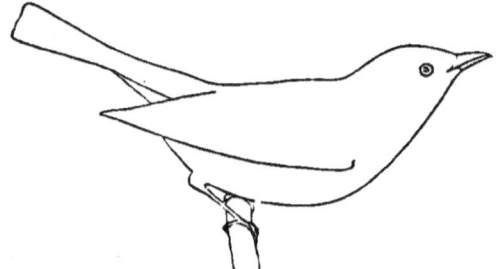

Fig. 6. Warbling Vireo ($\frac{1}{2}$).

some localities they are very rare. Though they do not, I think, show quite so much familiarity towards man (at least here), as some authors have represented, yet they are certainly to be found, to some extent, in cities, towns, villages, and thickly populated neighborhoods — for instance among the elms of Boston Common. Though occasionally seen in the haunts of the Yellow-throated Vireos (B), they seem to be particularly fond of rows of, or solitary, elms, poplars, and basswood trees — particularly those beside roads or near houses. They usually remain among the higher branches as they search for insects; and, on account of their size and quiet colors, they might easily be overlooked, were it not for their music.

(d). Their ordinary notes are like those of the Red-eyed Vireos, but less loud and querulous. Their song is exquisitely sweet, and, though quite distinct, recalls vividly that of the Purple Finch (§ 15, III). Dr. Coues, in speaking of the Warbling Vireo, says that "its voice is not strong, and many birds excel it in brilliancy of execution; but not one of them all can rival the tenderness and softness of the liquid strains of this modest vocalist. Not born 'to waste its sweetness on the desert air,' the warbling vireo forsakes the depths of the woodland for the park and orchard and shady street, where it glides through the foliage of the tallest trees, the unseen messenger of rest and peace to the busy, dusty haunts of men."

(E) PHILADELPHICUS. (*Brotherly-love Vireo.*) *Philadelphia Vireo.*

(*a*). This vireo, if a distinct species, differs from *Vireo gilvus* (D) in a doubtful technicality only. Dr. Coues pronounces it "almost indistinguishable from *gilvus*, except by absence of spurious quill," and says that the colors of the latter species are "precisely" the same. Is it not doubtful if one feather among hundreds (though, perhaps, an important one) can characterize a bird as more than a variety?

(*b*). (*d*). I suppose that the nest, eggs, and song of this bird are essentially the same as those of the Warbling Vireo.

(*c*). The Philadelphia Vireo is probably a migrant through Massachusetts, having been obtained at Philadelphia, also in Maine, and at Moose Factory (to the southward of Hudson's Bay and James Bay). I have never seen it here, so far as I know, nor have I seen any specimens shot here. I have no observations to make upon its habits, which I suppose to correspond closely to those of its immediate relations. I have since learned that this bird has been obtained in this State. Mr. Brewster, in the "Bulletin of the Nuttall Ornithological Club," says: "On Sept. 7th, 1875, I shot a female of this beautiful little species in Cambridge, Mass. It was feeding in company with several individuals of *Vireo olivaceus*, in a low willow tree."

In a more recent number, Mr. Ruthven Deane says that several specimens have been obtained in Maine, both in June and September, and that the Philadelphia Vireos may be considered summer-residents about Lake Umbagog.

(F) NOVEBORACENSIS. *White-eyed Vireo.* "*Politician.*"
(In southern New England a rather common summer-resident, though very locally distributed.)

(*a*). About five inches long. Above, bright olive-green; below, white. Sides of the body, eye-ring, wing-bars, etc., (bright) yellow. Iris white.

(*b*). The nest is almost invariably placed in a low tree, bush, or vine, two or three feet from the ground, generally, but not always. in the woods, whether dry or wet. It is pensile, and essentially like that of the "Red-eye," though prettier and often characterized by being largely composed of newspaper, or paper from wasps' and hornets' nests. The eggs, moreover, are strongly like those of the Red-eyed Vireo, but are generally a little smaller, and longer in shape. They are laid, near Boston, about the first of June.

(*c*). The White-eyed Vireos differ from their relatives in several respects. They are summer-residents in Eastern Massachusetts, but are so locally distributed as to be extremely rare or wanting in some places, though quite common in others. To the westward of the Connecticut River, in New England, they are so uncommon that the few specimens obtained may almost be considered stragglers. They reach the neighborhood of Boston, at least those who breed here, in the second week of May; but as to their general distribution and migrations I have not clearly made up my mind. Massachusetts has been generally considered their northern limit, but I feel quite confident of having seen them, in past years, apparently migrating through this State, in April and October. I have once or twice seen the Solitary Vireos in the latter month, when they were obliged to feed upon berries, as the "Red-eyes" do in September, and I find in my note-book that I observed a "White-eye" (or a species, hitherto undescribed, much resembling it) on the 18th of October, traveling with many other birds in a "wave."

These "bird-waves" are extremely interesting, and, to show their nature, I shall quote from my Journal:

"Nov. 15th, 1873. This morning, while wandering about

the place under the delusion that the passage-birds (or most of them) had fairly gone, an immense flock of birds suddenly appeared, evidently traveling from the North southward, and were soon scattered over the place. Among them were many Snow-birds, White-throated, Fox-colored, Tree, and Song Sparrows, Ruby-crowned 'Wrens,' Golden-crowned 'Wrens,' Nuthatches, Brown Creepers, and Chickadees. Never have I seen an assemblage of birds exhibiting such a variety of species. At noon most of them had disappeared."

The White-eyed Vireos frequent lightly timbered woods, particularly those which are in low land and contain a second growth about the taller trees, and also swamps, thickets, and the "scrub." They have a habit of moving their tails, much like the Shrikes. They keep nearer to the ground than our other vireos, and are so shy, that, if they were silent, they would rarely be seen as they busy themselves in the common pursuit of their family, that of insects.

(*d*). When, however, their nest is approached, they display themselves, and are usually very vehement in their expressions of anger (unlike their relations, particularly the Solitary Vireos), and utter a harsh scold or chatter, and sometimes a peculiar mewing, or other querulous cry. Their song is very peculiar or even eccentric, and is very loud for such small birds. It is full of character, energy, and vehemence, though some of the lower whistles are sweet and quite different in tone. It partakes of the owners' nature, much as the human voice does, and indicates the almost fiery temperament of these little vireos, which is so markedly in contrast with the cheerfulness, gentleness, and calmness, of other members of their family. Their music is constantly varied, and in it one may occasionally hear the apparently mimicked notes of other birds.

§ 14. **Laniidæ.** Shrikes. (See § 13.)

I. COLLURIO

(A) BOREALIS. (*Great Northern*) *Shrike.* "*Butcher-bird.*"
(A winter-visitant to Massachusetts, but never very common.)
(*a*). 9–10 inches long. Above, *light* bluish-ash, very light

on the rump. Below, white, very finely waved with black (often almost imperceptibly). Edging of crown, eye-ring and middle of the forehead, white. Rest of forehead, continuously with broad stripes through the eye, black. Wings and tail black, with white markings.

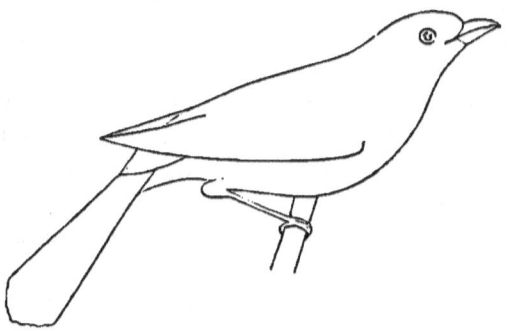

Fig. 7. Butcher-bird ($\frac{1}{3}$).

(*b*). The nest is placed in the woods, in the fork of a bush, not far from the ground. It is composed of leaves, grasses, and roots, is often lined with feathers, and is finished early in the season. One set of eggs contains from four to six, averaging 1·10 × ·80 of an inch. A specimen before me is blotched and spotted, most thickly about the crown, with faint lilac, and light sandy and yellowish brown; others are darker.

(*c*). The shrikes possess the cruelty of the hawks, but not the stateliness of some, nor the gracefulness of others. Neither do they possess the charms of many passerine birds, for they are wild, and, moreover, incapable of uttering musical sounds. Yet, there is attached to them that interest, which is naturally attached to birds who differ so distinctly from others, and about whom much is yet to be learned.

The Great Northern Shrikes, or the well-known "Butcher-birds," are virtually the sole representatives of their family in New England. They breed in the forests of Northern Maine, but in other parts occur principally as winter-visitants, remaining near Boston from the first of October until April " or even May." They vary greatly in abundance from year to year, following, to a great extent, the migrations of our very irregular visitors, the "Red-polls" and Pine Finches.

While with us, they are usually to be seen singly or in pairs about farms, orchards, fields, and meadows, though so extremely bold as to take up their abode in the Public Garden and Common of Boston, where they prey upon the English Sparrows and have several times been shot. When on the watch for their prey, they take a perch not far from the ground, and may be observed to flirt their tails much like the Pewees, now and then taking low and rapid flights from bush to bush, or tree to tree, particularly if pursued. On detecting what they wish to seize, they pounce upon it, if upon the ground, or pursue it through the air, if a bird, with force, great rapidity, and an almost infallible certainty of aim. As their bills are particularly powerful, the muscles about their head highly developed, and their feet naturally weak, they use the latter solely for perching. They use their bills, on the other hand, to seize the birds which they pursue, generally by the neck, thus suffocating them, and afterwards to tear their flesh.

Their food consists of grasshoppers, mice, and principally our smaller winter-birds of the finch-tribe who associate in flocks,— the Snow-birds, Snow Buntings, Tree Sparrows, "Redpolls," and Pine Finches. I have seen one dart after a flock of Goldfinches, who escaped by flying upwards. The Shrike followed with effort and a rather laborious flight, until, despairing of success, he turned and dropped with the speed of an arrow, arresting himself instantaneously on approaching the earth. He afterwards dashed into a company of Tree Sparrows, who showed much less address in escaping his clutches. They separated and fled to the bushes, whilst he followed one through a thicket and seized him on the other side. The Shrikes have several times been known in their boldness to enter cages, and to kill the inmates, though sometimes fortunately trapped themselves afterwards, and made captive.

The "Butcher-birds" are best known by their notorious

practice of impaling their food upon thorns or the like, thus securing, according to an European superstition, nine victims every day, whence they are in some places called "nine-killers." There are three theories often advanced to explain this extraordinary and characteristic cruelty, which are as follows: That the shrikes are fond of tainted meat; that they are naturally provident for the future; and that they employ their food, to a certain extent, as bait. The former of these theories may be refuted by the evidence, which has, I believe, been generally given, even from observations upon specimens in confinement, that the "Butcher-birds" never feed upon these stores. The last theory is absurd, as Wilson has already demonstrated, since they can at any time, by swiftness and dexterity of flight, seize a small bird who ventures near them, and need never resort to guile or deceit, and since, if grasshoppers be the creatures impaled, our winter-birds, upon whom the shrikes prey, are all granivorous or seed-eating, never touching insects (except, perhaps, in summer), and since in many cases the victims impaled are birds, who certainly would not serve satisfactorily as bait to attract their friends. I regret very much that I have not had enough opportunities for studying thoroughly the habits of the "Butcher-birds" to decide this question, but, in want of evidence, I am inclined to suppose that they keep up this murderous practice solely from instincts of cruelty, and perhaps other instincts, allied to the thieving and hiding propensities of the magpies and their relations, though, indeed, their acts are murder in the first degree and without secrecy. In brief, is it not probable that they exercise this barbarity and ferocity simply in sport, and for their amusement? I cannot, at present, present to the public any more satisfactory explanation.

(d). Audubon and Nuttall both state that the Great Northern Shrikes imitate the notes of other birds to attract their attention and to allure them into danger, but I have known no modern ornithologists to confirm these statements, which at present need corroboration. Whilst here in winter, the Shrikes are usually silent, and I have but once heard them uttering any sounds. About the middle of March I observed a pair in a field overrun with mice, and heard their extraordinary note, brief and often repeated, which resembled the buzz of a small insect (with somewhat of a squeal intermixed?). I at first, in my haste and ignorance, attributed this sound to the field mice, but afterwards supposed that it was probably a cry confined exclusively to the mating-season of the birds, to whom it certainly belonged.

I shall close this biography by inserting a very entertaining passage from an old English book on Falconry, which I find quoted in Mr. Wood's interesting book, "Homes without Hands."

"Sometimes upon certain birds she doth use to prey, whome she doth entrappe and deceive by flight, for this is her desire. She will stand at pearch upon some tree or poste, and there make an exceeding lamentable crye and exclamation, such as birds are wonte to do, being wronged or in hazard of mischiefe, and all to make other fowles believe and thinke that she is very much distressed and stands in need of ayde; whereupon the credulous sellie birds do flocke together presently at her call and voice, at what time if any happen to approach neare her she out of hand ceazeth on them, and devoureth them (ungrateful subtill fowle!) in requital for their simplicity and pains.

"Heere I end of this hawke, because I neither accompte her worthy the name of a hawke, in whom there resteth no valor or hardiness, nor yet deserving to have any more written upon her propertie and nature. For truly it is not the property of any other hawke, by such devise and cowardly will to come by their prey, but they love to winne it by main force of wings at random, as the round winged hawkes doe, or by free stooping, as the hawkes of the Tower doe most commonly use, as the falcon, gerfalcon, sacre, merlyn, and such like."

(B) LUDOVICIANUS. *Loggerhead Shrike.*

(But rarely obtained so far to the northward as Massachusetts.)

(*a*). 8-9 inches long. Like the Butcher-bird (A), but more slaty above, and generally with no white on the head (except on the throat), the eye-stripes meeting on the forehead.

(*b*). The nest is said to be much less elaborate than that of the "Butcher-bird," though the eggs are very similar to those of that bird. Dr. Brewer says: "The spots are usually larger and more scattered than in the eggs of *C. borealis*."

(*c*). The Loggerhead Shrike is chiefly an inhabitant of the Southern States, and I have heard of but few instances of its capture in New England or the State of Massachusetts. It is, however, says Mr. Allen, in his "Notes on the Rarer Birds of Massachusetts," a summer-resident at Hamilton, in Canada West, on the Northern Shore of Lake Ontario (McIlwraith), and has been known to breed at Buffalo, New York. Wilson says that "this species inhabits the rice plantations of Carolina and Georgia, where it is protected for its usefulness in destroying mice. It sits, for hours together, on the fence, beside the stacks of rice, watching like a cat; and as soon as it perceives a mouse, darts on it like a Hawk. It also feeds on crickets and grasshoppers."

(*d*). He adds that "its note, in March, resembled the clear creaking of a sign board in windy weather."

§ 15. The **Fringillidæ,** or *finches*, form our largest family (the warblers being second in size), and include the sparrows, buntings, linnets, grosbeaks, and crossbills. They are chiefly granivorous (or at least vegetarians), and consequently are less migratory than insectivorous birds. They are very sociable among themselves, and in some cases gregarious. They are clad both plainly and brilliantly, sometimes with crests, but are in nearly all cases musical, sometimes very highly so. Some of them are eminently field-birds, and on this account are easily observed in the country. As architects they are not to be ranked high, though their nests are often very neatly built. Their eggs exhibit great variety in colors and markings, and two (or even three) sets of four or five are laid by several species in one season, even so far to the northward as Massachusetts.

They (or at least our species) are characterized as follows. Bill, for the most part, not twice as long as high, but stout, more or less conical, with the mandibles generally meeting at their tips; commissure usually with a more or less evident angle; bristles often wanting; tarsi scutellate; primaries nine. They may be divided into three groups: (Gen. I–VI and VII?) Wings long; feet not strong; sexes generally unlike; males brightly colored. Birds of rather boreal distribution, of comparatively strong flight, and largely arboreal (except in genus VII). (Gen. VII?–XVIII.) Birds chiefly terrestrial; also plainly colored, and sexes generally alike; commissure frequently with the angle feebly marked. (Gen. XVIII?–XXIII.) Birds chiefly arboreal, and handsomely or brilliantly colored; sexes unlike. Distribution rather southern. Bill stout, somewhat curved above; angle well marked. (Gen. XXIV, XXV, are placed at the end, because not properly parts of our fauna.) (Figs. 8, 9, 10.) Possibly the starlings should be united with the finches, and ranked as a subfamily. (See § 17.)

The following genera require special notice:—

Curvirostra. Bill, with the mandibles crossed (pl. 1, fig. 16).

Pinicola. Bill stout, *hooked*, and with curved outlines.

Chrysomitris and *Ægiothus.* Bill conical, and pointed. Upper mandible often growing beyond the lower, as sometimes seen in other finches and blackbirds (pl. 1, fig. 12).

Plectrophanes. Hind-claw very long (pl. 1, fig. 17). In subgenus *Centrophanes* (including *Lapponicus* but not *nivalis*) hind-claw straightish; bill unruffled.

Ammodromus. Bill comparatively slender. Tail-feathers narrow and pointed. (Pl. 1, figs. 14, 15.)

Coturniculus closely related.

Passerella. Birds partially rasorial, as also in certain allied species.

Hydemeles. Bill deep, stout, and bristled; upper outline much curved, commissure strongly angulated (pl. 1, fig. 13). The details of structure vary with every group or genus, but the finches in general are easily recognized by their coloring.

I have arranged the genera (represented in New England) in what seemed the best sequence.

The position of the larks (*Alaudidæ*, § 16) is apparently doubtful. Though the typical Sky Lark of Europe (*Alauda arvensis*) has been introduced into this country, yet the true American larks belong to the subfamily,

Calandritinæ (fig. 11). They are characterized as follows: Bill (in *Eremophila*) twice as long as high, pointed, and with the upper outline convex; nostrils concealed; primaries nine; tarsi "scutellate and blunt behind as in front, with a deep groove along the inner side, and a slight one, or none, on the outer face;"[42] hind-claw very long. The common Shore Lark is the type.

I. CURVIROSTRA

(A) RUBRA. *Red Crossbill. Common Crossbill.*

(To be found in Massachusetts as an extremely irregular visitor from the North.)

(*a*). *Mandibles crossed* (as in B). About six inches long. ♂, chiefly of an almost brick-red, with wings and tail dusky or nearly black. ♀, often with a strong yellowish suffusion. Wings and tail, dark. Above, of a shade varying from brownish to olive, with dusky streaks. Rump, almost yellow. Beneath, paler, more or less streaked.

(*b*). The nest is built in the early part of spring, or even, it is said, in winter. Mr. Paine found one in a leafless elm, in East Randolph, Vermont, early in the month of March. The parents were so tame that it was necessary to remove them forcibly from their eggs, which "were four in number, and measured ·85 × ·53 of an inch. They have a greenish-white ground and are beautifully blotched, marbled, and dotted with various shades of lilac and purplish-brown."

(*c*). The Crossbill, on account of his many peculiarities, is an interesting subject for study. His most marked oddity is

---

[42] In the *Oscines*, "the tarsus is *normally* covered on either side with two entire horny plates, that meet behind in a sharp ridge." (Coues.)

that which Wilson has spoken of in admirable language. That author says:—"On first glancing at the bill of this extraordinary bird one is apt to pronounce it deformed and monstrous; but on attentively observing the use to which it is applied by the owner, and the dexterity with which he detaches the seeds of the pine tree from the cone, and from the husks that enclose them, we are obliged to confess on this as on many other occasions where we have judged too hastily of the operations of nature, that no other conformation could have been so excellently adapted to the purpose;" etc. (WILSON, VOL. IV, p. 44).

The exact distribution, the regular breeding-habits, and the migrations of the Crossbills are not, at present, perfectly understood. These birds migrate (it is supposed and wellnigh proved), in accordance with the abundance of food in their usual habitat (northward of the 44th parallel of latitude). Hence they are sometimes not seen at all in Massachusetts during the year, and at other times appear as early as August, and remain until June (whence it has been assumed that they breed here).

Though often here in autumn and spring, they are commonly driven to our latitudes in the winter-months; then, usually in flocks varying in number from three or four to hundreds, they are to be seen busily engaged in extracting seeds from the cones of our evergreens. They are good climbers, moving much like parrots, but with more agility. They occasionally eat berries; and they also descend to the ground, having a fondness, it is said, for saline substances. It is somewhere stated that in Arctic countries they often become so engrossed in their feeding, when on the ground, that they can easily be caught with a net, or knocked over with a club. Whilst near Boston in winter, they exhibit neither shyness nor stupidity, but, when started from a tree, often return to it, after manœuvring in the air in the manner of the "Red-polls." They generally fly at a considerable height, and sometimes at a very great elevation, at least great relatively to the powers of flight which belong to this family of birds. In spring, the Crossbills do mischief in attacking the buds of various trees; and Mr.

Maynard speaks of their eating the tops of oats in autumn, at Albany, Maine.[43] They are said to build their nests often in February or March, and therefore their presence in summer may not properly indicate the districts in which they breed, though such immature specimens were obtained by Mr. Horace Mann, at Weston, Massachusetts, in May, 1862, that Mr. Allen thinks it "hardly possible" that they were born far from that place.[44] The nest of the Crossbills has been found at Milltown, Maine, by Mr. Boardman,[42] and these birds may, therefore, breed quite extensively in that State and North-eastern New Hampshire, having been "common at Umbagog, according to Mr. Deane, during the summer of 1870," and according to Mr. Brewster, being "very common at Franconia in summer."[45] Their habitat in the breeding-season, may be generally considered as the vast hemlock and spruce-forests of the North.

(*d*). As Wilson says, they "have a loud, sharp, and not unmusical note" and "chatter as they fly." They sometimes utter in spring quite a sweet song, which has the character of their ordinary cries, as is noticeable in the music of the birds nearly related to them, the Pine Grosbeaks, "Red-polls," Goldfinches, etc.

(B) LEUCOPTERA. *White-winged Crossbill.*

(Much less common in Massachusetts than even the preceding species.)

(*a*). *Mandibles crossed* (as in A). About six inches long. Essentially like RUBRA, but with *white wing-bars*, and a much rosier hue in the male.

(*b*). An egg described by Dr. Brewer "is pale blue, the large end rather thickly spattered with fine dots of black and

---

[43] "The Naturalist's Guide." p. 111.
[44] "Notes on Some of the Rarer Birds of Massachusetts," in pamphlet [pp. 30. 31, 32], and in "American Naturalist" Vol. III, pp. 505-519; 568-585; 631-648; and numbers for Nov., Dec., and Jan., 1869-70.
[45] C. J. Maynard. "A Catalogue of the birds of Coos Co., N. H., and Oxford Co., Me.," etc., 5th species, p. 16, pamphlet.

ashy-lilac; is regularly or rather slightly elongate-oval, the small end rather obtuse. It measures ·80 of an inch in length by ·56 in breadth."

(c). The White-winged Crossbills are much rarer here than the Red Crossbills, since they habitually reside in more northern countries, though, indeed, on the authority of Mr. Deane and Mr. Brewster said to be "common at Umbagog in June, 1870, and at Franconia in summer."[46] They are seldom seen in Massachusetts, though occasionally common in winter, and known to migrate much further to the southward. So far as I have had opportunities to observe, they resemble closely in their habits the other species, feeding chiefly upon the seeds of our evergreens, both obtaining these and climbing dexterously, and sometimes seeking food upon the ground, having a partiality for saline matter. Mr. Maynard says that they feed "upon the seeds of beach-grass," "at Ipswich, Massachusetts," and that he "obtained a specimen on June 13, 1866, which was shot on an apple-tree in Newtonville," and was "filled with canker-worms."[47] This, says Mr. Allen, was "a male in fine breeding plumage," and therefore it is possible that these birds may occasionally breed in this State, though at the same time it is possible that the specimen in question may have wandered from the North, having previously reared his young in April or May. Instances of equally strange freaks among birds have been known to occur, such as wandering more than a thousand miles from a regular habitat. It is to be remarked that these instances take place almost wholly at the time of the migrations in autumn or early winter.[48]

(d). The song of the White-winged Crossbills, says Dr. Brewer, is "irregular and varied, but sweet and musical." These birds have a plaintive cry, distinct from the notes of the Red Crossbill.

---

[46] C. J. Maynard, 55th species (p. 16. pamphlet), "Birds of Coos Co., N. H.," etc.
[47] "The Naturalist's Guide," pp. 111-2.
[48] For example, the occurrence in Massachusetts of the Varied Thrush, Lark Finch, and Gray King-bird.

II. PINICOLA

(A) ENUCLEATOR. *Pine Grosbeak.*

(In Massachusetts a winter-visitant of very irregular appearance.)

(*a*). 8–9 inches long. ♂, carmine. Back dusky-streaked. Belly, almost white. Wings and tail, dusky (or black) ; former with much white. ♀, "ashy-gray above and streaked. Paler below, and not streaked." Crown (and rump) marked with rusty-yellow.

(*b*). Dr. Brewer says: "No positively identified eggs of the American Pine Grosbeak are as yet known in collections." A European specimen measures about $1.00 \times .75$ of an inch, and is greenish, blotched and spotted with brown and purplish, chiefly dark tints. Mr. Boardman found near Calais, Maine, "in an alder-bush, in a wet meadow," a nest and two eggs, referable to this species.

(*c*). The Pine Grosbeaks spend the summer-season in the cold regions which lie to the northward of New England, and though, I believe, common winter-residents in Maine and New Hampshire, are rather rare, or at least irregular, in their appearance about Boston, and other parts of this State. They are sometimes common here throughout the winter, wandering in large flocks from place to place, but at other times are wholly absent during the year, or at the most are seen but once or twice after a cold "snap" or a heavy storm. I have seen them from the first of November until the latter part of March, though their departure usually occurs earlier in the season, since they habitually breed in March and April. It is to be remarked that among our winter-birds of this family, the young almost invariably predominate, and often are unaccompanied by mature specimens. This interesting fact has not, so far as I know, been satisfactorily explained, though it may possibly be due simply to an inability of the young to withstand the cold so well as their parents. Yet these birds are supposed to be regulated in their migrations almost entirely by supplies of food, and not to be affected by cold, since in severe winters they are often much less abundant here than in mild seasons. To determine questions of this sort, much philosophical study, technical knowledge, comparison of notes, and coöperation of different sciences, is greatly needed.

The Pine Grosbeaks frequent the pines and other evergreens almost exclusively, feeding largely upon their seeds, but also upon buds and berries. Mr. Maynard speaks of their being so unsuspicious that they can be easily captured by a noose attached to a pole, but I myself have never observed any like indiscretion on their part. In general appearance they bear a strong resemblance to the Robin, but possess powers of flight even superior to those of that bird. Large flocks often travel many miles, from time to time, in the course of a day, moving at some height, and the individuals rising and falling in their flight. The Pine Grosbeaks are also very much at ease among the trees, though not such clever climbers as the crossbills. They seem, whilst here, to remember those long winter-nights of the North, which " become less and less separated by daylight, the farther to the northward that they occur, until at the pole they become fused into a period of darkness which lasts for six months." I have observed that they generally retire before sunset, whilst other birds are still occupied in feeding, and collect among the branches of some thickly foliaged evergreen. The "Red-polls," on the other hand, are given to late hours, so that their respective habits are probably to be accounted for solely by a difference of taste, since both species inhabit much the same regions. Certainly nature has created much for the sake of pleasing man by variety alone.

(d). The Pine Grosbeaks have a characteristic single note, a loud, clear, but somewhat plaintive whistle, which is often repeated several times, and also a few subdued whistles, not audible at any great distance. I here quote briefly from my journal. "March 13, 1875. This morning I arose at 5.15, and went out at 5.40, when crows were beginning to fly over. At 5.55 a Red-poll, who was among some pines, awoke and gave his call, which was answered by two or three of his companions, who were near him, likewise in pines. * * *

He finally woke up a solitary Pine Grosbeak, who uttered his call-note several times, and remained in the neighborhood until 6.15, when he perched on the top of a pine, and sang for several minutes. His song was sweet and very much like that of the Purple Finch, but was now and then interrupted by his ordinary cries."

III. CARPODACUS

(A) PURPUREUS. *Purple Finch.* "*Linnet.*"

(In New England, a common resident in summer, but only occasional in winter.)

Fig. 8. Purple Finch (¼).

(*a*). About six inches long. Crown-feathers erectile. ♂, carmine, of very different shades and intensities in different specimens. Back dusky-streaked; belly, almost white. Edgings of the wings, reddish. ♀, olivaceous-brown, and streaked, except on the belly, which as well as a superciliary line is white. Wings and tail like those of the male, but with no reddish.

(*b*). The nest is usually composed of fine rootlets, weedstalks, and grasses, being lined with hairs, but its materials vary greatly in some cases. It is placed in a pine, cedar, or orchard-tree, or occasionally a bush or hedge, from five to twenty feet above the ground. The eggs of each set are four or five, and average ·75 × ·55 of an inch or more. They are of a light greenish blue, marked rather thinly and chiefly at the larger end, with specks, blotches, and scrawls, of very faint lilac, and of blackish. The first set is laid about the first of June or earlier, and a second one often appears in July.

(*c*). The Purple Finches are well known on account of their charming song, and the gay or brilliant coloring in summer of the males, who attract, especially if in flocks, the attention of many a person who is habitually inobservant. A few pass the less severe winters in Eastern Massachusetts, but in doing so usually frequent swamps of cedar-trees, or retired places where seeds and berries are sufficiently abundant. The "Linnets" generally arrive here from the South on the first of April or earlier, but sometimes not until May, and then appear in the open country, when the males and females often congregate in small flocks, usually feeding upon the buds of various trees. The males are not at this time of the year in full dress, and perhaps on this account, if these birds may be supposed to have human vanities, are often alone or apart from the females. They are, however, in full song, and, perched on some high branch, sing loudly, as if under the delusion that winter disappears in April.

When much startled, the "Linnets" usually fly for some distance at a considerable height. In May they usually become very abundant, and also mischievous, since they "feed on the stamina of various fruit-blossoms." They also gather in large flocks on the ground, where, not unfrequently in company with the Goldfinches or other members of their family, they pick up various seeds and perhaps other food. They are summer-residents throughout New England, though less common to the northward, and frequent principally cultivated or open lands, though occasionally to be met with in woods. Their song may not unfrequently be heard in September, when most other birds do not sing. In October they become quite rare, and finally, usually before November, forsake their summer-haunts. Those seen here in the former month are very possibly migrants from the North.

(*d*). The music of the Purple Finch is a warbled song, which would be monotonous, were it not sweet, mellow, and full-toned. Both sexes sing. In autumn they often give utterance to a few notes, which recall those of the Blue Bird. Besides their customary "chink," which they utter particularly when on wing, they have a variety of less important notes. The most pleasing of these is their "pewee," which is often softly repeated by the females, and the most striking a single whistle, to be heard chiefly or wholly in autumn, and which recalls that of the Great-crested Flycatcher.

The "Linnets" are much more common and generally distributed through this State than formerly, and are gradually becoming quite fearless of man. They are now so tame as often to build their nests in hedges, and on account of their several attractions should be allowed to increase, in spite of the injuries that they may do us in spring. They resemble in habits the Pine Grosbeaks, from the irregularity of both their appearance and abundance from year to year. In studying the Purple Finches, one must not confuse their song with that of the Warbling Vireo,[49] or even with those of the Robin and some other birds, nor the notes already mentioned with those of the Great Crested Flycatcher[50] and Blue Bird.[51]

IV. CHRYSOMITRIS

(A) TRISTIS. (*American*) *Goldfinch*. "*Yellow Bird*."[52] "*Thistle-bird*."

(Common in New England throughout the year, but more abundant in summer than in winter. Like the Cedar-birds, they breed very late in the season.)

(*a*). About 4¾ inches long. ♂ (from April 1st, until September 20th?), bright yellow, "inclusive of lesser wing-coverts." Crown, wings, and tail, black. Upper tail-coverts, whitish; but wing-markings and tail-spots entirely white. ♀, dusky olivaceous yellow above; paler or yellowish beneath. Wings and tail less purely colored than in the male, who in winter resembles the female, though much browner.

(*b*). The nest is usually composed of fine grasses (or strips of bark), and is lined with down from thistles and other plants, but sometimes with hairs. It is quite deep or cup-shaped, but is substantial, neat, and compact. It is placed in a pasture-bush, a shade-tree (especially on roadsides), perhaps an apple-tree, or a like situation, commonly between five and twenty feet above the ground, and almost invariably in a crotch. I have known it to be just completed as early as the twelfth of

---

[49] § 13, I, D.   [50] § 19, II, A.   [51] § 2.
[52] There is a warbler (§ 9, X, A) also called the Yellow Bird.

June, and as late as the first week in August. The eggs of each set are five or six, average about ·63 × ·50 of an inch, and are faint bluish-white (rarely with a few faint markings?).

(c). The Goldfinches, perhaps the most graceful members of their large family, are very common and well-known, and one could hardly select from all the finches, or from all birds, more charming objects of study. They are summer-residents throughout a greater part of the eastern United States, are common in Massachusetts, and are very abundant in (certain parts of) Northern New Hampshire, and probably the whole of northern New England. They are very hardy, and remain in the neighborhood of Boston throughout the year.

Ornithologists very generally have advanced the theory that those birds who pass the summer in a locality, where the species which they represent are resident throughout the year, retire in winter to the South, leaving their place to be supplied by others of the same kind from the North. Mr. Maynard, however, ingeniously argues that this is not the case, at least with the Hairy Woodpecker.[53] However the case may be, it is certain that many Goldfinches pass the winter near Boston.

In those months during which snow generally covers the earth, they wander, usually in small flocks, feeding, as at other times of the year, upon the seeds of pines or weeds, and such suitable things as they can find upon the ground. The males are then in their winter-dress, and do not assume their gay summer-livery until April. In March the "Yellow Birds" become rather common, and in April abundant. About the first of May, or even later, they often associate in large companies with the Purple Finches and other members of their family, and frequent orchards and various places where they can procure food from the ground. The song of the male (for the female does not sing) may often be heard at this time, previous to and during which they ramble over open country and cultivated lands, rendered noticeable by the jet black and bright yellow of the gayer sex. These flocks are gradually

---

[53] "The Naturalist's Guide," p. 129.

broken up, but at all seasons of the year the so-called "Yellow Birds" show a social spirit, whence, even in summer, two or three often enjoy one another's society and fly about together.

The following observations on their habits in summer were made among the White Mountains, where, in certain districts, they were very numerous. The Goldfinches there inhabited the pasture-land, in which they often built their nests, over which they wandered, and from which chiefly they obtained their food. There were in the place but few trees on the roadsides, except such as formed the part of some wood (and in woods these birds never build their nests), but the large bushes, which in many places supplied this want, answered the Goldfinches' purpose as well. On these bushes, or the telegraph-wires and posts, males and females, or when the latter were on their nests, a solitary male or several often perched. They occasionally alighted in the road to pick up food, but not very commonly. The daintiness and evident enjoyment of their bath was very charming. They usually waded into a gently flowing brook, which rolled over clean sand, and then showered themselves with the water tossed up by the splashing of their wings, bobbed their heads into the clear stream, next dressed their feathers, and finally flew away, twittering expressions of their pleasure. In the early part of the summer they often appeared in the gardens and fruit-trees of the village, but in September congregated where thistles were abundant. On the heads of these weeds they perched, until the stalks swayed to the ground; and, when this brief ride was finished, they bent over to feed upon the seeds. In the same way do they often treat the garden-iris in summer, when the rich blue or purple of that flower forms a most gorgeous contrast with their plumage. Whilst assembled, the Goldfinches are always extremely harmonious, and seem to express their happiness by their delightful cries. Their flight, as every one who knows them must have observed, consists of a series of marked undulations, and occasionally of great circles in the air. If pursued by any bird of prey, they mount in circles often to a great height, knowing well that they are safe only when above their enemies; and, though their powers of flight are not great, I have never seen a hawk or shrike who was sufficiently persistent to exhaust them, and thus to secure his prey.

To return to those "Yellow Birds" who have passed the summer in Massachusetts, they (or latterly substitutes from the North) are tolerably abundant in September, but less so in October. Sometimes at this season they associate with the sparrows, and feed in asparagus-beds, old vegetable-gardens, and like places. Before October has passed away, they become quite uncommon, and assume many of their winter-habits. Their haunts are much the same throughout the year, and include the whole country, with the exception of the woods, meadows, and swamps.

(*d*). The male Goldfinch has a lively and sweet, but not full-toned song, characterized by his ordinary notes, and resembling that of the "Canary," his near relation. In listening to it, one may hear harsh notes, and then a sweet *che-wé* or *che-we-wé*. I have heard it in April, October, and the intervening time, most often in the first-named month and in May. He has also a very sweet and almost pathetic cry, which to me has a singular fascination, but it is not easily to be distinguished from the corresponding notes of the "Red-poll," Siskin, or Canary-bird. Both sexes own a low whistle, heard chiefly in summer, and rarely then, and their characteristic twitters, which these birds commonly utter at every undulation of their flight, and often when perched. Such other sounds as they occasionally produce are less noticeable, and are among those details regarded only by one intimate with birds and with their individual traits.

In writing this volume, I have been struck with the thought that the biographer of birds has, at least in one respect, a pleasanter task than the biographer of a human friend, for he has never to speak of death; for, since we regard all of a species as virtually one being, and rarely regard distinctions between individuals, we are necessarily led to consider them as a perpetual being, though, indeed, instances are known to modern history of the apparent extinction of a race, such as that of the Great Auk, owing to persecution, and the comparative helplessness of this creature in escaping his enemies, particularly man.

Should the Goldfinches ever cease to exist, let this be their eulogy. The Goldfinches were peculiarly attractive on account of their apparently happy disposition, and their sprightly, expressive twitters, which were never exchanged for the weak and almost mournful notes which many other birds adopt in autumn and winter. What more could have been reasonably asked than that these birds should be finely colored, sing sweetly, have a variety of charming notes, possess a peculiar flight and attractive habits, be common and resident throughout the year, and frequent the neighborhood of man?

(B) PINUS. *Pine Finch.* "*Siskin.*"

(An irregular winter-visitor to Massachusetts, occasionally lingering here until June, and having been known to breed at Cambridge.)

(*a*). About 4¾ inches long. Flaxen; paler below. Thickly streaked with darker, rather finely so on the head and under parts. Wings and tail, black, with much yellow, which, in the breeding-season, is more or less suffused throughout the plumage.

(*b*). Dr. Brewer says: "Early in May, 1859, a pair of these birds built their nest in the garden of Professor Benjamin Pierce, in Cambridge, Mass., near the colleges. It was found on the 9th by Mr. Frederick Ware, and already contained its full complement of four eggs, partly incubated." "The eggs are of an oblong-oval shape, of a light green ground-color, spotted, chiefly at the larger end, with markings of a light rusty-brown. They measure ·71 by ·50 of an inch."

(*c*). So irregular are the habits of the American "Siskins," that I have never clearly understood their distribution and annual movements. Though these birds have been known to breed exceptionally at Cambridge, in Massachusetts, they usually breed in New England, only to the northward of that State, such as in certain places among the White Mountains and about Lake Umbagog. They are sometimes common in Massachusetts during the winter, and at other times are altogether absent then, presumably in the latter case, not passing to the southward of their summer-range. And yet they are said by Wilson to have been common in Pennsylvania for a number of successive winters, and are known to occur occasionally on the shores of the Gulf of Mexico. The most interesting fact in their Natural History is their frequent appearance near Boston in April and May, or even June and July, even when not observed in the preceding winter. Mr. Maynard supposes that their journeys are chiefly governed by the snow, but my own observations do not altogether confirm this theory, which I do not think supported by the facts relative to the feeding of these birds, or to their appearance here, for the Pine Finches occasionally reach Boston in autumn, before the snow, and even as soon as the young are able to travel, though indeed these latter are rarely hatched before August.

The Siskins may be observed in winter to wander in flocks from place to place, being, like their various near relations, entirely nomadic at that season. They fly in undulations like those of the Goldfinches, to whom they bear a very strong resemblance in other ways.[54] They live upon the seeds of weeds, and those of the several evergreens, feeding both upon the ground and in trees. They may often be seen clustered at the top of some tall pine, busied in extracting the seeds, or clinging to the cones of a spruce, with an ease which clearly indicates their habits. They are also fond of birch-seeds, which are highly esteemed by many of our winter-birds, particularly the Ruffed Grouse. They are graceful in their movements, and their attitudes, when feeding, are always pretty, but they are not such climbers as the "Red-polls."

(*d*). The Pine Finches are closely allied to the Yellow Birds and "Red-polls" by their notes, and their sweet call is almost

---

[54] Mr. Allen, in his "Winter Notes of an Ornithologist," published in the "American Naturalist," considers the Siskins swifter in flight, their notes "wilder and more wiry."

indistinguishable from the call-notes of those birds. Their song and their twitters, though distinct from those of the Goldfinch, are yet much like them, but their twitters, most often uttered as they fly, are much louder and less musical. They have also a very characteristic note, resembling the word *wee*, uttered in a peculiar tone with a rising inflection, and, moreover, if I remember correctly, a loud and rather unmusical trill.

V. ÆGIOTHUS

(A) LINARIUS. "*Red-poll.*" *Red-poll Linnet. Lesser* "*Redpoll.*"

(Another irregular visitant to New England, in the winter-season only, being in some years very common and in others altogether absent, at least in Massachusetts.)

(*a*). About 5½ inches long. Upper parts, flaxen, dark-streaked. Beneath, whitish, more or less dusky-streaked. Wings and tail dusky, with white edgings; the former with two narrow whitish bars. *Crown carmine;* "rump white or rosy, always streaked with dusky." In the mature ♂ the breast is bright rosy, and the under tail-coverts paler and streaked.

[Dr. Coues has endeavored to establish one or two varieties of this species, which it is perhaps necessary to accept. They are VAR. *fuscescens, Dusky Red-poll*, a darker form; with "rump scarcely lighter," and "sides heavily streaked," which Dr. Coues supposes may occur from the wearing of the feathers, and VAR. *exilipes, American Mealy Red-poll*, with flaxen paled to whitish, and rump unstreaked in adults, "representing," says Dr. Coues, "the true Mealy Redpoll, *A. canescens*, of Greenland."]

(*b*). The "Red-polls" breed in Arctic Countries on the ground, and lay four or five eggs, which are light greenish-blue, with a few brown spots, and which average about $\cdot 65 \times \cdot 50$ of an inch.

(*c*). The "Red-polls" are occasionally the most abundant of our winter-birds, but, on the other hand, several successive winters often pass, without their occurrence in Massachusetts.

They breed in the Arctic countries, and when obliged to travel to the southward, as they sometimes are, it is supposed, by lack of food, occur in the United States in November, April, and more often the intervening months. They move in flocks, which vary in size, but sometimes consist of two hundred or even more, and which are frequently augmented by the companionship of Goldfinches and other birds. These flocks always seem, however, to consist of more than one species, since the individuals, among whom the young predominate, represent various colorations at the different periods of their growth.

The "Red-polls" wander continually during their visits, and hence are very irregular in appearance at different localities. I have never observed them to feed from the evergreens, but they have a marked fondness for the seeds of white birches and of alders, and according to Brehm, the German ornithologist, pass the summer among the former trees in the most northern part of Europe. They often gather where the coarse field-weeds project above the snow, on banks or roadsides, and also feed upon the ground. They allow quite a near approach, and when finally so startled as to take flight, often return to the spot just left, after circling in the air. Though not alarmed by man's approach, they are often shy of venturing near to buildings, though I remember to have seen two staying for a moment to feed with Snow-birds on some grain scattered before the window of a dining-room.

The following extracts from my Journal will illustrate the habits of these birds. " March 4th. Sunrise in Boston at 6.30 a. m., sunset at 5.55 p. m. * * * At twenty minutes before six this afternoon, whilst I was exercising the dogs, a 'Redpoll' alighted near me in a small apple-tree. He paid almost no attention to me or my companions, though we were noisy, and I was at one time within five feet of him. The dogs I finally sent away. The bird at first uttered his sweet call-note, in order, I suppose, that he might obtain the companionship of his mates, if any were near, and occasionally other sounds to express his satisfaction, as he obtained from the bark bits of food so minute as to be invisible to my eye. He displayed thoroughly his great skill in climbing, and often, in searching the crannies of the bark, hung with his head downwards. He soon became silent, and I remained motionless until five minutes after six. I then observed another 'Red-poll,' who flew over at some distance, and at a considerable height from the ground, apparently about to 'take perch' in a neighboring pine-grove. My friend, a moment later, took to flight and seemed (it was then dusk) to alight in a pine."

"March 13th. This morning I went out at twenty minutes before six, when Crows were already beginning to fly over. Quarter of an hour later, a 'Red-poll,' who was in the pines which border —————— street, awoke and gave his call, which was answered by two or three of his companions, who were near him, likewise in the pines. These birds then warbled for about five minutes and afterwards flew away."

"March 22d. This morning * * * * the 'Red-polls' awoke at quarter of six among the pines, but not those in which they were before, and at once sang. I next observed a solitary one, who flew over at a great height, but the rest gathered into flocks and set about the business of the day, flying to a distance. The Goldfinches showed much the same habits. At six I found one in a pine, singing very sweetly, but he soon flew away, after uttering a few twitters."

"March 28th. This morning I left the house at half-past five, but spring has made the birds rise very early, for on going out, I saw the Crows and 'Red-polls' flying over. At six two of the latter, who have lately been very common, alighted near me, to rest in their early rambles."

"April 6th. A few 'Red-polls' flew over to-day, but they are becoming scarce."

"April 24th. This afternoon a 'Red-poll' (*Ægiothus Linarius*), who shows no wounds, nor as yet any signs of decomposition, was picked up in the barn-cellar, the doors of which were shut."

(*d*). The "Red-polls" have a sweet call-note, like that of the Goldfinch or Siskin, and a simple "chit," often so repeated, especially by a flock, as to resemble the twitterings of the former bird, or even those of the latter. Their song is quite like the Yellow Bird's (*C. tristis*), but is distinct, since all their ordinary notes are introduced.

The winters when these happy, pretty little birds are common are always much enlivened by their presence, and those years are richer for the naturalist, which bring us visits from the Arctic birds.

VI. LINOTA

(A) BREWSTERI[55] *Brewster's Linnet.*

(One specimen, not clearly referable to any known species or variety, was obtained by Mr. William Brewster, at Waltham, Mass., from a flock of common "red-polls.")

(*a*). It is described as follows in Messrs. Baird, Brewer, & Ridgway's "North American Birds."

"General appearance somewhat that of *Æ. linarius*, but no red on the crown, and the sides and rump tinged with sulphur-yellow; no black gular spot. ♀ *ad.* Ground-color above light umber, becoming sulphur yellow on the rump, each feather, even on the crown, with a distinct medial stripe of dusky. Beneath white, tinged with fulvous yellow anteriorly and along the sides; sides and crissum streaked with dusky. Wings and tail dusky; the former with two pale fulvous bands; the secondaries, primaries, and tail-feathers narrowly skirted with whitish sulphur-yellow. A dusky loral spot, and a rather distinct lighter superciliary stripe. Wing 3·00; tail 2·50; tarsus ·50; middle toe, ·30. Wing formula, 1, 2, 3, etc."

VII. PLECTROPHANES

(A) NIVALIS. *Snow Bunting.*[56] "*Snow-flake.*"

(An inhabitant of the "far North," visiting New England in winter, in large assemblies.)

(*a*). 6½–7 inches long. *In the breeding-season*, pure white

---

[55] Since named *Ægiothus flavirostris* var. *Brewsteri.*
[56] Sometimes called "White Snow-bird," in distinction to the so-called Black or Blue Snow-bird.

with black variegations, and a black bill. *In winter*, bill brown, and the plumage endlessly varied. A specimen before me, a very fair type, is chiefly white, with a rich dark brown on the crown, becoming lighter and warmer on the back of the neck and on the rump. The interscapulars are vaguely streaked with white, black, and brown, these colors extending to the scapulars. Wings and tail, chiefly black and white. Under parts, snowy-white, with a light warm brown patch on each side of the breast. Specimens have been obtained pure white, and unmarked.

(*b*). Mr. Macfarlane found on the Arctic coast a "nest situated in a cave in a sand-bank." "The eggs, five in number, are of a dull white, with perhaps a faint bluish cast, sprinkled and spattered with dilute yellowish-rufous, the markings most numerous toward the larger end; they measure ·95 of an inch in length by ·64 in breadth."

(*c*). The Snow Buntings are quite regular as winter-visitors to New England, appearing in November, April, and the intervening months. They are very restless, and roam over the country in flocks, which sometimes contain thousands of individuals. They have very good powers of flight, and hence can take long flights whenever their wishes or instincts prompt them to do so. They generally move to the northward when long-continued fine weather occurs, and to the southward on the advent of heavy snow-storms, and therefore have acquired, in their winter-haunts, the name of "bad-weather birds," a title which originated in Europe, where they are well known. The Snow Buntings for the most part breed in Arctic countries, but a pair have been known to build their nest near Springfield, Massachusetts, and, says Mr. Maynard,[57] "this species may breed on the tops of some of the ranges of Maine and New Hampshire. I have a note of a well authenticated instance of a large flock being seen on Mount Katahdin, in early August, 1869." None, however, have ever been reported in summer

---

[57] "A Catalogue of the Birds of Coos Co., N. H., and Oxford Co., Maine," etc.; 57th species, p. 17 of pamphlet.

from Mt. Washington, the highest peak in New England, and I saw none on walking up Mount Lafayette, another prominent peak, in the early part of September, though it was very cold at the summit, and the true Snow-birds (*Junco hyemalis*) were very abundant at comparatively great altitudes, where the vegetation was stunted. Audubon speaks, however, of a nest found among the White Mountains, in July, 1831, and seen by Wm. M. Boott, Esq., of Boston. It is probable that the Snow Buntings normally belong to the United States as winter-visitors only, and as such occur so far to the southward as Kentucky, if not still further. They are not so shy as one might reasonably suppose them to be from their habits in summer, but near Boston frequent the "Back Bay lands," the roads, and roadsides. They often obtain seeds from the weeds in fields and ploughed lands, but they are most common on and near the sea-shore, where they feed much upon small shell-fish. Wilson says: — "In passing down the Seneca river towards lake Ontario, late in the month of October, I was surprised by the appearance of a large flock of these birds feeding on the surface of the water, supported on the tops of a growth of weeds that rose from the bottom, growing so close together that our boat could with great difficulty make its way through them. They were running about with great activity; and those I shot and examined were filled, not only with the seeds of this plant, but with a minute kind of shell fish that adheres to the leaves. In these * * * aquatic excursions they are doubtless greatly assisted by the length of their hind heel and claws. I also observed a few on Table rock, above the falls of Niagara, seemingly in search of the same kind of food." Mr. Maynard speaks of thousands feeding on the seeds of beach-grass, at the Ipswich Sand-hills.[58] The Snow Buntings run with ease and rapidity, like the larks, and fly with considerable swiftness, when in flocks often whirling like a flurry of snow before alighting on the ground. They are the most picturesque of our winter-birds, and often enliven an otherwise dreary scene,

---

[58] "The Naturalist's Guide," p. 112.

especially when flying, for they then seem almost like an animated storm, driven before a gusty wind.

(*d*). Their principal notes are a clearly piped whistle, and a peculiar *chirr*, which they often utter when on wing. Their song, rarely to be heard in Massachusetts, is short and simple, but quite sweet.

(B) LAPPONICUS. *Lapland Longspur. Lapland Bunting.*

(Rare in Massachusetts, where it is present in the winter-season only; "common on the Ipswich Sand-hills.")

(*a*). 6–6½ inches long. ♂, in the breeding-season, with the crown, forehead, sides of the head, throat, and upper breast, continuously black. Superciliary line, whitish, continuing down the side of the chestnut-red patch on the back of the neck. Interscapulars, dark brown or blackish, with lighter edges. Lower breast and belly, whitish; the former more or less streaked. Wings and tail dusky; the former marked with bay (and white), the latter with conspicuous white patches. ♂, in winter, with the black interrupted and the chestnut-red less pure. ♀, with the throat much like the breast, crown like the back, and the chestnut almost wanting.

(*b*). In eggs from Anderson River, "where distinctly visible, the ground-color appears to be of yellowish-gray, * * *. The blotches are of various shades of brown, with shadings of olive, purple, or red, and at times almost black." "They measure ·80 × ·60 of an inch."

(*c*). The "Longspurs," as their name indicates, have remarkably long hind-claws, such as also belong to the Snow Buntings, to whom they are as closely allied by habits and notes as otherwise. They are still more northern in their range than those birds, and pass the summer in Arctic countries only. Brehm says, from his own observations at this season in the extreme North of Europe, that they may be found among the birch-woods there, where they often perch upon the trees, feed much upon the gnats which swarm in the toondras, and sing only when on the wing, often hovering like the Lark when doing so, whereas the Snow Buntings usually perch on rocks, and are not naturally shy. They occur in Massachusetts as rare winter-visitors only, and as occasional stragglers in large flocks of Snow Buntings or Shore Larks, though, says Mr. Maynard, "common on the Ipswich Sand-hills." They frequent almost exclusively the coast or the lands near it, feeding on seeds and small shell-fish. They run nimbly, fly swiftly, and chiefly affect the ground, but occasionally perch in trees.

(d). They have a shrill *chirr*, and a rather melancholy call of two syllables. Their song is said to be simple but sweet, with their call-notes often introduced.

VIII. CHONDESTES

(A) GRAMMACA. *Lark Finch.*

(An inhabitant of the western United States, one, however, being "taken in Gloucester, in 1845, by S. Jillson."[59])

(a). About 6½ inches long. "Crown chestnut blackening on forehead, divided by a median stripe, and bounded by superciliary stripes, of white; a black line through eye, and another below eye, enclosing a white streak under the eye and the chestnut auriculars; next, a sharp black maxillary stripe not quite reaching the bill, cutting off a white stripe from the white chin and throat. A black blotch on middle of breast. Under parts white, faintly shaded with grayish-brown; upper parts grayish-brown, the middle of the back with fine black streaks. Tail very long, its central feathers like the back, the rest jet-black, broadly tipped with pure white in diminishing amount from the lateral pair inward, and the outer web of the outer pair entirely white." (Dr. Coues.)

(b). The nest of these birds is most often built upon the ground. "The maximum number of their eggs" says Dr. Brewer "is five. Their average measurement is ·85 by ·65 of an inch. The ground-color is usually a grayish-white, rarely a light brown, marbled and streaked with waving lines, and a few dots of black or a blackish-brown."

---

[59] Maynard, Naturalist's Guide, p. 112. Gloucester is on the coast of Massachusetts, north of Boston.

(c). The Lark Finches, since but one specimen has been taken in this State, namely, at Gloucester, in 1845, have no more claim to be considered or treated as birds of Massachusetts, than a Turk who passes a day and night at Paris to be called a Frenchman ; but, in conformity to the strict but not unreasonable demands of modern science, I shall give a brief account of its habits, formed from the observations of other naturalists. The Lark Finches feed principally upon seeds which they obtain upon the ground. They are most abundant in prairies and other open lands, though they also visit trees, or resort to their immediate neighborhood. In general habits, they resemble the White-throated Sparrows (*Zonotrichiæ*, next to whom they should properly stand). Mr. Ridgway considered their delightful song, which is usually delivered from a perch, as the finest belonging to the finches.

IX. AMMODROMUS

(A) MARITIMUS. *Sea-side Finch.*

(Almost wholly absent from Massachusetts, though said by Dr. Coues to be, or to have been, abundant in New Hampshire.)

(*a*). About six inches long. Tail-feathers narrow and pointed, as also in *caudacutus*. Superciliary line from bill to eye, and edge of the wing, yellow. Upper parts, and side-shading below, brown or gray, olive-tinted, the former more or less streaked. Under parts, white ; breast tinted with brown, and faintly or obsoletely streaked. Wings and tail, plain, scarcely marked. Side-markings on the head, vague.

(*b*). "The nest is usually placed in a tussock of grass, in the fresh water marshes, or on the sea-shore beyond the reach of high-tide." The eggs measure about ·80 × ·57 of an inch, and are white, gray-tinged, thickly, finely, and most often evenly marked with brown, which is sometimes confluent or predominant at the crown.

(*c*). I regret that I know nothing of the habits of the Sea-side Finches, and that I cannot add to what has appeared in the various meagre accounts of these birds already published.

Dr. Coues considered this species abundant on the coast of New Hampshire, but "Mr. Brewster * * * * has looked for it in vain at Rye Beach." Mr. Maynard doubts the occurrence of these birds on the coast of Massachusetts, but, says Mr. Allen, in his "Notes on the Rarer Birds of Massachusetts," "they were formerly known to breed in the Chelsea marshes, and probably do still." Wilson speaks of the Sea-side Finch as "keeping almost continually within the boundaries of tide water," and adds that "amidst the recesses of these wet sea marshes it seeks the rankest growth of grass, and sea weed, and climbs along the stalks of the rushes with as much dexterity as it runs along the ground, which is rather a singular circumstance, most of our climbers being rather awkward at running."[60]

(d). Their notes are said to be a *chirp*, and a song, hardly worthy of the name, which is somewhat like that of the Yellow-winged Sparrow.

(B) CAUDACUTUS. *Sharp-tailed Finch.*

(A summer-resident in Massachusetts, but rare, being confined to a few marshes and other places.)

(a). About 5½ inches long. Tail-feathers more sharply pointed than in *maritimus*. (Edge of the wing, yellowish.) Crown, brownish, black-streaked, and with a median line. *Superciliary line, and sides of the head, orange-brown.* Ear-patch, and back, brown or gray, olive-tinted; the latter dark-streaked (with feathers pale-edged). Beneath, white; breast, brownish-yellow, black-streaked.

(b). The nest and eggs resemble very exactly those of the Sea-side Finch, being found in marshes and on the sea-shore. The eggs measure about ·77×·55 of an inch, and are white, gray-tinted, thickly, finely, and usually evenly marked with brown, which sometimes predominates about the crown, or is confluent. Mr. Brewster says that they are not laid here until the first week of July, but these may belong to a second set.

(c). With the Sharp-tailed Finches I can claim no intimate

---

[60] Vol. IV, p. 68.

acquaintance. They probably do not occur to the northward of Massachusetts, where they are chiefly confined to a few localities, such as the salt-water marshes of Charles River, and those at Ipswich. These places they reach in April, and do not leave until October, or even the latter part of that month. They sometimes frequent the fresh-water marshes, but generally prefer the sea-coast and its neighborhood. They run very nimbly, and make their way so cleverly among the rushes and tall grass that one cannot easily see them except by "flushing" them, when they take a short flight and immediately drop to conceal themselves. They are already very rare in this State, and, I fear, will be soon exterminated here, as, from their scarcity, they are unwisely persecuted every year by enterprising naturalists. Their extermination is facilitated by their confinement to a few places, where they may be considered, in a broad sense of the term, colonial. Dr. Brewer says that their flight " is quite different from that of any other bird," and as I have myself observed, that " in flying they drop their tails very low."

(d). Their single ordinary note is "rather more mellow than that of the Sea-side Finch," but their song has little or no merit, and consists of but a few notes.

X. COTURNICULUS

(A) PASSERINUS. *Yellow-winged Sparrow.*

(A summer-resident in Massachusetts, but in many parts rare.)

(a). About five inches long. Crown, very dark, with a brownish-yellow median line, and a lighter superciliary line. Interscapulars, dull bay, black-streaked, and edged with brownish-yellow. Rump, brown and gray intermixed. Beneath, brownish-yellow or buff (obsoletely streaked); belly, almost white. Wings edged with bright yellow, and with a patch (the lesser covert) yellowish; otherwise corresponding to the back and tail.

(b). The nest is usually placed on the ground, in a field or pasture, is often lined with hairs, and is here finished in the

last week of May. Four or five eggs are then laid, averaging
·78×·60 of an inch, and normally are white, with a wreath of
blended reddish-brown and obscure lilac spots about the greater
end, and a few scattered spots of the former color elsewhere.
In some cases the markings cover the greater end, so that there
is no distinct ring.

(c). My own observations have shown me that the Yellow-winged Sparrows are rare, at least in some parts of Eastern Massachusetts, though common in others, during their comparatively brief residence here through May and the summer-months. Mr. Maynard, however, considers them as "not uncommon" throughout this district, being "very numerous on Nantucket Island;" but Mr. Allen is, I think, right in believing them to be more abundant in the western than in the other portions of the State, as, for instance, near Springfield. To the northward of Massachusetts they perhaps do not occur. They frequent almost exclusively dry fields, particularly such as are sandy or do not contain a luxuriant vegetation, and feed upon seeds and insects. They are rather shy, and often nimbly escape a near approach. They run with ease, and never leave the ground, except to take a short, low flight, or to perch upon the top of some weed, or on some fence. Though often more or less collective, they are never strictly gregarious.

(d). Their ordinary notes are a *chirr*, much like the note of some insect, and an occasional *chick*. Their song is so peculiar as to be quite characteristic, and may be represented by the syllables "*chick', chick-a-sëë*," with the chief accent on the last and highest of these. Wilson speaks of their "short, weak, interrupted chirrup."

(B) HENSLOWI. *Henslow's Bunting. Henslow's Sparrow.*
(A summer-resident in Massachusetts of rarity.)

(*a*). Five inches long (or less). Like *passerinus* (A, a) but "more yellowish above, and with sharp maxillary, pectoral and lateral black streaks below." (Coues.)

(*b*). The nest, which is somewhat coarse, is built upon the ground. "The eggs," says Dr. Brewer, "five or six in number, somewhat resemble those of the *C. passerinus*. Their ground-color is a clear bright white, and they are spotted with well-defined reddish-brown markings and more subdued tints of purple. The markings, so far as I have seen their eggs, are finer and fewer than those of *C. passerinus*, and are distributed more exclusively around the larger end. The eggs measure ·78 × ·60 of an inch, and are of a more oblong oval than those of the common Yellow-wing."

(c). The Henslow's Buntings are very rare in Massachusetts, though said by Mr. Maynard[61] to seem "more common at some localities in the State than" their immediate relations, the Yellow-winged Sparrows. Like these latter birds they frequent fields (and chiefly, so far as my observations prove, those which are dry or sandy), and are always on or near the ground. They feed on seeds and insects, and easily secure the smaller beetles, etc., from the facility with which they run and make their way among the weeds and grass. Mr. Maynard[62] has recorded that he "took two males in a wet meadow on May 10, 1867," whose "song-note" was "like the syllables '*seé-wick*,' with the first prolongedly and the second quickly given." I have seen the Henslow's Sparrows here only in May and the warmer part of summer; but, though Massachusetts is considered as their northern limit, I have suspicions, upon which I shall not here enlarge, that they occur in at least one spot among the White Mountains. I may add that this species was at first recorded in this State as Bachman's Finch (*Peucæa æstivalis*), an error afterwards corrected.

(d). Mr. Ridgway, as quoted by Dr. Brewer, speaks of "the tail being depressed, and the head thrown back at each utterance" of their notes.

---

[61] As quoted by Mr. Allen in his "Notes on Some of the Rarer Birds of Massachusetts."
[62] In his "Naturalist's Guide," p. 117.

XI. PASSERCULUS

(A) PRINCEPS. *Ipswich Sparrow.*

(A northern species, but lately discovered, reaching New England in winter.)

(*a*). Mr. Maynard describes as follows the first specimen obtained (though the italicizing is my own) : " Back grayish ; the middle of the feathers having a black centre edged with rufous. *Top of head* streaked with dusky and pale rufous, *divided by a broad stripe of pale yellowish white.* There is also a whitish superciliary stripe extending from the base of the bill to the back of the head. Ear-coverts grayish, with a rufous tinge." (Description of wings here omitted.) White wing-bars "rather indistinct." "*Tail brownish*, with the tips of the feathers and *terminal half of the outer web of the outer tail-feathers pale yellowish white;* the rest of the tail-feathers narrowly edged with the same. Under parts, including under tail-coverts, pure white. Feathers of the sides of the throat, with a broad band across the breast and sides, streaked with rufous, with dusky centres. The throat is indistinctly spotted with dusky. A triangular spot on the sides of the neck, below the ear-coverts, pale buff; ears dusky. Bill dark brown, with the base of the under mandible paler: Eyes and feet brown." Length, six inches (or more).

(*c*). That I may do full honor to Mr. Maynard, as the discoverer of a bird, not before described, in a country well populated by naturalists of all sorts, I shall here transcribe at length his own remarks about the Ipswich Sparrow, which he at first erroneously supposed to be the Baird's Sparrow,[63] Professor Baird having pronounced it to be that species. This mistake, however excusable on the part of the latter gentleman, who is ranked as the foremost of American naturalists,

---

[63] Until within the last two or three years this latter bird, a species confined to the western United States, was known to ornithologists by one specimen only, one of those shot by Audubon "upon the banks of the Yellowstone River, July 26, 1843." Lately others have been shot, and their habits studied in northern Dakota.

shows the necessity of strict accuracy and the utmost care in scientific investigation.

Mr. Maynard says: "The Ipswich Sand-hills, where the specimen was procured, is a most peculiar place. I never have met with its equal anywhere. Years ago these Sand-hills, which are three miles long by three-fourths of a mile across, and contain about one thousand acres, were covered with a thick growth of pine-trees. Protected by these trees, and among them, dwelt a tribe of Indians, whose earlier presence is indicated, not only by tradition, but by numerous shell heaps scattered over the Sand-hills at irregular intervals. Indeed, even now the ashes of camp-fires may be seen, apparently fresh. Upon the advent of the white man, the usual event transpired, namely, the disappearance of the trees; and to-day, with the exception of a few scattering ones at the south-easterly corner, near the house of the proprietor of the Sand-hills, Mr. George Woodbury, not a tree is to be seen. All is bleak and barren. The surface of the ground, once covered with a slight deposit of soil, has become a mass of shifting sands. Many times has the present owner had cause to regret the want of foresight in his ancestors in removing the trees, as the several acres of arable land around the house are now covered with sand, including a valuable apple-orchard. Upon this orchard the sand has drifted to the depth of thirty feet. Some of the trees present the curious phenomenon of apples growing upon limbs that protrude a few feet only above the sand, while the trunk and lower branches are buried! The Sand-hills, in places, are covered with a sparse growth of coarse grass, upon the seeds of which, as I have remarked elsewhere, thousands of Snow Buntings feed. There are, in some places, sinks or depressions with the level of the sea. In these sinks, which, except during the summer months, are filled with fresh water, a more luxuriant growth of grass appears. Walking, on December 4, 1868, near one of these places, in search of Lapland Longspurs, I started a sparrow from out the tall grass, which flew wildly, and alighted again a few rods away. I approached the spot, surprised at seeing a sparrow at this late day so far north, especially in so bleak a place. After some trouble I again started it. It flew wildly as before, when I fired, and was fortunate enough to secure it. It proved to be Baird's Sparrow. When I found I had taken a specimen which I had never seen before,—although at that time I did not know its name or the interest attached to it,—I instantly went in search of more. After a time I succeeded in starting another. This one, however, rose too far off for gunshot, and I did not secure it. It flew away to a great distance, when I lost sight of it. After this I thought that among the myriads of Snow Buntings that continually rose a short distance from me I again detected it, but I was perhaps mistaken. I am confident of having seen it in previous years at this place, earlier in the season."

* * * * * * *

" * * * As might be expected, I heard no song-note at this season, but simply a short chirp of alarm."

The Ipswich Sparrows are now known to be regular winter-visitants from the North along the coast of New England. They also occur inland, as I observed two, who were extremely shy, in a sandy field at the distance of several miles from the sea.

(B) SAVANNA. *Savannah Sparrow.*

(A rather colonial species, locally common in the summer-season throughout New England.)

(*a*). About 5¼ inches long. With no bright tints (especially about the interscapulars), and rarely a prominent pectoral blotch, as in the Song Sparrow (XIII, A, who sometimes, however, lacks the latter feature), and *never* with a chestnut patch on the wing, or conspicuous white on the tail as in the Grass Finch (XII, A). Feathers above, brownish-gray, on the tail scarcely marked, but elsewhere pale-edged, and darkly streaked, most finely upon the crown. Superciliary line and edge of the wing, yellowish; a faint line dividing the crown, whitish. Beneath white (or buffish), with dark streaks, brown-edged. A little bay is to be found on the wings, and among the interscapulars.

(*b*). The nest is built on the ground, in the various summer-haunts of this bird. It is composed chiefly of dry grasses, and in Eastern Massachusetts is finished in the second week of May. Four or five eggs are then laid, averaging ·75 × ·55 of an inch, exhibiting great variation, and often approaching those of other sparrows. Some are dull white, faintly and minutely marked, most thickly at the crown. Dr. Brewer says : " In some the ground-color, which is of a greenish-white, is plainly visible, being only partially covered with blotches of brown, shaded with red and purple. These blotches are more numerous about the larger end, becoming confluent and forming a corona. In others the ground-color is entirely concealed by confluent ferruginous fine dots, over which are darker markings of brown and purple and a still darker ring of the same about the larger end."

(*c*). The Savannah Sparrows show a marked preference for the sea-coast, and the islands near it, and are to be found much farther to the northward along the coast-line than in the interior, where, however, they frequently occur to the southward of the mountain-chains in northern New England. To the inland, rather than along the shore, they are locally distributed, being the most colonial of all our sparrows. Though collective, they do not cluster as the swallows do, but many often pass the summer in one place, and several pairs frequent the same field, or the same strip of shore. They reach Eastern Massachusetts, where they are particularly "abundant in the salt-water marshes and their neighborhood," in the second or third week of April, but many soon pass to the northward.

They have a settlement, if I may so call it, at a place in the White Mountains, where I made the following observations. They there inhabited the fields and pasture-lands. In the earlier part of July they were seen in small flocks, or families, to visit gardens in the search of food ; and, even so late as the twenty-third of that month, a nest was found containing freshly laid eggs. As well-grown young were also then observed, they doubtless reared two broods ; and certainly until the latter part of August they remained in the fields where they had built their nests. Although they were eminently terrestrial in habits, and fed and nested on the ground, yet they not unfrequently alighted on the fences between the pastures, and by the roadsides, or rarely on the telegraph-wires. They were very nimble on the ground, often chasing the insects, which constituted their chief food; and usually, when frightened from their nests, they feigned lameness, and endeavored to lead one from the spot,—whereas the Bay-winged Buntings generally flew at once to some near fence. Unlike these latter, they did not often venture to the roads, except when autumn drawing near, they associated with the "Grass Finches," and followed their habits more closely than during the breeding-season. In September they seemed less numerous than in July, but wandered much more freely over the country.

In Massachusetts, a few stay until November, but a majority pass to the southward earlier, and I have never known any to spend the winter in New England. There is nothing very characteristic in their flight, which is usually short and low. They are often shy, and can never be closely approached when on the ground, and though they sometimes feed in gardens near houses or barns, they commonly prefer the more remote fields, where civilization is not busy.

(*d*). Their notes are interesting, as distinct from those of other birds, and so far as I know, are appreciably like only those of the Yellow-winged Sparrows. Besides a low *chip* (?) they have a peculiar *chirp*, which one might reasonably attribute to some loud-voiced cricket or beetle, and which also bears resemblance to the Night "Hawk's" ordinary cry. Their song-notes are very characteristic, and are drawly but musical. They nearly resemble the syllables *chip-chirr*, sometimes extended to *chip-chee, chee-chee-chirr*, or so varied as to be a song.

In describing three common birds, frequently confused by the ignorant or inexperienced, namely :—the Savannah Finch, the Bay-winged Bunting, and the Song Sparrow, I have endeavored to mark the characteristic differences so as to render their identification a matter of no difficulty. These streaked species, as well as their ground-nesting relations, are often indiscriminately called "Ground Sparrows;" and likewise a sparrow's nest found in a bush is referred to the equally vague "Bush Sparrow." One may often hear it said that "the Ground Sparrow sings charmingly," but whether this refers to the Field, Song, or Bay-winged Sparrow, it is impossible to say, though doubts are lessened if the bird is described as streaked beneath. It is to be observed that the Savannah Sparrows (with generally dull tints) are most common near the sea, often frequenting marshes, and, like the Yellow-winged Sparrows (unstreaked beneath) who have a preference for dry and sandy fields, are quaintly but not sweetly musical. The Song Sparrows (with generally bright tints) to a certain extent, as the Swamp Sparrows (unstreaked beneath) do exclusively, pass their time in swamps and meadows, and are both sweet musicians, as the Bay-winged Buntings, characterized by their conspicuously white outer tail-feathers, also are. The little "Chippers" and Field Sparrows (*unlike* the above mentioned "Yellow-wings") are brightly tinted above, and (*like* them) unstreaked below, the former having the breast light gray, the other pale brown or buff. The former is often found in the immediate neighborhood of man, and is unmusical, but the latter sings most charmingly from the fields, pastures, and bushy "scrub," which he is ever in. The little streaked female of the Purple Finch, a mellow warbler, should be kept distinct, as should the Lincoln's and the Henslow's Sparrows, who are, however, very rare in Massachusetts, especially the Lincoln's Finch.

XII. POÖCETES

(A) GRAMINEUS. "*Grass Finch.*" *Bay-winged Bunting. Bay-winged Sparrow. Vesper Sparrow.*

(A common resident in New England, except in the winter-season.)

(*a*). About six inches long. *A patch on the wing* (the lesser covert), *chestnut. The outer tail-feathers, white.* Above, grayish-brown, darkly streaked, most finely on the crown, which is not divided. Below, white (often buff-tinged); breast and sides streaked with brown or black. Wings marked with bay. Eye-ring white.

(*b*). The nest is invariably placed on the ground, generally in a pasture or field. It is lined with fine roots, dried grasses, or horse-hairs. In Massachusetts two sets of eggs are laid, one in the last week of May or earlier, and the other a month or more later, each containing four or five. These average ·80 × ·60 of an inch, but exhibit several variations in coloration. One specimen before me is white, irregularly spotted and blotched with a rather light reddish-brown and extremely faint lilac, and measures ·87 × ·65 of an inch. Another is dull livid white, with fine but almost invisible markings scattered over the egg, and a few large umber-brown spots, some of which are surmounted with black. These forms are almost two extremes. A third has scrawls and vermiculations on it, and there are still others entirely distinct in character.

(*c*). The Bay-winged Buntings, with the exception of the Song Sparrows and "Chippers," and perhaps the Goldfinches, are the most abundant members of their family to be found in New England, during summer. Though they sometimes reach Eastern Massachusetts in March, they more commonly appear in the second or third week of April, and become plenty before May. Usually a few only can be found here in November, the majority returning to the South in the preceding month. A very few may possibly spend the winter in this State, but I have never known such to be the case. In early spring, they are to be found in fields, pastures, vegetable-gardens, and ploughed lands, often in association with other species, or gathered by themselves. They are not so persistent in remaining on or near the ground as the Savannah Sparrows (being rather less nimble), are not so much confined as those birds are to certain localities, and are not, I think, usually so common near the sea-shore as in the interior. They have, however, a much more limited distribution, being found in summer neither so far to the northward or southward.

The so-called Grass Finches, though they spend much of their time on the ground, often alight on the ridge-poles of barns, and on fences, or on telegraph-wires,— generally those by the roadside, where fields are near at hand. They often venture to the roads, where they pick up food, and sometimes dust themselves, generally being undisturbed by a near approach. When approached in the fields, they often run ahead, if a person walks behind, occasionally "squatting," so to speak, as if to rest. The whole or partial whiteness of their outer tail-feathers, noticeable as the birds fly, renders the Bay-winged Buntings easily recognizable. These finches build their nests in fields and pasture-lands, usually produce their first set of eggs in the early part of May, and raise two or even three broods in the course of one summer, so that their duties to their young are often not completed until August. In the latter part of that month, and later in the season, they are chiefly gregarious, and, perhaps associated with Song or Savannah Sparrows, frequent in large flocks the roadsides, and their other feeding-grounds. Their flights are less confined than those of the Savannah Finches, though they are not much on the wing. They are, however, bolder than those birds, though like them they avoid to a certain extent the neighborhood of houses.

(*d*). The song of the Bay-winged Buntings is quite loud and clear, and resembles that of the Song Sparrow, but is entirely distinct, and rather sweeter though less lively. It often may be heard in the heat of a summer-noon, but is more often repeated towards dusk, whence the name of "Vesper Sparrow." It is my impression that I have heard it once or twice at night, and I have certainly heard it in October. Their ordinary note, a *chip*, is in no way characteristic.

XIII. MELOSPIZA.

(A) MELODIA. *Song Sparrow.*

(A resident in Massachusetts throughout the year. In summer very abundant in all the New England States.)

(*a*). 5¾-6½ inches long. (Head-markings, never prominent, are as follows : — crown bay, finely streaked with black ; median and superciliary stripes, impure white; side-markings often vague). *Interscapulars*, *bright reddish-brown* (or "bay"), pale-edged, and *black-streaked*. Tail brown, sometimes faintly barred. (Rump, brown with a few markings.) Under parts, white (shaded with brown behind), with black streaks, brown-edged, on the breast and sides, generally coalescing into a conspicuous blotch on the former (and into maxillary stripes). Wings in no contrast to the back.

(*b*). The nest is composed of dried leaves, stalks, grasses and the like, and is often bulky. The lining consists of finer materials of the same sort, or of horse-hairs. The nest is most often placed upon the ground in fields and pastures, frequently under shelter of a bush or tussock; less commonly in bushes and thickets on or near meadows, or in shrubbery and hedges near houses. Wilson speaks of one found in a cedar-tree, five or six feet from the ground; and I have seen or heard of several peculiar specimens, such as one built in a broken jar. The eggs vary considerably in size, and greatly in coloration, often resembling those of other species. In Eastern Massachusetts two or three sets of four or five (rarely six) are usually laid in the course of the season, the first appearing about the first of May, or even earlier, when snow is on the ground. Several different specimens are now before me. The first measures ·85 × ·60 of an inch, and is dull white (perhaps green-*tinged*), faintly but thickly blotched with a purple-tinged brown. The second is elliptical, measuring ·78 × ·60 of an inch, and is dull white, thickly but irregularly marked with the same purple-tinged brown of a somewhat darker shade, and with traces of lilac. The third is almost elliptical, measures ·80 × ·58 of an inch, and is marked thickly but finely with brown and lilac. The fourth measures ·78 × ·55 of an inch, and is white, tinged with greenish gray, and minutely marked with sandy brown, a little lilac, and one or two black scrawls near the crown. The fifth is light blue, greenish-tinged, finely marked and also irregularly blotched, chiefly at the crown, with Vandyke-brown and a little lilac, and measures ·78 × ·58. of an inch. The sixth measures ·77 × ·55 of an inch, and is of a light but bright greenish blue, chiefly marked by cloudings of Vandyke-brown (in some places umber) and lilac, grouped in an irregular ring about the larger end. A seventh resembles strongly the ordinary egg of the Swamp Sparrow, and another is dull white, with markings so feeble as to be almost invisible. Still other forms exist, with various combinations, to detail all of which would be impossible.

(c). On winter-days one may sometimes see certain small birds, skulking from thicket to thicket in the swamps, or other cheerless places, occasionally hopping on the ground to pick up the seeds which have fallen from the weeds upon the snow, now and then emitting a rather melancholy note; and these are the Song Sparrows, for a few always pass the winter in Eastern Massachusetts, though strange to say much less common, at least in one township, during the past very mild winter than in the preceding one, an extraordinarily severe season. This was also the case with the Robins. Besides having seen the Song Sparrows, I have also heard their song near Boston, in every month of the year,[64] but in winter they are rare. About the middle of March they first practise their spring carols; and those who have passed the colder weather in the South then return to their spring-haunts. During the latter part of March and early April they are extremely abundant, particularly in swamps and about vegetable-gardens, and in those places associate with other species, especially the Fox-colored Sparrows. They also become less shy than they are in winter, and some, to a certain extent, frequent shrubbery about houses, where, however, I have known one to remain throughout the year. Wherever they may be, at this season, they are in full song, and their haunts resound with the confusion of a hundred melodies poured out by these birds and their associates. Though the Song Sparrows cannot properly be called gregarious, yet in spring they often collect in large

---

[64] Mr. Maynard also says (in "The Naturalist's Guide," p. 118):—"Mr. Brewster informs me that he has taken it (*i. e.* the Song Sparrow) every month in the year; has even heard it sing in January."

numbers at their feeding-grounds; but gradually many leave us to pass the summer in a more northern country, and others begin to build their nests here. During the breeding-season they occupy the neighborhood of these nests, the various situations of which have already been mentioned. In many localities, other than those in which I have made my own observations, such as the fields and pasture-lands of the interior, and those of New Hampshire or Maine, they perhaps pass the spring as they do the summer, in those fields and their immediate surroundings. In such places they are probably in the former season less common and less gregarious than in the country previously described. As they raise two or three broods every year, it is not until August (or a little earlier) that they are freed from their household cares. Like several other birds, they divide the labors of rearing their young, and the males, while their mates rear one brood, often build the nest for another, and are busied until summer is well advanced. Later in the year they collect at their feeding-grounds, but not so abundantly as in the spring, since the fall-migrations of this species extend through a greater length of time than the others. During the former the Song Sparrows are most common throughout a part of September and October, and associate with various other finches, rather preferring, at this season, dry grounds to the swamps. It is impossible, however, to exactly define the nature of the places in which they may then be usually found. After the middle of October, they appear and disappear until only those are left who pass the winter with us. At all times of the year, except during the mating-season, they are rather shy, and, when startled, almost invariably dive into some near brush-heap or thicket, where they are well concealed. They commonly prefer the neighborhood of the ground, running quite nimbly on it, but much more often perch in trees, even at a considerable height, than is commonly supposed. They have a gently undulating flight, flying low and never very far.

In summer they are to be found throughout a greater part of northern North America, even so far to the southward as the Gulf of Mexico (though in the West represented by several varieties), being abundant and well known in almost all parts of New England; and, indeed, in a majority of places they are, with the exception of the Chipping Sparrows, the most common of all the finches. It is impossible to define accurately all their haunts, since these vary according to the nature of the country, and somewhat according to the seasons; but their haunts, and moreover all those minor habits which have not been fully detailed, may easily be learned by the ornithological experience of one or two years.

(d). The song of the Song Sparrow is sweet, lively, and poured out with an energy which doubles its charm. It has several variations, which might excusably be attributed to two or three species; but the one most often heard is that which they give utterance to in the spring. This is an indescribable song, characteristic of itself. It usually begins with a thrice repeated note, followed by the sprightly part of the music, concluding with another note, which, like the first, is often tripled.[65] The Song Sparrows have also eccentric music, peculiar to the mating-season, and in autumn often soliloquize. In the earlier part of spring they sing most loudly, in summer they are much less often heard; in fall they sing unfrequently, and in winter seldom. Occasionally they pour out their music, when dropping to the ground from some perch above the fields, with wings outstretched. Their ordinary notes are a characteristic, sharp *chuck*, or "hoarse *cheep*," as it variously sounds, and a *chip*, less often heard, which resembles that of several other sparrows.

The Song Sparrows, regarding man's so-called "interests," are neutral, feeding principally upon seeds or small berries, but with those who know them are justly favorites, particularly on account of their sprightly song, which, if we except the Blue Birds' note, is the first to be heard in spring.

---

[65] See account of the Red-winged Blackbird's notes (§ 14, IV, A, d).

(B) LINCOLNI. *Lincoln's Finch.* *Lincoln's Sparrow.*
(Of great rarity in Massachusetts, occurring as a summer-resident.)

(*a*). 5½ inches long. Below, white; dusky-streaked, except on the belly. *Breast band* (and side-shading), *brownish-yellow.* Above, grayish-brown; crown and back streaked with blackish, brownish, and paler; tail scarcely marked. Wings with some bay and white. (Abridged from Coues.)

(*b*). The nests hitherto found have all been placed upon the ground. An egg in my collection measures about ·75 × ·55 of an inch, and is light green, finely blotched all over with a medium brown, which is purple-tinged. Dr. Brewer describes others, having "a pale greenish-white ground," "thickly marked with dots and small blotches of a ferruginous-brown," etc.

(*c*). The Lincoln's Finches are very rare in Massachusetts, a few specimens only having been hitherto obtained in this State. Their summer-habitat is an extensive one,—"the United States from Atlantic to Pacific,"— including the North, for they were "first met with by Mr. Audubon in Labrador." As I have seen them but once, my brief description of their habits is gathered from Dr. Brewer's account of them.[66] The Lincoln's Finch is allied in habits to the Song Sparrow, singing "for whole hours at a time" from the top of some shrub, often diving into thickets, and, when frightened, flying "low and rapidly to a considerable distance" (as the Song Sparrow does not) "jerking its tail as it proceeds, and throwing itself into the thickest bush it meets." Audubon found the Lincoln's Sparrows chiefly near streams; and apparently these birds are often gregarious, at least during the migrations.

(*d*). Their song is said to be a fine one, and is described "as composed of the notes of a Canary and a Woodlark of Europe." They have also a "chuck."

---

[66] My biography of this species was written before I had access to the works of Audubon.

(C) PALUSTRIS. *Swamp Sparrow.*

(In Massachusetts, on the whole, a common summer-resident.)

(*a*). 5½–6 inches long. Crown, bay (in ♂ in autumn and ♀, black-streaked, and divided by a light line). Forehead ("and nuchal patch"?), often black. (Side-markings on the head not prominent.) Side of head, and the breast, warm gray or "ash." Latter sometimes marked with obsolete streaks, which become more distinct on the sides (which are often brown-washed). Chin and belly, almost white. Interscapulars, bay, boldly black-streaked (and pale-edged). Rump the same. Tail not strongly marked; wings much edged with bay.

(*b*). The nest is placed in swamps, and on or near meadows, usually in a tussock of grass, but sometimes in a low bush. It is much like that of the Song Sparrow, and is finished about the middle of May. The eggs of each set, two sets being often laid in the season, are four or five, and average about ·80 × ·60 of an inch. They are white, tinged with gray, green, or blue, finely marked with brown (and lilac), and irregularly blotched or even splashed, usually more thickly about the crown than elsewhere, with two or three shades of a brown, varying in tint from sandy-brown to umber. I have seen eggs, both of the Song and Tree Sparrows, very closely resembling them.

(*c*). There are few things more charming in Nature than her first music in spring; and the simple chant of the Song Sparrow in March makes the heart gladder than the melody of the Wood Thrush in June. Yet the cheerful song of the former, when first heard to ring through the meadows, inspires but delusive hopes of spring, and it is therefore that the sweet but more modest notes of the Swamp Sparrow, heard later, may afford to those who hear them a more lasting pleasure. But this bird is unfortunately almost unknown except to the student of birds, owing to his continual residence in swamps, meadow-thickets, or even marshes, his rareness in many places, and above all his shyness. It is, therefore, with pleasure that

I shall endeavor, so far as possible, to introduce him to my readers.

The Swamp Sparrows are locally common throughout New England, but most so to the southward and eastward. They reach the neighborhood of Boston in the earlier part of April, and remain there until October or even November. They inhabit exclusively wet lands, chiefly those which are rather secluded, or which contain bushes and the like. They are shy, and it is almost impossible to study their habits except by penetrating their haunts and resting there motionless. They may be there observed to move from bush to bush, but not "jerking their tails as they fly," or to run quite nimbly on the ground, where they find much of their food, which consists of seeds, berries, and insects. They are not so collective as the Song Sparrows often are, nor have I often seen them perched in trees. On the contrary, they are very terrestrial, often scratching like the Fox Sparrows, or wading in shallow water.

(*d*). The Swamp Sparrows excel all our other finches in the variety of their distinct notes, and on this score are perhaps to be ranked as the first musicians of their family. Of these notes their mellow *chuck*, their harsh scold, and their song, bear a strong resemblance to the corresponding notes of the Catbird. This song is much less pleasing than the sweet, clear trill, much like that of the Pine Warbler or Snow-bird, which generally replaces it in spring, or their low warble occasionally to be heard in autumn. They have also a soft *chip*, a querulous note, and certain expressive twitters. Like the Song Sparrows, who sing chiefly in the early morning and at dusk, they keep comparatively late hours, and often do not retire until it is almost dark. I remember to have seen one at evening in the eccentric expression of his passion during the season of love, dart from a thicket, mount in the air, and take quite a rapid, circuitous flight, continually uttering a fine, steady trill, until, having returned to the thicket, he dived into it, ejaculating a few broken musical notes, after which all was still. Song with birds is often a passion, or the effect of one, and the chaffinches in France are said, when caged, and placed as rivals near one another, to sing until one finally succumbs, often falling dead on the floor of his cage!

XIV. SPIZELLA

(A) SOCIALIS. *Chipping Sparrow.* "*Chipper.*" Etc. "*Hair-bird.*"

(A very common summer-resident in Massachusetts, and almost throughout the United States.)

(*a*). About 5½ inches long. Crown, chestnut; forehead, black (former in ♀ often black-streaked). Interscapulars, reddish-brown, edged with paler and black-streaked. Rump, ashy (slightly streaked?). Tail forked, and dusky with pale edgings. Superciliary line, light; eye-stripe, dark. Under parts, white; lower throat and breast, very light warm gray (= "pale ash"). Two narrow white bars on the wings, which otherwise accord with the back and tail. (Bill black, occasionally paler; never reddish as in *pusillus*.)

(*b*). The nest is almost invariably composed of fine rootlets (occasionally—in pastures—of straw, and therefore comparatively bulky), and is lined with horse-hairs, whence the name "Hair-bird." I have one made entirely of white hairs, and strikingly different from all other specimens of bird-architecture. The nest is usually placed, not far from the ground,[67] in shrubbery near houses, in piazza-vines, or in cedar-trees — particularly those in pastures; also not infrequently in pines or orchard-trees, and less often in shade-trees. The eggs average ·68 × ·48 of an inch, and are light but bright bluish-green, with dark purplish and black markings, which form a ring about the large end (and are rarely like the scrawls on the eggs of the blackbirds, § 17, IV). In Massachusetts, two sets of four or five are usually laid every year, the first of which commonly appears about the first of June.

(*c*). The Chipping Sparrows are the most familiar and abundant summer-residents in Massachusetts, of all the numerous finches. They reach the neighborhood of Boston about the

---

[67] In a few exceptional cases it has been found upon it.

twentieth of April, but are not at that season gregarious, and about the first of May become abundant, soon afterwards beginning to build their nests. They inhabit more or less pasture-land, but particularly affect the neighborhood of man — to such a degree that they were formerly abundant on Boston Common, though they have lately been somewhat supplanted by the English sparrows. They frequent lawns, orchards, gardens, the neighborhood of houses, and public ways. They often obtain on the roadsides the small seeds which constitute a part of their food, and, when so doing, are rarely disturbed by the approach of man. They feed also very largely in summer upon small caterpillars, inclusive of the dreaded canker-worms, and are thus beneficial to man. Towards one another they are rather pugnacious, but perhaps playfully so. Their flight, never a long one, is in no way peculiar. They often perch upon fences, and sometimes between two narrowly separated pickets, which well illustrates their littleness. They rarely perch or fly at any great height from the ground, and indeed are not commonly to be seen in tall trees, unless in the lower branches, for instance of the pines, in which they often build their nests. There is hardly a populated district of Massachusetts where they are not common, but to the northward of that State they gradually become rarer, though in summer found in Arctic countries. In Northern New Hampshire, they are not very numerous, and they there collect in small flocks so early as August. In Massachusetts they congregate in September, sometimes to the number of a hundred, but do not associate much with other species. They disappear in the early part of October, and retire to pass the winter in the South. Before their departure they frequent the roadsides, or vegetable-gardens, where they can obtain abundant food, and may often be seen to pursue one another, uttering their rather weak battle-cries.

(*d*). Their ordinary note is a single *chip*, like that of the Tree Sparrow. But the "Chippers" also possess a variety of combined *chips*, and a series of querulous twitters, which they employ as a battle-cry. Their nearest approach to a song is a long, dry-toned, unmusical trill, which, from their perch on fence or tree, they often repeat during the breeding-season and summer. These trills have several variations, which are sometimes combined, one with a rising inflection being followed by a more open one with a reverse inflection. It is said that individuals have actually been known to sing, and very sweetly, but such cases are wholly exceptional, " et lusus naturæ."

The Chipping Sparrows are "so tame as to be fed with crumbs from the table," so fearless of man as to be much favored by him, and so common that they may eventually become as intimate in our households as certain birds of Europe are in those of their country.

(B) MONTICOLA. *Tree Sparrow.*[68] "*Arctic Chipper.*"

(In Massachusetts, a winter-resident, generally quite common and regular in appearance.)

(*a*). About six inches long. ("Bill black above, yellow below.") Crown, chestnut, in winter slightly marked. Superciliary line, dull white; eye-stripe (and maxillary line), dark. Interscapulars, bright bay, pale-edged, and black-streaked. Rump unmarked; tail, dusky ("black") with white edgings. Under parts, white. Sides of head, lower throat, and upper breast, ashy-*tinted; the latter with a dark central blotch.* Sides, however, and rarely the whole under parts, brown-washed or buffy. Two conspicuous wing-bars, white; part of the wing black. Wings otherwise as in *socialis*, "in keeping with" the back.

(*b*). The Tree Sparrows breed in Arctic countries only. Their eggs are strikingly like those of the Swamp Sparrow and allied species (XIII, C), exhibiting some variation. A specimen before me measures about ·77 × ·55 of an inch, and is of a faint and vague blue or green, finely marked with brown all over, clouded with umber-brown about the crown, and splashed in one or two places with a pale and peculiar tint of the same color. Dr. Brewer says that the eggs "measure

---

[68] Not to be confused with the English Tree Sparrow (XXV).

·85 × ·65 of an inch." "Their ground-color is a light green," "freckled with minute markings of a foxy brown."

(c). With the exception of the Snow-birds, the Tree Sparrows are the most regular in appearance of all the finches who visit us in winter, but who pass the summer in a colder climate. They are, moreover, more or less common during their spring (and fall) migrations. They first make their appearance in Eastern Massachusetts in the last week of October, or the first of November, but many are then on their way to the South. In the last part of the latter month they become common, and continue to reside here throughout the winter. They usually go about in small flocks, sometimes, however, in pairs or singly, but, when such is the case, several may usually be found in the same immediate neighborhood. They feed entirely (?) upon various seeds, and consequently spend their time mostly in fields where the weeds are not entirely covered by the snow,—in vegetable-gardens where the stubble of the summer's crop, or the withered asparagus-stalks, furnish them with food,—or in the roads and on the roadsides. When on the ground, the Tree Sparrows are quite nimble, which is highly consistent with their mode of life, since they generally feed when on the ground itself, though they sometimes perch upon the tops of weeds, and still more often may be seen in trees, frequently collecting in apple-trees. They prefer open grounds, and rather avoid the neighborhood of houses, though I have known one to join Snow-birds who were feeding on a piazza. They are not usually shy, and, indeed, I have seen them in village-streets, and have at other times approached within five yards of them, when occupied in picking up their food. When frightened, they do not dive into thickets or bushes as some other sparrows do. Their flight when short is low, when long is high, but at all times is rapid. The Tree Sparrows do not mingle much with other species, but seem to prefer one another's society, generally living in peace, though occasionally an unpleasantness takes place, when a brief combat ensues. In April they return to the North, but those who have passed the winter further to the southward than Massachusetts return at this season, sometimes lingering here until the second week of May.[69] These spring-migrants associate somewhat with other birds, and are, moreover, rather more shy than those who have been winter-visitors in the same neighborhood. I have occasionally seen them in the "scrub," when they were quite wild and quickly took to flight on a near approach.

(d). The ordinary note of the Tree Sparrows is a *chip*, which is more or less characteristic, and yet resembles that of the Chipping Sparrow. When they fight, these birds utter querulous but still musical twitters, which recall their own song, rather than any of the Chipper's notes. The following passage is a quotation from Dr. Brewer's account of the Tree Sparrows, and describes their music as fully as it would be possible for me to do: " * * * during November, the marshes of Fresh Pond,[70] are filled with them, when their wailing autumnal chant is in marked contrast with the sweet and lively song, with which they enliven the spring, just before they are about to depart for their summer homes." " In regard to their song, Mr. William Brewster informs me that they usually commence singing about the 25th of March. Their song is a loud, clear, and powerful chant, starting with two high notes, then falling rapidly and ending with a low, sweet warble. He has heard a few singing with their full vigor in November and December, but this is rare." " During the love-season, the Tree Sparrow is quite a fine musician, its song resembling that of the Canary, but finer, sweeter, and not so loud. In their migrations, Mr. Audubon states, a flock of twenty or more will perch upon the same tree, and join in a delightful chorus. Their flight is elevated and graceful, and in waving undulations." Just before their departure the Tree Sparrows, when in flocks and feeding on the ground, often produce an agreeable chorus, though at other times simply twitters. Occasionally in winter an individual emits a few musical notes.

From my acquaintance with the Tree Sparrows, I have almost

---

[69] They must not then be confused with the Chipping Sparrows. (A.)
[70] At Cambridge.

involuntarily learned to associate them with a winter's afternoon drawing to its close, a clear sunset, with perhaps dark clouds above, and a rising north-west wind, which sweeps across the fields, to warn us of to-morrow's cold. The almost mournful *chip* of these birds, as they fly to their nightly rest, has always seemed to me a fitting accompaniment for such a scene.

(C) PUSILLUS. *Field Sparrow.*

(A common summer-resident in Massachusetts, frequenting pasture-lands and the "scrub.")

(*a*). 5¼ inches long. ("Bill pale reddish.") Crown, rufous-red. Sides of the head vaguely marked. Interscapulars, bright bay, black-streaked, with pale edging (or rarely none). Rump, median, unmarked. Tail, dusky-black; feathers pale-edged. Wings (as in *borealis*, and) with two inconspicuous white wing-bars. Beneath, white; breast and sides *distinctly* washed with brown. (Line dividing the crown, and nuchal patch, both faintly ashy, or wanting.)

(*b*). The nest is placed on the ground or in a low bush, in my own neighborhood generally the latter, and in a field, a pasture, or the scrub-land. When placed in a bush, it is usually composed of fine straws, and sometimes fine twigs also, and is occasionally lined with horse-hairs, which is nearly always the case when it is on the ground. Each set of eggs, two sets being often laid in a season, of which the first appears here in the last week of May, consists of four or five eggs, which average about ·70 × ·50 of an inch, and are white (gray-tinged), with scattered spots of *light*, almost flesh-colored, reddish-brown, which are rarely so confluent as nearly to conceal the ground-color.

(*c*). The Field Sparrows, though quite common here in summer, are not so generally well known as they deserve to be. Though found in Maine, New Hampshire, and Vermont, yet Massachusetts is the most northern of the New England States in which they are common. In spring they come to the neighborhood of Boston in the latter part of April, at about the same time as do the Chipping Sparrows, like them not collecting in flocks at this season; and about the middle of May they begin to build their nests. Their usual haunts, in summer, are pastures, fields (rather seldom those near swamps), and the "scrub." In these places they feed upon seeds and caterpillars, and occasionally, to obtain the former, venture to the roads and roadsides. But they are habitually much less familiar towards man than their near relations, the well known Chipping Sparrows, and lead a more retired life. In September they collect in flocks, and leave us before October is far advanced. At this time they are bolder than before, and associate somewhat with other species — especially the "Chippers"; feeding on the roadsides, and in pastures, stubble-fields, and vegetable-gardens. Their powers of flight are not great, though they are quite nimble on the ground, and they do not ordinarily perch at a greater height than on fences or bushes. When frightened, they often disappear among the latter, but the female, when on her nest, is often courageous, and permits a near approach.

(d). As has just been said, the Field Sparrows occasionally remain on their nests (particularly when these are in bushes), until one can see them looking up with an anxious, appealing expression, which is very charming. Sometimes, however, almost always when the nest is on the ground, they take to flight, when one intrudes too boldly, though they at once return to the immediate neighborhood, and express their feelings by the utterance of repeated *chips*. Wilson speaks of their *chiruping*, by which he probably refers to their occasional twitters, but he says that they have no song. But the Field Sparrows do sing, and very sweetly, most often in the early morning and towards evening, though also at other times of the day. Their notes are sweet and very clear, and have been likened to the tinkling of a bell. They open with a few exquisitely modulated whistles, each higher and a very little louder than the preceding, and close with a sweet trill. But they are often varied; and, says Mr. Allen, "the songs of the males" in Florida " were so different from those of the northern bird that the species was almost unrecognizable by me from its notes." The little Field Sparrows, however, are always charming singers, and no sounds are more refreshing, on a warm afternoon of early summer, than those which they produce.

XV. ZONOTRICHIA

(A) ALBICOLLIS. *White-throated Sparrow.* "*Peabody-bird.*" "*White-throat.*"

(A common migrant through Massachusetts, many breeding in northern New England.)

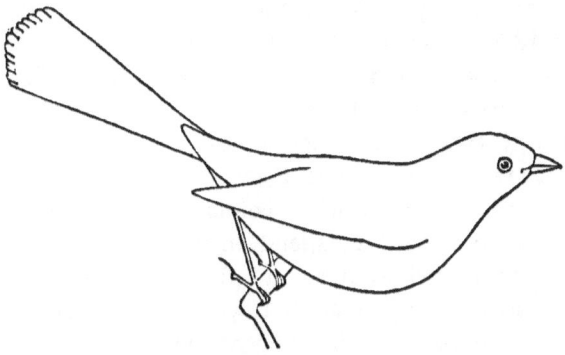

Fig. 9. White-throated Sparrow (⅓).

(*a*). 6–7 inches long. Crown, to just below the eyes, black, with a median line and superciliary line white, the latter, however, bright yellow from the bill to the eye. Sides of the head, ash, or warm gray; breast and sides, lighter. Throat and belly, white (the latter being separated from the ash of the head by a narrow black maxillary line). Back, reddish-brown, black-streaked, and feathers pale-edged. Rump and tail unmarked; latter of a vague grayish brown, former ashy-tinted. Wings with two white bars, which are not prominent, and a yellow edge. ♀, with less pure and defined colors than the male.

(*b*). The nest is built on or near the ground, in woodland, or sometimes pastures, and generally resembles that of the Snow-bird or Song Sparrow. The first set of four or five eggs is laid in New Hampshire about the first of June, a second often coming later. The eggs average ·85 × ·65 of an inch, and are grayish-white, finely marked and clouded with a *dark* brown. Paler types also exist, resembling some eggs of the Song Sparrow.

(*c*). The White-throated Sparrow is one of the largest, handsomest, and most charmingly musical, of all the New England sparrows.[71] These birds habitually pass the winter in that country which is so often indefinitely referred to as "the South;" and I have heard of but one supposed instance of their remaining in Massachusetts throughout the winter, which instance came to my notice (from an insufficient authority) in the year 1874, when another specimen was reported from a town near Boston, in the latter part of July. The White-throated Sparrows usually come to that neighborhood, when on their way to their summer-homes, about the twentieth of April or a few days later, but in severe seasons not until May. During their stay here, which is commonly of between one and three weeks' duration, they spend their time in stubble-fields, roadsides, cultivated estates, and like places (also rarely in swamps); associating somewhat with other finches, particularly with those who are migrating at the same time; generally

---

[71] Since I have begun this article with the use of the singular number, I will here quote an explanation of why, in ornithological writings, it has been objected to, in reference to birds. "It necessitates the general use of either the pronoun *she* (which is not customary, except in sometimes speaking of a bird of prey), or the pronoun *he* (which hardly generalizes to a sufficient extent one's remarks when applied to a species, and which sometimes causes an unintentional apparent distinction between the male and female or their habits), or the pronoun *it*, which is the worst of all. For to speak of animated birds as *its* and *whiches*, to any one who has studied them and regards them as friends, is as unpleasant as it would be to hear an acquaintance referred to by the neuter. By the use of the singular better expressions can sometimes be formed than by that of the plural, and the use of the pronouns *he* and *she* is sometimes effective or necessary, but, in general, the plural is preferable for obvious reasons. The following exaggerated examples require no explanation. 'The Crow is black. *He* builds his nest in pines, and lays four eggs in May.' 'The Robin is a common bird, and *she* is well known.' 'The Goldfinch, which is abundant here, is resident throughout the year. It sings in May, and lays its eggs in June, etc.' Though strictly incorrect, it is allowable by custom even to say:—'they lay their eggs in June,' but the plural sometimes is certainly undesirable."

being themselves in small flocks, though separate individuals may now and then be seen. They feed almost entirely upon seeds, which they pick up from the ground, but they are not very quick in their movements. They are rather shy, and, when frightened, usually fly to trees, not often perching at a greater height than thirty feet above the ground. They are not, however, so shy as never to come near houses, if they find the precincts attractive,. but they seem to be most bashful when they sing. Unfortunately they do not sing very much in spring, and, indeed, some naturalists have told me that they have heard them utter *here* only their ordinary notes. In summer, the "White-throats" inhabit northern New England (or the countries beyond), as for instance Mount Desert or the White Mountains. In both these places they frequent the woodland, especially that of "light growth," or the spruce-trees, and I have often heard them there near the tops of high wooded hills. I say "heard them," for one rarely sees them, because of their shyness. If I remember rightly, it is about the first of August that they almost cease to sing; and, as autumn approaches, they show less attachment to their summer-haunts. It is in September that they again make their appearance in Massachusetts, and, from the middle of that month until the latter part of October, they are tolerably common, though a little irregularly so. In the autumn their habits are much the same as in the spring, but they are rather less gregarious. I have seen a solitary individual so late as the fourteenth of November, and I have, moreover, occasionally heard these birds sing during their fall-migrations.

(*d*). The ordinary note of the White-throated Sparrows is a rather feeble "*tseep*," much like that of the Fox-colored Sparrows, and indeed of other birds. Their song is sweet, clear, and exquisitely delicate, consisting of whistled notes, which have been likened to the words :—"Old Sam Peábody, peábody, peábody, peábody."[72] This song is often somewhat varied,

---

[72] It usually begins with a note pitched at about D on the piano, followed by one higher, which is succeeded by several triplets (2–3), each of which is pitched a little lower than the preceding. It is sometimes prefaced by a few low twitters.

and again snatches or parts of it are sometimes sung. It is more often whistled in the morning and at evening than any other times of the day, and it may be sometimes heard at night. How often have I listened to its almost plaintive tones in the stillness and cool of the New Hampshire woods, and how charmed have I been to hear it sung at night, as one may sometimes hear it in the summer-homes of these attractive birds.

(B) LEUCOPHRYS. *White-crowned Sparrow.*
(A generally rare migrant through New England, breeding in the North.)

(*a*). About seven inches long. Crown like that of *albicollis* (A), but with the *median and superciliary lines* much broader, and *meeting behind*. Rump and tail, and the under parts also, as in *albicollis*, but with the colors beneath less distinct. Nape and sides of head, light-colored. Back streaked with brown (= "purplish-bay") and ashy-white. Wings with two white bars.

(*b*). "Eggs of this species, from Wyoming Territory, measure from ·90 to ·95 of an inch in length by ·70 in breadth, and are of an oblong-oval shape. The ground-color is a light greenish-white, thickly marked with reddish-brown and lighter markings of an obscure purplish-brown. The intensity, depth of coloring, and size of the darker brown markings, vary. They are principally disposed about the larger end."

(*c*). I shall not here give a detailed account of the White-crowned Sparrows, since they are closely allied to the White-throated Sparrows, of whose habits and notes a full description has been given in the preceding pages. They are very rare in Eastern but not so in Western Massachusetts, through which State they pass about the middle of May, and again in September or early October. It is in spring, when traveling to the land north of the United States, that they are most common. They do not often mingle with the "White-throats," but often reach the neighborhood of Boston rather later, and, instead of gathering in flocks, usually go about individually or paired. They feed on the seeds, and perhaps the insects, which they can obtain in swamps, stubble-fields, or on the roadsides; but they also frequent woodland. They are so shy as to escape general notice, the more so from their strong resemblance to the "Peabody-birds" (*Z. albicollis*).

(*d*). I have heard them sing during their brief stay here but once or twice. Their song, and their "tseep," are almost exactly like those of the White-throated Sparrow, already described.

XVI. PASSERELLA

(A) ILIACA. *Fox-colored Sparrow. Fox Sparrow.*

(A common migrant through New England, but never resident there.)

(*a*). About seven inches long. Above, bright rusty-red or fox-color; back with large, and crown with small, ashy streaks. Wings, rusty, with two slender white bars. Below, white; marked, except on the belly, with *chains* of rusty or fox-colored blotches, which are here and there confluent.

(*b*). The nests and eggs, as is the case with many others which are not to be found in New England, I must describe through other writers. Dr. Brewer says: "Their eggs measure from ·92 to an inch in length, and ·70 in breadth. They are oblong in shape. Their ground-color is a light bluish-white, thickly spotted with a rusty-brown, often so fully as to conceal the ground."

(*c*). The Fox-colored Sparrows are the largest and most strikingly handsome of all our sparrows, and as musicians are unsurpassed by any birds of that group. They are among the few land-birds that are known to occur in New England as migrants only, passing the summer in Labrador and other cold countries. While journeying to the South, they are in Massachusetts during the latter part of October, as well as throughout the following month, and I have seen them here so late as the ninth of December. Though they are then less often found in swamps, and do not sing, their habits are otherwise the same as in the spring. At that season, on their return to the North, they usually reach Boston about the middle of March, and are common for a month or so, a few even lingering until May. They frequent for the most part swampy woodland, unless the water be frozen, though also gardens, stubble-fields, the roadsides, and occasionally the immediate neighborhood of houses (usually, in the last case, only as individuals). They generally gather in parties of from five to twenty, and often associate with other birds, such as the Song Sparrows or Snowbirds, particularly the former. In the early morning their songs, when blended with those of these sparrows, form a loud and very striking, but confusing and misleading chorus. The Fox Sparrows are rather shy, when frightened taking flight to trees (especially the pines), but they pass most of their time upon the ground, where they feed principally upon seeds, and such morsels as they find beneath the fallen leaves. They have a peculiar habit of scratching much like hens, and thus turn over the pine-needles, etc., or rake the grass.

(d). Their most pleasing characteristic is their song, which is rich, full, loud, clear, and ringing, though tinged with a slightly mournful tone. It can be well imitated by the human whistle, but cannot be well described, owing to its several variations. It may often be heard here, chiefly in the cooler hours of the day, in March or April. It is sometimes abridged to a sweet warble, to which twitters are occasionally added. The Fox-colored Sparrows have also a rather dreary lisp or "*tseep*," and a loud *chuck*, which is more rarely heard. In my Journal is the following anecdote of a young bird of this species. "Nov. 24th. * * * * Observing him on a branch above me, I whistled the spring-song of this sparrow, being curious to observe his conduct. Whereupon the youngster swelled his throat, opened his bill, and apparently tried to sing, producing, however, only a few weak hisses. This he repeated several times, as often as I whistled. Finding, however, none of his companions about, as I had probably led him to suppose, he soon returned to the asparagus-bed near by." His instinct of song, and his futile efforts to answer my deceptive notes, afford much food for interesting thought.

If anything can add freshness to the freshness of a bright

morning in spring, it is the music which the Fox Sparrows produce at that season, and it is well worth the effort of early rising.

XVII. JUNCO

(A) HYEMALIS. *Snow-bird.*[73]

(In Massachusetts, common from September until May; in winter, for the most part, only present with the snow, or just before storms.)

(*a*). 6–6½ inches long. Outer tail-feathers, always pure white. In full plumage, slaty-black, with the breast and belly abruptly white. Often, especially in winter-specimens or the females, the black and white of the under parts are shaded into one another, and all the black is less pure, with brown edgings on the wings (and back), or is even replaced by a rich, warm, dark brown, which also tints the breast and sides.

(*b*). The nest is built on the ground (often near roadsides), sometimes on a stump or log, and rarely in a bush or low evergreen. Four or five eggs are laid about the first of June among the White Mountains, and often others in July. These average ·80 × ·60 of an inch, and vary from pale grayish-white, marked thickly and delicately, but very faintly, with lilac, to bluish or greenish-white, spotted and blotched, chiefly about the crown, with reddish-brown, umber, and often purplish. The nest may be found both in woods and pasture-land, differing from those of the various warblers in being much larger and sometimes coarser.

(*c*). The Snow-birds spend the summer in the woodland of the White Mountains, and other parts of northern New England (occasionally in the highlands of Western Massachusetts?), but in the autumn pass with regularity to the southward of their summer-range. They are common in winter from New Hampshire to Florida, and near Boston occur so early as the latter part of September, and so late as the middle of May.

---

[73] Often called the Black or Blue Snow-bird in distinction from the Snow Bunting, or " White Snow-bird."

They frequent, while here, the woods, roadsides, stubble-fields, etc., for the most part in small flocks, and often accompanied by sparrows. They are so tame as fearlessly to approach our houses and barns in the country, and they may be attracted to piazzas, particularly those with shrubbery near, by the scattering of cracked-wheat or oats. In spite of their familiarity, they are easily startled, and fly immediately, at the presence of real or imaginary danger, to trees or shrubbery. They hop quite nimbly on the ground, and while so doing constantly open and shut their tails with rapidity. They occasionally scratch like the Fox-colored Sparrows, or by a quick backward motion toss up the snow. I have seen them make passage-ways in this manner to reach the wheat placed for them on a stand, and such long ones that they disappeared in the recesses. They are quarrelsome, and in them we may see feebly reflected many of the human passions. They have, I believe, a topographical instinct, as is indicated by the prompt collection of apparently the same individuals on the above-mentioned stand, after the first fall of snow, at the beginning of two or three successive winters. They follow quite strictly, except in autumn and spring, the snow-line, often rather disappearing from Boston during the heavy thaws, and returning just before or with the storms. They are said to be common about Plymouth, New Hampshire, during the warm "spells," though absent in cold weather. In March and April they become rather shy, and are much among trees, such as the pines, from the branches of which they utter a great variety of musical notes. As soon as the milder weather comes, they migrate to the northward, and they are often scarce here in spring.

They are sometimes affected by a faintness or dizziness, which may apparently cause death, as I have several times found them lying dead, without a feather ruffled, or without a perceptible wound, and yet food was abundant at the time. Once, in walking through the woods, my attention was attracted by the sound of some object falling, and, upon turning, I saw upon the ground a Snow-bird lying on his back. When I gently picked him up, he fluttered away to a branch, from which he soon afterwards reeled and again fell. After a brief chase, during which he flew feebly, usually alighting on the ground, I again captured him. On being taken to my room, he was for some while listless, but afterwards picked up a few of the grains spread for him on the floor, though he refused water. He soon began to fly about the room, most often against the window-panes, and was finally allowed to escape, when he perched in a bush, where half an hour later he was found, looking rather forlorn, though sufficiently active to escape a recapture.

The Snow-birds, as I have discovered from several observations made in March, though early risers, are very drowsy at sunrise. They at that season usually passed the night in evergreens, and before six o'clock in the morning gathered at some lilacs and other bushes, where many slept or rather napped, for several minutes, near the ground, though others were actively employed. So great was their drowsiness that I could approach them closely before they made the effort to rouse themselves. Other birds, observed at the same time, such as the "Red-polls," Crows, and Robins, seemed to awake with a desire for immediate activity, except those who sang before leaving their roosts.

(*d*). The Snow-birds have a loud *chuck*, and cries of *chit*, *chit-a-sit*, or the like, which they utter particularly as they take to flight.[67] They have also in spring a great variety of twitters, trills, and even tinkling sounds, which are often so combined as to form a lively song. The notes which they employ when excited or quarreling strongly resemble the sound produced by the shying of a stone across the ice. Their trills are often so like those of the Pine Warblers, though more open and more like twitters, that it is difficult to distinguish them when the birds are together in the pines. These notes also differ but little from those of the Swamp Sparrow, in whose haunts, however, the Snow-birds rarely occur.

As the most common and regular of our winter-visitors, and

---

[67] See § 1, I, D.

almost the only ones who ever seek the neighborhood of man, the Snow-birds are certainly entitled to our affections; and their liveliness cannot but afford pleasure, when brought directly in contrast at our very doors, so to speak, with the cold and storms of midwinter.

NOTE. — According to Mr. William Brewster (Bulletin, Nuttall Ornithological Club, April, 1876, Vol. I, No. 1) a female Oregon Snow-bird (*Junco Oregonus*) was "shot in Watertown, Mass., March 25th, 1874." ♂ black; ♀ browner. Lower breast, etc., white. Back and wing-edgings, "dull reddish-brown;" sides paler.

XVIII. PIPILO

(A) ERYTHROPTHALMUS. *Towhee Bunting.* "*Towhee.*" "*Chewink.*" "*Ground Robin.*" "*Marsh Robin.*" "*Swamp Robin.*"[68]

(A common summer-resident in Massachusetts, but not common to the northward of this State.)

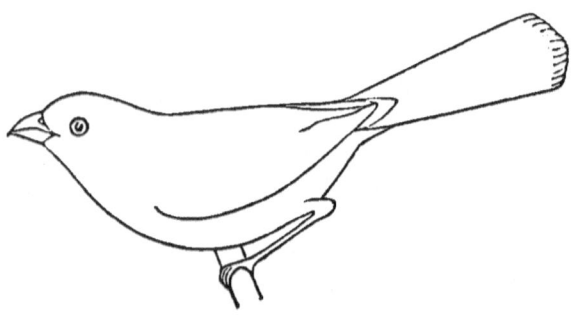

Fig. 10. Towhee Bunting (⅓).

(*a*). 8–8½ inches long. (Iris, in the summer-season red, except in the young; otherwise, white or nearly so.) ♂, black; lower breast, belly, and nearly the whole of the outermost tail-feathers, white. A conspicuous patch on the side of the breast, chestnut (with paler traces of it behind). Wings and tail

---

[68] This name has been applied indiscriminately to several different birds.

with some white, besides that mentioned. ♀ , of a *deep*, warm brown where the male is black.

(*b*). The nest, which near Boston is generally finished in the last week of May, is to be found in the "scrub" and low wet woods. It is placed on the ground, or near it in a pile of underbrush, and is composed of twigs, dead leaves, grasses, and roots. The eggs of each set are usually four, averaging 1·00 × ·75 of an inch ; and their ground-color is white, often tinged with brown or gray. The markings are usually very fine, rarely in blotches, and never coarse. They are sometimes most prominent about the crown, and sometimes are scattered evenly over the egg, often being very minute and numerous. Their colors are various browns, and occasionally lilac also.

(*c*). The Towhee Buntings are common almost throughout the eastern United States, though rare to the northward of Massachusetts, and not known to occur beyond the White Mountains. In other parts of the country they are represented by numerous closely allied species and varieties, as are other of our common birds, such as the Song Sparrow, of whom there are said to be no less than six distinct races in the West and North-west.[69] The "Towhees" usually reach Boston (which now includes much country within its limits) in the first week of May, sometimes earlier, sometimes later, and leave it in September or early October. On their arrival they sometimes appear in the copses and shrubbery of cultivated estates, but they usually desert these later in the season, and frequent almost exclusively swampy woodland, and the "scrub," often that growing on hillsides. The "scrub" is a low or bushy "growth" of trees, consisting chiefly of oaks and birches, which occurs for the most part in dry and hilly lands, particularly such as once contained pines. Here among the underbrush the "Chewinks" busy themselves, always on or near the ground, except when the males mount some low perch to sing. They search for seeds and insects underneath the leaves and decayed vegetation, which they turn over by scratching much

---

[69] Dr. Coues.

like hens; when disturbed, leaving the ground to eye the intruder, but, unless pursued, immediately returning to their former occupation. They may often be seen flying across the road or paths, with their broad, white-edged tail wide-spread. They never are gregarious, except so far as to gather in family-parties during the autumn and their migrations at that season. It is not always easy to catch sight of them, particularly when they are near their nests, which they conceal with extraordinary care, and often with much success. Though shy, they often seem saucy; and, while one person complains of their chirruping to and starting his horse, another says that, on the discovery of their nest, they express their sorrow so impudently as to rouse his indignation.

(*d*). Their most characteristic note is a "*tow-hée*," of which the last syllable resembles in tone the chirp of the Wilson's Thrush, though sometimes much more petulant. They have also a whistled "whit'-a-whit'-a-whit'," often repeated in the fall, when it sounds quite melancholy, and a loud *chuck*. The males have a simple but sweet song, often poured out in the early summer from some dilapidated fence or brush-heap, which may be represented by the words "che wé we wé, wee," the last being an indefinite trill. This chant is frequently prolonged by the addition of other notes, and, says Mr. Allen, in his "List of the Winter Birds of East Florida," "as is well known, the song of" this bird "at the north consists of two parts, nearly equal in length but otherwise quite different," though in that of "the Florida bird the last half is almost entirely omitted." Mr. Samuels speaks of their having moreover "a quavering warble difficult of description."

XIX. EUSPIZA

(A) AMERICANA. *Black-throated Bunting.*

(Very rare in Massachusetts, where it has occasionally been found in the summer-season.)

(*a*). About 6½ inches long. ♂. Crown, yellow, rendered olive by an admixture of black, which here and there appears in streaks. Back of the neck, and side of the head, ashy.

Superciliary line, and edge of the wing, bright yellow; breast paler. Other under parts, white; lower throat with a broad black patch, forming a cross-bar. Upper parts, dull brown; interscapulars black-streaked. Wings with bright chestnut, wanting in the ♀, who has less yellow, and no black beneath except in streaks.

(*b*). The nest is usually built upon the ground in dry fields, and the eggs are bright, light blue, green-tinged, averaging ·75 × ·55 of an inch.

(*c*). The Black-throated Buntings are extremely rare so far to the northward as Massachusetts, where, says Dr. Brewer, only two of their nests have been found, to which may now be added a third, which I myself found with fresh eggs, in the early part of June, at Canton. It was in a dry grassy field, near cultivated land, and such a place as these birds are said usually to inhabit. The female left her nest on my approach, and, after running through the grass, perched on a low fence, from which she, together with the male, watched me silently. These were the only living specimens that I have ever seen. The Black-throated Buntings, says Wilson, " arrive in Pennsylvania from the south about the middle of May; abound in the neighbourhood of Philadelphia, and seem to prefer level fields covered with rye-grass, timothy, or clover, * * *." They are " never gregarious; but " are " almost always seen singly, or in pairs, or, at most, the individuals of one family together." " Their whole song consists of five notes, or, more properly, of two notes; the first repeated twice and slowly, the second thrice, and rapidly, resembling *chip, chip, che che ché.* Of this ditty, such as it is, they are by no means parsimonious," and like " the Yellow-Hammer of Britain * * * they are fond of mounting to the top of some half-grown tree, and there chirruping for half an hour at a time." Wilson's description of their eggs is wholly incorrect.

XX. CYANOSPIZA

(A) CYANEA. *Indigo Bird.*

(A common summer-resident in southern New England, but less so to the northward.)

(a). About 5½ inches long. ♂, bright indigo-blue, darker on the head, reflecting green in the light. Wings and tail, darker, with much blackish. ♀, above, a peculiar shade of warm brown; below, lighter, flaxen-tinted, sometimes streaky.

(b). The nest is built in bushes or open shrubbery, not infrequently near a house. It is composed outwardly of dead leaves, dry weed-stalks, grasses, etc.; and is lined with finer materials of the same sort, or with hairs; often being quite bulky. In Eastern Massachusetts four or five eggs are laid in the last week of May, or later. They average ·75×.55 of an inch, and are white, often blue-tinged, and perhaps occasionally marked.

(c). The Indigo Birds are common in New England as summer-residents, occurring so far to the northward as Bethlehem among the White Mountains,[70] though, according to Dr. Brewer, locally distributed through Eastern Massachusetts. They arrive at Boston in the second week of May, and, during their residence here of about four months, frequent not only the pastures, woodland of low growth, and the "scrub," but shrubbery near houses, where they frequently build their nests, one of which, says Dr. Brewer, was occupied by a pair for five successive summers. They feed both upon insects and seeds, but principally the latter, which they often search for on the ground, even on the roadsides. They can fly quite rapidly, and in summer, even when there is no necessity for such wandering, often fly more than a mile at a considerable height, moving from one pasture to another. They are rather shy, and sometimes find this a convenient manner of escaping the annoyance of intrusion. In autumn they are gregarious, and associate in small flocks with other finches. The females are insignificant little birds, occupied, during their stay here, chiefly with household cares, but the males, from their bright plumage, glistening with the reflections of the varying lights, and from their music, so persistently repeated, except near

---

[70] Mr. Wm. Couper says that they breed near Quebec, in Canada, where, however, they are not common.

their nests, are always conspicuous, and ever insist on making their presence known.

(d). The song of the males is of varying length, sweet and lively, but rather weak, forcibly reminding one of the warblers. The Indigo Birds have also a *chip* and a loud *chuck*. Wilson, in speaking of this species, says:—"It mounts to the highest tops of a large tree and chants for half an hour at a time. Its song is not one continued strain, but a repetition of short notes, commencing loud and rapid, and falling by almost imperceptible gradations for six or eight seconds, till they seem hardly articulate, as if the little minstrel were quite exhausted; and after a pause of half a minute or less, commences again as before. Some of our birds sing only in spring, and then chiefly in the morning, being comparatively mute during the heat of noon; but the Indigo-bird chants with as much animation under the meridian sun, in the month of July, as in the month of May; and continues his song, occasionally, to the middle or end of August."

XXI. GUIRACA
(A) CÆRULEA.[71] *Blue Grosbeak.*

(I know no instance of this bird's capture in Massachusetts, but it has been shot on Grand Menan Island.)

(a). About 6½ inches long. ♂. Above, dark blue, almost indigo, with no reflections. Wings and tail, black; the former with a few brown markings. ♀, warm brown above, lighter and flaxen-tinted below. Wings with light bars.

(b). The nest is built in a tree or bush; and the eggs are light blue, averaging about ·95 × ·70 of an inch.

(c). The Blue Grosbeaks, so far as I know, cannot be properly considered as birds of New England, though they have occurred both in New York and New Brunswick. Mr. Herrick, in his "Partial Catalogue of the Birds of Grand Menan," an

---

[71] I am strongly inclined to place this species in the genus *Cyanospiza*, or at least a genus intermediate between that and the one in which it now is, but I have not ventured to do so. *Guiraca* may stand, if the Rose-breasted Grosbeak, etc., be called *Hydemeles*, as is now generally done.

island off the coast of the latter country, says that "in the spring of 1861, Mr. Cheney shot a fine ♂ specimen and sent it to G. A. Boardman, Esq., in whose cabinet it now is." This specimen has been spoken of as having been obtained in Maine, which I suppose to be an error.[72] The Blue Grosbeaks are probably closely allied to the Indigo Birds otherwise than merely by their coloration and structure, but I can ascertain but little about their habits. "They are" says Wilson "timid birds, watchful, silent and active," feeding "on hemp seed, millet, and the kernels of several kinds of berries."

(*d*). "Their most common note is a loud *chuck;* they have also at times a few low sweet toned notes." Their song is elsewhere described "as a rapid, intricate warble, like that of the Indigo Bird, though stronger and louder." They also sing at night.

XXII. HYDEMELES

(A) LUDOVICIANA.[73] *Rose-breasted Grosbeak.*

(A common summer-resident in Massachusetts, though still scarce in many places.)

(*a*). About eight inches long. ♂, with the upper parts, whole head and neck, black. Rump and under parts, white. A large patch on the breast, and also the fore-part of the wing inside, bright carmine. Wings and tail, black, marked conspicuously with white. ♀, with no white on the rump or tail, and but little on the wings, and with none of the male's carmine, that on the wings being replaced by saffron, which sometimes tints the breast. Upper parts, flaxen-brown, and under parts, white, dark-streaked, most thickly above, and most finely upon the crown. Eye-stripe, dark; line below, superciliary stripe, and median line, dull white. Wings and tail, plain.

---

[72] I have since learned that I am probably mistaken about the occurrence of this bird in New England, since Mr. Boardman (Proc. B. S. N. H., IX, p. 127) speaks of it as "very uncertain" at Calais, Maine, though "common in the spring of 1861."

[73] This species, having been placed in various genera, at last stands in *Hydemeles*.

(*b*). The nest, a rather frail structure, is composed of straws, leaves, or twigs, and is sometimes lined with hairs. It is often built in the shrubbery or trees of cultivated estates, but is also to be found in barberry-bushes in pasture-land, or oaks, etc., in the woods, especially damp woods. An instance is known of its being found in a pine, fifty feet from the ground, though usually not placed very high. The eggs, which are here laid generally in the first week of June, are three or four, and average $1.00 \times .75$ of an inch. They are marked quite thickly but coarsely, usually with rather dull reddish or purplish umber. Their ground-color varies from greenish-blue to dull olive-green. They strongly resemble several other eggs. (See the Key.)

(*c*). The male Rose-breasted Grosbeak possesses, combined in such a degree as few other birds do, gay beauty of plumage, and fine powers of song, though the female is plain, inconspicuous, and for the most part silent. He, therefore, absents himself from the immediate neighborhood of his nest, except when obliged to approach it, or when relieving his mate from the fatigue of incubation, as he occasionally does. He is rare to the northward of Massachusetts, where he is common in many places, though still locally distributed. He reaches Boston in the second week of May, and returns to the South in September, not being sufficiently hardy to withstand the cold accompanying a hard frost. He frequents not only lightly timbered or swampy woods, but orchards, groves, and shrubbery on cultivated estates. He feeds chiefly upon berries and seeds, and obtains the latter from various trees, such as the birches and alders. He also eats buds, often committing depredations on our fruit-trees, and he must be considered as injurious to agriculture. He frequently plucks blossoms, and, dexterously cutting off the petals, etc., lets them fall, while he retains the ovary which contains the seeds. He occasionally seeks for morsels on the ground, and may be seen rustling among the fallen leaves and decayed vegetation. He usually, however, remains at some height above the ground, and rarely flies near it. He is rather shy and watchful, there being nothing in his habits to render him noticeable.

(d). He is not always silent during the day, when feeding, but it is at evening in May or June that he sings most loudly and sweetly. Then, perching near the top of some low tree, he pours out an extremely mellow warble, like that of the Robin, but very much finer. Sometimes, in the love-season, he sings at night, and with an ardor which adds to the beauty of his song. There is a peculiar charm in hearing birds sing at night, for their music is more distinct and impressive in the general silence which there then is, and awakes the imagination. The cries of the owls would not seem so unearthly, were they heard only in the day, nor would they inspire such terror to the superstitious, a terror which the darkness naturally increases or partly creates.

The Rose-breasted Grosbeaks have as an ordinary note a sharp *chink*, which bears some resemblance to the cry of the little spotted or Downy Woodpecker, but is more like a certain note of the Black and Yellow Warbler. They are never gregarious, but occur here for the most part in isolated pairs, who in autumn are sometimes followed by their young. They are said sometimes to sing well in confinement, " though," says a correspondent, " one, which I had for several months, was for a long while silent, until one morning he burst into song, and sang gloriously for almost an hour, when he fell dead on the floor of his cage ! " The males sometimes warble when on wing, and they probably mount in the air, as they sing at night. Their merits as musicians will, it is sincerely to be hoped, ever protect them from persecution as occasional depredators on our shrubs and trees.

XXIII. CARDINALIS

(A) VIRGINIANUS. *Cardinal Grosbeak. Cardinal Red Bird. Cardinal-bird.* "*Cardinal.*" *Red Bird.*[74] "*Virginia Nightingale.*"

(Accidental in Massachusetts, and rare so far to the northward.)

---

[74] Not to be confused with the vermilion *Summer Red Bird* (§ 10, I, B). The Cardinal has a red bill.

(a). About 8½ inches long; *crested*. ♂, black about the bill, but otherwise of a brilliant vermilion, which is dull upon the back. ♀, dull brown above, much paler beneath, with vermilion on the crest, and traces of it elsewhere.

(b). The nest seems to resemble strongly that of the Rose-breasted Grosbeak, though more substantial. The eggs average 1·05 × ·80 of an inch, and are white, evenly spotted with (dull) brown and faint lilac.

(c). The gorgeous Cardinal Grosbeaks seem to have occurred occasionally in Massachusetts as wanderers from the South, and not merely as escaped cage-birds. They are habitually summer-residents for the most part in the Southern States, where they inhabit shrubbery, groves, thickets, and like places. They feed principally upon various seeds and grain, and are probably somewhat injurious on this account. Not only are the males extremely brilliant, and very conspicuous in their haunts, but both sexes sing finely.

(d). "They are in song" says Wilson "from March to September, beginning at the first appearance of dawn, and repeating a favorite stanza, or passage, twenty or thirty times successively; sometimes with little intermission for a whole morning together; which, like a good story too often repeated, becomes at length tiresome and insipid. But the sprightly figure, and gaudy plumage of the Red-bird, his vivacity, strength of voice, and actual variety of note, and the little expense with which he is kept, will always make him a favorite."

It is said that a stuffed specimen can never convey an adequate idea of the Cardinal Grosbeak's beauty, as the intensity of his color disappears very soon after death.

XXIV. PASSER

(A) DOMESTICUS.[75] *House Sparrow. English Sparrow.*

(An imported bird, common in many of our cities and towns, but not yet to be found in the country, with a few exceptions.)

(a). About six inches long. *Nostrils covered*. ♂. Above,

---

[75] This species apparently belongs to the genus *Pyrgita* (XXV).

reddish-brown, black-streaked; but crown, rump, etc., ashy. Forehead, lores, and *throat, black;* other under parts, brownish or grayish. ♀. Without black on the head; brown of the back rather grayish.

(*b*). The eggs are often somewhat elongated, the length being about ·85 of an inch, and the breadth sometimes no more than ·55. They are dull white, or grayish, marked with ashy, and sometimes purplish or dark brown. These markings are commonly spread over the egg numerously and evenly.

(*c*). The House Sparrows, or, as they are better known to Americans, the English Sparrows, have been introduced into the United States within twenty years, and into Boston within ten years. They are now abundant in many cities and towns, but the wisdom of their introduction is greatly to be doubted. They are extremely prolific, and it is not improbable that a pair may often produce thirty young in one year, for they begin to build their nests even in winter. This disproportionate increase, and their tyrannical disposition, render them dangerous to our birds, many of whom they have already driven from Boston Common. So long, however, as they confine themselves to their present haunts, and do not invade the country, they will not be insufferable. As to their value, though it is said that they have greatly checked the ravages of cankerworms, they are very destructive to fruit-blossoms, and they are now too pampered by luxury to be efficiently useful, being constantly provided with food and with lodgings. They are regardless of cold, and nearly so of man, but, except in their familiarity, they possess no charms, being unmusical.

(*d*). Their only notes are chirps or twitterings, which may be almost constantly heard.

XXV. PYRGITA

(A) MONTANA. *Tree Sparrow.*[76] *Mountain Sparrow.*

---

[76] Not to be confounded with the American Tree Sparrow, XIV, B. Several other European birds, such as the Serin Finch, and Goldfinch of that country, are said to have occurred in Massachusetts, but they were, almost without doubt, escaped from cages.

(But recently detected among our English Sparrows, being likewise imported birds. The following account of their appearance is quoted from the "American Naturalist," for January, 1876.)

"It will interest ornithologists to know that the tree sparrow of Europe (*Pyrgita montana*) has lately been discovered to be a resident of the United States.

"The resemblance of this species to the English house sparrow has led me to be on the watch for it since the introduction of the latter, but without success until I found it in St. Louis, Mo., last spring. Here I found the new species abundant, but was unwilling to take any until the breeding-season was over. Four skins sent to Mr. G. N. Lawrence, of New York, are pronounced by him to 'agree accurately with the plate and description of this species.' He also informs me that about five years ago Mr. Eugene Schieffelin noticed fifty or sixty of these birds in the store of a bird importer in New York, where they were unrecognized; and these were probably afterwards sold as or with *P. domestica*. This is undoubtedly the explanation of their occurrence here, and further search will very likely show their presence in other localities.

"With a general resemblance to the common house sparrow, *Pyrgita montana* is readily distinguished by its chestnut crown and the similarity of both sexes and the young. In St. Louis it considerably outnumbers *P. domestica*, and, as is the case in Europe, it prefers the outskirts of the city and the country. In other respects these two species closely resemble each other."—*Dr. James C. Merrill, U. S. Army.*

§ 16. **Alaudidæ.** Larks. (See § 15 *ad finem*.)

I. ERIMOPHILA

(A) ALPESTRIS. *Shore Lark. Horned Lark.* "*Sky Lark.*"

(Quite common in Massachusetts in winter, chiefly on or near the sea-shore.)

(*a*). 7–7½ inches long. Above, salmon-colored brown, vaguely streaked with dusky brown. Outer tail-feathers, black;

outermost white-edged. Throat and superciliary line, pale yellow. Large patch or crescent on the breast, and smaller one under the eye, black. Belly, etc., white. (In fall and winter-specimens, tints generally duller, and markings more obscure.) In living specimens the lengthened feathers above the ear form two slight "horns." Feet black. Hind-claws very long.

Fig. 11. Shore Lark (½).

(*b*). The Shore Larks breed far to the westward and northward of New England; but, though " seen by Mr. W. Brewster, in July, 1869," they have never been known to breed in this State. Their nests are built on the ground, and their eggs are grayish, thickly marked with brown, and sometimes lilac, and average ·90 × ·65 of an inch.

(*c*). The Shore Larks come to New England, from the North, in October, and remain until April. They may be found in Massachusetts, throughout the winter, in loose scattered flocks, often associated with other birds, such as Snow Buntings, chiefly on the beaches and marshes along the shore, and never, as a rule, very far from the sea-coast. In spring, however, when the snow has been much melted, they sometimes venture inland, and in ploughed lands, fields, and roads, pick up many of the seeds, and perhaps a few of the insects, upon which they habitually feed, or which at least afford them satisfactory nourishment. They are very nimble, when on the ground, where they are most of the time, but they have a singular habit of hiding behind stones or in holes, so that when man approaches he is obliged to play at "hide-and-seek" with them, before gaihing their acquaintance. They retire in summer to Labrador, where they build their nests near the sea, on the moss-covered rocks.

(*d*). The Shore Larks seem to possess notes much like those of their celebrated European relation, for, says Wilson, they "have a single cry, almost exactly like that of the Sky Lark of Britain," and " are said to sing well; mounting in the air, in the manner of the Song Lark of Europe; but this is only in those countries where they breed." Audubon speaks of the male uttering a very soft and plaintive note, when his nest has been disturbed.

The famous trait of the English Sky Lark, is probably known to most readers of this volume,—his manner of flying toward the sky, constantly pouring out his delicious music, until almost lost to sight. The poet Shelley has addressed this bird in these spirited lines : —

> "Hail to thee, blithe Spirit!
> " Bird thou never wert,
> " That from heaven, or near it
> " Pourest thy full heart
> " In profuse strains of unpremeditated art."
>
> "Higher still and higher
> " From the earth thou springest
> " Like a cloud of fire;
> " The blue deep thou wingest,
> " And singing still dost soar, and soaring ever singest."
>
> " In the golden lightning
> " Of the sunken sun
> " O'er which clouds are brightening,
> " Thou dost float and run,
> " Like an unbodied joy whose race is just begun."

"The pale purple even
"Melts around thy flight;
"Like a star of heaven
"In the broad daylight
"Thou art unseen, but yet I hear thy shrill delight."

* * * * * * *

"Teach me half the gladness
"That thy brain must know,
"Such harmonious madness
"From my lips would flow
"The world should listen then, as I am listening now!"

The last stanza of Wordsworth's ode to the Sky Lark is also very fine: —

"Leave to the nightingale her shady wood;
"A privacy of glorious light is thine,
"Whence thou dost pour upon the world a flood
"Of harmony, with instinct more divine;
"Type of the wise, who soar, but never roam —
"True to the kindred points of Heaven and Home."

NOTE.—"The famed Skylark of the Old World" (*Alauda arvensis*), says Dr. Brewer, "can rest on a twofold claim to be included in a complete list of North American birds. One of these is their occasional occurrence in the Bermudas, and in Greenland. The other is their probably successful introduction near New York."

(*a*). Nearly eight inches long. Above, grayish-brown; beneath, white, or buff-tinged; above and below, much streaked with dusky. Outer tail-feathers, white. (Details omitted.) Young much more yellowish, and less streaked.

(*b*). Of two eggs in my collection, one measures $\cdot 95 \times \cdot 65$ of an inch, and is grayish-white, thickly and minutely marked with ashy brown, forming a dark ring about the crown. The other is tinged with green, is more evenly marked, and measures $\cdot 90 \times \cdot 70$ of an inch. The nest is built upon the ground.

§ 17. The **Icteridæ** (or *starlings*) include the blackbirds, orioles, etc. As Dr. Coues says; "the relationships are very close with the *Fringillidæ* on the one hand; on the other, they grade toward the crows (*Corvidæ*). They share with the fringilline birds the characters of angulated commissure and nine developed primaries [also scutellate tarsi, etc.], and this distinguishes them from all our other families whatsoever; but the distinctions from the *Fringillidæ* are not easily expressed. In fact, I know of no character that, for example, will relegate the bobolink and cowbird to the *Icteridæ* rather than to the *Fringillidæ*, in the current acceptation of these terms. In general, however, the *Icteridæ* are distinguished by the length, acuteness and not strictly conical shape of the unnotched, unbristled bill, that shows a peculiar extension of the culmen on the forehead, dividing the prominent antiæ of close-set, velvety feathers that reach to or on the nasal scale."

With the exception of the *Sturnellæ* (or meadow larks), who show an affinity to the true larks, the sexes are unlike, and the males are largely or wholly black, often highly lustrous.

The orioles are arboreal, but the other starlings are in a great measure terrestrial, being walking birds. They are generally granivorous rather than insectivorous, and are migratory and gregarious. The orioles, however, form a distinct group, ranked as a subfamily, *Icterinæ* (Gen. V). Bill rather slender, and acute, with upper and lower outlines both more or less curved; tail rounded. Birds non-gregarious, and scarcely granivorous; fine musicians, and clever architects, building pensile, woven nests. (Fig. 13.) The other subfamilies are:

Agelæinæ (I–IV), (fig. 12). Bill generally stout; upper and lower outlines both incurved; tail nearly even. I, II, sweetly musical; tail-feathers pointed. II, III, bill fringilline. IV, bill as in pl. 1, fig. 18. I, bill similar, but elongated. *Quiscalinæ*, or *grakles* (VI, VII), (fig. 14). Bill with the edges noticeably turned inward, with upper outline much curved, but lower nearly straight. Birds scarcely musical, but eminently gregarious. Nests rather rude, and never on the ground.

I. STURNELLA

(A) MAGNA. *Meadow Lark.* *Old-field Lark.* "*Marsh Quail.*"

(A common summer-resident of New England, and known to have occurred here in winter.)

(a). *About 10½ inches long.* Upper parts, sides, etc., brown, with much pale edging, and blackish chiefly in streaks. Outer tail-feathers, largely white. Median and superciliary lines, pale; a part of the latter, the edge of the wing, and the *under parts, bright yellow, with a black crescent on the breast.* The female is rarely more than ten inches long.

(b). The nest is built often on or beside a tussock, and usually on or near a meadow. It is composed chiefly of grass, except perhaps the lining, and is often ingeniously concealed by a more or less perfect arch. The eggs of each set are four, or sometimes five, average $1 \cdot 10 \times \cdot 80$ of an inch, though variable in size, and are white, marked with (reddish-) brown and lilac, sometimes finely and faintly, though occasionally with splashes. They are laid near Boston in the latter part of May, though possibly a second set may be laid later.

(c). During what are called the "open" winters, the Meadow Larks may be found scattered throughout southern New England, where they are common in summer even so far to the northward as the White Mountains. Usually, however, they appear in Massachusetts about the middle of March, and they may then be found in almost every broad meadow which is bordered by rising ground. Though they often perch in tall trees and in bushes, yet they are most often upon the ground, where, like the true larks, they walk and do not hop. They obtain their food, which consists of insects and seeds, from meadows, fields, and occasionally ploughed land. They fly with a rapid but intermittent quivering of their wings, usually near the ground, but not unfrequently at a considerable height. They are, when mated, very affectionate, often flying to meet one another, or calling back and forth. They are also shy, rarely admitting a near approach, and they frequently conceal their nest by an arch of the long grass in which it is usually built. In autumn, when collected in flocks, they are sometimes pursued by gunners, from whom, I suppose, they have received the name of "Marsh Quail," which is not altogether inappropriate, since "they are generally considered, for size and delicacy, but little inferior to the quail." They are in the fall even more shy than before, though in winter, at the South, "they swarm among the rice plantations," says Wilson, "running about the yards and out-houses, accompanied by the Kill-deers,[84] with little appearance of fear, as if quite domesticated."

(d). The Meadow Larks have a single rather shrill note or whistle, another note which is much like that of the Night "Hawk," a peculiar guttural chatter, and a plaintive whistle, consisting of four or five notes (of which the first and third are usually higher than those immediately succeeding, and the last most dwelt upon). Though subject to such variation as sometimes to suggest the songs of two different species, their music always expresses the same sweetness, plaintiveness, and almost wildness. It is uttered, not only from the ground and from the tree-tops, but very often when the birds are on the wing.

II. DOLICHONYX

(A) ORYZIVORUS. *Bobolink. Reed-bird. Rice-bird. "Skunk Blackbird."*

(A common summer-resident throughout the north-eastern United States.)

(a). ♂, about 7½ inches long. From arrival in New England until August, *black;* hind-neck, buff, interscapulars streaked with the same; shoulders, rump, and upper tail-coverts, nearly white. At other times like ♀; yellowish-brown above, darkly or blackly streaked (as are also the sides); wings and tail, dark, with pale edgings; median and superciliary stripes, and under parts, brownish-yellow.

(b). The nest is built upon the ground, in fields of long grass, or in meadows, and is more or less concealed. It is usually finished, near Boston, in the last week of May. The eggs are four or five, averaging ·90 × ·70 of an inch, and are white, tinged with brown, gray, or rarely green, and generally

---

[84] A kind of plover.

blotched, splashed, or clouded, with a dark, dull brown. The colors are, however, variable, occasionally resembling those of the Rose-breasted Grosbeak's egg.

(c). The Bobolinks are common summer-residents of New England, but chiefly in the southern parts. From other writers it may be gathered that they pass the winter far to the southward (being, according to Gosse, migrants through Jamaica), enter the Gulf States in large flocks during March or April, and thence proceed northward, plundering on their way the farmers, and in Virginia doing "great damage to the early wheat and barley, while in its milky state." They reach Boston (but never in flocks) about the tenth of May, and are soon dispersed over the grassy fields, orchards, and meadows, which are their summer-homes. There they may be seen in pairs, perched on some tree or fence, while the male carols to his mate, or walking on the ground in search of their food, which consists of seeds, of spiders, beetles, and other insects. There they build their nests, which are by no means easily found, being often artificially concealed by the parents, and naturally protected by the uniformity of the long grass everywhere near them. In the latter part of July, or in August, the males gradually lose their summer-dress, and resemble the females, with whom, as well as with their young, they associate, sometimes in great numbers. They then frequent the sea-shore, visit the grain-fields, and do mischief by eating oats and corn. They also begin their journey to the South, and may be heard flying overhead even at night, when their note is distinct in the general silence. What instinct or sense enables birds to migrate so accurately is yet unexplained, but how they can, as many species do, travel several hundred miles by night, is still further a mystery.

The Reed-birds "about the middle of August" says Wilson "revisit Pennsylvania on their rout to winter quarters. For several days they seem to confine themselves to the fields and uplands; but as soon as the seeds of the reed are ripe they resort to the shores of the Delaware and Schuylkill in multitudes; and these places, during the remainder of their stay, appear to be their grand rendezvous. The reeds, or wild oats, furnish them with such abundance of nutritious food, that in a short time they become extremely fat; and are supposed, by some of our epicures, to be equal to the famous Ortolans of Europe. Their note at this season is a single *chink*, and is heard over head, with little intermission, from morning to night." After attacking the rice-fields of the South, many proceed to the West Indies, reaching Jamaica, where they are called "Butter-birds," "in the month of October." Gosse adds that they visit "the guinea-grass fields, in flocks amounting to five hundred or more."

(*d*). What adjectives can describe the Bobolink in May and June? He is jolly, rollicking, madly happy, recklessly happy. Nothing sober pleases him; he perches on the elm, because its branches rock and wave in the breeze more than those of another tree; then he spreads his wings, and, bursting into ecstatic song, sails to the ground, perhaps caresses his mate, then soars again to another perch, and again carols. Who imagines that *he* has any control over his merry music? It is a scientific fiction. His song is like champagne, and his notes bubble out, when he opens his bill; and yet, just as too much champagne is surfeiting, so may be too much of his merry jingle.

From his notes originate his name "Bobolink," and perhaps the Indian name "Conqueedle" (of the orthography I am uncertain); and from them has been formed the following amusing version of his song, which, if repeated rapidly with a rising inflection in each part, illustrates it very well:

"Tom Noodle, Tom Noodle, you owe me, you owe me, ten shillings and sixpence:

"I paid you, I paid you; you didn't, you didn't; you lie, you lie; you cheat!"

The ordinary note of the Bobolink is a peculiarly metallic *chuck*, but there are also others less often heard, some of which are slightly querulous.

III. MOLOTHRUS

(A) PECORIS. *Cow-bird. Cow Blackbird. Cow Bunting. Cow-pen Bunting,* etc.

(A common summer-resident of New England, and notorious for the practice of laying eggs in the nests of other birds.)

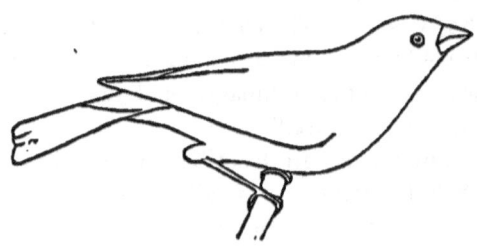

Fig. 12. Cow-bird (⅓).

(*a*). About 7½ inches long. ♂, iridescent black; head of a warm silky brown. ♀, smaller, entirely brown; beneath, paler (and often streaky?).

(*b*). The eggs average ·90 × ·65 of an inch, though greatly varying in size, and are white, thickly sprinkled, or finely blotched, with brown and generally faint lilac.

(*c*). The Cow-birds, like the Cuckoos of Europe,[85] present a most interesting phenomenon in nature, for, instead of providing for their young, they deposit their eggs in the nests of other birds. They are also, unlike all our other birds, polygamous, being equally without conjugal and parental affection. I shall here follow their history from the earliest period of their life, when they are left to the mercies or care of their foster-parents, among whom I may enumerate from my own observations, the Blue Birds, Golden-crowned "Thrushes," Maryland "Yellow-throats," Black and White "Creepers," Summer Yellow Birds, several other warblers, Red-eyed and White-eyed Vireos, "Chippers," several other sparrows, and

---

[85] Our cuckoos, who build their own nests, have been called "Cow-birds" from their notes.

the Pewees; also, on the authority of others, the Goldfinches, Meadow Larks, and Brown Thrushes. Commonly one egg, sometimes two, and rarely three, or even four, are found in the chosen nest. I am satisfied, from indirect evidence, that the eggs are often laid near the nest, if on the ground, and afterwards placed in it. They are generally laid later than those of the rightful owners, though sometimes earlier. The proprietors, on discovering the intrusion, occasionally destroy the foundling, still more rarely build over it a second story, or even a third, which becomes the nursery for their own young, or, in some cases, even desert their home; but more often, after manifestations of their displeasure, they adopt the helpless stranger. As the Cow-bird's egg is almost invariably somewhat larger than others in the nest, it receives a larger share of warmth, in consequence of which the others frequently become stale, when they are removed and destroyed by the parents. Even should the legitimate eggs receive an equal share of warmth, those of the parasite are first hatched, since they, in many cases, apparently require a shorter period of incubation. Thus the young Cow-bird, who is, as I have once or twice observed, hatched in the middle of the nest, is able to dislodge his companions, who soon perish, while he grows to fill up gradually the space left.[86] Carefully nourished and brooded over until well grown, and more than old enough to provide for himself, he at last leaves his foster-parents, and, with a wonderful instinct, searches out and joins his own fellows and kin. The Cow-birds lay from April until the middle of June; each female probably (from analogy) laying four or five eggs in one season, and presumably at irregular intervals rather than in regular succession from day to day.

These birds are gregarious throughout the year. Before November they leave Massachusetts, and migrate to the South, where they often associate in large numbers with the "Redwings" or other blackbirds. About the first of April, they

---

[86] As he claims all the time of his foster-mother, her own eggs are often suffered to decay before being hatched.

return to the neighborhood of Boston, where, at that season, they are most often seen in small flocks, in which the females predominate. In moving about the country, they generally perch on or near the tops of trees, and from the very summit of some pine their notes may often be heard. They feed upon seeds, and upon insects, particularly beetles, to obtain which they frequent roads, pastures, and ploughed lands. From their fondness of seeking food about cattle their common name has arisen. When on the ground, they move with an extremely awkward gait, which is ordinarily a walk, though occasionally more rapid in the pursuit of some insect. The male pays his court, such as it is, to several females indifferently, and these latter, when ready to lay, retire from the flock. They become anxious, skulk about from bush to bush and tree to tree, as if troubled by a guilty conscience, and watch the motions of the smaller birds. On discovering a nest, they seize the opportunity of absence on the part of its owners to drop their eggs, and then return to their companions, relieved of anxiety. After these ceremonies one both hears and sees less of the Cow-birds than before, until the autumn, when, joined by their young, they often form large flocks. They are then chiefly dependent upon seeds, and are less common in pastures.

(*d*). There is something ludicrous, and yet pitiable, in the efforts of the male to express his passions musically. It is often as painful to hear him and see him, as to converse with one who stutters badly. He ruffles his feathers, spreads his wings and tail, gives a convulsive movement to his body, and yet produces nothing but a shrill, unmusical *cluck-seé*. He often adds to this, or splutters out at other times, a chattering call, quite distinct from that of any other bird, or utters a few low guttural notes, not audible at a distance. He has in common with other members of his family a loud *chuck;* but he is not wholly destitute of musical powers. One may often hear in spring from the top of some tree, a clear, pensive, but rather shrill whistle, usually followed by a few similar but falling notes. These belong to the Cow-bird, who also whistles sometimes as he takes to wing.

There is much yet to be studied in the habits of these birds, and much that requires the attention of a specialist. Even the ornithologist who devotes his time to his proper pursuit is too much occupied in May and June to make the necessary observations. Few monographs in Natural History could be more interesting than one of the Cow-birds.

IV. AGELÆUS

(A) PHŒNICEUS. *Red-winged Blackbird. Swamp Blackbird. Marsh Blackbird. " Red-wing."*

(A very common summer-resident throughout Massachusetts.)

(*a*). ♂, about nine inches long, lustrous black; shoulders, scarlet, bordered by a color varying from brownish yellow to whitish. ♀, about 7¼ inches long. Back, etc., dark brown or blackish, with lighter edgings, median and superciliary lines. Beneath, white or whitish, sharply and thickly dark-streaked (except on the throat).

(*b*). The nest is built in swamps, and on meadows or marshes, either on the ground, when it is generally placed upon a tussock, or in a bush, the alder being frequently chosen for this purpose. Says Mr. Maynard: " I have found the nests on an island in the marshes of Essex River, placed on trees twenty feet from the ground ! In one case, where the nest was placed on a slender sapling fourteen feet high, that swayed with the slightest breeze, the nest was constructed after the manner of our Baltimore Orioles, prettily woven of the bleached sea-weed called eel-grass. So well constructed was this nest, and so much at variance with the usual style, that had it not been for the female sitting on it, I should have taken it for a nest of *I. Baltimore*. It was six inches deep." The nest of the Red-winged Blackbird is generally constructed of dry grasses or partly hairs (— occasionally also of roots), which are firmly attached to any neighboring branches or stalks, or which form a very neat hollow in the grass. In Eastern Massachusetts it is finished soon after the middle of May. The eggs of each set are four or five, average $1.00 \times .75$ of an inch, and are very faintly blue, with a few scrawls and often blotches (chiefly at the larger end) of dark brown, black, and rarely lilac.

(c). The Red-winged Blackbirds pass the winter in many of the Southern States. Wilson, in recording his observations there, says: " Sometimes they appeared driving about like an enormous black cloud carried before the wind, varying its shape every moment. Sometimes suddenly rising from the fields, around me with a noise like thunder; while the glittering of innumerable wings of the brightest vermilion amid the black cloud they formed, produced on these occasions a very striking and splendid effect. Then descending like a torrent, and covering the branches of some detached grove, or clump of trees, the whole congregated multitude commenced one general concert or chorus, that I have plainly distinguished at the distance of more than two miles, and when listened to at the intermediate space of about a quarter of a mile, with a slight breeze of wind to swell and soften the flow of its cadences, was to me grand and even sublime. The whole season of winter that with most birds is passed in struggling to sustain life, in silent melancholy, is with the Red-wings one continued carnival. The profuse gleanings of the old rice, corn, and buckwheat fields, supply them with abundant food; at once, ready and nutritious; and the intermediate time is spent either in aerial manœuvres, or in grand vocal performances, as if solicitous to supply the absence of all the tuneful summer tribes, and to cheer the dejected face of nature with their whole combined powers of harmony." Though Wilson does not deny the great injuries which these birds do to crops, where agriculture is extensively carried on, yet he estimates at the time of his writing that they ate, in four months spent in the United States, 16,200,000,000 noxious insects!

The Swamp Blackbirds are to be found in summer so far to the northward as the 57th parallel of latitude, though in many parts of northern New England altogether absent. They are sometimes the first birds to visit us in spring, though generally preceded by the Blue Birds. They are said to have reached

Massachusetts in February, and even exceptionally to have passed the winter here. Ordinarily, however, they appear in March, though with no great regularity, the males preceding the females; and previously to mating, which occurs about the first of May, they are more or less gregarious. During the period of arrival, they may be observed flying at a considerable height in the air, and often uttering their loud *chuck*, though sometimes silent. Later in the season, they visit ploughed lands and fields, to obtain whatever suitable food they can find, walking over the ground in search of it, and, when frightened, betaking themselves to the nearest trees, where they frequently cluster in large numbers. They roost at night in bushy meadows and in swamps. When the weather permits, they frequent these by day, and also the open meadows, from which their notes are constantly heard. They soon mate, and in May begin to build their nests. At this time there is always more or less commotion in the communities which they usually form, and they constantly fly back and forth, frequently chattering. This is particularly the case with the males, who often perch upon some tree to sing or whistle, and who consequently make much noise about their family-cares. They are certainly most devoted parents, and often defend their nests bravely, even when intruded upon by man. In July they become gregarious, some flying southward, and in the early part of autumn they desert the inland meadows, resorting to their various feeding-grounds. " In the salt marshes, or near the sea, they collect in large flocks, which not unfrequently contain more than a thousand individuals." Hawks, farmers, and unambitious sportsmen, diminish their numbers in a certain measure, but not, I suppose, very appreciably. The " Red-wings" fly rapidly and strongly ; moving their wings with more swiftness but less regularity than the Crows. When perching, they often flirt their tails. Owing to the nature of their haunts, rather than to any natural shyness, they are not easily approached very closely.

(*d*). Their ordinary note is a loud, mellow *chuck*, or sometimes *check*. The variety of sounds, however, which they can produce is correspondent with their general noisiness. The chorus of a flock in spring suggests the combined creaking of many wheelbarrows, being an indescribable confusion of various unmusical notes. Later, their chatter, which has some resemblance to the Cow-bird's, though distinct, may often be heard, particularly when the birds are excited. The male's song note, "conk-a-rée," is familiar to all who live near his haunts; but also, as if not satisfied with this musical (or unmusical) effort, he frequently warbles during the season of courtship. Perching prominently on some bush or tree, he spreads his tail, slightly opens his wings, and produces what is no doubt agreeable to his taste and that of his mate, even if not wholly so to ours. It suggests the Cat-bird's song deprived of melody. He has, however, a far pleasanter note, a clear, plaintive whistle, which is sometimes merely "pheù," but which at other times consists of three distinct syllables.

I can at present add nothing of interest to the history of the "Red-wings," but any omissions may easily be filled by the study of their habits, which is attended with little or no difficulty.

NOTE.—One specimen of a western species, the Yellow-headed Blackbird (*Xanthocephalus icterocephalus*), "was shot in an orchard, at Watertown, about the 15th of October, 1869." (Maynard.) About 10 inches long. Black; head, etc., largely yellow; wing-patch, white. Female and young; smaller, much duller.

V. ICTERUS

(A) BALTIMORE. *Baltimore Oriole. Golden "Robin." "Fire-bird." "Hang-nest."*

(In New England, a generally common summer-resident, though rare to the northward.)

(*a*). About 7½ inches long. ♂, with the head, interscapulars, wings, and a part of the tail, black. Otherwise orange of varying intensity, but with white on the wings. ♀, with duller colors, the black being skirted or glossed with olive, and "sometimes entirely wanting."

(*b*). The nest is one of the most interesting specimens of bird-architecture to be found in New England. It is pensile, being from five to eight inches deep, and is generally fastened (near the end) to the bough of an elm or orchard-tree, where, often beyond the direct reach of all enemies, it swings with the slightest breeze, though secure from destruction by the most violent gale. It consists of plant-fibres, dry grasses, and such materials as may be accidentally obtained, such as thread, string, yarn, wool, and bits of cloth, all of which are firmly interwoven. Though its structure and shape exhibit much variation, yet it is usually enlarged near the bottom, and warmly lined, most often with hairs. It is frequently built be-

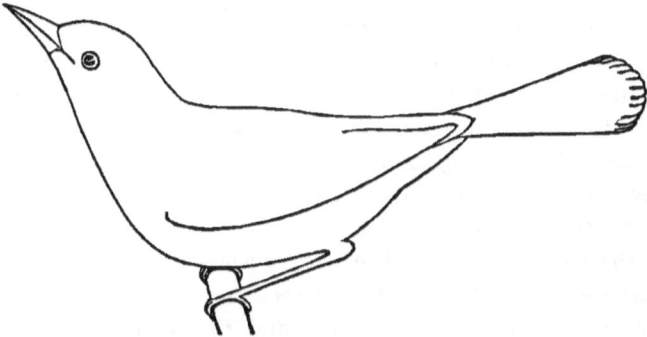

Fig. 13. Baltimore Oriole (⅔).

neath a canopy of leaves, so as to be sheltered from the rays of the sun. In Massachusetts, it is generally finished in the last week of May, or about the first of June. Dr. Abbott believes it to be built, when in exposed situations, so as to conceal the sitting bird, especially from hawks, but otherwise to be more open at the top.

The eggs of each set are four, five, or sometimes six, average ·90 × ·60 of an inch, and are white, feebly tinged with an indefinite color, or bluish, and are marked (but not thickly) with lines, scrawls, and spots, of brown, black, and often faint lilac.

(*c*). The male Golden "Robins" are among the few brilliant

birds that come so far to the northward as New England. They reach Massachusetts about the tenth of May, and are soon followed by the females. Though abundantly distributed through this State, they are not common beyond it. Wherever they go, they attract attention by their bright colors, their loud notes, and their peculiar nest. This latter structure requires the labor of a pair for a week or ten days. It is most interesting to watch its progress, but I have generally found it unsatisfactory to observe birds while building, so far as regards learning exactly the manner in which they work. The "Firebirds" are exceedingly clever architects, and a most skilful knitter would be puzzled to construct a piece of work like theirs, or even to understand how the original manufacturers produce it. They do so by fastening at both ends a piece of string, or grass, to the twigs between which their nest is to hang, by winding and twisting it around them. Having fastened many other pieces like these, so as to cross one another, and to form a loose pouch, they interweave other materials with care and skill, finally adding the lining. As Nuttall says: "There is sometimes a considerable difference in the manufacture of these nests, as well as in the materials which enter into their composition. Both sexes seem to be equally adepts at this sort of labor; and I have seen the female alone perform the whole without any assistance, and the male also complete this laborious task nearly without the aid of his consort, who, however, in general, is the principal worker." The young, soon after being hatched, clamber to the edge of the nest, and are there fed by their parents. They climb well, but sometimes tumble to the ground.

The Baltimore Orioles frequent our orchards, gardens, and the woods. They have a marked fondness for elms, and among them may often be seen in villages, or even on Boston Common. I do not doubt that they are beneficial to man, for, though they certainly destroy the blossoms of fruit-trees, they are chiefly dependent upon insects, and check the ravages of caterpillars more than any other of our birds. They feed also upon berries, and occasionally search for food upon the ground, where, however, they are but seldom seen. The male generally spends his time in wandering from one group of trees to another, often flying vigorously for quite a distance. Then perching near the top of some flowering shrub or tree, he deals destruction around him, while he whistles exultingly. He is apparently never burdened with family-cares, but, on the contrary, suggests the jovial man who frequents a convivial club.

(*d*). His whistled notes are loud and clear, but, though subject to variation, are often monotonous. They never form a continuous or rapid melody, but the same sounds occur again and again, especially his loud "*tu-wée, tu-wée*." They are much less often heard after the middle of June than before, and finally cease some time before his departure in September. When engaged in combat (as frequently happens in May) he twitters; at other times he utters a querulous *ank*. His ordinary note, however, is a harsh chatter, which becomes vehement, whenever he is excited.

(B) SPURIUS. *Orchard Oriole.*

(In Massachusetts, the northern limit of this species, a rare summer-resident.)

(*a*). About seven inches long. ♂, with the head, interscapulars, wings, and tail, black; a narrow wing-bar, white. Otherwise chestnut, or chestnut-red. ♀, rather smaller; olive-yellow or olivaceous above, brownish on the back, and yellowish (or "greenish-yellow") beneath. Wings, darker, with two whitish bars.

(*b*). The nest differs from that of the Baltimore Oriole in being less cylindrical and rarely or never more than five inches deep; in Massachusetts it is seldom finished before the second week of June. Wilson, speaking of a specimen, says: "I had the curiosity to detach one of the fibres, or stalks, of dried grass from the nest, and found it to measure 13 inches in length, and in that distance was thirty-four times hooked thro' and returned, winding round and round the nest!"

The eggs are generally smaller, less elongated, and more

spotted than those of the Golden "Robin"; averaging about
·80 × ·60 of an inch.

(c). The Orchard Orioles do not reach Massachusetts until
after the middle of May, and leave it on the approach of autumn. I have but seldom seen them, since they are rare so far
to the northward, though said to have occurred at Calais, in
Maine. As has been observed by various authors, they are
livelier than the Baltimore Orioles, and flirt their tails in a
much more marked manner. Audubon speaks of their sociability towards one another, observable in the South, where they
are abundant.

(d). They whistle more rapidly than the Golden "Robins,"
but their notes are very generally considered inferior and less
mellow.

VI. SCOLECOPHAGUS

(A) FERRUGINEUS. *Rusty Blackbird.* *Rusty Grakle.*

(Not known to occur in Massachusetts except as a migrant.)

(a). ♂, about nine inches long. In "high" plumage, black,
with chiefly green reflections. Otherwise, black, interrupted by
brown or "rusty." ♀, smaller and much browner than the
male.

(b). Mr. Samuels, in speaking of several nests observed by
him on the Magalloway River in Maine, says that they "were
all built in low alders overhanging the water: they were constructed of, first, a layer of twigs and brier-stalks; on this
was built the nest proper, which was composed of stalks and
leaves of grass, which were mixed with mud, and moulded into
a firm, circular structure, and lined with fine leaves of grass
and a few hair-like roots. The whole formed a large structure,
easily seen at the distance of a few rods through the foliage."

The eggs average about 1·00 × ·75 of an inch, and are bluish
or greenish, much spotted with brown, but apparently rarely
marked with scrawls or lines. These characteristic markings
are also sometimes wanting in the eggs of the Crow Blackbird.

(The irrelevancy of the following opening is due to the omission of an introductory paragraph, relative to the Rusty Blackbirds and their distribution.)

(c). As is well known, the animals belonging (or indigenous) to a country constitute its *fauna*. But, in a large country like North America, it has been found that different districts (bounded by isotheral lines) are inhabited by distinct groups of birds, or ornithological *faunæ*. In New England there are two *faunæ*, the Canadian and Alleghanian, which are chiefly separated by the approximate latitude of 44°, or the isotheral line of 65°. This line is just to the southward of Mount Desert and the White Mountains. Most species belong to several *faunæ*, but not, as a rule, to merely a part of any one. There are several Alleghanian species, however, who have not been found, so far as I know, to the northward of Massachusetts. On the other hand, several Canadian species have been known to breed in this State, chiefly, I believe, along water-courses (such as the Nashua Valley), or along mountain-ranges. Birds may often be detained or prevented from reaching their usual summer-homes, and therefore obliged to remain in a warmer climate, especially in the case of young birds who do not breed. Some species are distributed in an exceptional manner; thus the Red-bellied Nuthatches are common summer-residents in the Canadian district, and breed in the Carolinian *fauna*, but *not* in southern New England. I have likewise observed that the Great Crested Flycatchers are more common among the White Mountains than in Eastern Massachusetts. The Long-billed Marsh Wren, moreover, has been found in Greenland. During the migrations, especially in autumn, birds frequently wander several hundred miles from their usual *habitat*, and, even in summer, may occur to the northward of their usual range. Several kinds have even crossed the Atlantic, being driven to sea by winds, and afterwards alighting on ships. Finally in the list of wanderers are to be included escaped cage-birds.[87]

The Rusty Blackbirds pass the summer in northern New

---

[87] In the appendix is a list of the species belonging to our two *faunæ*.

England (chiefly Northwestern Maine?) and in all the countries beyond, except the Arctic regions. They winter in the Southern States, where they are frequently met with in large flocks. They reach Massachusetts in March, lingering into April, and return in autumn, when they are most abundant in October, though often seen in November. Whilst migrating, they are gregarious, and also associate, from time to time, with other blackbirds. They frequent wet places, particularly if bushy, though, in fall, they may be observed in woodland, often resting grouped in some low pine. They probably do but little mischief to the farmers near Boston, though they sometimes collect in ploughed lands. Their food consists of seeds, insects, and *crustacea*. To obtain these, they pass much of their time upon the ground, where they walk in the manner of their family, frequently jerking their tails. Though much less often seen near the habitations of man than the Crow Blackbirds, they are not very shy of man's approach, usually flying, when disturbed, to some neighboring tree or bush.

(*d*). While they are here, their ordinary note is a *chuck* like that of the next species. Their song-notes are not, as I have heard them, musical, but resemble those of the other blackbirds, particularly when united in chorus. The Rusty Grakles, however, are *comparatively* very silent, though said to have in their summer-homes a musical and agreeable note. Mr. Samuels says that a female, whose nest he approached, on flying "uttered a chattering cry, almost exactly like that of the female Redwing when disturbed in a similar manner."

VII. QUISCALUS

(A) PURPUREUS (var. *purpureus?*) *Crow Blackbird. Purple Grakle.*

(In Massachusetts, a common summer-resident in certain localities.)

(*a*). The following description, and that of *æneus*, is quoted (with abridgment) from Messrs. Baird, Brewer, and Ridgway, to show what distinctions these gentlemen believe to exist between the typical Crow Blackbird and the variety *æneus*.

"General appearance glossy black; whole plumage, however, brightly glossed with reddish-violet, bronzed purple, steel-blue, and green; * * * wings and tail black, with violet reflections, more bluish on the latter; the wing-coverts frequently tipped with steel-blue or violet. Bill, tarsi, and toes pure black; iris sulphur-yellow." About 12½ inches long. Female considerably smaller, and less lustrous.

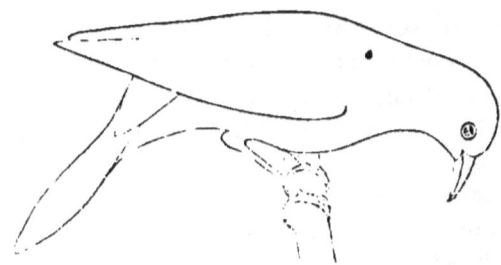

Fig. 14. Crow Blackbird (⅓).

(*b*). The nest is placed from six to sixty feet above the ground, most often in an evergreen, or perhaps occasionally in the hollow of a tree. It is a rather coarse structure, often cemented with mud. Its chief materials are small sticks, dry grasses, and other vegetable matter. In Eastern Massachusetts, it is finished about the middle of May, after which four or five eggs are laid. These average about $1\cdot25 \times \cdot90$ of an inch, and exhibit great variation. The following descriptions are taken from several eggs before me. (1) Strongly bluish, with almost imperceptible lilac markings, and a few spots and thick scrawls of blackish-brown. (2) Strongly greenish, marked abundantly with dull, faint brown, and a few blackish scrawls. (3) Light creamy gray, with some scrawls much subdued, as if washed out, or washed over with the ground-color, and others heavy and prominent, suggesting a tremulous hand-writing made with a very broad-nibbed pen. (4) Of an indefinite light shade, with numerous small blotches of a subdued, dull brown. (5) Dirty white, minutely marked with light purplish brown, and one blackish blotch. (6) Very light greenish, faintly and evenly marked with lilac and dull brown. In short, the ground-color varies from a rather strong bluish-green to various faint and indefinite shades, and the markings (which are often coarse scrawls or blotches) from blackish to light and vague colors, all of which are for the most part dull, the brightest being rusty-brown.

(c). The Crow Blackbirds are common summer-residents in southern New England, though very much confined to certain localities (as Cambridge), where they live more or less in communities. They are said to reach Eastern Massachusetts in March, but I have not observed them until April, when they often appear in very large flocks, flying at a considerable height, and commonly moving northward. They then roost in low pine-woods at night, and during the day resort to ploughed lands and fields. If frightened from their roost, they rise with a loud roar of their wings, and many noisy exclamations. In the latter part of September, and in October, they may be found near Boston in flocks of several hundreds, visiting open woods, for beech-nuts or acorns; also lawns, orchards, and farms. While thus assembled, they continually chatter so loudly as to be heard at the distance of a mile or even more. They obtain most of their food from the ground, over which they walk, occasionally with greater agility than one might expect. They feed upon seeds, small nuts or sometimes berries, and various insects, especially those which infest the soil. Though in this way beneficial, they do great injury by their depredations on grain-fields, and their fondness for the eggs and young of other birds. Disagreeable as it is to witness the extermination of any feathered creature, I should not hesitate to sign a death-warrant in the case of these robbers. They are remarkably fearless, and unhesitatingly familiar toward man, often closely approaching houses or entirely disregarding the various scare-crows employed to intimidate them. Their flight is somewhat undulatory, but is very vigorous.

(d). The Crow Blackbirds have a loud *chuck* or *check*, variously uttered, an occasional chatter or whistle, and in spring a rather unmusical warble, hardly to be graced with the name of song. When united in chorus, their varied notes, which, though unmusical, have a certain cadence, being not disagreeable when heard at a proper distance, suggest a concert of wheel-barrows. The Crow Blackbirds are by no means silent thieves.

(B?) PURPUREUS (var. *æneus*). *Bronzed Blackbird. Bronzed Grakle.*

(In Massachusetts, perhaps a migrant only.)

(*a*). This variety (recently established, whether rightfully or not I cannot say) is described as follows by Messrs. Baird, Brewer, and Ridgway. "Metallic tints rich, deep, and uniform. Head and neck all round rich silky steel-blue, this strictly confined to these portions, and abruptly defined behind, varying in shade from an intense Prussian blue to brassy-greenish, the latter tint always, when present, most apparent on the neck, the head, always more olivaceous; lores velvety-black. Entire body, above and below, uniform continuous metallic brassy-olive, varying to burnished golden olivaceous-bronze, becoming gradually uniform metallic purplish or reddish violet on wings and tail, the last more purplish; primaries violet-black; bill, tarsi, and toes pure black; iris sulpher-yellow." About thirteen inches long. Female smaller and less lustrous.

(*b*). The Bronzed Blackbirds are thought to build in hollow trees, " a manner of breeding now known to be also occasional in the habits of the *purpureus*." The eggs are like those of the Purple Grakle, exhibiting great variation.

(*c*). The Bronzed Grakles do not probably differ in habits from the well-known Crow Blackbirds; at least no salient point of difference has yet been discovered. In New England, they are summer-residents in Northern Maine, but are only migrants in more southern portions, appearing near Boston in (April and) October. Their chief habitat consists of the Mississippi Valley and British Provinces.

§ 18. The **Corvidæ** include the crows, ravens, rooks, daws, pies, and jays. All those of the eastern United States are characterized as follows: More than seven inches long; bill very stout, but pointed; nostrils concealed; tarsi scutellate; primaries ten, with the first short and only half as long as the second. The sexes are alike in coloration.

The crows and jays are the most nearly omnivorous of our birds, and much the most mischievous. Like the blackbirds, they are social, more or less gregarious, noisy, and almost wholly unmusical. Moreover, they are partially migratory. They build comparatively neat nests of sticks, etc., generally in evergreens. Their eggs are most often green (or brown), darkly spotted; with four, five, or sometimes six, in a set. In this climate, but one brood is usually raised.

Our *Corvidæ* are divided into two subfamilies:

Corvinæ or crows (genus I). Wings much longer than the tail; feet large and stout; colors dull, or dark and lustrous.

Garrulinæ or jays (II and III). Wings not longer than the tail; feet comparatively weak; colors dull or bright (chiefly blue); birds often crested.

I. CORVUS

(A) AMERICANUS.[88] *Crow. Common Crow.*

(A common resident throughout New England.)

(*a*). Twenty inches long or less. Lustrous black; reflections chiefly violet.

(*b*). The nest is placed from twenty to eighty feet above the ground, commonly in a pine (or a cedar), and often so as

---

[88] The Raven (*C. corax*) does not now occur in New England, unless in the extreme North-east. It is twenty-four inches long, lustrous black, "with the throat-feathers acute, lengthened, disconnected." The Fish Crow (*C. ossifragus*) may occasionally occur on the shores of Connecticut. It is sixteen inches long or less. Wilson says that their voice is "hoarse and guttural, uttered as if something stuck in their throat, and varied into several modulations ———," and that they frequently sail "without flapping the wings, something in the manner of the Raven." Mr. Wm. Brewster is confident that he saw a Fish Crow at Cambridge "on the morning of March 16th, 1875."

to be almost entirely concealed from beneath. It is usually hollowed to the depth of several inches, and is, for so large a bird, a very neat structure. It is composed of various materials (frequently including dry grass), of which the most characteristic are generally the sticks outside, and the lining of bark (consisting of strips taken from cedars or grape-vines).

It is, in Massachusetts, finished between the tenth of April and the tenth of May, and four or five eggs are then laid. These average about $1 \cdot 60 \times 1 \cdot 25$ of an inch, and are spotted sometimes coarsely and sparsely, sometimes thickly and finely, occasionally in both ways. The ground-color is a green of varying shade; the markings are variously brown, olive, dusky, and rarely purplish. The eggs of the Raven and Fish Crow differ but little except in size, the former being more than an inch and three quarters long, the latter much less. The Ravens usually build on cliffs.

The eggs of the Crow often exhibit abnormal forms, among which Dr. Brewer enumerates some which are green but unmarked, some which are white but spotted with reddish-brown, and one which has different grounds on the opposite sides. Another, in my collection, has a strong bluish tinge, like that of a thrush's egg, and only a few dark spots.

(c). The Crows are common residents in Eastern Massachusetts throughout the year. How far to the northward they may be found in winter I cannot say. During that season they are not uncommon near the sea, where they most readily obtain food. As their habits vary with the seasons, it is interesting to observe the changes. I shall therefore begin their biography by detailing the life which they lead from the opening of the year until the period of courtship.

The Crows are said to suffer extremely from cold weather in certain parts of the country, and even to die of starvation; but, near Boston, they seem to fare very well. At night they roost in thick evergreens, to which they retire promptly at evening, and from which they arise in the morning before any other birds. As they are very sociable (among themselves) throughout the year, they are seen often in small parties, and

occasionally in very large flocks. They obtain most of their
food by the sea, to which they fly in the early morning. They
there eat various shell-fish, and the refuse, such as dead fish,
which may usually be found along the shore. They are, however, omnivorous, eating grain, fruits, insects, and all sorts of
flesh; and a winter-day never passes, when they may not also
be seen searching in the interior for such morsels as may be
found there. 'On the approach or arrival of spring, their numbers increase appreciably, and mating takes place. At this
time, they frequently amuse themselves, before roosting, by
playing in the air, flying round and round, or chasing one
another. This forms a picturesque sight, especially if seen
against the glow of a setting sun. The Crows sometimes begin to build so early as the middle of March. For this purpose, they gather, chiefly from the ground, large sticks, which
they pick up and carry in their bills. In April, when the softer
materials are needed, they visit fields or orchards, and pluck
the long, dry grass. In the woods they strip off the bark of
cedars, and from the pastures often obtain cow-hair or horse-
hair. They are so wary and cautious that it is extremely difficult to watch them while building, for, on the discovery of
danger, they fly about in a purposely indefinite way, so that
one cannot learn more than the general direction in which they
carry their materials. If their nest be approached, when finished but not occupied, the parents are soon to be seen overhead, frequently *cawing*, but careful not to betray its situation.
After incubation has begun, they sit on the nest bravely, generally not leaving it until the tree is rapped. Upon this, the
female disappears, but often, in case of further intrusion, soon
returns with numerous sympathizing companions, who loudly
proclaim the distress of the community. During April, the
Crows are beneficial, and frequent ploughed lands or fields for
the purpose of obtaining various destructive insects. But,
when obliged to provide for their young, they themselves become injurious and very destructive, exhibiting more than at
other times a carnivorous taste. They do most mischief in
destroying the young and eggs of various eminently useful

birds; and this is the most serious charge which can be brought against them. They occasionally kill field mice, and even, it is said, chickens. I have also seen them feeding on snakes, but whether killed by themselves or not, I do not know. In the latter part of summer, and in autumn, they feed chiefly upon berries and grain. The young, constantly nourished by their parents, grow rapidly, and, at the end of about five weeks, show no pin-feathers, appearing in full dress when half-grown. They can then walk readily, and even fly for a short distance. I have never had but one pair, who when found, apparently had tumbled from their nest, as a dead one was lying near by. Previously to experience, I had vaguely supposed it necessary to feed young birds at least once an hour, in order to keep them alive. To my surprise, I was able to reduce the diet of my *protégés* to three meals a day, even before they were well fledged. The young are easily nourished upon meat, particularly if raw, and upon worms, or occasionally even bread soaked in water. In October I have often remarked a scarcity of Crows, who probably then pass to the South, to be replaced by others from the North, who resume their winter-habits in November.

Our Crows walk with a slow, measured step, which Audubon considers "elevated and graceful." That author adds that they frequently alight "on the backs of cattle, to pick out the worms lurking in their skin, in the same manner as the Magpie, Fish-Crow, and Cow-bird." This I have never observed. They fly with a regular, but seemingly slow beat of the wings, which is occasionally relieved by sailing, especially when the birds are about to alight, which they most often do at some height from the ground. It is common to see them with ragged wings, as if injured by shot; but the loss of several feathers, even if confined to one side, does not seem to interfere with their naturally vigorous flight. As they often fly at a great height, and very rarely near the ground, they are frequently obliged to fight against the winds, and even to "tack," that they may reach their destination.

The natural characteristics of the Crows are sagacity, cunning, and a tendency to thievishness. The difficulty of approaching these birds with a gun is proverbial. They are brave in defending their nests from the approach of other birds, but, in turn, are very commonly pursued and annoyed by the pugnacious King-bird. They frequently follow hawks, who easily avoid, and seemingly disregard them; and they take great pleasure in mobbing owls, whom they surround with noisy greetings, whenever discovered in the day-time. Wilson, however, quotes an anecdote of one being killed by a large owl at evening.

(d). The notes of the Crow, which are highly unmusical, are ordinarily a slightly prolonged *caw*, or a shorter *och* frequently repeated. There is another distinct cry, more guttural, which suggests the rattling of a rope through a pulley. This I at first attributed to individuals with "broken" voices, but I am now inclined to believe that it is merely peculiar to the season of spring. It is perhaps also used as a note to their young, whose voice is feebler and distinct from that of their parents. The Crows, in producing their notes, are obliged to gesticulate, when perched, and occasionally (in individuals) to suspend the motion of their wings, when flying.

Of all our birds, the crows and jays are doubtless most worthy of being destroyed. The former have not, however, I think, diminished in numbers, as Mr. Allen believed to be the case when he wrote his catalogue, but, on the contrary, have steadily increased. They are in summer abundant throughout a larger part of New England.

II. CYANURUS

(A) CRISTATUS. *Blue Jay*.
(A common resident throughout Massachusetts.)

(*a*). 11-12 inches long, and crested. Above, purplish-blue; beneath, white, becoming distinctly gray on the breast, and bluish on the throat. Wings and tail, bright blue, more or less black-barred, and white-tipped (except the primaries). Collar and frontlet, black.

(*b*). The nest is generally placed in a low pine, or other

evergreen, often near the trunk, from five to twenty feet above the ground. The chief materials are usually sticks or twigs, and fine roots, which form the lining. Four or five eggs, averaging $1 \cdot 20 \times \cdot 80$ of an inch, are laid, near Boston, about the twentieth of May. They are brown or green (resembling the lighter shades used in frescoing), more or less spotted with subdued brown and often obscure lilac.

(c). If the old proverb be true, that "handsome is what handsome does," the Blue Jay is not to be admired, in spite of his strikingly beautiful plumage. On the contrary, he is to be despised as a murderer, a thief, a rioter, and a disturber of the general peace. In the slaughter of babes (if I may extend the use of this word) he "out-herods Herod." He sneaks into the nests of smaller birds, sucking their eggs, or killing their young (of which he often eats the brains, but leaves the rest), and spreading sorrow wherever he goes. In the stealing of grain, he rivals the Crow. He even sneaks into the storehouse, and like a rat, devours the corn there. As a leader of riots, though a coward, he does not hesitate occasionally to tease the hawks (for which, says Wilson, he sometimes pays dearly), or to take advantage of the owls, when confused by the daylight, to heap insults upon them. As a disturber of the general peace, he delights to spread terror among other birds by imitating the cries of hawks, or to deceive them by pretending distress; no less often do his cries disturb man, and drown the sweet melodies which one might otherwise hear in all our woods and groves. On account of his bad habits, his noisiness, his fine colors and crest, he is frequently shot; and the number of Jays near Boston has lately, I think, materially diminished, whereas the cunning Crows much less often fall victims to the revenge of their numerous enemies.

The Blue Jays are residents in Massachusetts through all the seasons, but in winter are somewhat rare, as they also are to the northward, even during summer. They are gregarious throughout a greater part of the year, but are necessarily more or less separated, as is always the case during the breeding-season. They are, like the Crows, omnivorous, but they have a peculiar fondness for acorns and beech-nuts, which they are said to store for the winter. They frequent the woods chiefly, in which they build their nests, particularly among the evergreens. They may often be seen, however, in open lands, but comparatively seldom on the ground. They fly vigorously, but not with the steady, monotonous beat of the Crows. They are said to be amusing pets, having in confinement the gaiety and roguishness natural to their tribe. I am told that they may be easily caught, by being made drunk through corn dipped in whiskey. Grain impregnated with poison is also used to kill them. Though common in summer, they are, perhaps, most abundant in autumn, when I have once or twice seen as many as twenty together not far from Boston. In winter they are often scattered, but in spring they reünite, remaining in flocks until May, when they separate to build, becoming less impudent and more shy.

(*d*). Their notes vary endlessly from loud, characteristic screams to soft and musical whistles, though all are somewhat characterized by the same tone. The Blue Jays are very noisy, and possess not only the power of ventriloquism, but also that of mimicry. They imitate the cries of the Sparrow Hawk, and those of the "Hen Hawks," with great exactness, so that, were not these sounds so often heard near houses, they might easily deceive even an experienced naturalist. There is one note, to which I would particularly call attention, a guttural cry not unlike the sound produced by the rapping of woodpeckers. This may be heard in spring especially, and is apparently a love-note. The Jays, on uttering any sounds, are obliged to gesticulate in a most ludicrous manner, unless when screaming on the wing.

III. PERISOREUS

(A) CANADENSIS. *Canada Jay.* "*Whiskey-Jack.*"

(A resident of northern New England and the countries beyond.)

(*a*). 10–11 inches long. Ashy or leaden above; dull gray

beneath. Head, and tips of tail and certain wing-feathers, dull white; but hind-head very dark.

(*b*). A nest of the Canada Jay, found by Mr. Boardman, and described by Dr. Brewer, " is woven above a rude platform of sticks and twigs crossed and interlaced, furnishing a roughly made hemispherical base and periphery. Upon this an inner and more artistic nest has been wrought, made of a soft felting of fine mosses closely impacted and lined with feathers." An egg in my collection measures 1·20 × ·75 of an inch, and is grayish, evenly marked with brown. Unlike other specimens, it is green-tinted.

(*c*). The Canada Jays do not much inhabit New England, so far as I know, except in Northern Maine, where they are resident. As Audubon has apparently had many opportunities of observing these birds, I shall here quote his biography nearly in full, as I have already quoted one of Wilson's. " I have found this species of Jay," says Audubon, " breeding in the State of Maine, where many individuals belonging to it reside the whole year, and where in fact so many as fifteen or twenty may be seen in the course of a day by a diligent person anxious to procure them. In the winter, their numbers are constantly augmented by those which repair to that country from places farther North. They advance to the southward as far as the upper parts of the State of New York, where the person who first gave intimation to Mr. Wilson that the species was to be found in the Union, shot seven or eight one morning, from which number he presented one to the esteemed author of the ' American Ornithology,' who afterwards procured some in the same neighborhood. This species is best known in Maine by the name of the ' Carrion-bird,' which is usually applied to it on account of its carnivorous propensities. When their appetite is satisfied, they become shy, and are in the habit of hiding themselves amongst close woods or thickets; but when hungry, they show no alarm at the approach of man, nay, become familiar, troublesome, and sometimes so very bold as to enter the camps of the ' lumberers,' or attend to rob them of the bait affixed to their traps. My generous friend, Edward Harris,

Esq., of Moorestown, New Jersey, told me that while fishing in a birch canoe on the lakes in the interior of the State of Maine, in the latter part of the summer of 1833, the Jays were so fearless as to alight in one end of his bark, while he sat in the other, and help themselves to his bait, taking very little notice of him.

"The lumberers or woodcutters of this State frequently amuse themselves in their camp during their eating hours with what they call 'transporting the carrion bird.' This is done by cutting a pole eight or ten feet in length, and balancing it on the sill of their hut, the end outside the entrance being baited with a piece of flesh of any kind. Immediately on seeing the tempting morsel, the Jays alight on it, and while they are busily engaged in devouring it, a wood-cutter gives a smart blow to the end of the pole within the hut, which seldom fails to drive the birds high in the air, and not unfrequently kills them. They even enter the camps, and would fain eat from the hands of the men while at their meals. They are easily caught in any kind of trap. My friend, the Rev. JOHN BACHMAN, informed me that when residing in the State of New York, he found one caught in a snare which had been set with many others for the common Partridge or 'Quail,' one of which the Jay had commenced eating before he was himself caught.

"In the winter they are troublesome to the hunters, especially when the ground is thickly covered with snow, and food consequently scarce, for, at such a time, they never meet with a Deer or Moose hung on a tree, without mutilating it as much as in their power. In the Bay of Fundy I observed, several mornings in succession, a Canada Jay watching the departure of a Crow from her nest, after she had deposited an egg. When the Crow flew off, the cunning Jay immediately repaired to the nest, and carried away the egg. I have heard it said that the Canada Jay sometimes destroys the young of other birds of its species, for the purpose of feeding its own with them; but not having witnessed such an act, I cannot vouch for the truth of the report, which indeed appears to me too monstrous to be credited.

"I have often been delighted by the sight of their graceful movements on alighting after removing from one tree to another, or while flying across a road or a piece of water. They have an odd way of nodding their head, and jerking their body and tail, while they emit their curiously diversified notes, which at times resemble a low sort of mewing, at others the sound given out by an anvil lightly struck with a hammer. They frequently alight about the middle of a tree, and hop with airy grace from one branch to another until they reach the very top, when they remove to another tree, and thus proceed through the woods. Their flight resembles that of the Blue Jay, although I do not consider it quite so firm or protracted.

"The Canada Jay breeds in Maine, in New Brunswick, Nova Scotia, Newfoundland, and Labrador. It begins so early as February or March to form its nest, which is placed in the thickest part of a fir tree, near the trunk, and at a height of from five to ten feet. The exterior is composed of dry twigs, with moss and grass, and the interior, which is flat, is formed of fibrous roots. The eggs, which are from four to six, are of a light grey color, faintly marked with brown. Only one brood is raised in the season. I found the young following their parents on the 27th of June, 1833, at Labrador, where I shot both old and young, while the former was in the act of feeding the latter."

The remainder of Audubon's biography is chiefly quotations from other authors, or descriptions of the birds. The following paragraph is, however, of interest. Still referring to the Canadian Jay, Audubon says:

"Its range is very extensive, as I have specimens procured by Mr. Townsend on the Columbia River, and it has been observed by Dr. Richardson as far northward as lat 65°. The former of these naturalists states that he found 'these birds at the site of old Fort Astoria, on the Columbia river. They were very noisy and active; the voice is strong and harsh. The Indians however say that thay are rarely seen, and that they do not breed hereabouts.' Mr. Titian Peale has obtained it in the neighborhood of Philadelphia, and I have the body of one procured there by himself in October, 1836."

(*d*). The cry of the Canada Jays seemed to Mr. Samuels like that of the Blue Jay, to Mr. Maynard, like that of the lynx. These birds have also a low chatter, but their notes vary, like those of their familiar relatives, though not, so far as I know, ever imitative.

§ 19. The **Tyrannidæ** (or true *flycatchers*) are the sole North American representatives of the *Clamatores*,[89] and in turn are themselves represented only by the *Tyranninæ* or typical flycatchers. (With the exception of the *Pyrocephali*) they are characterized as follows. Sexes alike in coloration; colors plain, being green, brown, or gray, usually olive-tinted, yellow and white. Birds, subcrested, or with erectile crown-feathers. Bill about one third as deep as long, but half as wide, conspicuously hooked, notched, and bristled (Pl. I, figs. 20, 21); mandibles rather thin and hollow; tarsi scutellate as already described; primaries ten, tail-feathers twelve. (Fig. 15.) The flycatchers are eminently insectivorous and migratory, though some species feed partly upon berries, and migrate quite late in the fall. They are, as a rule, rather pugnacious, and are never gregarious. They rarely touch the ground, though not possessed of much power of flight. They are, however, admirably clever on the wing, and, darting from their posts of observation into the air, often snap up several insects at a time, and with distinct clicks of the bill. They are extremely energetic, and often show it in their indefinably characteristic voice, which, though never strictly musical, is yet pleasing and striking. The Great Crested Flycatchers build their nests in the *hollows* of trees, and the Pewees about buildings or on rocks; but the others build their nests (varying in neatness) in bushes or trees. The eggs are four or five, and white, creamy, or buff, in most cases unmarked or spotted with brown and lilac.

---

[89] See beginning of Chapter I.

The three genera of smaller flycatchers may be distinguished as follows:
Sayornis (III). Tail forked, frequently flirted; tarsus longer than the middle toe. *Contopus* (IV). Tail slightly forked, never (?) flirted; tarsus shorter than the middle toe. *Empidonax* (V). Tail even or rounded, and depressed upon the utterance of the very abrupt energetic, *song*-note, when the head is thrown back also.

I. TYRANNUS
(A) CAROLINENSIS. (*Tyrant Flycatcher.*) *King-bird. Bee "Martin." Field "Martin."*
(A common summer-resident in New England.)
(*a*). About eight inches long. Above, very dark gray, slightly brownish on the wings. Crown and tail, black; the latter broadly white-tipped, the former with erectile crown-feathers touched with orange or vermilion. (Many wing-feathers, and the outermost tail-feathers, white-edged.)

[The Gray King-bird (*T. Dominicensis*) is about nine inches long, and is rather grayer, with the "tail conspicuously forked," and *not* broadly white-tipped. "An immature specimen was taken by Mr. Charles Goodall, at Lynn, on October 23, 1868;" "its usual habitat being Florida and the West Indies."]

(*b*). The nest of our King-bird is commonly placed, from five to fifteen feet above the ground, in a horizontal fork, or on the limb, of an orchard-tree. Sometimes it is built, even nearer to the ground, in the crotch of a low sapling or stout bush, in some field or pasture. It is composed of the fine stalks of various weeds and grasses, intermixed with plant-down, to which are often attached bits of "sweet fern," dead leaves, or moss, and it is frequently lined with horse-hairs. It is, in this State, finished about the first of June. The eggs of each set are four or five, and average $1·00 \times ·75$ of an inch. They are creamy-white, with a *few large* spots of lilac, and umber, or occasionally reddish-brown. These spots are sometimes replaced by blotches, and, in two specimens before me, by large splashes of several shades of brown.

(c). The male King-bird is so well known for his pugnacity from the time of mating until his young are reared, that it is scarcely necessary for me more than to allude to this important trait in his character. He particularly dislikes Crows, whom he often pursues for at least half a mile. As he generally teases them by descending on their backs, he is frequently obliged to mount to a considerable height in the air. From his courage in driving away from his summer-home both hawks and crows, he deserves protection among the farmers, and, though he may occasionally feed upon bees, he destroys an immense number of other winged insects, upon which he chiefly depends for food.

The King-birds are common summer-residents almost throughout New England, but they inhabit principally cultivated lands and populated districts. They frequent orchards, gardens, and fields, rarely or never resorting to the woods. On the contrary, they may often be seen immediately about houses, especially on farms. They reach Massachusetts in the second week of May, and leave it in September. They are never, whilst here, strictly gregarious, but small parties of three or four may often be seen in spring. It is common to see two males paying attentions to a female. The victorious one soon after follows his mate to search for a building-site. I am inclined to believe that among all birds the female has most to do in the selection of a situation for her nest, as is very natural, since she is generally the chief builder and occupant.

The King-birds feed almost exclusively upon winged insects, which they seize with a click of the bill, and in the manner of all true flycatchers. They perch on some bough, fence, or wire, carefully watching for their prey, then make a sally, and snap up a fly or even several, often returning to their former post, which is usually not far from the ground, being sometimes merely the stalk of a weed. They also vary this mode of capture, by darting upon some insect in the grass, or by hovering and skimming over the surface of the water. They usually fly with a rapid, nervous beat of the wing, and frequently hover, either to reconnoitre, or to feed from some flock of gnats who are likewise hovering and swarming in the air. They bathe by plunging into the water, after which they fly to some twig, and dress their plumage. They perch rather erectly, and rarely alight upon the ground, unless to pick up something for their nests.

(d). Their notes are shrill twitters, which often resemble those of the swallows. They are loud, sharp, and rather vehement. Among them may be heard the syllable *king*, which constantly recurs. Though the King-birds are plainly dressed, and though they have no song, they are entitled to both our respect and affection.

II. MYIARCHUS

(A) CRINITUS. *Great Crested Flycatcher.*

(In New England, a rather rare summer-resident.)

(a). About nine inches long. Crown-feathers erectile, often forming a loose crest, and dark-centred. Above, " dull greenish olive," inclining to dusky on the wings and tail. Beneath, pale yellow; but throat gray (or " pale ash "). Tail-feathers, largely chestnut; primaries edged with the same. (Rest of the wing with much white edging, forming two inconspicuous bars. Outer tail-feathers edged with yellow.)

(b). The nest and eggs differ strikingly from those of all our other birds. The nest, which in New England is finished in the first or second week of June, may be found in woods or orchards. It consists of a few materials, placed in the hollow of a tree, among which cast-off snake-skins are almost invariably to be found. The eggs of each set are four or five, and average about $1·00 \times ·75$ of an inch. They are buff or creamy, spotted with lilac, and curiously streaked, or " scratched," with purplish and a winy brown.

(c). The Great Crested Flycatchers are summer-residents in all the States of New England, but they are apparently nowhere common. They reach Massachusetts about the middle of May, and ordinarily remain there four months, but once, so late as the first of November, I saw one not far from Boston, who was fat and in excellent condition, in spite of the cold season. The Great Crested Flycatchers for the most part frequent woods, though sometimes seen in orchards or in small groups of trees. They rarely enter the evergreens, but prefer some collection of hard-wood trees, where there are clearings and tracts of dead timber. In such a place they select their summer-home, over which they assume a despotic right, and from which they drive any other birds whom they may consider as intruders. They usually remain at a greater height than the King-birds, frequently perching near the tops of tall trees. Moreover, they often fly more rapidly and freely than those birds, though often with a striking similarity. They catch insects in the same manner, and feed upon them during spring and the early summer; but, in autumn, unlike our other flycatchers, they seem to be almost wholly dependent upon various berries, among which may be mentioned huckleberries. In the latter season, they may occasionally be seen in family parties, but, in spring, I have never observed more than two together.

(d). In regard to their notes, my experience obliges me to differ from other writers. Wilson and Audubon both speak of their note as a loud, harsh, disagreeable squeak, and subsequent writers have repeated this statement. I have watched the Great Crested Flycatchers many times at all seasons, except in winter, for the express purpose of hearing this cry, but I have never heard them utter any sound to which the above description is applicable. On the contrary, I have at all times heard them utter a single loud, brusque note (not unlike the ordinary call of the Quail), which it is difficult to imitate well, though one may do so by whistling and suddenly drawing in the breath. These flycatchers have also a few low notes, which are likewise whistled. I do not wish to deny the accuracy of my predecessors, but merely to state that there is certainly one sound familiar to me, which seems to have escaped their attention, and that what they describe is very probably a querulous cry.

III. SAYORNIS

(A) FUSCUS. *Pewee* (*Flycatcher*). *Phœbe-bird*. *Bridge Pewee*.

(A common summer-resident throughout the cultivated parts of New England.)

(*a*). Seven inches long or less. Tail, forked; crown-feathers erectile, and very dark. Above, dark olive-brown, in autumn (after the moult) *approaching* olive-green. Sides always, and the breast often, shaded with the same. Under parts, otherwise white (or very pale yellow, chiefly behind, and brightest in autumn. Eye-ring, edging of the wings and of the outer tail-feather, inconspicuously white.) The throat is sometimes streaked. *Bill wholly black.*

(*b*). The nest of the Pewee is most often built on a beam or pillar, or under the eaves of some building, occasionally those of a bridge. It was primitively attached to a wall of rock, either on a cliff, or in a cave, but, so far as I know, it is no longer often to be found in Massachusetts thus placed. It is rendered firm by mud, to which are added various materials, of which the most conspicuous is generally moss, and it is commonly lined with horse-hairs. The eggs of each set are usually five, average about ·75 × ·57 of an inch, and are pure white (rarely spotted?). Near Boston, one set is generally laid in the first or second week of May, and another in June. I have known a pair, who built in a shed partly surrounded by glass, to raise three broods in one season, of which the first was hatched about the fifth of May. An egg from the third set measures ·65 × ·50 of an inch or less.

(*c*). There are few birds dearer to an ornithologist than the Pewee, and no birds are better entitled to the affection of a friend, if usefulness, cheerfulness, familiarity towards man, and charm of manner, deserve our regard. In fact no bird is more home-like than this species, who is almost the first to announce spring at our very doors, and who is the foremost to establish his home where we have established ours, and who returns persistently, if unmolested, to the same shed or barn, year after year. Audubon even proved in one case that the young returned with their parents, thus increasing the little colony which already existed on his plantation. No bird is more peaceable or less jealous than the Pewee, who looks hospitably upon all his neighbors, and it is common to find several pairs on the same estate, living in happiness and peace.

As I sit down to write out of doors, I find that my attention is but little confined to my biographical labors. I have placed in the shrubbery around the piazza several bits of cotton-wool, which readily attract the attention of the various birds who are now building. A male Redstart is singing in the oak on the bank, while his mate cautiously approaches a vine, from which my chair is scarcely a yard distant, and, seizing several shreds of the wool, flies off. Eager to discover her home, just as I have already discovered those of nearly all her friends (and mine too), I step on the lawn to watch her motions. She flies to the nearest group of trees and disappears, while I fix my eyes upon the cotton-wool, to watch her return; but, when some sound causes me to turn my head, I see her pulling at another piece, in the opposite direction. How cautious she is of betraying her purpose, and what a vacillating course she takes from tree to tree! Is she not evidently an unusually cautious bird? A neighbor, one of her own species, without waiting for warmer weather, has already finished a nest, and laid eggs, in a birch on the edge of the swamp, and a "Black-throated Green," who built in the piazza-vines, last year, showed no hesitation in building while persons were near. But here is the Redstart again; she is now refreshing herself by catching flies. It is after nine o'clock, and she has probably worked for several hours; but she denies herself rest, and again approaches the vine, this time to gather several little strips of bark, with which she flies directly to the orchard. As she enters a pear-tree, pauses a moment, and then flies off, I feel sure that her nest is there, and so post myself close to the trunk of a neighboring apple-tree, motionless and silent, to await her return. She immediately reappears, and, apparently not realizing my presence, enters her nest, which is already shaped, and firmly presses her materials into position with her bill. She next gathers something from a tree in the orchard, but, on seeing me as I move, she is frightened, and utters a *chip*, though her mouth is quite full. Just then a most familiar sound falls upon my ear, and recalls me to my biography. On looking up, I see two Pewees providing food, either for their own young, or for some helpless Cow-bird, who has been left to their care. What labor they are obliged to undergo! Probably no less than a thousand insects must be procured each day for several weeks. One spring, when the season was backward, and the same pair were behindhand in building, they proceeded to construct, side by side in a shed, two nests, which were finished at the same time. While the male fed the young of the first brood in one nest, the female laid the eggs of a second brood in the other; but, whether this was their original design or not, I cannot say.

The Pewees reach Massachusetts about the first of April, and rarely, if ever, before the last week of March. They arrive singly, and the males seem quite dispirited until the appearance of their mates, when they at once assume their usual cheerfulness. The same pair return every year to the same spot, during their life-time, and, should one of them die, the other often finds a new mate, with whom, in the following spring, he returns to his old quarters. The Pewees are summer-residents in all the States of New England, but in the northern sections are not common, though elsewhere abundant and generally well-known. They frequent farms, and cultivated or open lands. They are nowhere shy, but occasionally the rapidity with which they check their course on entering the building which contains their nest, and on seeing there some person, shows that they possess a share of the timidity natural to most birds. They are chiefly insectivorous, though they frequently feed upon berries, such as those of the poisonous "ivy." In hunting for their usual prey, they choose a perch in some open spot, and rarely at any great height from the ground. They then flirt their tails, or from time to time utter their notes; but, on seeing an insect, they fly, and commonly seize it instantaneously, though sometimes obliged to give chase, which they do most adroitly. They often resort to the edge of ponds or streams, where gnats or mosquitoes abound. In feeding from a swarm of very small insects, they frequently hover with the body almost erect, and sustained by a rapid beating of the wings. Their flight is quite characteristic, but cannot be well defined; it is rarely protracted, unless directed toward their nest. They never alight on the ground, unless to pick up some material for building, or to perch upon a heap of earth. In autumn, they are not confined to their usual haunts, but wander quite freely about the country, though rarely to be found in woods. I have never seen them near Boston later than the sixteenth of October, and a majority pass to the southward much earlier.

(*d*). The Pewees possess a greater variety of notes than a superficial observer would suppose. They have a loud *chip* (more or less characteristic), being, I believe, the only non-oscine (or unmusical) birds who possess this note. They have also a *whit*, a single rather melancholy whistle, but seldom heard, and various twitters, of which some are querulous and others not unlike those of the King-bird. Besides these sounds, of which the latter are heard chiefly in spring, they utter quite constantly during the breeding-season, though much less often in summer, and rarely in autumn, their familiar and cheerful note, *pee-wee*, which is subject to more or less modification. Occasionally, in April, a Pewee darts into the air, and, hovering or fluttering in a circle, repeats this note so rapidly and excitedly as to produce eccentric music, which might almost without impropriety be called a song. There is, I believe, nothing which I can say to endear these birds to the naturalist, more than they are now endeared to all who know them.

IV. CONTOPUS

(A) BOREALIS. *Olive-sided Flycatcher.*

(A rather rare summer-resident.)

(*a*). About 7½ inches long. Tail considerably forked; crown-feathers erectile and dark-centred. Above, of an indescribable "dark olive-brown;" sides (almost meeting across the breast), shaded *streakily* with the same. Under parts, otherwise white or yellowish. Wings, with more or less obscure white edging. *Bill black above only.*

(*b*). The nest is much less finished and artistic than that of the Wood Pewee, and is, moreover, nearly always placed in an evergreen or orchard-tree. It is frequently built in a pine, from fifteen to even fifty feet above the ground, being placed in the fork of a horizontal limb. One before me is shallow, and is composed of twigs, fine strips of bark, stalks of field-weeds, and a little moss. The eggs of each set are usually five, average about $.85 \times .65$ of an inch, and are in Massachusetts laid in the second week of June. They are white, or creamy, spotted with lilac and reddish-brown.

(*c*). The Olive-sided Flycatchers may be classed among those birds, who are, at least in Massachusetts, neither rare nor common. They reach this State about the middle of May, and leave it in September. They may more often be found among evergreens than any others of their tribe, and most often occur in orchards or among pines. They are expert flycatchers, and have the habit of selecting a post, frequently a dead stump or decayed limb, to which they continually return. In common with other members of their family, they have a quarrelsome disposition, in consequence of which they often engage in broils, even among themselves. They are, however, no more gregarious than other flycatchers.

(*d*). Their notes possess the tone which largely characterizes this family of birds. Sometimes they are merely querulous whistles, like *pu-pu-pu* (often somewhat lengthened), and at other times form a distinct song-note, "*eh phèbèē*, or *h'phebéä*, almost exactly in the tone of the circular tin whistle or bird call, being loud, shr'll, and guttural at the commencement." (Nuttall.) These notes are subject to marked variations, which I find it impossible to describe satisfactorily.

(B) VIRENS. *Wood Pewee.*
(In Massachusetts, a common summer-resident.)

(*a*). Six inches long or more. Tail forked; crown-feathers erectile. *Bill black above only.* Wings *always* with two narrow whitish bars. Otherwise the coloration is essentially that of the Common Pewee (III). (See p. 273.)

(*b*). The nest is artistic, and in its character quite unique, though in some respects not unlike that of the Hummingbird. It is composed chiefly of fine grasses, or weed-stalks, which are mixed with the silk of spiders or caterpillars. It is rather shallow, and, being thickly covered outside with lichens, seems a part of the moss-grown limb to which it is "saddled." It is usually placed on a horizontal branch of the oak, or some like tree, in a grove or rather lightly timbered wood, from ten to forty feet above the ground. Near Boston, four or five eggs are laid about the middle of June. They average $.70 \times .55$ of an inch, and are buff or creamy, with a few large markings, at the greater end, of lilac and umber or reddish-brown.

(*c*). The Wood Pewee is one of the four common flycatchers in southern New England, and even in the northern parts is not a rare summer-resident. He is one of the latest migrants in spring, and does not reach Massachusetts until the third or often the fourth week of May. He announces his arrival by his plaintive notes, which he utters in his favorite haunts, the woods and groves. These places he rarely leaves, for he is rather reserved and unsocial, having little to do with man or other kinds of birds, though very affectionate to his mate and young. There is sometimes an air of seeming melancholy about him which is quite touching, but undoubtedly he either takes a pleasure in sadness, or else he is not sad. He is not very often seen, but he may easily be observed from his habit of returning to one spot. I have known one to choose the dead limb of a pine, to which he resorted every evening for about an hour, and sometimes in the course of the day. There I often saw him with his mate, but since the building of their nest the place has been deserted. The limit of his wanderings from his nest seems to be about one-eighth of a mile, and, to a certain extent, he may at certain hours be found at nearly the same place from day to day.

The Wood Pewees, when perching, do not flirt their tails in the manner of the Common Pewee, though they sometimes move them, when nervously quivering their wings. They usually choose a perch between ten and forty feet above the ground, from which they sally, often snapping up a dozen insects at a time. Although they fly quickly, they are rarely on wing for more than a minute, unless playing together and chasing one another through the branches. They frequent almost exclusively woods and groves, either of pines or deciduous trees, either dry or swampy, and they rarely wander even to orchards. They resort to wet places, chiefly in the evening, when they are, perhaps, most active. The insects which abound near pools of stagnant water afford them rich repasts, and opportunities of displaying their adroitness to its best advantage. Audubon says that "this species, in common with the Great Crested Flycatcher, and the Least Wood Pewee, is possessed of a peculiarity of vision, which enables it to see and pursue its prey with certainty, when it is so dark that you cannot perceive the bird, and are rendered aware of its occupation only by means of the clicking of its bill."

(d). The Wood Pewees possess a sufficient variety of notes to characterize several species. All these sounds are nearly whistles, uttered in a plaintive and often a drawly tone. None of them are loud, and many are audible only at a very short distance. The most characteristic of these notes is *pee-u-ee*, often abbreviated to *pee-u*, and this is frequently repeated. Other syllables, less often heard, are (*ch'*) *pe-ö-e, whit, whit-pée,* and *pu pu pu pu* uttered very softly. In addition to these there are certain querulous and guttural cries, which are employed chiefly during the season of love. The Wood Pewees become more or less silent in autumn, but I have heard and seen them in the White Mountains so late as the 17th of September. They usually leave Massachusetts about the middle of that month.

V. EMPIDONAX

(A) TRAILLI. *Traill's Flycatcher.*

(Rare in Eastern Massachusetts; most common in the latter part of May.)

(*a*). Six inches long, or less. Tail, even; crown-feathers, erectile, dark-centred; bill, not black. Above, dark olive-green, usually tinged with brown. Beneath, white, shaded with the color of the back on the sides, with grayish on the breast, and with yellow behind. Eye-ring, and two wing-bars, (yellowish) white.

(*b*). The nest of this species is usually placed, not far from the ground, in a swamp or near a brook, and frequently in an alder-bush. It is composed of grasses, stalks of weeds, and narrow strips of barks. Several eggs which I obtained among the White Mountains average about ·65 × ·50 of an inch, and are creamy, or pale buff, with a few dots of reddish-brown at the larger end. Dr. Brewer describes others as white, "marked almost entirely about the larger end with larger and well-defined spots and blotches of purplish-brown."

Fig. 15. Traill's Flycatcher ($\frac{1}{2}$).

(*c*). The Traill's Flycatchers are common summer-residents in many parts of northern New England, and of Western Massachusetts, but near Boston they are very rare. They are most common in the latter part of May, when they may occasionally be seen in copses, thickets, and swampy woodland. They are then migrating, and are often entirely silent. Nearly all pass on to the northward. Among the White Mountains, they frequent wet woodland, sheltered water-courses, and bushy, swampy fields. Unlike many other flycatchers, they are somewhat shy of man's approach. They usually remain within fifteen feet of the ground, but they sometimes take both higher and longer flights than I have ever known the Least Flycatchers to take. They are in fact much less stationary than most of their relations, though their general habits are the same. They live much on the edges of the woods, and often occur along the roadsides, where, from the tops of the bushes and lower trees, they utter their peculiar notes. I have been led, partly from observations on this species, to believe that probably the line, separating two *faunæ* (such as the Alleghanian and Canadian[90]), can never be precisely defined, since birds of the same district vary considerably in their latitudinal range. This is even the case in more or less restricted localities. While walking southward through the Crawford Notch, I saw or heard Traill's Flycatchers from the Willey House to a point several miles nearer Conway, and beyond this point the Least Flycatchers (who are comparatively rare in the Canadian district) were soon heard. No more of the former were seen, but the latter were frequently observable down to North Conway, where (at least in one grove) the Swainson's Thrushes and Black-throated Blue Warblers were apparently common. The dividing line, already spoken of, must necessarily be irregular, because affected by altitude as well as latitude. Among the White Mountains, one often finds it quite sharply defined by the general face of nature and by the atmosphere.

The Traill's Flycatchers do not, so far as I know, occur near Boston in the autumn, and it is probable that they return to the South by an inland route, as is the case with many other birds.

(*d*). Their ordinary note is a slightly querulous *pu*, which is often repeated, and which recalls the voice of the Great Crested Flycatcher. Another note is *pu-ée*, which is uttered in a peculiar tone, very distinct from that of the Wood Pewee,

---

[90] See § 17, VI, A, (*c*).

though somewhat like that of the Goldfinch's plaintive note. Their song-note is delivered energetically and forcibly, the head being tossed or thrown back, and the tail depressed. It resembles the syllables *che-beé-u*, and is distinct from all other notes that I have ever heard.

Nests of this species which I have lately examined are cup-shaped, but shallow. They are usually built very near the ground, and, according to Mr. Henshaw, in an *upright fork*.

(B) MINIMUS. *Least Flycatcher. Least "Pewee." "Chebec."*
(A common summer-resident throughout Massachusetts.)

(*a*). Five inches long or more. Except in size, scarcely different from *E. trailli* (A), unless somewhat grayer. Notes and eggs, however, distinct.

(*b*). The nest is placed from five to twenty feet above the ground, on a horizontal limb (frequently where it forks), occasionally one of a shade-tree, but more often one of a tree in some orchard or wood. It is sometimes built in a crotch, and then resembles the Goldfinch's nest. It is composed of fine grasses, rootlets (and pine-needles), firmly woven together with caterpillar's silk, cobwebs, cottony or woollen substances, and such accidental materials as thread or string. In Eastern Massachusetts, four or five eggs are usually laid in the first (or second) week of June; occasionally others in July. They average ·60 × ·50 of an inch, and are white, or creamy.

(*c*). The Least Flycatchers are common summer-residents almost throughout New England, though rare in some of the northern portions. They reach Massachusetts in the first week of May, and remain there until the middle of September. They frequent both woods and orchards, in cultivated districts rather preferring the latter, particularly if somewhat neglected and unfrequented. As a rule, they do not resort to pine-groves, or to very thick woods, as the Wood Pewees often do. They prefer woodland composed of birches, maples, and beeches, and do not show the fondness for low growth and wet lands, so often observable in Traill's Flycatcher. They generally return every year to their chosen home, and apparently, when once mated, are wedded for life. Occasionally, however, an intruder presents himself, in the hope of winning the affections of the female, and in these cases the male becomes irritated and furious. But ordinarily he is not very pugnacious, though of a rather jealous disposition. After becoming settled in their summer-homes, the Least Flycatchers often limit their movements, and confine themselves to some group of trees much more closely than I have observed any other birds to do. This may be due to a desire to protect their homes. They are both less expert and less active than many other flycatchers, and sometimes remain for a considerable length of time on one perch, uttering their loud song-notes. They do not depend exclusively upon insects in the air, but occasionally pick them up in the foliage of trees, among which they pass their days, sometimes, however, alighting on a fence, or on the top of a weed. They flirt their tails, but never in the decided and continuous manner of the Common Pewee, and, on delivering their song-note, throw the body back, in the manner of Traill's Flycatcher.

(*d*). This song-note is loud and emphatic, but wholly unmusical, and resembles the syllables *che-béc*. It is frequently repeated, occasionally at night, often for half an hour at a time, and sometimes so hurriedly as to become an unmusical song. The other notes are a single *whit*, and querulous exclamations (*wheu, wheu, wheu*) which are more or less guttural and subdued.

The Least Flycatchers, though common and well characterized by their striking notes, escaped the attention of Wilson, and apparently that of Audubon, until it was called to the then new species by Professor Baird. This is an excellent instance of the rule that the more one knows, the more one sees, though it is natural to suppose that the reverse might be the case. Hence, "most discoveries are accidental, or, at least, indirect." Young students, on beginning to study birds, will almost invariably from year to year discover species which they have never before *observed*, though they may often have *seen* them, and will find many species common which they before considered rare. And this is not merely because beginners set too high a value on all common objects, but because their observation, on being cultivated, is greatly increased. It has, however, been said, somewhat sarcastically, that inexperienced students see more rare birds and nests than an experienced naturalist can ever find.

(C) FLAVIVENTRIS. *Yellow-bellied Flycatcher.*
(Not common in New England.)

(*a*). About 5½ inches long. Above, olive-green; sides, shaded with the same; otherwise *beneath, decided yellow.* Lower mandible, eye-ring, wing-bars, etc., yellowish (or even yellow). *Tail* even or *rounded.*

(*b*). Dr. Brewer found a nest of this species which closely resembled that of the Indigo Bird, at Grand Menan, near the shore, "about two feet from the ground, placed in the fork of a bush." The eggs were white. "Those procured by Mr. Boardman were sprinkled with minute dots of reddish-brown. Their measurement is ·68 × ·52 of an inch." Two eggs in my collection measure about ·75 × ·55 of an inch, and are pure white, unmarked.

(*c*). The Yellow-bellied Flycatchers are the rarest members of their family in New England, and, though their distribution is probably similar to that of Traill's Flycatcher, yet they are apparently in no district very common. I have rarely found them near Boston, and generally have seen only two or three in June or the latter part of May. There is little to observe, other than their shyness, their fondness for shrubbery and wet lands, their low and characteristic note (approached only by one of the Goldfinches which is rarely heard), and the occasional flirting of their tail. Mr. Maynard's notes are very interesting. He says: "On May 31, 1869, I shot the first specimen *I* had ever seen living; the next day (June 1st) I took *eight* of both sexes in a few hours! Between this time and the 10th I took two or three more. I do not doubt that it has occurred in previous seasons, but, being unaccustomed to its low note,—which is like the syllable *Pea* very plaintively and prolongedly given,—and its retiring habits, I had not detected it before. The specimens captured were all, with the exception of the first,—which was shot on a tall oak,—taken in low, swampy thickets. It keeps near the ground, is rather shy, and upon the appearance of the intruder instantly ceases its song."

(*d*). In his "Catalogue of the Birds of Coos Co., N. H., and Oxford Co., Me., etc.," Mr. Maynard says: " We found it in dark swamps at Upton. Here, for the first time, I detected this species with any other note than the low *pea*. It was like the syllable *kil-lic* very gravely given, with a long interval between each utterance. The song was even less energetic than that of *Traillii*.[91] While singing, the birds were perched on low limbs. Both male and female used this note."

Dr. Brewer says that Mr. Boardman " has heard this bird give forth quite a pleasing, though somewhat monotonous trill. This, according to Dr. Hoy, resembles *Pēa-wäyk-pēa-wäyk*, several times repeated in a soft and not unpleasant call or song."

(D) ACADICUS.[92] *Small Green-crested Flycatcher. Acadian Flycatcher.*

(Hardly to be ranked as a bird of New England.)

(*a*). About six inches long. Tail even ; crown-feathers erectile (as in all flycatchers), and dark-centred (?). Like *E. flaviventris* in coloration, but rather less bright above, with the yellow beneath very pale, or confined to the hinder parts. Eye-ring, etc., yellowish ; breast shaded with olive-green.

(*b*). The nest is built in a tree, not very far from the ground.

---

[91] I do not know whether the song-note of Traill's Flycatcher, as described by this author, is one which I have already described, or one which I have never heard. I can hardly reconcile it to my own observations. He says: "This species has a most peculiar note like the syllables *ke win'k;* this is not so quickly given as the *se wic'k* of *E. minimus*, and is somewhat harsher. There is perhaps thirty seconds interval between each *ke win'k.*" Mr. Brewster, likewise, in speaking of the male, says: " His song consisted of a single dissyllabic strain, *ke'wing*, uttered in a harsh, peevish voice," etc. (Quoted by Dr. Brewer.)

[92] This species is considered by some authors as probably identical with *E. Traillii*, next to which it should stand. As it is questionably a bird of New England, I have placed it at the end of the group.

An egg in my collection measures about ·85 × ·65 of an inch, and is white, with a *few* brown markings at the larger end.

(c). Mr. Henshaw, in comparing this species with Traill's [93] says: "In New England, if the Acadian Flycatcher be found at all, it is in the character of a very rare visitant, and I am inclined to believe that all of the various quotations assigning this bird to a place in the New England fauna may be set down as instances of mistaken identification, not excepting the evidence of Mr. J. A. Allen, who states that *E. acadicus* is a rare summer visitant near Springfield, Mass. I am inclined to think that Mr. Allen's *acadicus*, were really *Traillii*, more especially since, in recounting the habits, he says, 'it breeds in swamps and thickets, which are its exclusive haunts.' This accords perfectly with the habits of *E. Traillii*, and is utterly at variance with those of *acadicus*, as elsewhere shown.* " As at present made out the Acadian Flycatcher reaches no further along the coast than New Jersey. Nor in the interior does its range appear to extend much if any higher." " * * * the nest is disposed in a *horizontal* fork." Dr. Wheaton "is of the opinion, that the eggs of *acadicus* average a little longer and slenderer than those of *Traillii*, and have perhaps a *yellower* buff tinge." " * * * of the Acadian he says: 'It is never found in company with, or in such localities as are frequented by the Traill's. In all cases it is found in upland woodland, preferably, and I might almost say as far as my observation extends in beech woodland. I have never seen it even during the migration in other places.'"

NOTE.—*Empidonax pygmæus. Pygmy Flycatcher.*

(a). About five inches long *or less*. Crown-feathers erectile. Tail even. Coloration, so far as known, like that of other small flycatchers (*Empidonactes*), but apparently with little olive tinting above, and no yellow beneath. [Moreover,

---

[93] Quarterly Bulletin of the Nuttall Ornithological Club, Cambridge, Mass.

" * Since penning the above I understand that Mr. Allen allows this view to be correct."

with no buffish suffusion, etc.?] *Outer web of the outermost tail-feather* (and possibly, but not probably, more of the tail), *white*.

(c). On the twelfth day of May, 1875, whilst walking about my father's place near Boston, I caught sight of a small flycatcher in some shrubbery which stood near an open field, and which consisted of barberry-bushes, a white birch, etc., while near this place were several apple-trees, pines, isolated oaks, and other trees. There, soon after noon, I saw the subject of this memoir. By his habits, his erected crown-feathers, and his style of coloration, I knew him to be a flycatcher; on observing his size and even tail, I ascribed him to the genus *Empidonax* (or a closely allied genus); and, on noticing that his tail was edged with white to the depth of an eighth of an inch or more, when closed, I believed him to be a new species. In Dr. Coues' "Key to North American Birds," but two flycatchers, ever found in the United States, are mentioned, who have the outermost web of the tail white. Of these, *Empidonax obscurus*, Wright's Flycatcher (a bird of the south-western United States), is much larger than *pygmæus*—for by chance a Pewee alighted beside the latter, and I noticed then that the Pewee seemed to be at least two inches longer, if not more. On the other hand, I did not *observe* in *E. pygmæus* the buffish suffusion, and yellow lower mandible, said to be the characteristics of *Mitrephorus fulvifrons*, var. *pallescens*, a bird of the same size, but belonging to a Mexican genus (though first called by Dr. Coues "*Empidonax pygmæus*, Buff-breasted Flycatcher," when obtained by him at Fort Whipple, Arizona). It hardly seems possible that the Buff-breasted Flycatcher should have strayed to Massachusetts, though similar instances of wandering have occurred before among birds. I feel quite confident that the bird in question is a new species, probably belonging to the genus *Empidonax*, though possibly to *Mitrephorus*, or even to a new genus (to be called *Muscaccipiter*). After trying to identify my bird, and having hurriedly, and yet with as much care as possible, endeavored to learn all the details of his coloration, I proceeded to study his habits.

For about three minutes I watched the bird (for he was not

shy, and at first allowed me a very near approach), as he flew from his perch into the air, and, in the manner of the true flycatchers, caught the smaller insects, showing great dexterity during his aërial excursions, which were all short, so far as I observed. He returned each time to his former perch or to one near it, and then occasionally flirted his tail, in the manner of the Pewee, but with much less energy. Finally, either by an accidental sound I frightened him, or he cared no longer to stay, for he flew away to one of the higher branches of a neighboring oak, and so from tree to tree, until lost to sight. I suppose this Pygmy Flycatcher to have been a migrant, passing through on his way to the northward with various other small birds, who were abundant at the time.

Either owing to its great rarity, or its general likeness to other species (especially the Least Pewee), this species, if indeed genuine, has hitherto escaped the notice of our naturalists; but it is hoped that, now being on their guard, these gentlemen will succeed in obtaining specimens, or that I myself may do so, for, on first meeting it, I had no gun. That this bird was a partially albino Least Pewee (*E. minimus*) seems wholly improbable. Even its general appearance and habits seemed distinct from those of that bird. I think, moreover, that I should have discovered a Least Pewee there earlier in the season, having been there every day previously, and the Least Pewees having arrived several days before; for, as is well known, these birds usually frequent their haunts pretty persistently; finally, I have not seen my bird since. This matter must be left to the consideration of the public, until more satisfactory evidence can be produced.

CHAPTER II.

SECOND ORDER. PICARIÆ.

This order is a "way-farer's home," established to receive those birds who do not belong elsewhere (in science, a polymorphic group). The (North American) birds composing it are characterized by the combination of a bill without any cere or soft membrane, and *one* of the following features: tail-feathers ten; foot syndactyle by the union throughout of the middle and outer toe; front-toes two in number. There are also certain internal and other features which are more or less characteristic. Either the bill or the toes always present certain peculiarities.

There is an important element in classification, which is often overlooked, that of latent features. These are frequently undeveloped. For instance, the chief, and let us momentarily suppose, the only, difference between the typical thrushes and mocking-thrushes is in the tarsus, or so-called "leg." In the latter group it is always scutellate (or divided into scales)—at least, in front; whereas in the former thrushes, when adult, it is "booted" (*i. e.* without scales, unless near the toes). Yet a young robin with scutellate tarsi is no less a typical thrush; his tarsi are virtually "booted," and will become so upon normal growth. Those of a young Cat-bird never will. Is not abnormal growth frequently due to the persistent latency of normal features? As another example, the females of two closely allied species may be exactly alike in coloration, size, and structure. They may differ, however, in the latent power of producing distinct eggs; they may differ less in the latent instinct of building different nests, or still less in the latent power of producing eggs, many of which contain the germs of very distinct male birds. Hence the freshly laid eggs of two species may be indistinguishable except in latent, undeveloped features, though, since like produces like, they may be identified through the parent-birds.

NOTE. — The third order, *Psittaci* (parrots and their allies), is not represented in New England. Its members have toes in pairs, and an essentially raptorial bill. (See Chap. III.)

§ 20. The **Caprimulgidæ** (or *goatsuckers*, of which the American species are typical, and belong to the subfamily *Caprimulginæ*) and the *Cypselidæ* (or *swifts*, § 21, pl. 1, fig. 23) form a natural group possessing the following features: gape extensive, and about six times as long as the culmen (or upper outline of the bill); feet small and weak; primaries ten; tail-feathers ten. The goatsuckers may be distinguished from the swifts by the more or less bristled bill, the feet slightly webbed at the base, and the elevated hind-toe. This last feature, however, also belongs to the *Chæturinæ*, a subfamily containing the Chimney "Swallows," and differing further from the true swifts in having unfeathered tarsi. The *Chæturæ* (§ 21, I) have mucronate tail-feathers, in which the shaft projects beyond the webs. (Pl. 1, fig. 22.)

The *swifts* probably possess powers of locomotion superior to those of any other living creatures. With their long, pointed wings, they are said to fly sometimes at the rate of two hundred and fifty miles in an hour. They are strictly insectivorous and migratory, and more or less colonial. "They never perch, but many resort to hollows, as in trees, for the purpose of roosting and of nesting." Their nests are attached to some more or less perpendicular surface, and are constructed partly or even wholly of a gummy saliva. The eggs are white, and rather elongated.

The *goatsuckers* are generally nocturnal or crepuscular, and, as a rule, do not fly about in the day-time, unless when cloudy. When resting, they do so on the ground, or perch lengthwise on a bough or fence. They are insectivorous, capturing moths and smaller insects at some height in the air, also migratory and often gregarious. They are larger than the swifts, who are also somewhat crepuscular, and their plumage is much variegated. They build no nest, but lay two eggs on the ground, or near it. There are two American genera.

I. *Antrostomus.* Bristles very conspicuous; tail rounded. Birds strictly nocturnal.
II. *Chordicles.* Bristles short; tail forked; wings very long. (Fig. 16.)

I. ANTROSTOMUS
(A) VOCIFERUS. *Whippoorwill.* "*Night-jar.*"
(A well known summer-resident throughout New England.)
(*a*). About 9½ inches long. *Tail rounded.* Throat-patch, and tips of outer tail-feathers, in ♂ white, in ♀ light brown. Crown, black-streaked. Otherwise indescribably variegated or mottled with several quiet colors. The *Chuck-will's-widow* (*A. Carolinensis*) of the Southern States possesses a very similar coloration, but is a foot long.

(*b*). The eggs are laid on the ground in some dry part of the woods, no nest being made, unless a slight hollow be scratched among the fallen leaves. They are elliptical, average 1·25 × ·85 of an inch, and are creamy, spotted rather sparsely, chiefly with lilac and lavender. In Massachusetts, two eggs are laid about the first of June.

(*c*). The Whippoorwills, wherever known, are well-known, and yet by the common people they are rarely seen. Were it not for their loud and famous notes, they might well be considered by collectors very rare. As it is, they are known to be common at various points throughout New England, as well as other parts of the country; but their distribution is probably irregular and local. They reach the neighborhood of Boston in the latter part of May, and leave it before or soon after the arrival of autumn. They differ from the Night "Hawks" in habits very distinctly, though, according to Wilson, the two species were once confused even by naturalists. They are strictly nocturnal, unless occasionally active towards the end of a cloudy afternoon. During the day, they retire to some well shaded spot in the woods (or occasionally the "scrub"), and there repose, resting on the ground, or, more often, perched upon a limb. Their feet are so small and weak that they never (?) perch crosswise, but lie along the bough. I have but rarely found them sleeping, but on such occasions I have always observed this peculiarity. Like most of the owls, they are dazed by a strong light, and in the day-time usually allow a near approach. At evening they become active, and are said to continue so until dawn, particularly on moon-light nights. They are never, I believe, quite so gregarious as the Night "Hawks" very often are, though in spring there is often rivalry between the males, who seem to challenge one another. The Whippoorwills also fly much lower, and prefer to fly near the ground, rather than among the clouds or at any great height. Hence their food must differ considerably from that of their relative. Audubon in speaking of this species says: "It passes low over the bushes, moves to the right or left, alights on the ground to secure its prey, passes repeatedly and in different directions over the same field, skims along the skirts of the woods, and settles occasionally on the tops of the fence-stakes or on stumps of trees, from whence it sallies, like a Fly-catcher, after insects, and, on seizing them, returns to the same spot. When thus situated, it frequently alights on the ground, to pick up a beetle. Like the Chuck-will's-widow, it also balances itself in the air, in front of the trunks of trees, or against the side of banks, to discover ants, and other small insects that may be lurking there. Its flight is so light and noiseless, that whilst it is passing within a few feet of a person, the motion of its wings is not heard by him, and merely produces a gentle undulation in the air. During all this time, it utters a low murmuring sound, by which alone it can be discovered in the dark, when passing within a few yards of one, and which I have often heard when walking or riding through the barrens at night." The young run about much like young partridges.

(*d*). The most characteristic note of these birds is a loud whistle, which resembles more or less distinctly the syllables *whip-poor-will*. It is said to be never repeated, except after dark, and when the birds are perched, as on a fence or roof. It is most commonly heard in June, and is usually preceded by a *click*, as if produced by a snapping of the bill. The other notes of the Whippoorwills are low, sweet whistles (*whit, whit,*

whit) and occasionally a rather harsh and guttural chatter. Mr. Nuttall says that the young have a low, mournful *pé-ugh*. It is probable, at least in New England, that few or no superstitions are now attached to these birds.

II. CHORDEILES

(A) VIRGINIANUS. *Night "Hawk." "Bull-bat."*
(A common summer-resident throughout New England.)

(*a*). About nine inches long. Tail forked. Variously mottled, or variegated. ♂ with a white, and ♀ with a reddish, throat-patch. ♂ with *both* a white wing-patch and white tail-spots.

(*b*). The eggs, of which two are here laid about the first of June, are dropped upon rocks, upon the ground, or occasionally upon a flat roof. They have been found variously in cities, pastures, fields, and woods. They are elliptical, average about 1·25 × ·85 of an inch, and are light gray, or brown, thickly and finely marked with lilac, dark brown, and sometimes slate-color.

Fig. 16. Night "Hawk" (¼).

(*c*). The Night "Hawks" have not been named altogether appropriately, for, though to a certain extent crepuscular (belonging to twilight or dusk), they are not nocturnal. There is, however, a strong resemblance in their general method of flight to that of certain hawks, as well as to that of the swifts, and the latter part of their name is warranted by their general appearance at a distance. They fly with ease, and sometimes, when favored by a wind, with much rapidity. They often mount to a great height, so as to be fairly lost among the clouds, and comparatively seldom skim over the earth, in the manner of the Whippoorwill. They move through the air very irregularly, and often change their course at nearly every flapping of their wings, as they dart about in the search of the winged insects upon which they feed. They fly about freely in the day-time, especially if it be cloudy, but they are generally rather silent in very sunny weather. They occasionally alight upon the ground, and move about, but whether in search of earth or insects I am uncertain, probably the former.

The Night "Hawks" are common summer-residents throughout New England, but, according to Mr. Allen,[1] do not winter in Florida, as many Whippoorwills do. They usually reach Massachusetts in the earlier part of May, or sometimes, it is said, in April. Separate individuals or pairs are not uncommon, but they may often be seen migrating in companies, containing even two dozen, for they are more or less gregarious throughout the year. They show a fondness for pasture-land, and uncultivated districts, though quite common in Boston and other cities, where they have been found to lay their eggs on flat roofs. They are probably more abundant in northern New England than in Massachusetts, in some places forming large colonies. Near Wilson's Mills in Maine, says Mr. Samuels, "in the space of every four or five rods, a female was sitting on her eggs." Both Wilson and Audubon speak of the female's endeavors, when frightened during incubation, to lead the intruder away by feigning lameness and distress. In this case, though less so than with many other birds who build no nest, it is difficult to find the eggs. If these latter be left undisturbed when found, they are sometimes removed, very probably in the capacious mouths of their parents, as Audubon states to be the case with the Chuck-will's-widow. The Night "Hawks" like the Whippoorwills perch lengthwise, but unlike them frequently utter their notes on wing.

(d). Their ordinary note is peculiar and indescribable, though I have heard it well imitated by the human mouth. It is usually called a loud, harsh squeak, but I know no sounds

---

[1] "List of the Winter Birds of East Florida, with Annotations." J. A. Allen.

like it, except the notes of one or two other birds. It is very striking, and, if heard from a near standpoint, rather startling. The male Night "Hawk" produces an equally extraordinary sound, which is heard chiefly during the season of courtship. Mounting to some height, he falls, head foremost, until near the ground, when he checks his downward course, and then the "booming" is heard, a sound "resembling that produced by blowing strongly into the bung hole of an empty hogshead." I am uncertain as to what causes this noise, having found it impossible to make any close observations. Wilson thought it produced by the mouth, Audubon, by the concussion caused by a change of position in the wings. The Night "Hawks" all leave New England in September.

§ 21. **Cypselidæ.** Swifts. (See § 20.)

I. CHÆTURA

(A) PELAGICA. *Chimney Swift.* Chimney "*Swallow.*"

(A common summer-resident throughout New England.)

(*a*). About five inches long. Sooty-brown, glossed with green above; throat, much paler. Lores and wings, black.

(*b*). The Chimney "Swallows" soon after their arrival construct their curious nests, which are composed of twigs firmly glued together by "a fluid secreted with the birds." These nests are now placed in chimneys, almost universally throughout civilized parts of the country, but they have been found attached to boards, and the eggs were originally laid in hollow trees or stumps. The eggs of each set are four, average ·70 × ·50 of an inch, and are pure white, unmarked.

(*c*). The Chimney Swifts possess powers of flight which are probably unsurpassed by those of any bird not belonging to this family. It is almost certain that they often fly no less than a thousand miles in the course of twenty-four hours. When providing for their young, they are sometimes busy during a greater part of the day, and even continue their labors at night. Usually, they become active at a very early hour, sometimes even before dawn, and retire during the warmer part of the day, unless it be cloudy, when they continue their exercise. At evening, they renew their activity and do not retire until a comparatively late hour. The Chimney "Swallows" are common summer-residents throughout New England. They reach Massachusetts in the first week of May, and leave it in August or September. They have altered their habits conformably to civilization, and here roost and nest exclusively in chimneys. Formerly they occupied hollow trees, and Audubon describes as follows a visit to one of their haunts, a large, hollow sycamore near Louisville, in Kentucky. "Next morning I rose early enough to reach the place long before the least appearance of daylight, and placed my head against the tree. All was silent within. I remained in that posture probably twenty minutes, when suddenly I thought the great tree was giving away, and coming down upon me. Instinctively I sprung from it, but when I looked up to it again, what was my astonishment to see it standing as firm as ever. The Swallows were now pouring out in a black continued stream. I ran back to my post, and listened in amazement to the noise within, which I could compare to nothing else than the sound of a large wheel revolving under a powerful stream. It was yet dusky, so that I could hardly see the hour on my watch, but I estimated the time which they took in getting out at more than thirty minutes. After their departure, no noise was heard within, and they dispersed in every direction with the quickness of thought." Audubon estimated their number at nine thousand. The Chimney Swifts never rest except in their roosting-places, to the walls of which they cling, partly supported by their stiff tail; and, so great is their muscular vigor, that they never rest by perching. As has already been mentioned, they often rest at noon, or seek refuge during violent storms. On this account, they are very abundant sometimes, and at other times are not to be seen. On entering a chimney, they fall boldly head-foremost in a very unconcerned way. Their general manner of flight is so varied that it is difficult to describe. It consists of rapid sailing, combined with quickly repeated strokes of the wings, and sudden turnings in every direction. Their flight possesses so much force that they break off twigs for their nests without any diminution of speed. It is almost unnecessary to say that they feed entirely upon winged insects, the indigestible parts of which they are said to disgorge in pellets.

The Chimney Swifts may easily be distinguished from the true swallows by their peculiar and more rapid flight, their long wings, and their apparent want of tail (as seen from a distance). They sometimes skim over water, but more often fly at a considerable or even a very great height.

(*d*). Their only note is a loud *chip*, often repeated quickly and vehemently, so as to bear a resemblance to the twittering of the swallows. Their young, who are born blind, have a much feebler voice.

§ 22. The **Trochilidæ** (or *hummingbirds*) are in North America represented only by the typical subfamily, *Trochilinæ* (while the other group, "*Phæthornithinæ*, representing about one-tenth of the whole, is composed of duller colored species especially inhabiting the dense forests of the Amazon"). The Ruby-throated Hummingbird is an excellent type of the group. The bill is very long and slender, being of a nearly equal depth throughout; the feet are small; the wings long and with ten primaries; the tail is ten-feathered.

The *Alcedinidæ* (or *kingfishers*, § 23) are in America represented fragmentarily by the subfamily *Cerylinæ*. They differ strikingly from all the families to which they are allied by position in classification. The common Belted Kingfisher is a good type. The bill is stout and pointed, about one-fourth as deep as long; the tarsi are extremely short; the feet small, and syndactyle from the union of the outer and middle toes nearly throughout (pl. 1, fig. 24); [2] primaries ten, but tail-feathers twelve.

The *Coccyginæ* (or *American cuckoos*) form a distinct subfamily of the large and much varied family, *Cuculidæ* (or cuckoos, § 24). They are quite closely related to some of the

---

[2] In many other birds the toes are partly united at the base.

woodpeckers; but show little affinity to the other picarian groups. They are characterized as follows: bill deepest at the base (?), with upper outline convex, and the lower concave; toes arranged in pairs; tail-feathers ten; feathers above the tarsus long and flowing.

The cuckoos are insectivorous, and eat great numbers of caterpillars; but unfortunately they often rob the nests of other birds, though not, like the European cuckoos, parasitic. On account of their peculiar notes, however, they have been called "Cow-birds." They are migratory but not gregarious. They build rude and frail nests, of sticks or the like, in a bush or tree, and lay several bluish or greenish eggs, often at irregular intervals.

I. TROCHILUS

(A) COLUBRIS. *Ruby-throated Hummingbird.*[3]

(A summer-resident throughout New England.)

(*a*). About 3¼ inches long. Golden green above; white beneath. Wings and tail, brownish-purple. ♂, with the sides green, and the throat metallic, reflecting ruby-red. Tail simply forked. ♀, with the tail slightly forked, and "double-rounded," more or less black-barred, and, on the outer feathers, white-tipped.

(*b*). The Hummingbird's nest may be considered a perfect type of bird-architecture, and, as such, is one of the most beautiful objects in nature, though composed of simple materials, gathered chiefly from weeds, and though constructed by but a single instrument. Had not man *ideal* in art, his works could not be favorably compared with such a production as this. "What enlightened person," says an anonymous writer, whom I have already quoted, "can gaze upon this nest without regretting that man should in the progress of civilization so often forget nature, fail to appreciate her, or even wrong her?"

---

[3] A "Linnée's Emerald" (*Argyrtira maculata*) "was captured by Mr. William Brewster, at Cambridge, in August, 1894; it was moulting, and apparently a female." Though this bird may actually have wandered here from its home in South America, yet such an incident is not likely to occur again.

The Hummingbird's nest is usually placed on the limb of an orchard-tree or oak, though occasionally fastened to the stalk of a large weed.[4] Its depth is about half an inch, and its diameter inside is rarely more than twice that. The walls are thick, and are composed of plant-down, bits of fern, the silky husks of certain seeds, and other soft materials. These are so thickly coated with lichens as to closely resemble the branch to which they are attached. Near Boston, two eggs are laid in each nest, in the early part of June. They are white, elliptical, and half an inch long or even less.

(c). Our little Hummingbirds deserve renown, not only for their small size, exquisite colors, and eminently pleasing architecture, but also for their hardiness, courage, and admirable flight. They are known in summer to occur so far to the northward (if not further) as the fifty-seventh parallel of latitude, which crosses Hudson's Bay and Northern Labrador. They are summer-residents throughout a larger portion of the eastern United States, and as such are common in New England. They reach Massachusetts in the second week of May, and I have seen them near Boston so late as the twenty-third day of September.[5] They generally arrive in pairs, and return to the same home every year. The male protects his honor and rights with undaunted courage, and often teases very large birds in expression of his anger, though he may be "incompetent" says Wilson "to the exploit of penetrating the tough sinewy side of a crow, and precipitating it from the clouds to the earth, as Charlevoix would persuade his readers to believe." He also finds occasion to battle with intruders of his own kind, but it is impossible to understand the details or result of such a duel, so confusing is the intense quickness of the combatants. In fact, the Hummingbirds are so small, and so extremely swift

---

[4] Wilson says that he has "known instances where it was attached by the side to an old moss-grown trunk; and others where it was fastened on a strong rank stalk, or weed, in the garden." I have been told that the Hummingbirds were once very abundant on the Isle of Shoals, where there were no trees.

[5] Coincidentally Mr. Maynard gives the same day as his latest date of observation.

in all their movements, that it is as difficult to observe them, unless stationary or seemingly so, as to follow the course of a shooting star. So rapid is the beating of their little pinions, that they produce a loud humming whenever flying, and seem to be immovable, when pausing before a flower, while the presence of their nearly invisible wings is scarcely indicated except by the constant buzz and whirr. The Hummingbirds have two distinct methods of feeding, easily observable upon studying their habits. They may be seen darting from flower to flower, and thrusting their long slender bills into the heart of the blossoms, not only to procure the honey, but to obtain the smaller insects which feed upon it. Of all the various flowers which they visit, they show a marked fondness for those which are trumpet-shaped, such as belong to the bignonia and honeysuckle. They do not frequent the lower and more humble kinds, but prefer those which are large and showy, and grow on shrubs, bushes, and vines. The taller garden-flowers also attract their attention. They are not wholly nectar-fed, as has poetically and popularly been supposed to be the case, but are chiefly insectivorous. They may be seen perched on some twig, from which they shoot into the air, and with great address seize the gnats and smaller insects, many of which are invisible to the naked human eye. They sometimes perch as if merely to rest, the female especially. They never alight upon the ground, but they sometimes perch upon weeds, and have been known to perish from being caught in the burs of the burdock.[6] They choose for their haunts not only orchards, gardens, and groves near them, but also forests, as I have several times observed among the White Mountains. It is probable that they much more often frequent the woods in civilized districts than is commonly supposed. Though they are jealous, and

---

[6] This fact has been communicated to the "Naturalist" by Mr. A. K. Fisher. The original discoverer of the dead bird (or rather its remains, a skeleton) "found a live one on a plant near by." Mr. Fisher himself found a Yellow Bird (*Chrysomitris tristis*) thus caught, who "tore itself away, leaving a number of its feathers on the burs." He also found a Yellow-rumped Warbler "fastened to the same kind of plant."

daringly pugnacious, yet they are known to congregate occasionally in flocks, chiefly during the migrations. Though they are apparently very hardy, yet they have never, I believe, been successfully kept in confinement for a longer period than a few months. The principal obstacles in rearing them are the injuries which they receive, if allowed to fly about a room, their suffering from cold, and the difficulty of providing proper food, since any prepared syrup apparently does not satisfy them except when young.

(d). Their only note is a *chirp*, which immediately suggests the voice of an insect.

No birds are more generally beloved and admired than our Hummingbirds, and America may well boast of a treasure which no other country possesses.

§ 23. **Alcedinidæ.** *Kingfishers.* (See § 22.)

I. CERYLE

(A) ALCYON. *Belted Kingfisher. Kingfisher.*

(A resident of New England in summer, and occasionally in winter.)

(a). About 12½ inches long. Upper parts, sides, and a breast-band, ashy-blue. Head-feathers darker, forming a loose crest, and giving a rough outline to the hind-head. Wings and tail also partly darker, and white-spotted. Broad collar (interrupted behind), lower breast, etc., white. The latter in ♀ with a band (often imperfect) of a chestnut-color, which extends along the sides, and sometimes mixes with the band above.[7]

(b). From the abundant evidence recently offered on the subject of the nest, and from my own limited experience, it may be gathered that it varies in length, though sometimes nine feet long, that it may be either straight or have a bend, and that it is rarely lined at the end, except with fish-bones, as is sometimes the case. That the Kingfishers always make

---

[7] "Several specimens in the Smithsonian collection marked female (perhaps erroneously) show no indication of the chestnut."

a *burrow* in a bank of sand or gravel, in which to lay their eggs, and that they most often do so near water, and not far from the ground, are undisputed facts. The eggs of each set are six or seven, average 1.35×1.05 of an inch, and are pure white.

(c). The Belted Kingfisher is well known, and " in the summer is found in every portion of North America, to the Arctic Ocean on the north, and from the Atlantic to the Pacific."[8] In New England, this species is occasionally resident throughout the year, but more often appears about the first of April, and remains until late in the autumn. Near Boston it probably cannot be much longer ranked as a common bird, since, being naturally shy, unsocial, and averse to the intrusion of man, it prefers wilder and less cultivated portions of the country.

Our common Kingfishers are more conspicuous than actually abundant, and two pairs are rarely found to occupy the same hunting-grounds. They may be found scattered throughout the State, and stationed at mill-ponds, lakes, rivers, and trout-streams. Such places are their chosen haunts, and there they search for their prey, while some neighboring sand-bank affords them a place to excavate their long burrows, which they do with both bill and feet. They are frequently obliged to wander in search of their food, as I have seen them in warm weather flying across the country at some distance from any large body or stream of water. They fly rapidly, with an intermittent beating of the wings. When watching for fish, upon which they feed almost exclusively, they perch on a fence or tree which stands immediately next to or overhangs the water. From this post they regard the water closely, sometimes flirting their tail or sounding their loud rattle. On seeing a fish, they plunge, so as to be completely immersed, and seizing it with their sharply pointed beak, carry it to shore, where they quickly swallow it. Sometimes they hunt like hawks, and, flying over the surface of the ponds, hover before plunging. On the approach of man, they usually retreat to

---

[8] Messrs. Baird, Brewer, & Ridgway's " North American Birds."

resume their occupation in a less disturbed quarter. They do not attack large fish, but prefer those which are collectively called "small fry." Audubon states that he has seen them plunge into the sea, but the ocean must ordinarily be too rough for them to detect easily the small objects for which they search. They frequently use their nest as a resort, probably making it regularly a retreat for the night. Gosse speaks of these birds as reaching Jamaica "about the beginning of September." In speaking of a pair, which he afterwards obtained, he says : "Once both birds seized the same fish, nearly at the same moment, and rising with it into the air, each tugged in contrary directions, until the grasp of one gave way. At last my assistant Sam * * * shot them both. The first was only wounded, and falling into the water swam out sea-ward, *striking out* boldly, the wings, however, partially opened. On being seized he proved very fierce, erecting the long crest, and endeavoring to strike with his pointed beak. He got hold of my thumb, and squeezed so powerfully, that the cutting edge of the upper mandible sliced a piece of flesh clean out. He was tenacious of life, for though I pressed the trachea until motion ceased, he repeatedly revived."

(*d*). The only note of the Belted Kingfisher is loud and harsh, resembling the sound produced by a watchman's rattle.

§ 24. **Cuculidæ.** *Cuckoos.* (See § 22, *ad finem*.)
I. COCCYGUS
(A) AMERICANUS. *Yellow-billed Cuckoo.*
(A summer-resident in Massachusetts, but rather rare.)

(*a*). About twelve inches long. Lower mandible, almost entirely yellow. Above, drab, or "quaker" brown (with bronzy reflections). Wings edged with cinnamon. Outer tail-feathers, wholly black and white. Beneath, white.

(*b*). The nest is hardly worthy of the name, but is generally a frail structure composed of a few twigs, and placed in a bush or low tree, not far from the ground. I have usually found it in dry places, such as dry woods, bushy pastures, and occasionally orchards, or even the "scrub." Near Boston, it is built about the first of June; "built," however, is not a term invariably applicable to this nest, as I have known it to consist of a cotton-rag, which was firmly caught in the thorns of a barberry-bush. The eggs, which in many cases are laid at irregular intervals, average 1·25 × ·87 of an inch, and are light greenish-blue, but rarely or never elliptical.

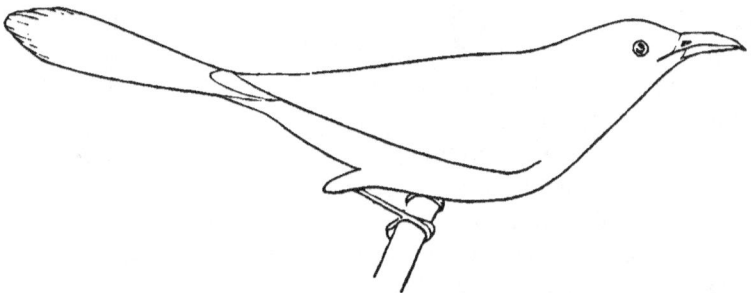

Fig. 17. Yellow-billed Cuckoo ($\frac{1}{3}$).

(c). The Yellow-billed Cuckoos have evidently become very much less common near Boston than they once were, and are now considered rare in many if not all parts of New England. In general habits they are closely allied to the more common Black-billed Cuckoos, whose habits will be fully detailed in the next biography. They differ chiefly in having a rather less rapid flight, a greater fondness for high, dry, and wooded lands, and a somewhat different diet. Their habit of laying eggs at intervals of several days, also observable in the other species, is enough to distinguish them from nearly all our other land-birds. It is not rare to find their nest containing both young and eggs at very different stages of development. I once found a Robin's nest in the same condition, but such a case was wholly exceptional. The female Cuckoo, when approached while on her nest, usually sits bravely, but finally throws herself upon the ground, and flutters away, uttering piteous and uncouth sounds, which can hardly fail to distract the attention of an egg-hunter; but this device rarely succeeds, since it is resorted to too late.

(*d*). The notes of the Yellow-billed Cuckoo do not differ distinctly from those of the Black-billed species, though often harsher.

(B) ERYTHROPTHALMUS. *Black-billed Cuckoo*.

(A summer-resident of all the Eastern States, but more common to the southward.)

(*a*). Nearly a foot long. Eye-ring, red. Above, drab or "quaker" brown (with bronzy reflections). Beneath, white, often slightly tinged. Outer tail-feathers white-tipped (and slightly sub-tipped with blackish).

(*b*). The nest differs from that of the Yellow-billed Cuckoo in being most often built in wet lands, and in being less carelessly constructed; strips of bark, or leaves, are often added to the usual sticks and twigs. It is placed in a bush, low tree, or briar, not far from the ground, and here is finished in the first week of June. The eggs are darker and greener than those of the other species, and are *elliptical*. They average about 1·15 × ·87 of an inch.

(*c*). The Black-billed Cuckoos are moderately common summer-residents in southern New England, but to the northward become rare. They reach Massachusetts in the third week of May, and leave it in the earlier part of September. They arrive singly or in pairs, and at once announce their arrival by their peculiar and characteristic notes. They frequent woods and shrubbery, particularly in low grounds or swamps, and visit orchards or cultivated lands. They fly rapidly, and often quite far, moving their wings with regularity. On alighting in a bush or tree (for they seldom alight on the ground), they choose a perch sheltered by the foliage, and often move their tail in an odd, deliberate manner, as if just about to fly off. They are eminently cowards, and rely much upon concealment, but, perhaps on this account, they may often be closely approached by man. They feed partly upon berries, and also, it is said, upon "fresh-water shell fish and aquatic larvæ," but they are chiefly insectivorous. They undoubtedly confer great benefits upon agriculturists, and are *our principal birds to attack and devour caterpillars in the nest.* On the other hand, they do great mischief in destroying the eggs of other useful birds. Like arrant cowards, as they are, they take opportunities to approach stealthily the nests of many birds, whom they would be afraid to encounter, and then feast on the eggs of the absent parents, after which they hurry away. They are scarcely less destructive in this way than the Black Snakes, though I have never known them to kill young birds. In this connection, it may be remarked that the common red squirrels (often called red "ferrets") greatly check the increase of our birds, though the little "chipmonks" are, I believe, quite harmless in this respect. These latter, often called Striped or Ground Squirrels, are much less adroit climbers than the former, and are comparatively seldom seen in trees. Recently, however, I observed one who was feeding at noon on a large stone, which he had established as his dining-table, and who, after his meal, climbed up a stump luxuriantly covered with the poisonous "ivy," evidently to enjoy a siesta. There, curled up on one of the branches, at some height from the ground, he rested for some while, occasionally allowing himself "forty winks," but usually keeping his eyes open to aid in the detection of danger. He was undoubtedly disturbed by his children at home; but he must provide for them; so he reluctantly descended, and, filling his pouches to an almost incredible extent, disappeared down his hole in the lawn. The red "ferrets" are said to throw young birds wantonly from the nest. This I have never observed, but I have frequently seen them apparently hunting for nests and actually robbing them of eggs. They climb cleverly, leap without hesitation from bough to bough, or tree to tree, and scamper over the ground with rapidity, even doing so while carrying one of their young between their teeth.

(*d*). The notes of the Cuckoo are all unmusical, and more or less uncouth and guttural. They are much varied, being sometimes *cow-cow-cow-cow-cow*, *cow-cow*, sometimes *cuckoó-cuckoó-cuckoó*, sometimes *cuckucow′*, *cuckucow′*, and at other times low. Many of them are very liquid, but I have heard one cry which has an affinity to that of certain woodpeckers. The Cuckoos may sometimes be heard at night.

§ 25. The **Picidæ** (or *woodpeckers*) form a remarkably distinct group, characterized by having two toes in front, and two (or only one) behind; ten primaries, of which the first is spurious, and a stiff tail of twelve feathers, of which the outermost are also spurious.

In *Colaptes* (standing at one end of the group, and next to the Cuckoos), the bill is three or four times as long as high, rather slender, pointed, and with the commissure, as well as the upper outline, convex; the nostrils are exposed. In *Picus* (a genus near the other end, containing typical woodpeckers), the bill is stouter, the outlines nearly straight, the end blunted or truncate, and the nostrils concealed. In other genera, the bills are more or less intermediate. In this family, as in some others, it has not been thought advisable to present certain divisions in classification, which have been recently established in scientific works. (See figs. 18 and 19, and pl. 1, fig. 25.)

In *Colaptes*, the birds are largely terrestrial, feed much upon ants, and frequently perch on branches crosswise.

In *Sphyrapicus*, the birds possess a peculiar tongue, and do mischief by stripping off bark, and feeding on the lining.

In *Picoides*, the birds are three-toed, and boreal.

In *Hylotomus*, the birds are crested and wholly (?) non-migratory. The woodpeckers are all more or less brightly colored, at least the males, and the sexes are differently colored. They are principally noted for hopping about the trunks and larger limbs of trees, supported by their tails, and rapidly hammering with their bills to extract the grubs, etc., upon which they feed, as well as on berries, or even sometimes grain. They are often social, but never strictly gregarious, so far as I have observed, partly, perhaps, because permanent residents in their summer-homes or only partially migratory. They frequent forests, woods, and orchards, where they build their nests by excavating a very neat hole in sound or decayed wood. In this, which contains no lining, from four to six very smooth white eggs are laid. The notes of the woodpeckers are unmusical, being variously screams, or rather shrill notes, pitched on a high key.

I. COLAPTES

(A) AURATUS. *Golden-winged Woodpecker. Pigeon Woodpecker.* "*Flicker.*" "*High-hole.*" "*Yellow-shafted Woodpecker.*" "*Yellow-hammer.*" (Also eight other names.)

(In Massachusetts, a common summer-resident, but much less abundant in winter.)

(*a*). About 12½ inches long. Above, umber brown, black-barred; tail and primaries, chiefly black; *rump, white.* Crown and nape, dark gray, with a scarlet crescent behind. Throat, and upper breast, cinnamon or "lilac-brown;" the latter with a black crescent, and ♂ with a black maxillary patch. Under parts, otherwise white, variously tinged, and black-spotted. *Wings and tail,* (chiefly) *bright yellow beneath.*

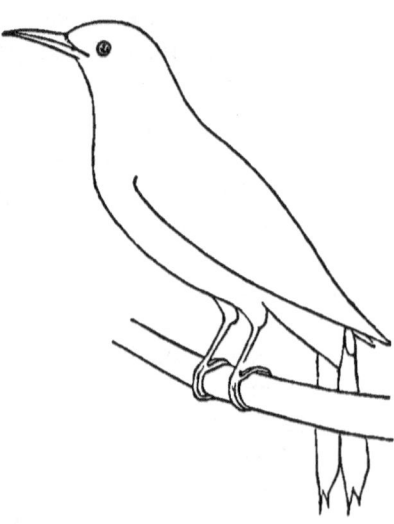

Fig. 18. Golden-winged Woodpecker (¼).

(*b*). The nests of our various woodpeckers differ but little except in size or situation. They always consist of a hole, generally excavated by the birds themselves in a tree, or rarely a post, which may be either sound or rotten. They are usually made more than six feet from the ground, and more often in a trunk than in a limb. They vary in length from six to even forty inches, and are enlarged near the bottom, though rarely or never lined. They are not always straight, but the entrance is almost invariably round, unless arched, as is often the case with those of the present species. No nests require more patience in construction than these; yet they are, in their way, master-pieces, being smooth, symmetrical, and, as it were, highly finished.

The nest of the "Flicker" may be found in maples, oaks, apple-trees, and occasionally pines or birches, but more often in some collection of trees than in an exposed place. In Massachusetts, it is finished about the middle of May, or earlier. The eggs, like those of all woodpeckers, have a smooth, white, unspotted[9] shell, and are often elliptical. They average about 1·15 × ·90 of an inch.

(c). As is indicated by the great number of nick-names bestowed upon them, the Golden-winged Woodpeckers are common and well-known throughout a large tract of country. In fact, they may be found in summer from the Gulf of Mexico to Hudson's Bay, and in many places, inclusive of Massachusetts, they may be found throughout the year. Near Boston, however, they are rather rare in winter. They usually become common between the middle of March and the first of April, and continue so until the approach of winter. Though social, and in autumn somewhat gregarious, they usually arrive in pairs, who return every year to their former haunts, but who generally build a fresh nest. This latter work they begin in April. Having chosen a suitable tree, by the roadside, in the orchard, or the woods, they proceed to excavate, the male and female laboring alternately. Observe one at work. Clinging to the trunk with his feet, but supporting himself by his rigid tail, he draws back his muscular head, delivers a vigorous stroke, and cuts a chip from the wood, which is generally dropped on the ground just outside. The hole (about three inches wide) is gradually deepened at the rate of between one-half and a whole inch each day, so that he can cling to the lower edge of the entrance while working. Finally he is lost to sight, and his operations can no longer be watched, for usually, if closely approached, he ceases his labors and flies away. Indeed, he is so suspicious as sometimes to be startled by the sound of distant foot-steps, and even to desert an unfinished nest if discovered. Moreover, he is fastidious, and often, displeased with

---

[9] There are frequently apparent markings, which can easily, however, be washed off.

the result of his first efforts, he begins again in another place or a different tree. It is nearly or quite as common to find the uncompleted excavations of this species and the Downy Woodpecker, as to find their finished nests. I have seen a tree with eight of the latter and three of the former. Immediately or soon after the middle of May (near Boston), six eggs are generally laid, sometimes at irregular intervals. A dozen eggs or more, however, have been found in the same nest, but these had probably been laid by two or more females. The female sometimes continues to lay, if robbed of her eggs, or, after deepening the hole, lays another set. Even this is often taken by boys, to whom few birds are more familiar than these. The young at an early age scramble out to the fresh air, and about their native tree, until old enough to fly.

The Pigeon Woodpeckers, as they are often called, frequent woods, orchards, pastures, fields, roadsides, and nearly all our kinds of trees, except the evergreens, for which they show no fondness. They may often be seen upon the ground, actively engaged in the destruction of ants (which chiefly constitute their diet), or hopping over our lawns in search of other insects. Sometimes, fluttering before a vine, they seize its berries; sometimes they visit gardens not only for grubs but for grain, and sometimes, like true woodpeckers, they hop about trees in the search of insects, or of their larvæ and eggs. They usually perch crosswise, which our other woodpeckers rarely do. They fly with ease, and often rapidity, moving through the air at a moderate height in gentle undulations, with an intermittent beating of the wings. They are naturally shy, and, though found in man's society, rather avoid his near approach. They are also affectionate, merry, and even noisy. Buffon supposed them to lead a dull, toilsome, and wearisome life,— an idea which both Wilson and Audubon have indignantly refuted.

(*d*). The three principal notes of the Pigeon Woodpeckers are: (1) A loud scream, wholly without the savageness observable in those of many birds of prey, but, on the contrary, rather jovial, (2) the rapid repetition of another unmusical though merry sound, and finally a lower note, chiefly of affection, to which many of their names owe their origin, such as that of "flicker." This last cry is a series of dissyllabic notes, and sounds like *wick'-a-wick'-a-wick'-a-wick'-a-wick'-a-wick'-a*. This is rarely heard unless two birds are together.

The Golden-winged Woodpeckers are undoubtedly less beneficial than many others of their tribe, but they never do enough injury to warrant their death at the hands of farmers. They are, however, but little molested, I believe, except by young sportsmen.

II. MELANERPES

(A) ERYTHROCEPHALUS.[10] *Red-headed Woodpecker.*
(Scarcely now to be ranked as a bird of Massachusetts.)

(*a*). About $9\frac{1}{2}$ inches long. Head, crimson. Interscapulars, wings, and tail, blue-black, highly glossed on the back and shoulders. Other parts (and the secondaries), white.

(*b*). The eggs average about $1\cdot10 \times \cdot85$ of an inch. See I, A, *b*.

(*c*). The Red-headed Woodpeckers were once common, about Boston, but I have seen but one within the last five years. I know no part of New England where they are not rare, and I shall therefore quote a large part of Wilson's biography of this species. "There is perhaps no bird in North America more universally known than this. His tri-colored plumage, red, white, and black glossed with steel blue, is so striking, and characteristic; and his predatory habits in the orchards and corn fields, added to his numbers and fondness for hovering along the fences, so very notorious, that almost every child is acquainted with the Red-headed Woodpecker. In the immediate neighbourhood of our large cities, where the old timber is chiefly cut down, he is not so frequently found; and yet at this present time, June, 1808, I know of several of their nests within the boundaries of the city of Philadelphia. Two of

---

[10] The Red-bellied Woodpecker (*Centurus Carolinensis*, with the crown and nape bright red, or in the female partly so) may rarely occur in New England.

these are in Button-wood trees (Platanus occidentalis), and another in the decayed limb of a large elm. The old ones I observe make their excursions regularly to the woods beyond the Schuylkill, about a mile distant; preserving great silence and circumspection in visiting their nests; precautions not much attended to by them in the depth of the woods, because there the prying eye of man is less to be dreaded. Towards the mountains, particularly in the vicinity of creeks and rivers, these birds are extremely abundant, especially in the latter end of summer. Wherever you travel in the interior at that season, you hear them screaming from the adjoining woods, rattling on the dead limbs of trees, or on the fences, where they are perpetually seen flitting from stake to stake on the road side, before you. Wherever there is a tree, or trees, of the wild cherry, covered with ripe fruit, there you see them busy among the branches; and in passing orchards, you may easily know where to find the earliest, sweetest apples, by observing those trees, on or near which the Red-headed Woodpecker is skulking; for he is so excellent a connoisseur in fruit, that wherever an apple or pear is found broached by him, it is sure to be among the ripest and best flavored. When alarmed, he seizes a capital one by striking his open bill deep into it, and bears it off to the woods. When the Indian corn is in its rich, succulent, milky state, he attacks it with great eagerness, opening a passage thro the numerous folds of the husk, and feeding on it with voracity. The girdled, or deadened timber, so common among corn fields in the back settlements, are his favorite retreats, whence he sallies out to make his depredations. He is fond of the ripe berries of the sour gum; and pays pretty regular visits to the cherry-trees, when loaded with fruit. Towards Fall he often approaches the barn or farm house, and raps on the shingles and weather boards. He is of a gay and frolicsome disposition; and half a dozen of the fraternity are frequently seen diving and vociferating around the high dead limbs of some large tree, pursuing and playing with each other, and amusing the passenger with their gambols. Their note or cry is shrill and lively, and so much resembles that of a species of tree-frog which frequents the same tree, that it is sometimes difficult to distinguish the one from the other."

Wilson eloquently defends this bird, proving his beneficial nature. He adds: "The Red-headed Woodpecker is, properly speaking, a bird of passage; tho even in the eastern states individuals are found during moderate winters, as well as in the states of New York and Pennsylvania; in Carolina they are somewhat more numerous during that season; but not one tenth of what are found in summer. They make their appearance in Pennsylvania about the first of May; and leave us about the middle of October."

III. SPHYRAPICUS

(A) VARIUS. *Yellow-bellied Woodpecker.*[11]

(In Massachusetts, chiefly a migrant.)

(*a*). About 8½ inches long. Wings and tail, black and white. Above, brownish or yellowish, marked with black. Beneath, yellowish; sides black-streaked. Crown-patch, scarlet; throat-patch, scarlet, or in ♀ whitish. Border of both patches, and eye-stripe, black. Head otherwise white or yellowish.

(*b*). The nest is to be found in woods or sometimes orchards. The eggs of each set are four or five, and average about ·95 × ·80 of an inch. See I, A, b.

(*c*). The Yellow-bellied Woodpeckers probably occur in Eastern Massachusetts as migrants only, though summer-residents to the westward ("beyond Springfield"), and to the northward, as in Canada, or the northernmost parts of New England, where they are quite common. Near Boston, I have seen them about the middle of April, and again in October, but I have always found them rare. They are somewhat shy, and usually silent. They travel singly or in pairs, and frequent woods rather than orchards. I have seen a pair, however, on a pine-tree, so near a house, that they were fired at with a parlor-rifle from the windows. As each bullet struck

---

[11] A Mexican species, *Centurus aurifrons*, bears the same name.

the tree, near the spot where the male was at work, if he moved, it was only to return immediately. He escaped apparently uninjured and continued for some time to dig out a hole in the trunk, for what purpose I am uncertain, as this was on the 4th of October, and on the following day he disappeared. If any of our woodpeckers are injurious, this species (including the next variety) is the only one. The Yellow-bellied Woodpeckers are well known to strip off the bark of various trees, not to obtain insects so often as to feed upon the inner bark. Sometimes, like the Downy Woodpeckers, they bore deep holes, especially in orchard-trees, whence they have been called "sap-suckers." They feed upon berries, and quite often, in common with other members of their family, catch insects in the manner of flycatchers, by darting at them from a perch. Their tongue is peculiarly constructed, and they cannot obtain an abundance of food in the characteristic manner of their tribe. They do not, however, so far as I know, ever seek it on the ground, though they sometimes visit fallen logs. They fly in undulations and rarely very far. Among the White Mountains, they may be seen not only in the woods, where removed from civilization, but also not unfrequently along the roadsides.

(*d*). Their ordinary note is an indescribable whine, like a puppy's moan, though Mr. Maynard thought that their alarm-note closely resembled that of the Blue Jay. But many of our woodpeckers delight in a music peculiarly their own, yet not unlike the drumming of the Ruffed Grouse. In spring, alighting on some tree, particularly one which is somewhat hollow and resonant, they rap loudly. The male and female often do this in response to one another, and it is, almost undoubtedly, a love-note. It is the only music which our woodpeckers can produce, and it is for them by far the easiest way of expressing their affection.

Sphyrapicus varius var. *nuchalis*, so-called, the Red-naped or Red-throated Woodpecker, is probably an abnormal form, or a distinct species, or else its occurrence in New England must be quite accidental. The last is probably the case, as it is said that only two specimens have been taken in this part of the country, and *nuchalis* may be treated as a western race. It differs from true *varius* in having a red patch on the hind-head or nape, and more or less red on the throat of the female. Yet, in Messrs. Baird, Brewer, & Ridgway's "North American Birds," it is stated that of true *varius* a female from Washington, D. C., has red on the throat, and a male from Carlisle, Pennsylvania, has it on the nape. The habits and notes of the Red-naped Woodpeckers are described as similar to those of the Yellow-bellied kind, and the biographical details of one (except as regards migrations and distribution) are applicable to the other.

IV. PICOIDES

(A) ARCTICUS. (*Northern* or) *Black-backed Three-toed Woodpecker.*

(A resident of northern New England, but of accidental occurrence in Massachusetts, in fall or winter.)

(*a*). About nine inches long. Wings and tail, black and white. Upper parts (and a maxillary line), glossy black. Beneath, white, banded on the sides with black. ♂, with a yellow crown-patch.

(*b*). The nest may be found in forests, chiefly in evergreens. The eggs seem to average about ·90 × ·75 of an inch; but two in my collection measure 1·05 × ·85. See I, A, b.

(*c*). The subjects of this biography have been given a name, which is no less resounding than their rapping in the forests, namely: Northern Black-backed Orange-crowned Three-toed Woodpeckers.[12] These birds are extremely rare or accidental in Massachusetts, and in no part of New England are common summer-residents, unless far to the northward, where they are resident throughout the year, though more common in winter. I have found the nest among the White Mountains, but I have not often seen the birds. They inhabit the extensive and thickly timbered forests, frequenting the evergreens rather

---

[12] This full title has actually appeared in print.

more than other species (unless the next). They lead an active life, and, like others of their tribe, are restless. They partly examine the trunk perhaps of a fine hemlock more than a hundred feet high, and then, as if dissatisfied, fly down to hop about a fallen log. They may occasionally vary this life by fly-catching, and in autumn undoubtedly feed on berries, in spite of the inexhaustible insect-wealth of the forests in which they live. They fly in undulations, but rather rapidly, often screaming as they do so.

(*d*). Their loud, shrill notes cannot easily be described. Audubon considered them "like those of some small quadruped suffering great pain;" but I have never heard the "shrill, harsh, rattling cry" which Dr. Cooper ascribes to this species. Authors must, however, necessarily differ in their descriptions of what it is nearly impossible to describe satisfactorily.

(B) AMERICANUS. *Banded Three-toed Woodpecker.*
(Much rarer in New England than the last species.)

(*a*). Essentially like the Black-backed Woodpecker (A), but with the back banded by white.

(*b*). "The nest and eggs do not differ from those of *P. Arcticus.*"

(*c*). The Banded Three-toed Woodpeckers have an Arctic (or circumpolar) distribution, and in New England are rarer than even the Black-backed Woodpeckers. They have not been captured in Massachusetts, except in a few isolated instances, of which I find only one recorded. They probably breed in northern New England to a limited extent, since "Mr. Brewster took two adult males at Gorham, July 30th, 1870, and one at Umbagog the first week in June, 1871." Mr. Maynard says: "I took a single specimen at Errol, October 31st, 1869. This species has a harsh, discordant note." Audubon never saw these woodpeckers, and drew his figures from specimens lent him by the Council of the Zoological Society of London. I have scarcely been more fortunate, having seen but one. This was on the roadside, not far from the Glen House in the White Mountains, and in August. During the momentary glimpse which I then had, I observed nothing peculiar in his habits. I have never found their nest or seen their eggs.

V. PICUS

(A) VILLOSUS. *Hairy Woodpecker.*

(Not common in Massachusetts, but abundant in the forests of northern New England, where it breeds.)

(*a*). About 9½ inches long. ♂, with a scarlet patch on the hindhead. Under parts, central back, and outer tail-feathers, white. (Feathers about the nostrils, yellowish.) Otherwise black and white.

[NOTE. There are Western varieties of this and the next species, with a soiling of gray on the breast, and without white spots on the wing-coverts.]

(*b*). The eggs of each set are four or five, and measure ·85 × ·65 of an inch, *or more.* The nest is built in woods, or sometimes orchards, and in Massachusetts is finished about the tenth of May. (See I, A, *b*.)

Fig. 19. Hairy Woodpecker (½).

(*c*). The Hairy Woodpeckers are resident throughout the eastern United States, and in summer, if not also in winter, may be found from the Gulf of Mexico so far to the northward as forests extend. Yet they rarely breed in Eastern Massachusetts, and are not even common in winter. The constant decrease of woodland in this part of the State has caused them in a great measure to desert it, but in the forests of Maine and New Hampshire they are abundant throughout the year. Near Boston, they frequent orchards as much as the woods. Excepting in being much less familiar toward man, and more fond of solitude, they scarcely differ in habits from the common little spotted or Downy Woodpecker. Audubon has represented these birds in no less than six assumed species, so great is the variation in size, and in the colors of the young. He even undertook to point out differences in manner and voice, between those of New Hampshire and those of Maine. Here his imagination almost undoubtedly led him astray, so easy is it for man to deceive himself by seeing, as he thinks, what he is determined to see.

(*d*). The Hairy Woodpeckers have both a loud, shrill cry, not unlike that of the "Flicker," and a sharp *chuck*, which resembles the characteristic note of the next species. Both of these notes, however, are somewhat peculiar, and need not often be confused with those of other species.

(B) PUBESCENS. *Downy Woodpecker.*

(A common summer-resident throughout New England, but less abundant in winter.)

(*a*). About $6\frac{1}{2}$ inches long. Outer tail-feathers barred with black. Otherwise like *P. villosus* (A).

(*b*). The nest is built in various trees, among which the apple-trees, birches, and poplars, are frequently selected. It has occasionally been found in a post. The entrance is two inches or less in diameter, whereas that of the "Flicker's" nest is usually from two to five inches high. The eggs, of which four or five are usually laid near Boston in the fourth week of May, measure ·80 × ·60 of an inch, *or less*.

(*c*). The Downy Woodpeckers, like their near relations the Hairy Woodpeckers, are resident throughout the wooded portions of eastern North America, in many places being common and well-known, as is the case in Massachusetts, where, however, they are less numerous in winter. In autumn they may be seen followed by titmice, creepers, nuthatches, and "wrens," whose society they seem to enjoy, though not themselves gregarious. They are not only sociable, but are very familiar towards man, showing no alarm at his approach, and preferring orchards, roadsides, and woods about houses or barns, to the forests, for which many of their relations have a marked fondness. Except on these points, they are fair types of their whole family.

They are only partially migratory, and are often resident in one locality throughout the year. They are usually mated for life, and on this account are frequently seen in pairs instead of singly. They are active or even restless. They sometimes eat berries, or catch insects on the wing, but I have never seen them on the ground. They generally pass the day in moving from tree to tree, from which they obtain insects, their larvæ and eggs, in the bark or beneath it. They fly in undulations, rarely far or high, and alight with both feet, on the trunk or larger limbs. They hop about with great ease, but generally move with the head pointing upward. Sometimes they merely pick up their food from the crannies of the bark, but at other times they extract wood-borers and other insects from the wood. For this purpose they dig out small circular holes of about the size made by a large awl, and with these often encircle even a large tree. In forming these holes, which are healthful to the trees and not injurious, they draw back their muscular head, and deliver their blows so rapidly as to produce a tremulous sound or rattling, which I find it impossible to imitate even by drumming with all my fingers on a board. They seize their prey by thrusting out their long tongue, which is coated with a sticky fluid. They work at their nest for about a month, chiefly in the early morning and in the afternoon. The male and female incubate alternately, and exhibit much alarm, if intruded upon after their young are hatched. They often fly above the heads of the men or dogs who may intrude, constantly uttering their loud note of alarm, and more often perching crosswise than at other times. They occupy their old nests or other cavities as retreats for the night or from very severe weather. They are very hardy, but not unfrequently in winter, during a blinding snow-storm or a pelting rain, they may be started from some decayed tree, on shaking it, or rapping it with one's cane. Should they pass the winter to the southward and return in the spring, they immediately resort to their former lodgings, unless some rude blast has destroyed these, in which case I have known them hurriedly to make an excavation in a neighboring stump.

(d). Their ordinary note is a *chink* or *chick*, which they most often utter on alighting on some tree or fence. Occasionally they repeat this rapidly (as *chick-a-chick-chick-chick-chick*). These notes, unless uttered in anger, seem indicative of the little woodpecker's contented disposition and constant happiness.

VI. HYLOTOMUS

(A) PILEATUS. *Pileated Woodpecker.* *Black* "*Log-cock.*" "*Wood-cock.*"

(In New England, almost entirely confined to the "timbered" districts of the North.)

(a). About eighteen inches long. Nearly black; a slight superciliary line, a broad stripe from the bill to the sides, wing-patch, etc., white. Crest, scarlet; in ♀, black in front. ♂, with a scarlet cheek-patch.

(b). "The eggs, which are six in number, average 1·25 × 1·00 of an inch, or more." See I, A, b.

(c). The Pileated Woodpeckers are in New England the largest, most spirited, and wildest of their tribe, but to the southward they yield to the larger "Ivory-bill," and in Central America to the magnificent *Campephilus imperialis*. They live exclusively in heavily timbered country, where they frequent the forests undisturbed by man, and the backwoods. There, solitarily or in pairs, they remain throughout the year, unless tempted by grain to wander to the fields. They are said to withstand alike the cold of Labrador and the heat of Florida, but in southern New England they are no longer found, though not rare in some parts of the White Mountains, and in like latitudes. They are rather shy, but they may sometimes be seen dexterously stripping off in large sheets the bark of decayed trees and logs, in order to lay bare the remains beneath. "If wounded on a tree, they cling desperately; if shot while flying, they defend themselves with courage, often inflicting severe wounds with their powerful bills." They fly in undulations, but rather laboriously, owing perhaps to their great size. They are probably the only members of their family in New England, whom the hawks never attack. One of our common woodpeckers may sometimes be seen adroitly dodging around some limb, while a disappointed hawk vainly endeavors to seize him. But should there be a pair of his enemies, he does not always escape, unless he can take refuge in a hole.

(*d*). The Log-cocks, besides the loud rolling sound of their hammering (audible for even a mile), often produce a loud cackling, not wholly unlike that of a hen. Hence, a countryman, asked by a sportsman if there were woodcock in a certain place, answered that he often heard " them hollering in the woods!"

CHAPTER III.

FOURTH ORDER. RAPTORES.

The *birds of prey* constitute this well-defined order. Their bill, like that of the parrots, is stout (about as deep as long), and strongly hooked; it is likewise furnished with a true cere, often concealed by feathers, which contains the nostrils. The toes, however, are not arranged in pairs, but on the general plan of three in front and one behind; the feet are highly muscular, and furnished with sharp, fully developed claws, called "talons." These are the principal external features.

The birds of prey are noted for the strength, rapidity, grace, or ease, of their flight, and in many cases, for their extraordinary power of sailing. With the exception of the vultures, they are famous for their spirit, variously displayed in energy, boldness, or courage, and for their carnivorous taste. For the most part, they feed upon smaller birds, quadrupeds, snakes, fish, or even insects, which they capture for themselves. They are hardy, being furnished with thick feathering, and an encasement of fat, which enables them to withstand the cold, and to live without food much longer than human beings can. They are to a large extent non-migratory, and those that migrate probably do so in a great measure to follow the migrations of their prey rather than to avoid the winter-weather in their summer-homes. They have been known to travel in large flocks, and the Fish Hawks are said to build their nests often in communities, but as a rule they are eminently unsocial, though faithful to their chosen haunts. The *vultures* are gregarious, cowardly, voracious, but rather slothful, and feed chiefly on carrion, which they frequently disgorge, when disturbed; whereas both the hawks, and the owls especially, eject in pellets only what is indigestible. Their only notes are said to be hisses or grunts. The hawks, on the other hand, possess various screams or whining whistles, while the owls are famous for their ludicrous or doleful cries, and for their hooting, so ill-boding to the superstitious.

§ 26. There are many things which cannot be defined except in their typical states, and, in the classification of birds, the typical species often characterize a group by certain features, which evidently allied species may possess only in part. Thus the *owls* may be defined as "nocturnal birds of prey," though some kinds hunt in daylight like the hawks. All our *Strigidæ*, however, possess the following structural features (besides those which characterize all *Raptores*) : head large, and capable of being turned in every direction without any movement of the body ; eyes looking more or less directly forward ; ear-feathers often forming noticeable tufts or "horns ;" nostrils concealed ; tarsi feathered ; general plumage very soft and thick. The colors are sober and much variegated, but alike in both sexes. The female is generally larger than the male.

The owls fly silently. Richard Hill, Esq., in Gosse's "Birds of Jamaica," says : "They search for their prey, as if they were pursuing it with the vigilance of the hound. They skim along the surface of the earth, glide among trees, explore avenues, sweep round, rise and fall, wheel short, and dart down, but never sail in circles. Their wide staring eyes are placed in what may be called their face, being right forward in front, and have scarcely any field of vision laterally. They therefore hunt with a forward and downward gaze, like dogs over a field. The globe of the eye of these nocturnal *raptores*, being immovably fixed in the socket by a strong elastic cartilaginous case, in the form of a truncated cone, they have to turn their heads to view objects out of the path of flight, and their neck is so adapted for this exertion, that they can with ease turn round the head in almost a complete circle, without moving the body."

Some owls lay their eggs on the ground or in the hollows of trees, but most kinds build a rude nest of sticks, or select an old nest of a like nature. Their eggs are 3–6, subspherical, white or whitish, and usually without a very smooth shell. Their peculiar notes, or hootings, are elsewhere noticed.

I. STRIX

(A) FLAMMEA (*var.* PRATINCOLA). (*American*) *Barn Owl.* (This bird has not recently occurred in Massachusetts more than once or twice.)

(*a*). "Tawny, or fulvous-brown, delicately clouded or marbled with ashy and white, and speckled with brownish-black; below, a varying shade from nearly pure white to fulvous, with sparse sharp blackish speckling; face, white to purplish-brown, darker or black about the eyes, the disk bordered with dark brown; wings and tail barred with brown, and finely mottled like the back; bill whitish; toes yellowish. * * * * ♀ 17 long; wing 13; tail $5\frac{1}{2}$; ♂ rather less. U. S., Atlantic to Pacific, southerly; rare in the interior, rarely N. to New England." (Coues.)

(*b*). "It is not uncommon in the vicinity of Washington, and after the partial destruction of the Smithsonian Building by fire, for one or two years a pair nested on the top of the tower." "Its nests have been found in hollow trees near marshy meadows" (Brewer), and, in certain parts of the country, the Barn Owls make burrows. The eggs average 1.70×1.30 of an inch, and are bluish or dirty (yellowish) white.

(*c*). The Barn Owls of America are much less well known than those of Europe, and no longer occur in New England, if, indeed, they ever have existed there except as stragglers. Mr. Allen, in his "Notes on Some of the Rarer Birds of Massachusetts," records the capture of one in this State, near Springfield, in May, and that of two others in Connecticut. The Barn Owls are common in many places to the southward and westward. Says Dr. Brewer: "The propensity of the California bird to drink the sacred oil of the consecrated lamps about the altars of the Missions was frequently referred to by the priests, whenever any allusion was made to this Owl."

Audubon says that "this species is altogether nocturnal or crepuscular, and when disturbed during the day, flies in an irregular bewildered manner, as if at loss how to look for a place for refuge. After long observation, I am satisfied that our bird feeds entirely on the smaller species of quadrupeds, for I have never found any portions of birds about their nests, nor even the remains of a single feather in the pellets which they regurgitate, and which are always formed of the bones and hair of quadrupeds."

(*d*). I can find no description of any note belonging to this species.

II. OTUS

(A) VULGARIS (*var.* WILSONIANUS). *Long-eared Owl.*
(In Massachusetts, a resident throughout the year.)

(*a*). About fifteen inches long. Ear-tufts conspicuous. General colors, fulvous and dark brown or blackish. Above, finely variegated, and mixed with whitish. Breast, etc., streaked, and also barred below. Tail (like the primaries, etc.) mottled and barred. Eyes *partly* encircled by black.

(*b*). The nest is most often that of a crow or hawk, slightly repaired. Sometimes, however, it is a fresh one, built by the birds themselves in some dark wood of evergreen, from ten to fifty feet above the ground ("on which," by the way, "the eggs are occasionally laid"). The eggs are pure white, as are those of most owls, and average about $1·60 \times 1·35$ of an inch. In Massachusetts, one set, varying in number from three to six, is laid about the middle of April.

(*c*). The Long-eared Owls are perhaps the most numerous of American owls, and are common near Boston, where they remain throughout the year. In spite of their comparative abundance, they are rarely seen, since they frequent the woods by day, and only fly abroad at night, unless, as often happens, they are driven out and rabbled by the Crows. They are easily approached in a strong light, as their vision is dependent upon darkness, but they usually roost in thick swamps, or dark and unfrequented woods of evergreen. At dusk they become active, and silently hunt for their prey, sometimes flying over fields and meadows, and sometimes perching to watch for it, with their keen eyes. Their hearing being no less acute than their sight, the slightest movement of any unfortunate mouse near them attracts their attention, and, sailing down from their post, they pounce upon their victim. They feed upon small birds and quadrupeds, or even large insects. They are unsocial, and generally lead a solitary life, though Wilson speaks of seven being found in one tree.

(*d*). I have never heard them utter any notes, and they are probably silent except during the season of love. Audubon, however, says: "When encamped in the woods, I have frequently heard the notes of this bird at night. Its cry is prolonged and plaintive, though consisting of not more than two or three notes repeated at intervals."

(B) BRACHYOTUS. *Short-eared Owl. Marsh Owl.*

(A resident of Massachusetts, most abundant near the sea.)

(*a*). About fifteen inches long. Ear-tufts inconspicuous. General colors, dark brown, and fulvous whitening beneath (on the belly, wings, etc.). Chiefly streaked, but on the tail, primaries, etc., barred (and slightly mottled). *Eyes completely encircled by black.*

(*b*). The nest is a rather slovenly structure, built on the ground, most often in rather wet places. The eggs of each set are usually four, averaging about 1.50×1.30 of an inch. They are white, and somewhat spherical. Several, taken from two nests not far from Boston, had apparently been laid about the middle of April.

(*c*). The Short-eared Owls are much less common than some other species, though resident in Massachusetts throughout the year. They are generally considered more abundant near the seashore than elsewhere, and even resort to marshes. They usually rest during the day on the ground or near it, and, when flushed, fly as if dazed, and soon alight. I have seen them abroad, however, on cloudy days. They sometimes occur in woods, particularly such as are swampy, but, in hunting, they more often fly over meadows or fields, moving their wings silently, and often sailing directly forward for a considerable distance. They also perch to watch for their prey, which seems to consist chiefly of mice and insects. Occasionally, when startled on the ground, they move off in leaps, more quickly than one might suppose them to be capable of doing, but they commonly take to wing. Audubon speaks of them as common in the Floridas during the winter, and says: "Indeed I was surprised to see the great number of these birds which at that period were to be found in the open prairies of that country, rising from the tall grass in a hurried manner, and zig-zagging for a few yards, as if suddenly wakened from sound sleep, then sailing to some distance in a direct course, and dropping among the thickest herbage." He adds: "I never started two birds at once, but always found them singly at distances of from twenty to a hundred yards; * * * ." The Short-eared Owls are partially migratory.

(*d*). Their notes, if they have any, I have neither heard, nor seen described.

III. SYRNIUM

(A) CINEREUM. *Great Gray Owl. Cinereous Owl.*

(Very rare so far to the southward as Massachusetts, where it occurs in winter only.)

(*a*). Extreme length, thirty inches. General colors, cinereous or ashy-brown, and a paler shade. "Waved" above; *streaked on the breast; barred on the belly,* tail, primaries, etc.

(*b*). One egg in Dr. Brewer's cabinet measures 2·25 × 1·78 of an inch.

(*c*). The Great Gray Owls exceed in size all other American species, and stand no less than two feet high. They seem, however, to be much less spirited than many others of their tribe. Mr. Dall considers them very stupid, and states that they may in day-time be caught by the hand. They are Arctic birds, and do not occur in New England except as very rare winter-visitors. I observed one in some pine-woods near Milton, in the early part of 1875, towards the end of an exceptionally severe winter. He was roosting in a partially dead tree, at about thirty feet from the ground. He instantly perceived my approach, and watched me dreamily. He refused to leave his perch until the tree was rapped violently, upon which he started with a few silent flaps and then sailed away. Owing to his great size, and his wings spread to their full extent, he presented a formidable appearance. He did not seem to experience difficulty in finding his way among the trees.

The Great Gray Owls, according to Mr. Dall's observations, "feed principally upon small birds, and he took no less than thirteen crania and other remains of *Ægiothus linaria* [or Lesser Red-poll] from the crop of a single bird."

(*d*). Their notes have been described as tremulous, and not unlike those of the Screech Owl.

(B) NEBULOSUM. *Barred Owl.* "*Hoot Owl.*"
(A resident in Massachusetts throughout the year.)

(*a*). About eighteen inches long. General colors, brown (cinereous above), and white (or tawny). Chiefly barred, *but on the belly streaked*. Eyes, small, very dark, and bordered on the inner edge with black.

(*b*). Evidence indicates that the Barred Owls usually build their own nests, choosing for a site some crotch next to the trunk of a pine or oak. The nests are finished in the latter part of April, and three or four eggs are then laid. These latter are white, and generally measure about 2.00×1.70 of an inch.

(*c*). The Barred Owls are apparently common residents in all the Atlantic States, but near Boston they have probably decreased in numbers proportionally to the decrease of woodland. They may, however, not unfrequently be seen during the day, reposing in some thick wood of pines or hemlocks. On such an occasion, they watch your motions as you approach, and should you walk from one side of the tree to the other, they follow you with their eyes, turning their head as if they must infallibly twist it off, but not moving the body. No creature through solemnity and soberness could be better fitted for the office of judge, and I am sure that every culprit would quail before such a stern, unvaried, and unceasing gaze. The effect of their behavior in a dark wood, is not unlike that of entering a darkened chamber, and observing the eyes of a grim ancestral portrait, as they everywhere follow one, as if to shame one out of some degeneracy. It is often difficult to start these owls, but sometimes, if your back is turned, they take the opportunity to glide away silently, and I have observed that on such occasions they do not seem to be much embarrassed by the light. They hunt at night, and are said to feed upon small birds, mice, snakes, frogs, and also larger game. I am inclined to believe that the males and females live apart except in the early spring-season, when their hootings are heard, even during the day.

(d). Their hootings are guttural, and rather startling, though ludicrous. Audubon thought that they might be compared to an affected burst of laughter. It has been asserted that the voice of the male is much weaker than that of his mate, as well as much less often heard.

IV. NYCTALE

(A) TENGMALMI (*var*. RICHARDSONI). *American (Sparrow) Owl. Richardson's Owl.*

(In Massachusetts, extremely rare.)

(a). About 10½ inches long. Except in size, essentially like *N. Acadica* (B).

(b). Dr. Brewer describes one egg as measuring 1.28×1.06 of an inch.

(c). The American Sparrow Owl is another species, whose occurrence in Massachusetts, even as a winter-visitor, is quite accidental, and about whose habits not much is apparently known by modern ornithologists. I have never seen one alive, and I shall therefore quote the brief biography of Audubon, who in his turn is obliged to quote from Richardson.

" I procured a fine male of this species at Bangor, in Maine, on the Penobscot, in the beginning of September, 1832; but am unacquainted with its habits, never having seen another individual alive. Mr. TOWNSEND informs me that he found it on the Malade River Mountains, where it was so tame and unsuspicious, that Mr. NUTTALL was enabled to approach within a few feet of it, as it sat upon the bushes. Dr. RICHARDSON gives the following notice respecting it in the Fauna Boreali-Americana:—'When it actually wanders abroad in the day, it is so much dazzled by the light of the sun as to become stupid, and it may then be easily caught by the hand. Its cry in the night is a single melancholy note, repeated at intervals of a minute or two. Mr. HUTCHINS informs us that it builds a nest of grass half way up a pine tree, and lays two white eggs in the month of May. It feeds on mice and beetles. I cannot state the extent of its range, but believe that it inhabits all the woody country from Great Slave Lake to the United States. On the banks of the Saskatchewan it is so common that its voice is heard almost every night by the traveller, wherever he selects his bivouac.'"

(B) ACADICA. *Acadian Owl. Saw-whet Owl.*
(In Massachusetts, not common, unless in autumn.)

(a). When erect, about six inches high. Above, chocolate-brown; head streaked, back spotted, and tail barred, with white. Beneath, white, streaked (in blotches) with reddish chocolate. (Tarsal feathers, tawny.) Eyes encircled by black. Bill black. (In A, "bill yellow.")

(b). "The eggs are generally laid in the hole of a tree, and are four to six in number." An egg, which was found in a pine-wood near Boston, about the first of May, evidently belonged to this bird. It was lying on the ground (not far from a tree, in which an Acadian Owl had previously been seen), and to it was attached two feathers, which correspond exactly to those of a stuffed "Saw-whet." The egg was cold, and slightly cracked. It has a remarkably smooth, white shell, and measures about $1 \cdot 00 \times \cdot 90$ of an inch.

(c). The little Acadian Owls are residents throughout New England, but near Boston, so far as I have observed, they are very rare in summer, being most numerous in autumn. They are apparently more social than other species, as "they have been known to occur in small parties." I have, however, always met them singly. During the day, they remain in woods and swamps, often ensconced in the hole of a tree, though they sometimes perch on a bough. They may be closely approached on a bright day, and do not fly far if disturbed. Immediately after sunset, however, they become full of animation and courage, and even venture into open lands. One would suppose it difficult for them to find enough food, but they undoubtedly surprise small birds at roost, easily detect the slightest movement of any small quadruped in the grass, and readily pick up such insects as sing through the night, or indeed others. They probably do not often feed on reptiles.

(*d*). Their extraordinary love-notes are doubly deceptive, from their strong resemblance to the noise of a saw-mill, and from the ventriloquism with which they are uttered. I have, however, vainly tried to produce similar sounds through various combinations of files and saws. The Saw-whet Owls, as they are called on account of these notes, have also a single low cry.

V. SCOPS

(A) ASIO. *Screech Owl. Mottled Owl. Red Owl.*

(A common summer-resident, but here rare, or absent, in winter.)

(*a*). Averaging nine inches in length. Gray, *or* brownish-red. paler below; variously marked, chiefly with black.

(*b*). The eggs are laid in the hollow of a tree, an apple-tree being frequently selected, in which are often placed a few simple materials, such as leaves or dry grass. The eggs, of which four are here laid about the middle of April, average $1·35 \times 1·20$ of an inch, though occasionally specimens measure $1·50 \times 1·30$ of an inch. They are white, and nearly spherical.

(*c*). The Screech Owls are probably the most well-known of the American Owls, owing to their general abundance in the United States, their frequent occurrence near the haunts of man, and their peculiar tremulous notes. During the day, they rest in the hollow of a tree, a thick evergreen, or even the hayloft of a barn, but from these retreats they are sometimes driven by impertinent Jays and other tormentors. They seem dazed by the light, and sometimes, when perched on a fence in the sunlight, as occasionally happens, they may easily be approached and even captured. At dusk they become active, often uttering their cries, which may be heard at all hours of the night until early morning, though never, so far as I know, in the day. They search the woods, fields, meadows, and often the neighborhood of houses and barns, now gliding like a shadow near the ground, or among the trees, and now perching to call to their mates or companions. They feed upon mice, various insects (many of which they catch upon the wing), and occasionally small birds. They are probably beneficial to the farmer, like some other owls, who differ in this respect from the hawks. Our night-owls, though aided by very keen sight, and by a flight so silent that their presence is often indicated only by their shadow, undoubtedly find it more difficult to obtain birds at roost than other creatures who betray themselves by moving. The Screech Owls as pets exhibit many of those traits, more or less characteristic of their whole family, which are less easily observed in the birds at liberty. I shall therefore quote from the "American Naturalist" an extremely interesting article by Mr. Maynard, on "The Mottled Owl in Confinement," from which, however, I am reluctantly obliged to omit several passages. He says: "On June 15, 1867, I observed some boys around a small owl which was perched on a stick. On closer examination I found that it was a young Mottled Owl (*Scops asio* Bonaparte). It was staring about in a dazed manner and seemed half stupefied. I easily persuaded the boys to part with it for a trifle, and took it home. I should judge that it was about two weeks old.[1] It was covered with a grayish down. I put it in a large cage, and gave it some meat which it ate, but not readily, for it seemed frightened at the sight of my hand, and at my near approach would draw back, snapping its beak after the manner of all owls. It soon grew tamer, however, and would regard me with a wise stare, as if perfectly understanding that I was a friend.

---

[1] This fact renders it probable that this species sometimes rears a second brood.

"In a short time it would take food from me without fear; I never saw it drink, although water was kept constantly near it. Its food consisted of mice, birds, and butchers' meat, on which it fed readily. I kept the bird caged for about two weeks, during which time it became quite tame, but would not tolerate handling, always threatening me with its beak when my hands approached it. As the wires of its cage broke its feathers when moving about, and as it hardly seemed resigned to confinement, I opened its cage and gave it the freedom of the room, leaving the windows open night and day. About this time I gave it the name of 'Scops,' to which in a little while it would answer, when called, with a low rattle, which sounded like the distant note of the kingfisher.

* * * * * * *

"When a bird is given it for food, it takes it in its claws, and with its beak invariably pulls out the wing and tail feathers first, then eats the head, then devours the intestines; then, if not satisfied, it eats the remainder of the bird, feathers and all.

"That this owl sees tolerably well in the daytime I have proved to my satisfaction. I caught a mouse and put it alive into an open box about two feet square. This I placed upon a bench near Scops, who was attentively watching my movements; the moment it saw the mouse, the owl opened its eyes wide, bent forward, moved its head from side to side, then came down with an unerring aim, burying its talons deep in the head and back of the mouse. Looking up into my face, and uttering its rattling note, as if inquiring, 'Isn't that well done?' it flew up to its perch with its struggling prey grasped firmly in its talons, where it killed the mouse by biting it in the head and back. During the whole act it displayed considerable energy and excitement.

* * * * * * *

"Scops will, in taking birds from my hand, almost always look up in my face and utter its subdued rattle. In sleeping, it usually stands on one foot, both eyes shut, but sometimes stretches out at full length, resting on its breast. When sound asleep it awakes instantly on its name being pronounced, and will answer as quickly as when awake. I have heard it utter its peculiar quavering note on one or two occasions, which, notwithstanding its reputed mournfulness, has much that sounds pleasant to my ears. When moving along a plane surface, Scops progresses, with a half walk, half hop, which is certainly not the most graceful gait possible.

"When out at night among the trees Scops acts in much the same manner as when in the house, hopping from limb to limb, looking about with a quick, graceful motion of the head, sometimes turning the head around so that the face comes directly behind.

"When it returns to the house in the morning, daylight is often long passed, and even sunrise. The alarm note is a kind of low moan; this was often uttered at the sight of a tamed gray squirrel (but with which it has now become better acquainted), and always at the sight of its old enemy, the dog.

"While flying, Scops moves through the air with a quick, steady motion, alighting on any object without missing a foothold. I never heard it utter a note when thus moving. When perching, it does not grasp with its claws, but holds them at some distance from the wood, clasping with the soles of the toes. When it has eaten enough of a bird, it hides the remaining portions in any convenient place near by. * * *

"Sometimes in the daytime it will take a sudden start, flitting about the room like a spectre, alighting on different objects to peer about, which it does by moving sideways, turning the head in various directions, and going through many curious movements; but it always returns to its perch and settles down quietly.

"I once placed a stuffed owl of its own species near it, when it ruffled its feathers, gave a series of hisses, moans, and snappings of the beak, and stretched out one wing at full length in front of its head as a shield to repulse what it took to be a stranger invading its own domains. As the stuffed bird was pushed nearer, Scops budged not an inch, but looked fiercer than ever; its ruffled back-feathers were erected high, its eyes sparkled, and its whole attitude was one of war.

"Some time since the building in which my pet was kept was torn down, and the bird was absent for two weeks; but a new building has been erected near the site of the old one, and to-day I found Scops in the new cellar, sitting on a projecting stone of the wall, as much at home as in the old place. From this it can be seen that its affection for locality is very strong. Notwithstanding Scops' long absence it is as tame as ever, taking its food from my hand, and behaving in the old manner. * * *"

(d). The ordinary note of the Screech Owl is a tremulous, continued hooting, repeated at short intervals. Wilson has likened this to the "shivering moanings of a half frozen puppy;" it resembles somewhat the distant baying of a foxhound, though not so deep. In spring, it is varied to what is more like an unearthly laugh, and it is not surprising that by the superstitions this cry should be considered ill-boding; yet there is almost a fascination in listening to it.

VI. BUBO

(A) VIRGINIANUS. *Great Horned Owl.*

(In Massachusetts, a resident throughout the year.)

(a). Extreme length, twenty-seven inches. Plumage variable; but large ear-tufts and white throat-patch constant. A fine specimen before me is marked with dark brown, whitish, and tawny. Above, finely variegated; tail, primaries, etc., distinctly barred. Beneath, more or less finely barred; under tail-coverts, pale, with a few waves of dark brown.

(b). The Great Horned Owls are said to sometimes lay their eggs in the hollow of a tree, or even in the fissure of a rock. Usually, however, they build a large nest of sticks, at some height above the ground, next to the trunk of a pine or occasionally a hemlock. For this purpose, they choose some dark and unfrequented wood, where in March, or even February, they lay their eggs, three or four in number. These measure 2.25×1.90 of an inch, or more, and are white, or sometimes yellowish.

(c). The Great Horned Owls are the most spirited and destructive of their tribe in North America, in many parts of which, including New England, they are not uncommon. They are resident in Massachusetts throughout the year. They frequent the thick woods, from which they roam at night over the open country, and pay visits to the farm-yard. They usually roost among some clump of evergreens during the day, and occasionally may be closely approached before they take to flight. But on cloudy days, they see well, and, exceptionally, even hunt for their prey, which consists of rabbits, squirrels, skunks, partridges, poultry, and the like. They fly with great strength and ease, often sailing, even in circles, like the buzzards. Apparently they inhabit the same neighborhood throughout the year, but lead a solitary life during the larger part of it.

Nothing can more gratify a romantic imagination than musings on the life of this owl. Imagine the scenes which characterize his existence. Fancy him perched on some tree: a silent watcher, he surveys the country shrouded in darkness, or fantastically lit by the moon, listens to the sighing of the breeze through the pines, and marks the waving of the mysterious shadows; then, spreading his wings, he sails away with the silence of a spirit, ready to pounce upon his unsuspecting prey, and alights in some still more romantic spot, perhaps by a lonely river in the forest; now, he wanders through a war of elements which man shrinks from, through darkness, cold, and falling snow, or goes abroad in a gloom impenetrable except to him and his fellow-wanderers, in furious winds, and in down-pouring rain; at last, he pounces upon some poor animal, and, tearing him piece-meal, begins his nocturnal repast. Next, he startles some traveler by his unearthly cries, perhaps united to the quavering note of the Loon.

What scenes he may have beheld, an unknown witness; what deeds of darkness he might disclose. But all this he enjoys. His savageness and wildness of disposition are evident. No other word than "devilish" can describe the Great Horned Owl in confinement. Approach him in some corner, remark his unconquerable spirit, observe his glaring eyes, as he slowly opens and shuts them, and listen to his hisses. Approach him with a light, see him contract the pupils of his eyes, and then, as you retreat, expand them until they seem like glowing orbs of fire. Approach him with food, and observe the eager ferocity with which he swallows it, doing so at a single gulp when possible. Approach him again, attempt to soothe him, and you cannot hesitate to pronounce him an irreclaimable savage.

(*d*). His cries are all unearthly. Sometimes he utters a horrid scream, sometimes notes which suggest the strangulation of some unhappy person in the woods, and at other times his loud hooting, *hoo-hoo-hoo-hoo*. Being, it is said, attracted by camp-fires, like other species, he often amuses the traveler with these agreeable and soothing sounds. In short, no bird has a character less pleasant to contemplate than the Great Horned Owl.

In the space left by a change in the text, it may not be amiss to give an amusing instance of the fictions credited by certain old writers. Charlevoix, says Wilson, wrote that certain owls caught mice for their winter's store, and, confining them, fattened them on grain.

VII. NYCTEA

(A) NIVEA.[2] (*American*) *Snowy Owl.*

(In Massachusetts, not uncommon in winter near the sea.)

(*a*). About two feet long. Snowy white; more or less marked with brown or blackish.

(*b*). The eggs are laid on the ground in Arctic countries. They are white, and nearly or quite 2½ inches long.

(*c*). The Snowy Owls, as their very thick and white plumage suggests, are Arctic birds, though in winter they wander southward in considerable numbers, being then more common in Massachusetts than any other species of this family with so high a range. It is said that, though rare in the interior, they are of not unfrequent occurrence along the coast, since they feed much upon fish, which they often catch for themselves.

---

[2] The specific name has recently been established as *scandiaca* var. *arctica*.

They have several times been captured on the islands of Boston Harbor, and I am quite confident of having seen one fly over the city. They may also be met with further inland, where they feed upon quadrupeds and birds. They hunt chiefly during the day, or just after sunset, and, instead of pouncing upon other birds, often pursue them on wing, thus resembling the hawks. As they feed upon grouse (or even, it is said, upon ducks and pigeons), they evidently possess great speed of flight. Owing to their size and handsome plumage, they are striking objects in winter-scenery, though often rendered inconspicuous by their likeness to the snow and ice. Though spirited, they exhibit much less ferocity than the Great Horned Owls, and are said to be more tractable as pets.

(d). Wilson says of this species that "its voice is so dismal that, as Pennant observes, it adds horror even to the regions of Greenland by its hideous cries, resembling those of a man in deep distress." The same author, in describing the method of fishing pursued by this owl, says: "Unlike most of his tribe he hunts by day as well as by twilight, and is particularly fond of frequenting the shores and banks of shallow rivers, over the surface of which he slowly sails, or sits on a rock a little raised above the water watching for fish. These he seizes with a sudden and instantaneous stroke of the foot, seldom missing his aim."

VIII. SURNIA

(A) ULULA (*var.* HUDSONIA). (*American*) *Hawk Owl.* Day Owl.

(A winter-visitant to Massachusetts of rare occurrence.)

(*a*). About sixteen inches long. General colors, dark brown and white, the former predominating above. Wings, tail, and under parts barred, but *throat streaked*. Face partly bordered by black, and narrow, approaching the hawk-type.

(*b*). "The nest is built in trees. The eggs, six in number, are white, and average about $1 \cdot 50 \times 1 \cdot 25$ of an inch."

(*c*). No other families of birds present such difficulties to the naturalist and biographer as the hawks and owls. Their general scarcity and shyness, their life of solitude and retirement, their frequent residence in inaccessible or little frequented places, and their silence during the greater part of the year, render it difficult to become intimate with their habits or, in some cases, with their notes. Such is eminently the case with the Hawk Owl, of whom apparently no adequate biography has yet been written. I have seen it but once, and can add little or nothing to former accounts. These birds, like several other species, inhabit the Arctic regions, not only of America, but also of the Old World. They very rarely visit Massachusetts, though "not uncommon in northern New England in autumn or winter" and said to have even bred in Maine. They are noted, not only for their physiognomy, which corresponds to their mode of life, but for their habit of hunting during the day like a hawk. It is probable, however, that they see well at night, as the one which I observed was active at dusk. His flight was much like that of a small hawk, and seemed less absolutely noiseless than that of other owls. Mr. Dall, as quoted by Dr. Brewer, says of this species "that it is very fond of flying, towards dusk, from the top of one small spruce to another, apparently swinging or balancing itself, calling to its mate at intervals, while chasing or being chased by it." Dr. Richardson says: "When the hunters are shooting Grous, this bird is occasionally attracted by the report of the gun, and is often bold enough, on a bird being killed, to pounce down upon it, though it may be unable from its size to carry it off. It is also known to hover round the fires made by the natives at night."

(d). "Its note is said to be a shrill cry, * * *." (Dr. Brewer.)

IX. SPHEOTYTO

(A) CUNICULARIA (*var.* HYPOGÆA). *Burrowing Owl. Prairie Owl.*

(One shot in Massachusetts, at Newburyport, May 4, 1875.[3])

---

[3] The authority for this statement is Mr. R. Deane.

(a). " Above, grayish-brown, with white, black-edged spots; below, tawny-whitish, variegated with reddish-brown, chiefly disposed in bars; face and throat whitish; crissum and legs mostly unmarked; quills with numerous paired tawny-white spots, and tail feathers barred with the same; bill grayish yellow; claws black; 9-10 long. * * * . Prairies and other open portions of the United States west of the Mississippi, abundant; lives in holes in the ground, in prairie-dog towns, and the settlements of other burrowing animals, using their deserted holes for its nesting place. There is certainly but one species in this country; it is a mere variety of the S. American bird." (Coues.)

(b). The eggs are described by Dr. Brewer as white, and as averaging about 1·35 × 1·15 of an inch.

(c). The peculiar Burrowing Owls habitually occupy the prairies and open lands to the westward of the Mississippi River, and there is but a solitary instance of their appearance in New England. They were formerly supposed to live habitually, as members of a "happy family," in the immediate company and dwellings of both the rattle-snakes and prairie dogs, but such a state of things has been shown to be fabulous. From the accounts furnished by Say to Bonaparte, the following facts may be gathered: The Burrowing Owls frequently occupy the villages of the marmots, whose deserted holes they use, instead of digging others for themselves. They are abroad during the day, and apparently feed chiefly on insects. "They manifest but little timidity, and allow themselves to be approached sufficiently close for shooting; but if alarmed, some or all of them soar away, and settle down again at a short distance; if further disturbed, their flight is continued until they are no longer in view, or they descend into their dwellings, whence they are difficult to dislodge."

(d). "The note of our bird is strikingly similar to the cry of the Marmot, which sounds like *cheh, cheh*, pronounced several times in rapid succession; * * * this cry is only uttered as the bird begins its flight."

§ 27. The **Falconidæ** are the typical *Raptores*, characterized by not having the ear-tufts, forward-looking eyes, and concealed nostrils of the owls, or the naked head, elevated hind-toe, and slightly webbed front-toes of our vultures (*Cathartidæ*, § 28). "The eyes, as a rule (but not always), are sunken beneath a projecting superciliary shelf, conferring a decided and threatening gaze." The tarsus is either naked or feathered, but the feathers above it are long and flowing (with certain exceptions, as in the fish-hawks).

The hawks and eagles are essentially diurnal birds of prey, not usually feeding on carrion. Some nest on cliffs, some on the ground, and others in the hollows of trees; but most of them build nests in trees, chiefly of sticks. The eggs of each set are from two to six, and are laid early in the season. They are rarely subspherical like owls' eggs, but are for the most part whitish, and generally blotched.

In this family there are several distinct groups.

The *harriers* (Genus I). Face with a slight ruff, forming an imperfect disk (such as belongs to the owls). Flight usually low, somewhat irregular, but not rapid. *Nest built on the ground.* Our species is characterized by the white upper tail-coverts.

The *falcons* (II). Upper mandible with a distinct pointed *tooth* behind the notch.[4] Highly raptorial birds of medium size. Flight in some respects inferior to that of

The *true hawks* (III, IV). Tarsi not scutellate behind, or feathered to the toes, which are always webbed at the base. Birds of comparatively slender form, with a rapid, protracted flight, occasionally interrupted by straight sailing, even at short intervals. They capture smaller birds with rapidity and energy.

The *buzzards*, including the *eagles* (V, VI, VII, VIII). Without the characteristics of the other groups. (In VI, VII, tarsus feathered to the toes.) Heavy and robust birds, with a

---

[4] The birds of this genus have been distributed into several subgenera not here presented. See Pl. 1, fig. 27.

beautiful and often sublime flight. They frequently sail upwards or forwards without moving the wings, generally doing so in circles. They usually pounce upon their prey from above, and often perch long to watch for it.

The *fish-hawks* (IX). "Plumage lacking aftershafts"' and oily. Feet very large. See IX.

I. CIRCUS

(A) CYANEUS (var. HUDSONIUS). *Marsh Hawk. American Harrier.*

(A common summer-resident throughout New England.)

(*a*). *Upper tail-coverts, white.* Mature ♂, extreme length about eighteen inches. Above, bluish-gray, becoming white beneath; often marked with brown. *Wings tipped with black.* ♀, extreme length about twenty inches. Upper parts, and streaks beneath, dark brown. Markings above, under parts, and bands on the tail, soft reddish-rusty.

(*b*). The nest, composed of grasses or occasionally sticks, is built, unlike those of all our other hawks, upon the ground, usually in a meadow, or other wet place. The eggs, of which in Massachusetts four are laid about the tenth of May, average 1·80 × 1·35 of an inch, and are white, often tinged with blue, and often marked with brown.

(*c*). The Marsh Hawks are among the least ambitious of their family, for the most part contenting themselves with such humble prey as mice, snakes, or frogs, and remaining near the ground. They may usually be seen flying low over meadows and fields, or wandering about the shores of some pond, but they also visit farms, and even molest poultry. Sometimes they beat about for their game; at other times they perch upon some fence to digest their last meal or to watch for another. They generally fly irregularly and leisurely, with intermittent sailing, up or down, to the right or left. But occasionally they mount higher, and sail about with ease; in autumn, when following the migrations of smaller birds, they even pursue these on wing, and often with success. Customarily, however, they drop upon their prey on the ground, and, after hurriedly poising, fall with a very certain aim, immediately rising, should they fail, but, if successful, feeding upon the spot. Their motions are characterized by ease and lightness, but their wings seem too long for rapid motion. The Marsh Hawks generally leave New England in autumn, and return in April. In summer they are among the commonest of our hawks.

(*d*). Their love-note is an indescribable scream, which is not, however, wholly characteristic, though distinct from any of the buzzards. Their winter-notes, says Audubon, "are sharp, and sound like the syllables *pee*, *pee*, *pee*, the first slightly pronounced, the last louder, much prolonged, and ending plaintively."

II. FALCO

(A) GYRFALCO. *Gyrfalcon. Gerfalcon. (Jerfalcon.)*
(In Massachusetts, an extremely rare winter-visitor.)

(*a*). About twenty-four inches long. Everywhere white, much marked with dark brown or black. Of several races, variety *islandicus* is said to be the only one which occurs in New England. In this form, white is especially predominant on the head.

(*b*). The eggs are said to measure about 2·40 × 1·70 of an inch, and to be much less darkly marked than those of the Duck Hawk. The nests are built on cliffs.

(*c*). Audubon describes as follows their habits in Labrador: "Their flight resembled that of the Peregrine Falcon, but was more elevated, majestic, and rapid. They rarely sailed when travelling to and fro, but used a constant beat of their wings. When over the Puffins, and high in the air, they would hover almost motionless, as if watching the proper moment to close their pinions, and when that arrived, they would descend almost perpendicularly on their unsuspecting victims.

"Their cries also resembled those of the Peregrine Falcon, being loud, shrill, and piercing. Now and then they would alight on some of the high stakes placed on the shore as beacons to the fishermen who visit the coast, and stand for a few minutes, not erect like most other Hawks, but in the position of a Lestris or Tern, after which they would resume their avocations, and pounce upon a Puffin, which they generally did while the poor bird was standing on the ground at the very entrance of its burrow, apparently quite unaware of the approach of its powerful enemy. The Puffin appeared to form no impediment to the flight of the Hawk, which merely shook itself after rising in the air, as if to arrange its plumage, as the Fish Hawk does when it has emerged from the water with a fish in its talons."

To this account I can add nothing, having never seen these birds, who are of accidental occurrence so far to the southward as Boston. I may here express my regrets at having had no opportunities of extending my researches to Labrador, from which a wealth of knowledge is undoubtedly to be obtained. Indeed, "an author should devote himself to travel and to one study," as has been said by a predecessor.

(B) COMMUNIS (*var.* ANATUM). (*American*) *Peregrine Falcon. Duck Hawk. Great-footed Hawk.**

(Very rare in Massachusetts, though known to have bred on Mount Tom, near Springfield.)

(*a*). About eighteen inches long. Above, dark ash (brownish or bluish, according to age), "waved" with a paler shade. Tail banded. Beneath, white or buffy; breast spotted, and sides barred, with black. Forehead, whitish; *cheeks, black*.

(*b*). The nest, if any, is built on a cliff, in some spot not easily accessible. A set of four eggs, found in this State, was laid in the early part of April. The Duck Hawk's eggs average about $2·20 \times 1·70$ of an inch, and are creamy, buff, reddish, or even brick-red, blotched and clouded with (several shades of) dark brown, often of a reddish tinge. A specimen in my collection presents a form or *appearance*, frequently observable in other eggs, that of having had the upper and darker markings removed.

(*c*). The spirited Duck Hawks (the American representatives of the famous Peregrine Game-falcons) belong to the highest nobility of their tribe, rarely descending from the dignity of open warfare, and pursuing birds on the wing with unsurpassed courage, speed, and skill. They are known to breed in several isolated parts of New England, where they are probably resident throughout the year, but in Eastern Massachusetts they are extremely rare, though they may occur along the coast in autumn or winter. Audubon, from his devotion to the pursuit of birds, was undoubtedly more familiar with the birds of prey than any other of our writers; and, having had no opportunities to study the habits of the Duck Hawk, I shall therefore quote from him.

"The flight of this bird is of astonishing rapidity. It is scarcely ever seen sailing, unless after being disappointed in its attempt to secure the prey, which it has been pursuing, and even at such times it merely rises with a broad spiral circuit, to attain a sufficient elevation to enable it to reconnoitre a certain space below. It then emits a cry much resembling that of the Sparrow Hawk, but greatly louder, like that of the European Kestrel, and flies off swiftly in quest of plunder. The search is often performed with a flight resembling that of the tame pigeon, until perceiving an object, it redoubles its flappings, and pursues the fugitive with a rapidity scarcely to be conceived. Its turnings, windings and cuttings through the air are now surprising. It follows and nears the timorous quarry at every turn and back-cutting which the latter attempts. Arrived within a few feet of the prey, the Falcon is seen protruding his powerful legs and talons to their full stretch. His wings are for a moment almost closed; the next instant he grapples the prize, which, if too weighty to be carried off directly, he forces obliquely toward the ground, sometimes a hundred yards from where it was seized, to kill it, and devour it on the spot. Should this happen over a large extent of water, the Falcon drops his prey, and sets off in quest of another. On the contrary, should it not prove too heavy, the exulting bird carries it off to a sequestered and secure place. He pursues the smaller Ducks, Water-hens, and other swimming birds, and if they are not quick in diving, seizes them, and rises with them from the water. I have seen this Hawk come at the report of a gun, and carry off a Teal not thirty steps distant from the sportsman who had killed it, with a daring assurance as surprising as unexpected. This conduct has been observed by many individuals, and is a characteristic trait of the species. The largest duck that I have seen this bird attack and grapple with on the wing is the Mallard.

"The Great-footed Hawk does not, however, content himself with water-fowl. He is sometimes seen following flocks of Pigeons and even Blackbirds. For several days I watched one of them that had taken a particular fancy to some tame pigeons, to secure which it went so far as to enter their house at one of the holes, seize a bird, and issue by another hole in an instant, causing such terror among the rest as to render me fearful that they would abandon the place. However, I fortunately shot the depredator.

"They occasionally feed on dead fish that have floated to the shores or sand bars. * * *

"Whilst in quest of food, the Great-footed Hawk will frequently alight on the highest dead branch of a tree in the immediate neighbourhood of such wet or marshy grounds as the Common Snipe resorts to by preference. His head is seen moving in short starts, as if he were counting every little space below; and while so engaged, the moment he spies a Snipe, down he darts like an arrow, making a rustling noise with his wings that may be heard several hundred yards off, seizes the Snipe, and flies away to some near wood to devour it.

"It is a cleanly bird, in respect to feeding. No sooner is the prey dead than the Falcon turns its belly upward, and begins to pluck it with his bill, which he does very expertly, holding it meantime quite fast in his talons; and as soon as a portion is cleared of feathers, tears the flesh in large pieces, and swallows it with great avidity. If it is a large bird, he leaves the refuse parts, but, if small, swallows the whole in pieces. Should he be approached by an enemy, he rises with it and flies off to the interior of the woods, or if he happens to be in a meadow, to some considerable distance, he being more wary at such times than when he has alighted on a tree."

Audubon elsewhere adds: "I never saw one of them attack a quadruped, although I have frequently seen them perched within sight of squirrels, which I thought they might easily have secured, had they been so inclined." He also says: "Many persons believe that this Hawk, and some others, never drink any other fluid than the blood of their victims; but this is an error. I have seen them alight on sand-bars, walk to the edge of them, immerse their bills nearly up to the eyes in the water, and drink in a continued manner, as Pigeons are known to do."

The Duck Hawks are so destructive, and so much opposed to the interests of sportsmen, that, in spite of their admirable spirit and strength, it is not to be regretted that they are rare in Massachusetts.

(C) COLUMBARIUS. *Pigeon Hawk. American Merlin.*

(Not very common in Massachusetts, though known to have bred here.)

(*a*). About twelve inches long. *Above,* dark ashy-blue; in the young (and ♀) ashy-brown. Forehead, tip and narrow bands of the tail, and markings on the wing, white or whitish. Tail, in ♂, also banded with black. *Beneath,* white, tinged with buff on the breast, with reddish behind, and marked with dark brown.

(*b*). The eggs average 1·50 × 1·20 of an inch, but otherwise strongly resemble those of the Duck Hawk, unless more finely marked. James Gatley, the so-called "Hermit of Hyde Park," obtained in that town, several years before his death, and before the pine-woods were extensively cut down, a small and neatly constructed nest of this species, together with the parents and young. I have another nest and five eggs, which were found near Boston in the early part of May. The latter, which was built in a pine about twenty feet from the ground, is composed of sticks, together with dry grass, strips of cedar-bark, and a little moss. The eggs are abnormal, being buff, slightly clouded with a darker shade.

(*c*). The Pigeon Hawks occur in the winter so far to the

southward as Florida, but at that season are rare in Massachusetts, much more so than in spring or fall. They vary in numbers from year to year, but occasionally breed here, and this I can from personal experience positively assert. They are probably more abundant as summer-residents to the northward, as I have observed them to be most numerous near Boston in fall, though never common. Occasionally they may be seen traveling, even in pairs, moving leisurely along at some height in the air. They do not sail so much as most of our hawks, but often perch on a tree to watch for their prey, which they pursue with indescribable speed and skill, and with a rapid beating of the wings. They feed principally upon birds (even attacking those of their own size), pursuing them through thick and thin, and following every turn with surprising agility, until, overtaking their victim, they thrust their talons into its vitals, causing instant death. They generally begin their repast upon the spot, and do not carry off their prey. They frequent the woods rather less than the Sharp-shinned Hawks, but more often occur in pastures with scattered trees, or about open lands. Their movements and haunts seem more or less dependent upon the progress of the smaller birds, whose migrations they often follow. They are somewhat shy of man, but are said to be so bold as to carry off chickens from the farm-yard. In summer, I have seen them among pines, where I have known them to build their nest.

On consulting other authors, I find the following facts, which I have either not mentioned or never observed. Wilson says of this species: "Sometimes when shot at, and not hurt, he will fly in circles over the sportsman's head, shrieking out with great violence, as if highly irritated. He frequently flies low, skimming a little above the field."

Samuels says: "The Pigeon Hawk, in alighting on a branch or other object, always descends below the level of it, and rises up; and usually turns abruptly about, and faces the direction from which it came, as soon as it has struck its perch. This habit is observable in many of the other hawks.

"While perching, the tail is often flirted up and down, and

the wings are partially opened and shut in a nervous manner, as if the bird were anxious to be off again in the pursuit of game."

Says Dr. Wood: "This bird when sitting on a tree so closely resembles a pigeon that it will oftentimes deceive the most expert hunter. One of the specimens brought me was shot for a pigeon, and the mistake was not discovered until the bird was picked up. It is from this striking singularity that I suppose it derives its name."

(d). The notes of the Pigeon Hawk, heard chiefly in spring, are quite characteristic, but, nevertheless, are not easily described. In fact, it is almost or wholly impossible to know the cries of our hawks, unless learned directly from nature.

(D) SPARVERIUS. (*American*) *Sparrow Hawk*. *American Kestrel*.

(In New England, a summer-resident, locally distributed.)

(a). About eleven inches long. Crown, ashy-blue, usually with a chestnut patch of varying size. Head, otherwise white, with generally seven large black markings, including one on the nape. Tail, often surrounded by white; and broadly (sub-) tipped with black. Primaries, etc., black, with imperfect white bars. Otherwise: — ♀, brown above, becoming chestnut on the tail, nearly everywhere black-barred. Beneath, white; breast (often buffy or reddish, and) streaked with black (or dark brown). ♂, smaller, and with few or no black bars or streaks. Wing-coverts, ashy-blue (sometimes spotted with black).

(b). The eggs are generally deposited in the hollow of a tree,—often of one rather isolated, a very rare circumstance in the case of other hawks. The eggs, four or five in number, or even more, are laid in Massachusetts about the middle of May. Two, taken from my cabinet, are fair specimens. One measures 1.35×1.20 of an inch, and is very light brown, with small blotches of reddish "Vandyke." The other measures 1.35×1.20 of an inch, is somewhat spherical and is finely freckled with two shades of russet, confluently so at the two ends.

Other specimens exhibit great variation in ground-colors, but they rarely have the large and prominent markings, often seen on the eggs of the Sharp-shinned Hawk.

(c). The Sparrow Hawks, though their flight is *comparatively* weak, it being rarely or never much protracted, are none the less active and daring. Perched on some tree or fence, and occasionally flirting the tail, they eagerly watch for their prey, which consists of mice, small birds, and even insects. Then, as if restless and dissatisfied, they leave their post, and fly off along the roadsides, over the fields, through the orchards, but less often among the woods than in open lands. Now pausing to reconnoitre, with a quivering of the wings, now sailing briefly but with eminent grace, they pass on swiftly, but not in the constant hurry which characterizes the Sharp-shinned Hawk. Sometimes they pounce upon a field mouse, which they often carry to a tree to eat; sometimes their quick eye detects a poor sparrow or thrush, and they then dive into some thicket or chase on wing, generally with fatal success. Their motions are characterized by more grace, but less speed and fury, than those of the other small hawks. They are, however, equally cruel and destructive, and the smaller birds find little or no protection in thickets or trees. They usually perch and fly not far from the ground, and never, so far as I have observed, mount to a great height. Several anecdotes serve to show that they are very scrupulous about their food, and do not like tainted flesh. They are the least shy of our hawks, and often exhibit a surprising degree of familiarity toward men. They are also rather social, and not uncommonly occur in family-parties or pairs.

The Sparrow Hawks are distributed through New England rather locally, but apparently are nowhere common. They are especially rare in Eastern Massachusetts, so far as I have observed in confirmation of others, and, having never seen them in winter, suppose them undoubtedly to be migratory. Mr. Maynard, however, considers them as resident throughout the year, though rare in winter. In Florida they are "abundant," remaining there at all seasons, though known to occur in high latitudes as summer-residents. They seem to have a marked fondness for home, and return to the same nesting-place, even several years, it is said, in succession. Wilson mentions a frequent circumstance in their life, which I have never observed, and says: "The Blue Jays have a particular antipathy to this bird, and frequently insult it by following and imitating its notes so exactly as to deceive even those well acquainted with both. In return for all this abuse the Hawk contents himself with, now and then, feasting on the plumpest of his persecutors; who are therefore in perpetual dread of him; and yet, thro some strange infatuation, or from fear that if they lose sight of him he may attack them unawares, the Sparrow Hawk no sooner appears than the alarm is given, and the whole posse of Jays follow."

(*d*). The notes of this species are loud and rather shrill, but cannot be defined. It may be useful, however, for some person familiar with British birds, to know that they were thought by Audubon to strongly resemble those of the European Kestrel.

III. ACCIPITER[5]

(A) FUSCUS. *Sharp-shinned Hawk.* "*Pigeon Hawk.*"

(A common summer-resident in many parts of New England.)

(*a*). About twelve inches long. Above, dark brown (becoming ashier with age), with a few white spots, chiefly on the hind-head and wings. Tail, lighter, with a few dark bands (which are more distinct than those of the wings), and tipped with pale brown or whitish. Beneath, white; breast, closely barred with light rufous-brown, and throat pencilled, but under tail-coverts often unmarked. The shafts of the wing and tail have a faint reddish gloss, as have also the basal portion of the webs.

(*b*). The nest is usually built in a pine, from twenty to forty feet above the ground. It is composed chiefly of sticks and

---

[5] *Nisus* has been lately established in place of *Accipiter.*

twigs, placed in a fork or crotch next to the trunk. The eggs, about four in number, are laid near Boston, in the second week of May. They measure 1·50×1·25 of an inch or less, and are white (tinged with blue or green), sometimes unmarked, but more often with a few large and prominent markings of dark brown, chiefly near the crown.

(c). The Sharp-shinned Hawks are common summer-residents throughout New England, but near Boston, so far as I have observed, are extremely rare in winter, though I have seen one boldly perched on the shafts of a wagon in a shed. Though naturally shy, they are very impudent, and, trusting to the rapidity of their flight, often commit some daring robbery before the eyes of the farmer. They frequent the woods much more than the Sparrow Hawk, and lie in wait there for some unfortunate passer-by. Should a Robin make his appearance, they give chase, and though he fly never so quickly, they soon overtake him. Sometimes, as they pass through the woods, they perceive some innocent bird feeding on the ground, whom they seize and bear off almost before the traveler can realize what has happened. So great is their eagerness and daring that their victims can hardly find any refuge from their fury. Nuttall says in illustration of their impetuous violence that "descending furiously and blindly upon its quarry, a young Hawk of this species broke through the glass of the green-house at the Cambridge Botanic Garden, and fearlessly passing through a second glass partition, he was only brought up by the third, and caught, though little stunned by the effort. His wing-feathers were much torn by the glass, and his flight in this way so impeded as to allow of his being approached." The Sharp-shinned Hawk characterizes all his movements with the same speed and continual apparent haste, the same restlessness and impetuosity. He often flies far, and even at a great height, but much less often straight forward or with a regular beat of the wings than the Pigeon Hawk. When flying to a distance, his flappings are quick but somewhat irregular, but, when hunting, he moves nervously, now high, now low, now to the right, now to the left, rarely having the patience to sail protractedly. On following his prey, he does so as if attracted by an irresistible magnet, his movements being instantly simultaneous with those of his quarry. He generally carries off his food, and eats it in a tree. But his prowess in comparison with his size is astonishing, and he often pounces upon birds much larger or heavier than himself. I have seen him fall upon Pigeon Woodpeckers, and upon plump Quail. In such cases, he feeds upon the ground, but it is useless to rescue his victims, as they are almost invariably found to be dead or past all recovery. These Hawks are said by Audubon to act often in concert, but they usually hunt singly. I have seen the Goldfinches escape from their clutches by mounting above them, even until almost lost to sight, but most birds, terrified by the fury of their onslaught, instinctively dive into thickets or trees, which unfortunately afford them but little protection. Whatever feelings of anger and indefinite longings for revenge may be excited by the Sharp-shinned Hawks, one cannot but admire their intrepidity and spirit. Though they feed partly upon insects, yet they must be considered eminently destructive, and be ranked among the audacious marauders who unhesitatingly plunder the farm. It is common to find traces of their murders in carefully picked bones or scattered feathers, along the wood-paths where they have secured some prize.

(d). Their notes are loud and shrill, but are not often heard except in spring.

(B) COOPERI. *Cooper's Hawk.* "*Chicken Hawk.*"
(In New England, a summer-resident.)

(a). About eighteen inches long. *Tail slightly rounded.* "Neck often marked with rufous." Otherwise like the Sharp-shinned Hawk (A).

(b). The nest has a strong outward resemblance to that of the Crow, and sometimes an imperfect resemblance throughout. It is composed chiefly of sticks, which are neatly laid together near the top of a pine, a rather slender tree being not unfrequently chosen. It is placed either in the topmost crotch, or more often at the junction of two branches with the trunk, from forty to sixty feet above the ground. Such are the nests observed near Boston, where the eggs are laid in the first week of May. Of these, the usual set of three or four average about 1·90 × 1·50 of an inch, and are white, tinged with blue (sometimes deeply), either unmarked, or with a few brown blotches.

(c). The Cooper's Hawks are common summer-residents in all the States of New England, but in many places are much less numerous than other species. Their general habits and manners are essentially the same as those of the Sharp-shinned Hawks, but they have much less "dash," and are not so bold. They are easily distinguished by their size. They may usually be seen flying just above the trees with a flapping of the wings, then a straight and rather measured sail, for they rarely move in circles. They feed upon rabbits, squirrels, water-fowl, and other birds, but not often on the smaller kinds, as I have seen these near them, or about their nests, disregarded. They may be seen to pursue flocks of wild pigeons or other migrants with a beat of the wings as rapid as that of their victims, and seizing one to bear it to some grove. Sometimes, in passing through the woods, they suddenly pounce upon the Ruffed Grouse, for they do not hesitate to grapple with creatures much larger than themselves. At other times, they mark a Robin, and follow it wherever it goes, dashing between branches, through trees, and over the fields, rarely being disappointed in the end. If possible, they carry their prey to the woods, and I am inclined to think that during a continued residence in one place, they often resort to the same tree. They are well known to the farmers as "Chicken" Hawks.

(d). Their cries suggest the exclamation of an alarmed hen, and consist of several successive notes, which Audubon considered similar to those of the Pigeon Hawk.

IV. ASTUR

(A) PALUMBARIUS (var. ATRICAPILLUS). (*American*) *Goshawk.* "*Partridge Hawk.*"

(In Massachusetts, a resident throughout the year, but very rare in the breeding-season and summer.)

(*a*). 20–24 inches long. Above, ashy or slate, becoming blackish on the head. Tail with dark bands and a white tip. Superciliary line and under parts, white; the latter waved or barred, and finely streaked, with ashy-brown or slate.

(*b*). The nest is usually built of sticks, etc., in a tall tree. The eggs measure about 2.25×1.75 of an inch, or more, and are white, strongly tinged with blue or green, and sometimes marked with brown.

(*c*). The handsome Gos-hawks are constant residents in northern New England, and also in Massachusetts, where, however, they are so extremely rare in summer that I have found but one nest, and have seen only two pairs. In winter, they are seldom common near Boston, though their numbers vary from year to year. They are very spirited and destructive, feeding principally upon rabbits, squirrels, pigeons, grouse, and ducks. They are also very active, perching and sailing comparatively little. They move, often at a considerable height, with a regular beating of the wings, which is redoubled, should they give chase to a flock of birds, when they move with a speed unsurpassed by that of any other hawk. I have seen one press into a company of Pine Grosbeaks and seize one in each foot. On perceiving a single bird of tempting size, they sometimes secure it by diving from above, when, without a moment's pause, they carry it to a perch. In the woods they fly rather low, ready to drop upon their prey, but so rapidly that one might imagine that their sight would be blurred. I have been surprised to observe how easily, when guiding themselves among the trees, they detect the presence of a partridge or squirrel. They are not, however, capable of constant activity, and occasionally, gracefully sailing up to some perch, they watch for their prey, sometimes doing so in open land. They stand with an erectness observable in other hawks, and are spirited even when at rest.

(*d*). For a greater part of the year they live singly and silently, but in spring I have heard them utter loud screams.

V. BUTEO

(A) BOREALIS. *Red-tailed Hawk* (or *Buzzard*). (*Eastern*) "*Red-tail.*" "*Hen Hawk.*"

(In Massachusetts, a resident throughout the year, but less common than the next species.)

(*a*). Extreme length, nearly two feet. Above, dark brown, marked with fulvous (chiefly on the head), and with white (chiefly behind). *Tail, chestnut-red,* tipped with white. and sub-tipped with black, but *beneath* of a uniform *silvery gray*. Under parts, white (or tinged), marked with a varying shade of brown, which generally forms an interrupted band across the lower breast. A fine *immature* specimen, now before me, is more than two feet in length. Above, dark umber, more or less interrupted by white, chiefly on the tail-coverts. Beneath, white; sides blotched with umber-brown, *forming a dark zone across the lower breast.* Feathers of the thigh spotted or imperfectly barred with a lighter shade. Tail, medium brown (often tinged with gray, but here with chestnut), barred with blackish, tipped with whitish; beneath, light gray, and faintly barred.

(*b*). The nest does not differ from that of the Red-shouldered Hawk, unless in being sometimes less well lined, occasionally rather less accessible, and more often built in dry woods. For a description of the eggs, see B, b.

(*c*). The Red-tailed Buzzards are the most majestic of our hawks, though surpassed by many in activity and speed. They are in southern New England resident throughout the year, but are said to occur to the northward only during the summer-season. Except in winter, they are much less common than the Red-shouldered Hawk, whose habits are so very similar, that I shall abbreviate this biography, and refer my readers to the next. They sometimes sail even a mile without moving the wings, or mount in circles till nearly lost to sight, but they are ordinarily dependent upon the impetus given by occasional flappings. They feed upon large birds, rabbits, squirrels, snakes, frogs, etc., and not unfrequently fall upon their prey from an elevation of several hundred feet. They also often perch upon some tree, as in a meadow, and watch for movements in the grass. They are somewhat shy and difficult to approach, but they are bold enough to carry off poultry, and I have been told of one actually caught in a hen-house.

(*d*). I can perceive no essential difference between their cries and those of the next species.

(B) LINEATUS. *Red-shouldered Hawk* (or *Buzzard*). "*Hen Hawk.*"

(In Massachusetts, a common resident throughout the year.)

(*a*). Much less stout than the "Red-tail," and less in average size, the female being rarely or never more than twenty-three inches long. The coloration is variable, but the following description of a fine mature specimen will answer for others. Above, dark brown. Head, streaked with rusty and white; back and rump marked with the same colors. Tail, and quill-feathers, black; the former tipped, and both barred, with white. *Shoulders, rich rufous* or pheasant-brown. Beneath, white. Breast, etc., streaked, chiefly with fulvous, with which the belly, etc., is tinged and finely barred. Under tail-coverts, white; tail the same, with bands of pearly gray. Immature birds have the white above and black impure, the rufous wanting or restricted. Beneath, white, streaked (and spotted) with dark brown. "Tail beneath silvery white." Under wing-coverts usually more or less fulvous as in the adult.

(*b*). The "Hen Hawks" generally build a fresh nest every year, though they may occasionally occupy the same nest "for several seasons," as Mr. Samuels states to be the case. Should their home be destroyed during the season of incubation, they usually repair an old nest for a second brood, as they sometimes do for their first. Their nest, when finished, is a large structure of sticks (from eighteen to thirty inches in diameter), and is commonly lined with small branches of hemlock, or with tree-moss. It may be found in rather secluded or unfrequented woods and pine-groves, particularly those which contain swamps, brooks, or ponds. It is placed next to the trunk of a pine, or sometimes an oak, from fifteen to seventy-five feet above the ground. It is seldom built in a young tree, or in one at all isolated, and is rarely concealed by surrounding foliage. Near Boston it is finished between the first week and last day of April, and two, three, or four eggs, are then laid. These often exhibit great variation, even when taken from the same nest. Though varying in size and shape, some being elongated, or somewhat pointed at the smaller end, they average about 2·20 × 1·70 of an inch. From a series in my cabinet, recently collected near Boston, the following descriptions are taken. (1) White, evenly blotched and spotted with lilac. (2) White, evenly but coarsely marked with a pretty reddish brown. (3) White, with a few thin and vague markings of chocolate. (4) Dirty white, not appreciably marked. (5) Dirty white, with a very few fine scrawls at the smaller end. (6) Dirty white, blotched at the smaller end with umber. (7) Dirty white, clouded at the smaller end with several shades of brown. (8) Dirty white, fadedly blotched, chiefly at the smaller end. (9) Impure white, blotched with faint reddish brown chiefly at the smaller end, and with a few dark markings. (10) Dirty white, faintly blotched all over, but with a few chocolate spots. (11) Dirty white, blotched faintly with purplish and reddish brown, but with dark blotches on the crown. (12) Impure white, with a ring of reddish brown blotches about the crown. Some specimens have reddish or buffy ground-colors, and others are marked but little and faintly, or with a few isolated blotches.

There is no salient point of difference between these eggs and those of the "Red-tail," of which several are now before me.

(c). The Red-shouldered Buzzards, so far as I have observed, are the commonest hawks near Boston, where they are resident throughout the year. They breed from Florida nearly to Hudson's Bay. Their range is therefore much less extensive than that of the "Red-tails," but their habits and manners are very similar. The following biography is applicable partly to both species, sometimes to one more than another, but it may be remarked that the " Red-tail" is more robust, spirited, and majestic.

The " Hen Hawks," and their immediate relations, are best characterized by their flight and mode of hunting. Sometimes, propelled by an occasional and slight motion of the wings, they sail in circles to a great height, and, if favored by a breeze, even rise until lost to sight, without any perceptible exercise of muscular power. Again, they often circle without ascending, though at a considerable distance from the ground. Thus the range of their vision is much extended, while the keenness of their sight enables them to detect the motion of a squirrel in the trees, or of birds and snakes in the open lands over which they more often fly. On perceiving the object of their search, closing their wings and tail, they fall with a loud rustle until near the earth, when, checking their speed, they drop unawares upon their victim. Should they fail, they rise, and in a second attempt it frequently happens that not even the cunning Quail can escape. They sometimes fly lower, with more or less sailing, according to the breeze or motion in the air, and, diving down, seize a chicken, or even a hen, and bear it off with apparent ease. At other times, they perch in a tree in their hunting-grounds, and with an eager, intent expression, watch closely the surrounding grass, down into which they drop when occasion requires, or over which they again sail, instantly checking their course and again alighting, should anything attract their attention. Then facing about, they wait until an opportune moment, when, spreading their wings and for an instant hovering, they pounce upon their prey. They rarely catch birds on the wing, and never, so far as I know, pursue them. On the contrary, if undisturbed, they sometimes remain perched for hours, either waiting for the appearance of game, or digesting a meal. In the woods, they not unfrequently catch squirrels, diving at them when in some exposed situation. They usually sail up to their perch, and stand erectly, often far above the ground.

Their ordinary fare is composed of hares, often called "rabbits," *squirrels*, minks, rarely rats or mice, *snakes* (especially the striped kind or garter-snake), *frogs*, grouse, quail, *and poultry*. They do not, however, often catch our so-called partridges, owing to the latter's rapid flight and rather persistent occupation of the woods, and it is not uncommon to find these game-birds in groves where the "Hen Hawks" have their nest.

It may be said that the natural home of the "Hen Hawks" is the woods (in our climate, particularly those of old pines, and such as are somewhat swampy), but it must be added that during the day they are much away from home. Their favorite hunting-grounds are open places, especially farms and meadows, but there are few kinds of land over which they do not fly, including even our smaller cities. Occasionally they may be seen in roads or perched on roadsides.

Towards man the "Hen Hawks" are naturally shy, though it is generally easy to approach them when gorged, or at other times to do so in a vehicle, or on horse-back. By this latter means, I have actually passed under one. They frequently leave their food when approached, instead of carrying it off in the manner of many hawks. Like other barbarians, they refuse to show signs of suffering, or to allow their spirit to become subdued. When shot and mortally wounded, they usually sail on unconcernedly while their strength lasts, until obliged to fall. If not dead, they turn upon their rump, and fight till the last, like others of their tribe. Their eyes gleam savagely, and they defend themselves with both bill and talons. With these latter they can inflict severe wounds, if incautiously treated, and they sometimes seize a stick with such tenacity that I have seen one carried half a mile through his persistent grasp. I have never known one to be tamed, but, on the contrary, they sometimes die from refusing to eat. This is in accordance with their natural pride, and their fondness for a wild life.

In autumn and winter the "Hen Hawks" lead a solitary life, but in summer, and more often spring, they may be seen in pairs. They then hunt together, or sail high in circles, as if to remove themselves from the common crowd of birds. Unless very seriously molested, they build their nest every year in nearly the same place. The females vary as regards courage or prudence, some leaving their nest on hearing one's approach, others waiting till the tree is rapped, and others until one has begun to climb or has even ascended several feet. I have never known them to attack man, when thus disturbed. The young are fed for several weeks after being hatched, and are often noisy.

(*d*). The screams of our two "Hen Hawks" do not materially differ, if at all. They are slightly prolonged, and are usually repeated several times at once, as *keé-o, keé-o, keé-o*. They are frequently heard, especially in spring, but are exactly imitated by the Blue Jays.

(C) PENNSYLVANICUS. *Broad-winged Hawk* (or *Buzzard*).

(To be seen in Massachusetts during summer, and occasionally winter, but more common as a migrant.)

(*a*). Eighteen inches long or less. Above, umber-brown, with more or less pale edging, and showing white on the hindhead. Tail banded and tipped with white. Under parts, white, variously streaked and barred with spots of medium or rufous brown, of which traces are often found above. *Throat bordered on each side by a dark maxillary patch.* Young with much white above, but that of the tail replaced by light brown.

This species, like the other buzzards, has the outer primary (and others) *emarginate*, i. e. with the inner web rather abruptly narrow towards the end. This buzzard has three, our others four emarginate.

(*b*). The nest does not essentially differ, so far as I know, from that of the Red-shouldered Hawk. An egg, which I took from a nest with three young, found near Boston on the sixteenth of May, measures 2·10 × 1·80 of an inch, and is white, blotched and spotted with brown, chiefly of a *purplish* shade.

(*c*). The Broad-winged Buzzards are reported as common summer-residents in many parts of northern New England. In Massachusetts, they are most common as migrants, but I have seen one in winter, and have found two nests near Boston, in neither of which cases did the female offer any resistance, though Mr. Boardman considers them so spirited as to attack intruders. Dr. Brewer, in the "Birds of North America," says: "Mr. McIlwraith, of Hamilton, Canada, has noted extensive migrations of this Hawk in March of different years, as many as twenty or thirty being in view at one time, passing at a considerable height, and moving in circles towards the north-west." These Buzzards, though readily distinguished by size from the "Hen Hawks," do not differ much in habits. In common with those birds, they are often teased by Kingbirds and Crows, but on such occasions they show a quiet dignity and unconcern, which is very striking.

(*d*). The Broad-winged Hawks have a loud, whining whistle, not unlike the familiar cries of the "Hen Hawks." These may most often be heard in spring.

VI. ARCHIBUTEO

(A) LAGOPUS (*var.* SANCTI–JOHANNIS). *Rough-legged Hawk* (or *Buzzard*). *Black Hawk.*

(In Massachusetts, a winter-visitor of great rarity.)

(*a*). *Tarsus feathered to the toes.* Extreme length, about two feet. Above, marked with various browns and white (or yellowish). *Tail* black-banded, but with the basal *half white* and unmarked. Under parts, white, variously marked with brown, which generally forms a broad band across the lower breast. There is a so-called *melanotic* race, with the plumage nearly uniform black or blackish, but with the forehead (throat), and more or less banding on the tail, white. This is the Black Hawk, supposed by some writers to be the adult of the other.

(*b*). The eggs, as described by other authors, do not apparently differ from certain forms, found among those of the "Hen Hawks." See V, B, b.

(*c*). The Rough-legged Buzzards occur in New England as winter-visitors only, and near Boston are rare, especially in black plumage. They are noted for the following traits: general sluggishness, fondness for hunting in the evening or toward dusk, fondness for meadows, marshes, and low, wet lands, and finally the simplicity of their fare, which consists chiefly of frogs and mice, but also, it is said, of wounded birds. They usually remain perched in their chosen haunts, regardless of weather, until some small quadruped attracts their notice, when, with the impulse received from a few beats of their wings, they drop down upon their prey. They may sometimes be seen sailing about with great ease and but little motion of the wings. They often stand motionless for a surprising length of time. I remember passing over the Boston and Providence Rail-road in March, and remarking, at about eleven o'clock in the morning, a hawk of this species stationed on the Fowl Meadows beyond Readville. On returning, toward sunset, I saw him in the same tree, though it is probable that he had made several sallies during the day. Such is the characteristic life of the Rough-legged Buzzards, but, in so cold a winter-climate as that of Boston, they are frequently obliged to resort to woods and higher grounds. I have seen one catch a squirrel, and another feed upon a Quail.

(*d*). Wilson speaks of their "making a loud squeeling as they arise, something resembling the neighing of a young colt; tho in a more shrill and savage tone." Dr. Cooper speaks of their "loud scream."

VII. AQUILA

(A) CHRYSAËTUS (*var*. CANADENSIS). *Golden Eagle. Ring-tailed Eagle* (young).

(In Massachusetts, extremely rare.)

(*a*). 30–40 inches long. *Tarsus thickly feathered.* Dark brown, varying from purplish to blackish, becoming rich fulvous on the hind-head and neck. Young, with the tail partly white.

(*b*). The nest is built on cliffs, or rarely in trees. The eggs are most often two in number, and are three inches long or more. They are white, usually blotched with brown.[6]

---

[6] This description, as one or two of the others, is gathered from those of other writers.

(c). Size has always a fascination for the world. The young collector prizes a hawk's egg more than that of the rarest warbler. The egg is big, the bird that laid it is big, the nest in which it was laid is big, the tree in which the nest was built is big, and the wood in which the tree grows is big. In much the same spirit, the world has called the eagle and lion king respectively of. birds and beasts, on account of their large size and carnivorous tastes. But modern writers have assured us that the lion is not a hero, that he is even a coward, that he does not deserve his title, which might better be bestowed upon the Royal Bengal Tiger. The eagle, however, though inferior in activity, speed, and spirit, to the little Sparrow Hawk, better merits the distinction, from the majesty of his appearance and the sublimity of his flight. But he cannot justly be considered superior to all other birds, since he is merely a large "hen hawk," who does not hesitate in many cases to feed on carrion or on the spoils which he robs from more industrious laborers than himself.

The Golden Eagles are extremely rare in Massachusetts, and are probably to be ranked as merely accidental winter-visitors. They are resident in mountainous and thinly populated districts of northern and possibly western New England. Mr. Brewster says that " a pair have bred for years on the cliff directly over the Profile House. They could be seen at almost any hour of the day sealing about their eyrie, uttering loud screams, but were especially noisy and active from sunset to dark."

The Golden Eagles are so averse to the encroachments of man, that I can find no mention of their being common in any much inhabited district, but the immense tracts of forest, and the high mountain-ranges, in their usual haunts, enable them to live remote from civilization. I have occasionally seen them among the White Mountains. They may sometimes be observed sailing at a vast height in wide circles, but with no perceptible effort. I have watched them for hours, but only once have I seen them plunge. One, who had been sailing for a long while at the elevation of several hundred feet, suddenly closed his wings and dropped with astounding velocity, which might well take one's breath away. In his fall he disappeared behind some woods, and I did not see him again. The keenness of vision which this species must possess is wonderful, but at how great a height they can distinctly perceive their prey is uncertain. I have seen one sail at some distance above the peak of Mount Lafayette, at least a mile above the sea-level, and, on crossing a valley beneath, suddenly descend, as if his attention had been attracted by an object four thousand feet beneath. Could man from the top of a monument twenty times as high as that of Bunker Hill distinctly see a cat directly beneath, or a fawn at the distance of two or three miles, even if not running through grass or woods? Yet man might distinctly see and recognize a tolerably small quadruped at the distance of a mile in a clear, level space, whence it seems possible that the powers of horizontal and perpendicular vision are somewhat distinct, even when the same surface of a body is seen. Audubon says of these birds that " young fawns, racoons, hares, wild turkeys, and other large birds, are their usual food, and they devour putrid flesh only when hard pressed by hunger, none alighting on carrion at any other time."

(d). The screams of the Golden Eagle are loud, harsh, and rather savage, " resembling at times," says Audubon, " the barking of a dog, especially about the breeding season, when they become extremely noisy and turbulent, * * * ."

VIII. HALIAËTUS

(A) LEUCOCEPHALUS. *"Bald" Eagle. White-headed Eagle. "Bird of Washington."*

(In some parts of New England not uncommon.)

(*a*). 30–40 inches long. *Tarsus naked.* Dark brown. Head, tail, and tail-coverts, white. Young with little or no white.

(*b*). The nest is much like that of the Fish Hawk in every respect. It is often, however, "partly composed of sods, and is commonly built in the top of a dead tree." The eggs, most often two in number, are laid in the early part of spring, or even in winter. They are nearly three inches long, or more, and are impure white or yellowish.

25

(c). The "Bald" Eagles, unfortunately selected as emblems of their country, are residents, at least in summer, from the Gulf of Mexico to the Arctic Ocean. They are common in many parts of northern New England, particularly along the coast of Maine. In Massachusetts, they no longer breed, except in a few places to the westward, but they occasionally appear along the shore, even in summer, when they undoubtedly often wander far in search of food. Wilson's picture of this bird is in spirit one of the finest portrait-paintings from nature, which it has ever been my good fortune to see, and, as his biography is scarcely less admirable, I shall quote several passages from it, adding a few observations not there recorded.

"This bird has been long known to naturalists, being common to both continents, and occasionally met with from a very high northern latitude, to the borders of the torrid zone, but chiefly in the vicinity of the sea, and along the shores and cliffs of our lakes and large rivers. Formed by nature for braving the severest cold; feeding equally on the produce of the sea, and of the land; possessing powers of flight capable of outstripping even the tempests themselves; unawed by anything but man; and from the ethereal heights to which he soars, looking abroad, at one glance, on an immeasurable expanse of forests, fields, lakes and ocean, deep below him, he appears indifferent to the little localities of change of seasons; as in a few minutes he can pass from summer to winter, from the lower to the higher regions of the atmosphere, the abode of eternal cold, and from thence descend at will to the torrid or the arctic regions of the earth. He is therefore found at all seasons in the countries he inhabits; but prefers such places as have been mentioned above, from the great partiality he has for fish.

"In procuring these he displays, in a very singular manner, the genius and energy of his character, which is fierce, contemplative, daring and tyrannical; attributes not exerted but on particular occasions; but when put forth, overpowering all opposition. Elevated on the high dead limb of some gigantic tree that commands a wide view of the neighboring shore and ocean, he seems calmly to contemplate the motions of the various feathered tribes that pursue their busy avocations below the snow white Gulls slowly winnowing the air; the busy Tringæ coursing along the sands; trains of Ducks streaming over the surface; silent and watchful Cranes, intent and wading; clamorous Crows, and all the winged multitudes that subsist by the bounty of this vast liquid magazine of nature. High over all these hovers one, whose action instantly arrests all his attention. By his wide curvature of wing, and sudden suspension in the air, he knows him to be the *Fish-Hawk*, settling over some devoted victim of the deep. His eye kindles at the sight, and balancing himself, with half opened wings, on the branch, he watches the result. Down, rapid as an arrow from heaven, descends the distant object of his attention, the roar of its wings reaching his ear as it disappears in the deep, making the surges foam around! At this moment the eager looks of the Eagle are all ardor; and levelling his neck for flight, he sees the Fish-Hawk once more emerge, struggling with his prey, and mounting in the air with screams of exultation. These are the signal for our hero, who, launching into the air, instantly gives chace, soon gains on the Fish-Hawk, each exerts his utmost to mount above the other, displaying in these rencontres the most elegant and sublime aerial evolutions. The unincumbered Eagle rapidly advances, and is just on the point of reaching his opponent, when with a sudden scream probably of despair and honest execration, the latter drops his fish; the Eagle poising himself for a moment, as if to take a more certain aim, descends like a whirlwind, snatches it in his grasp ere it reaches the water, and bears his ill-gotten booty silently away to the woods."

"When driven, as he sometimes is, by the combined courage and perseverance of the Fish-Hawks from their neighbourhood, and forced to hunt for himself, he retires more inland, in search of young pigs, of which he destroys great numbers. In the lower parts of Virginia and North Carolina, where the inhabitants raise vast herds of those animals, complaints of this kind are very general against him. He also destroys young lambs in the early part of spring; and will sometimes attack old sickly sheep, aiming furiously at their eyes."

"The appetite of the Bald Eagle, tho habituated to long

fasting, is of the most voracious and often the most indelicate kind. Fish, when he can obtain them, are preferred to all other fare. Young lambs and pigs are dainty morsels, and made free with on all favorable occasions. Ducks, Geese, Gulls and other sea fowl, are also seized with avidity. The most putrid carrion, when nothing better can be had, is acceptable; and the collected groups of gormandizing Vultures, on the approach of this dignified personage, instantly disperse, and make way for their master, waiting his departure in sullen silence, and at a respectful distance, on the adjacent trees."

"The flight of the Bald Eagle, when taken into consideration with the ardor and energy of his character, is noble and interesting. Sometimes the human eye can just discern him, like a minute speck, moving in slow curvatures along the face of the heavens, as if reconnoitring the earth at that immense distance. Sometimes he glides along in a direct horizontal line, at a vast height, with expanded and unmoving wings, till he gradually disappears in the distant blue ether. Seen gliding in easy circles over the high shores and mountainous cliffs that tower above the Hudson and Susquehanna, he attracts the eye of the intelligent voyager, and adds great interest to the scenery. At the great cataract of Niagara, already mentioned, there rises from the gulf into which the falls of the Horse-shoe descends, a stupendous column of smoke, or spray, reaching to the heavens, and moving off in large black clouds, according to the direction of the wind, forming a very striking and majestic appearance. The Eagles are here seen sailing about, sometimes losing themselves in this thick column, and again reappearing in another place, with such ease and elegance of motion, as renders the whole truly sublime.

"High o'er the watery uproar, silent seen,
"Sailing sedate in majesty serene,
"Now midst the sprays sublimely lost,
"And now, emerging, down the rapids tost,
"Glides the Bald Eagle, gazing, calm and slow
"O'er all the horrors of the scene below;
"Intent alone to sate himself with blood,
"From the torn victims of the raging flood."

Wilson elsewhere says: "The Eagle is said to live to a

great age, sixty, eighty, and as some assert, one hundred years. This circumstance is remarkable, when we consider the seeming intemperate habits of the bird. Sometimes fasting, through necessity, for several days, and at other times gorging itself with animal food till its craw swells out the plumage of that part, forming a large protuberance on the breast."

The Bald Eagles do not invariably sail when flying, but often progress by a continuous beating of the wings. They also occasionally plunge through the air, even doing so, it has been stated, from a height of several thousand feet, with a loud rustle, which may be heard at a considerable distance. Though notorious for their robbing of the Fish Hawks, they sometimes condescend to fish for themselves in the manner of those birds. This fact I have personally witnessed, and it has been corroborated by other naturalists. They also attack wild-fowl, especially if wounded, and have been known, on finding a crippled Brant, to plant themselves upon it, and, spreading their wings, to sail to shore.

(*d*). The Bald Eagles are usually silent. A young one, which I observed in confinement, snored when sleeping, and, when awake, frequently hissed or uttered extraordinary sounds, suggestive of the pig-sty, though not unlike disagreeable laughter. These are the chief items of interest which I can add to Wilson's account.

IX. PANDION

(A) HALIAËTUS (*var.* CAROLINENSIS). *Fish Hawk.* (*American*) *Osprey.*

(In New England, a summer-resident, but very rare in Massachusetts.

(*a*). About two feet long. Under parts, and the *head, white.* *Eye-stripe*, and the upper parts, *dark.* Tail, banded. Breast, spotted or streaked with brown. Feet, large and stout, presenting, as does the plumage, certain peculiarities.

(*b*). The nest is extremely large, being usually repaired and added to from year to year. It is composed of sticks, of which there is often a cart-load, and is lined with sea-weed, or other coarse materials. It is built in a tree, near some body of water, sometimes several being near together. It is placed at various heights above the ground, but often near the top, even of a dead tree. In New England, two, three, or four eggs are laid about the first of May, or sometimes later. They average 2·40 × 1·70 of an inch, and are usually creamy, buff, or reddish, thickly spotted and blotched with rich brown of several shades, some of which are dark and others reddish. Occasionally the eggs are white, with a few large markings of umber-brown.

(c). The Fish Hawks, like their tormentors the "Bald" Eagles, are summer-residents in Florida, Arctic countries, and the lands between, but, unlike them, are very migratory, and do not winter in New England, where from April until late in the autumn they are common. They are rare, however, in Massachusetts, except during the migrations, and are said to breed no longer along the coast of this State, though a few undoubtedly do so in the interior, of which I have had satisfactory evidence. They are everywhere most numerous on the sea-shore (as is observable in Maine), but they also resort to the neighborhood of rivers and large inland bodies of water. They are everywhere characterized by their sociability and affection, their perseverance and industry. They are well known frequently to migrate and build their nests in companies, to remain mated for life, and to feed their young longer, even more abundantly, than any other hawks. Though repeatedly robbed by the tyrannical eagles, they continue to fish undisheartened, and are said never to feed in any other way.

Their method of obtaining their prey is so interesting, that were it not known even to children, from being frequently described in books, it would daily excite wonder. It cannot, however, fail to hold the attention of any one who may see it for the first time, and I have never looked upon one of these birds without instinctively watching his motions. The flight of the Fish Hawk is much varied, but he may always be recognized by the prominent bend of his wings. When traveling directly forward, he flies with rather heavy flappings, not unlike those of a heron, which are relieved by sailing. When hunting, he more often moves in circles, and frequently at a considerable height. He often deceives some eager spectator by diving, as if to make a plunge, but he suddenly resumes his course, and continues to sail quietly. Finally he becomes absorbed in gazing at the movements of his prey; then, hovering for a moment, plunges head-long, and, disappearing beneath the surface, dashes up the foam. Sometimes he seizes so large a prize that a desperate struggles ensues, in which now the fish and then the bird appears out of his element, and it is said that he occasionally loses his life through being imprudent or too ambitious. Generally, however, he at once rises, and with his prey in his talons, flies to the shore, where, if not molested by robbers, he feeds in some tree upon his well earned meal. He is either no glutton, or has an insatiable appetite, for he is seldom or never seen gorged, but, when not eating, or necessarily at rest, he continues his active search. I do not know what are the largest fish that he catches, but I have been assured that one, which a bird dropped upon being frightened, weighed fully six pounds. The Fish Hawks are very spirited, and have been known to wound seriously intruders upon their nests, which, by the way, they are said by Wilson to repair in autumn to withstand the winter.

(*d*). Their notes are various, being sometimes piercing screams, but at other times a succession of agreeable whistles.

§ 28. The **American vultures** (CATHARTIDÆ) have the head chiefly naked, and the hind-toe not on a level with the others, which are slightly webbed. Two southern species, the Turkey "Buzzard"[7] (*Cathartes aura*) and the Carrion "Crow" (*C. atratus*), have accidentally occurred in Massachusetts once or twice. The former is very dark; "head red; feet flesh-colored; bill white. * * * * ; tail rounded. Length about 2½ feet; extent 6; wing 2; tail 1. U. S., from Atlantic to

---

[7] See, for authority, "The Naturalists' Guide," of Mr. Maynard, p. 137, 160th species.

Pacific, and somewhat northward; abundant in more southern portions; resident as far north as New Jersey. Nests on the ground, or near it, in hollow stumps and logs, generally breeding in communities; eggs commonly two, creamy white, blotched and speckled, $2\frac{3}{4} \times 1\frac{7}{8}$." Coues. The Carrion "Crow," or Black Vulture, has the wings paler beneath, and the hindhead feathered; "head dusky; bill and feet grayish-yellow. * * * ; tail square. Smaller than *aura*, in linear dimensions, but a heavier bird; length about 2 feet; wing $1\frac{1}{2}$; tail $\frac{2}{3}$. The difference in size and shape between this species and *aura* is strikingly displayed when the birds are flying together, as constantly occurs in the Southern States; there is also a radical difference in the mode of flight, this species never sailing for any distance without flapping the wings. Nesting the same: eggs similar, but larger, or at any rate more elongate; $3\frac{1}{4} \times 2$. Chiefly South Atlantic and Gulf States, there very numerous, far outnumbering the turkey buzzard, and semi-domesticated in the towns; N. regularly to North Carolina, thence straggling even to Massachusetts and Maine;" etc. (Coues.)

As the vultures are of wholly accidental occurrence in New England, and as their more characteristic habits are well known, I shall not here present their biographies, which I should be obliged to borrow from other writers. Some remarks as to their prominent peculiarities have already been presented among those on the birds of prey, at the beginning of this chapter.

CHAPTER IV.

FIFTH ORDER. COLUMBÆ.

"An essential character," says Dr. Coues, " of birds of this order is seen in the structure of the bill: horny and convex at the tip, somewhat contracted in the continuity, furnished at the base with a soft swollen membrane in which the nostrils open. There are four toes, three anterior, generally cleft, but occasionally with a slight basal web, and one behind, with a few exceptions perfectly insistent or not obviously elevated. The feet are never lengthened; the tarsus is commonly shorter than the toes, either scutellate or extensively feathered anteriorly, reticulate on the sides and behind, the envelope rather membranous than corneous. The plumage is destitute of aftershafts. * * * ." As this order is in North America represented but by one family, the well-known pigeons (including the doves), it is unnecessary to detail further its peculiar features. The two species of New England are excellent types. Their habit, however, of feeding their young by regurgitation from the crop may here be remarked.

The true "Game-birds" (Chapter V), all belong to the subclass, *Cursores*, or "terrestrial birds," and to the two orders, *Gallinæ* and *Grallatores*. The *Gallinæ* include the grouse, with the tarsi more or less feathered, and the partridges or quail, with naked tarsi. Dr. Coues ranks these as subfamilies, dividing our species into *Tetraoninæ*, or true grouse, and *Odontophorinæ*, or American partridges. The *Grallatores* include the Snipe and Woodcock, who both belong to the same family of the suborder *Limicolæ* or *shore-birds*. (It may be added that the *Odontophorinæ*, or *Ortyginæ*, are usually ranked as subfamilies of the *Perdicidæ*, or partridges, while the grouse are ranked separately as *Tetraonidæ*. This latter arrangement has been followed in this volume.)

It is to be remarked that the pigeons (*Columbidæ*, § 29)

show an affinity in several ways to the *Raptores*, or birds of prey, as well as in structure to the *Gallinæ*.

I. ECTOPISTES

(A) MIGRATORIUS. *Wild Pigeon. Passenger Pigeon.*
(In Massachusetts, most common as a migrant).

(*a*). *About sixteen inches long. Tail-feathers twelve.* ♂, above, dull-blue; beneath, dull red, paler behind. Sides of the neck highly metallic. Back, and part of the wings, olive-tinged. Shoulders black-spotted. Primaries, and long middle tail-feathers, black (or dark); the former variously edged. Outer tail-feathers white or bluish; their inner webs black, and chestnut, at the base. ♀, much duller above, and blue or gray beneath.

(*b*). The nest, a frail structure of twigs, is built on some branch in the woods. In April or May, according to latitude, one or two eggs are laid. These are elliptical, and pure white, and measure about 1·50 × 1·10 of an inch.

(*c*). No birds could more appropriately be chosen as emblems of their country than the Wild Pigeons. They occur throughout a large part of North America, and often in such prodigious numbers, that single companies have been estimated to contain fifty times as many pigeons as there are now inhabitants in the United States. They wander almost continually in search of their food, which consists chiefly of grain, seeds, beech-nuts, acorns, and berries. They possess great power of flight, and move with a rapid beating of the wings at the rate of sixty miles an hour or often more. On alighting, they flap the wings violently, as if to break the force of their impetus. If frightened from their roosts (to which they frequently resort several nights in succession), they rise with a loud roar. When on the ground, they invariably walk, but with no little grace. Many of their habits may be traced in those of tame pigeons, and in the appearance of a single individual there is often a striking analogy to that of a hawk. In many places they have become *comparatively* rare through the excessive persecution of man, in addition to the raids made upon them by birds of prey. This is eminently the case in New England, where they were once abundant. In summer they are now chiefly confined to the northern and wilder districts, but in winter they may occasionally be seen in more southern portions. They are most abundant near Boston as migrants in April and October. There is a low pine-wood within the present limits of the city, in which I have known flocks of several hundreds to roost every year, but I have never known them to be disturbed. The Wild Pigeons are still wonderfully numerous in many parts of the Western States, and it was there that Wilson made such observations as can no longer be repeated in any place, where I have seen these birds. Though toward the latter end of my work obliged to quote more often than I had hoped would be necessary, I do not hesitate to present to my readers several extracts from Wilson's extremely interesting biography.

After speaking of their range, he says: "But the most remarkable characteristic of these birds is their associating together, both in their migrations and also during the period of incubation, in such prodigious numbers as almost to surpass belief; and which has no parallel among any other of the feathered tribes, on the face of the earth, with which naturalists are acquainted.

"These migrations appear to be undertaken rather in quest of food, than merely to avoid the cold of the climate; since we find them lingering in the northern regions around Hudson's Bay so late as December; and since their appearance is so casual and irregular; sometimes not visiting certain districts for several years in any considerable numbers, while at other times they are innumerable. I have witnessed these migrations in the Genessee Country—often in Pennsylvania, and also in various parts of Virginia, with amazement; but all that I had then seen of them were mere straggling parties, when compared with the congregated millions which I have since beheld in our western forests, in the States of Ohio, Kentucky, and the Indiana territory. These fertile and extensive regions abound with the nutritious beech nut, which constitutes the chief food of the Wild Pigeon. In seasons when these nuts are abundant, corresponding multitudes of Pigeons may be confidently expected. It sometimes happens that having consumed the whole produce of the beech trees in an extensive district, they discover another at a distance perhaps of sixty or eighty miles, to which they regularly repair every morning, and return as regularly in the course of the day, or in the evening, to their general place of rendezvous, or as it is usually called, the *roosting place*. These roosting places are always in the woods, and sometimes occupy a large extent of forest. When they have frequented one of these places for some time the appearance it exhibits is surprising. The ground is covered to the depth of several inches with their dung; all the tender grass and underwood destroyed; the surface strewed with large limbs of trees broken down by the weight of the birds clustering one above another; and the trees themselves, for thousands of acres, killed as completely as if girdled with an axe. The marks of this desolation remain for many years on the spot; and numerous places could be pointed out where for several years after scarce a single vegetable made its appearance."

In speaking of their breeding-places, Wilson says: "In the western countries above mentioned, these are generally in beech woods, and often extend in nearly a straight line across the country for a great way. Not far from Shelbyville in the state of Kentucky, about five years ago, there was one of these breeding places, which stretched through the woods in nearly a north and south direction; was several miles in breadth, and was said to be upwards of forty miles in extent! In this tract almost every tree was furnished with nests, wherever the branches could accommodate them. The Pigeons made their first appearance there about the tenth of April, and left it altogether, with their young, before the twenty-fifth of May.

"As soon as the young were fully grown, and before they left their nests, numerous parties of the inhabitants, from all parts of the adjacent country, came with waggons, axes, beds, cooking utensils, many of them accompanied by the greater part of their families, and encamped for several days at this immense nursery. Several of them informed me, that the noise in the woods was so great as to terrify their horses, and that it was difficult for one person to hear another speak without bawling in his ear. The ground was strewed with broken limbs of trees, eggs, and young squab Pigeons, which had been precipitated from above, and on which herds of hogs were fattening. Hawks, Buzzards and Eagles were sailing about in great numbers, and seizing the squabs from their nests at pleasure; while from twenty feet upwards to the tops of the trees the view through the woods presented a perpetual tumult of crowding and fluttering multitudes of pigeons, their wings roaring like thunder; mingled with the frequent crash of falling timber; for now the axe-men were at work cutting down those trees that seemed to be most crowded with nests, and contrived to fell them in such a manner, that in their descent they might bring down several others; by which means the falling of one large tree sometimes produced two hundred squabs, little inferior in size to the old ones, and almost one mass of fat. On some single trees upwards of one hundred nests were found, each containing *one* young only, a circumstance in the history of this bird not generally known to naturalists. It was dangerous to walk under these flying and fluttering millions, from the frequent fall of large branches, broken down by the weight of the multitudes above, and which in their descent often destroyed numbers of the birds themselves; * * *."

"I had left the public road to visit the remains of the breeding place near Shelbyville, and was traversing the woods with my gun, on my way to Frankfort, when about one o'clock the Pigeons, which I had observed flying the greater part of the morning northerly, began to return in such immense numbers as I never before had witnessed. Coming to an opening by a side of a creek called the Benson, where I had a more uninterrupted view, I was astonished at their appearance. They were flying with great steadiness and rapidity, at a height beyond gun shot, in several strata deep, and so close together that could shot have reached them, one discharge could not have failed of bringing down several individuals. From right to left far as the eye could reach, the breadth of this vast procession extended; seeming everywhere equally crowded. Curious to determine how long this appearance would continue, I took out my watch to note the time, and sat down to observe them. It was then half past one. I sat for more than an hour, but instead of a diminution of this prodigious procession, it seemed rather to increase both in numbers and rapidity; and, anxious to reach Frankfort before night, I rose and went on. About four o'clock in the afternoon I crossed the Kentucky river, at the town of Frankfort, at which time the living torrent above my head seemed as numerous and as extensive as ever. Long after this I observed them, in large bodies that continued to pass for six or eight minutes, and these again were followed by other detached bodies, all moving in the same south-east direction till after six in the evening."

"* * * To form a rough estimate of the daily consumption of one of these immense flocks, let us first attempt to calculate the numbers of that above mentioned as seen in passing between Frankfort and Indiana territory. If we suppose this column to have been a mile in breadth (and I believe it to have been much more) and that it moved at the rate of one mile in a minute; four hours, the time it continued passing, would make its whole length two hundred and forty miles. Again, supposing that each square yard of this moving body comprehended three Pigeons; the square yards in the whole space multiplied by three, would give two thousand two hundred and thirty millions, two hundred and seventy-two thousand pigeons! An almost inconceivable multitude, and yet probably far below the actual amount. Computing each of these to consume half a pint of mast daily, the whole quantity at this rate would equal seventeen millions, four hundred and twenty-four thousand bushels per day! Heaven has wisely and graciously given to these birds rapidity of flight and a disposition to range over vast uncultivated tracts of the earth; otherwise they must have perished in the districts where they resided, or devoured up the whole productions of agriculture as well as those of the forests.

"A few observations on the mode of flight of these birds must not be omitted. The appearance of large detached bodies of them in the air, and the various evolutions they display, are strikingly picturesque and interesting. In descending the Ohio by myself in the month of February, I often rested on my oars to contemplate their aerial manœuvres. A column, eight or ten miles in length, would appear from Kentucky, high in air, steering across to Indiana. The leaders of this great body would sometimes gradually vary their course, until it formed a large bend of more than a mile in diameter, those behind tracing the exact route of their predecessors. This would continue sometimes long after both extremities were beyond the reach of sight, so that the whole with its glittery undulations, marked a space on the face of the heavens resembling the windings of a vast and majestic river. When this bend became very great, the birds, as if sensible of the unnecessary circuitous course they were taking, suddenly changed their direction, so that what was before in column became an immense front, straightening all its indentures, until it swept the heavens in one vast and infinitely extended line. Other lesser bodies also united with each other, as they happened to approach, with such ease and elegance of evolution, forming new figures, and varying these as they united or separated that I was never tired of contemplating them. Sometimes a Hawk would make a sweep on a particular part of the column, from a great height, when, almost as quick as lightning, that part shot downwards out of the common track; but soon rising again, continued advancing at the same height as before; this inflection was continued by those behind, who on arriving at this point dived down, almost perpendicularly, to a great depth, and rising followed the exact path of those that went before. * * *."

"Happening to go ashore one charming afternoon, to purchase some milk at a house that stood near the river, and while talking with the people within doors, I was suddenly struck with astonishment at a loud rushing roar, succeeded by instant darkness, which, on the first moment, I took for a tornado about to overwhelm the house and every thing around in destruction. The people observing my surprise, coolly said, 'It is only the Pigeons;' * * * ."

(d). The Wild Pigeons have a cooing not unlike that of the domestic birds. This is a love-note, and may be heard in spring. Audubon says: "The common notes resemble the monosyllables *kee-kee-kee-kee*, the first being the loudest, the others gradually diminishing in power."

II. ZENÆDURA

(A) CAROLINENSIS. *Carolina Dove.* "*Turtle Dove.*" *Mourning Dove.*

(In New England, a summer-resident.)

(a). *About twelve inches long. Tail-feathers fourteen*, and bluish; the outer ones singly black-barred and white-tipped. *Feet carmine* (and not yellow). Otherwise essentially like the Wild Pigeon (I), but more brownish, and with a black spot on the side of the head.

(b). The nest is a frail structure of twigs, built in the woods or sometimes in orchards. Two white and (nearly) elliptical eggs, measuring about $1\cdot 10 \times \cdot 80$ of an inch, are laid in May.

(c). The Carolina Doves differ distinctly from the Wild Pigeons in being regularly migratory, very much less gregarious, only small flocks being ever seen in New England, in not roosting closely together in trees, and in flying with a loud whistle of the wing, and seldom at a great height. They do not occur to the northward of Southern New England, where they are summer-residents of great rarity in many places, though common, according to Mr. Maynard, on Cape Cod. I have seen them from March until October. They frequent open woods and grounds, grain-fields, pastures, and even, it is said, barn-yards. There they may be seen, often in companies, now walking sedately, now more rapidly, and picking up the seeds, grain, berries, etc., upon which they feed. Occasionally they alight on fences, and flirt their long and handsome tails. They are eminently affectionate toward one another, but toward man they are often shy.

(d). Besides a low chuckle, they have a peculiar and very

striking cooing, one of the saddest sounds in nature, though sweet, and wholly inexpressive of the true feelings of the doves. It usually consists of four notes, which suggest the sobs and moans of a most disconsolate lover, or of a person in the deepest distress. The briefness of this last biography will, it is hoped, be excused. The author approaches the end of his long though pleasurable labors with a certain feeling of eagerness and relief, though glad to have paid even a slight tribute to nature, science, and the inauguration of a second century in the life of his country, for, through an unforeseen coincidence, as he writes these last words, the distant boom of cannon on Boston Common announces the hundredth anniversary of the Declaration of Independence.

CHAPTER V.

THE GAME-BIRDS. (See § 29.)

§ 30. **Tetraonidæ.** Grouse.

I. TETRAO (CANACE).

(A) CANADENSIS.[1] *Canada Grouse.* "*Spruce Partridge.*"
(A resident of northern New England, but in Massachusetts accidental.)

(*a*). About sixteen inches long. ♂, black; waved with a paler shade above, and extensively edged on the breast and sides with white. "Eye-brow" red. Head and wings with a few white markings. *Tail, usually of sixteen feathers, and broadly tipped with orange-brown.* Brown markings sometimes occur elsewhere in the male, and in the female are persistently numerous.

(*b*). The eggs, which are laid upon the ground, are described by Mr. Samuels as " of a beautiful yellowish-buff color, with spots and blotches of two shades of brown: one a purplish-brown; the other, a burnt sienna." In size they differ but little from those of the Ruffed Grouse.

(*c*). The Canada Grouse are common residents in many parts of northern New England, especially Northern Maine, but in Massachusetts they are of accidental occurrence, and I find records of only two captures in this State, one "in the hemlock woods of Gloucester, in September, 1851, another at Roxbury." These birds are rare among the White Mountains, so far as I know, as I have but occasionally seen them there.

---

[1] The White or Willow Ptarmigan (*Lagopus albus*) is said to occur as a winter visitant in Northern New England. At this time it is characterized by the pure white plumage, and its black confined to the tail. In summer it is marked with black and browns. It is about sixteen inches long. An allied but "rather smaller" species, confined to Arctic America, has a slenderer bill, and, in the male, a black eye-stripe. The ptarmigans have feathered toes.

N. B.—The Wild Turkey has for many years been exterminated in New England.

Their chief haunts are evergreen-swamps, where, if approached by man, they sometimes exhibit a surprising tameness, the mother of a young brood not hesitating boldly to defend her charge. Their habits are essentially like those of our "Partridges," who likewise, in wild places, if disturbed while with their young, often fly at the intruder, generally attacking his feet, after which they immediately retreat to collect the little ones, who have meanwhile hidden.

(*d*). The Canada Grouse, like their better known relatives, drum loudly; at least I have strong reasons to believe so, without having seen them in the act. Their ordinary note is a *chuck*.

II. CUPIDONIA

(A) CUPIDO. *Pinnated Grouse.* "*Prairie Hen.*"

(In New England, formerly somewhat common, but now almost or quite extinct.)

(*a*). About eighteen inches long. Above, marked transversely with black, white, and brown. Beneath, tawny, whitening behind. Throat often unmarked, but breast, etc., barred with white (and brown). Wings and tail, dull brown, generally marked with white. ♂, with long feathers on the neck, which when erected, form two *prominent* "wings," also with red "eyebrows," and beneath the "wings" a piece of skin, which can be distended so as much to resemble a half-orange.

(*b*). The eggs, which are laid on the ground, are brownish-drab or lighter, and average about 1·65 × 1·35 of an inch.

(*c*). The celebrated "Prairie Hens" are here included among the birds of New England, only on account of their possible presence on a few islands off the South-eastern Coast. I am informed, however, that they no longer exist on Naushon, where they are not known to have ever been indigenous, and that they are probably extinct on Martha's Vineyard. Having never seen these birds alive, I am obliged to draw my account from other authors. The Pinnated Grouse show a marked dislike for water, and choose dry, wooded soils for their haunts, such as are called "barrens." They feed chiefly upon berries, and also acorns. They usually roost upon the ground, but often resort to trees, especially in cold weather, during which they continue to reside in their summer-haunts. They fly less rapidly and with less whirr than the Ruffed Grouse, and walk rather less gracefully. At the mating-season, the males become very pompous and pugnacious. They meet in the morning at an early hour, and engage in fierce combat.

(d). It is at this time that they produce their peculiar booming, or "tooting," which is so loud that it may be heard at the distance of several miles. Their ordinary note is the chucking which belongs to other grouse.

The "Prairie Hens" are still abundant in the West, whence thousands are forwarded to Eastern markets. Their gradual extermination is greatly to be regretted.

III. BONASA
(A) UMBELLUS. *Ruffed Grouse.* "*Partridge.*" "*Pheasant.*"
(In many parts of New England, a common resident throughout the year.)

(a). About eighteen inches long. Above, reddish-brown, with numerous gray edgings. Erectile crown-feathers, and interscapulars, marked with black. Ruff-feathers on the sides of the neck, dark brown or black, with two or three metallic bars. Back, minutely speckled with black, and streaked with light grayish spots, which are black-edged. Tail, gray, with a broad subterminal black band; elsewhere paler, or reddish, barred and finely vermiculated with black. Primaries marked with whitish on the outer webs. Under parts, tawny, becoming white behind. Throat, unmarked or slightly waved; breast, with dull brown bars, dark-edged above; sides, with umber bars. The tail usually has eighteen feathers, and is rounded, as in the "Prairie Hen," but is considerably longer. The auriculars (or ear-feathers) are long and loose.

(b). The eggs average $1{\cdot}65 \times 1{\cdot}25$ of an inch, vary from drab-buff to rich reddish buff, and are sometimes spotted. From eight to fifteen are laid together in the latter part of May. The nest consists of a few leaves and grasses placed on the ground, beside a log, rock, or tree, in the woods. It is most often to be found in or near swampy lands. The last which I examined, which contained eight fresh eggs about the twenty-fifth of May, was placed in the "scrub," beneath an interlacing of fallen switches. It was a hollow, about nine inches in diameter, and was lined chiefly with bits of dry fern.

Fig. 20. Ruffed Grouse ($\frac{1}{4}$).

(e).[2] Had our forefathers been as intolerant of error in matters of science as in matters of faith, and had they wished, in applying familiar names to common objects, that the English should obtain by comparison an accurate impression of what was found here, our Ruffed Grouse would have been

---

[1] This biography, and the three following, have been contributed by a friend.

called "Wood Grouse," and not "Partridges," for they are grouse, though they differ strikingly from the English birds of that name, as well as from our own "Pinnated Grouse," in frequenting the woods, in the whiteness of their meat, in their want of sociability, and finally in their markings. The three birds differ but little in size.

The Ruffed Grouse have in common with their English relatives an indifference to danger early in the season, and, a little later, cunning and wariness, combined with swiftness on the wing. They resemble in habits the British Pheasants, whence the name given to them in the South and parts of the Middle States; and, since the English partridges scarcely resemble at all their name-sakes in New England, it must be confessed that the "Southerners" have come nearer the mark, in calling the present species a pheasant.

The Ruffed Grouse, or "Partridges," are very hardy, and, though not migratory, may be found from Newfoundland and the western British possessions to Georgia and New Mexico on the South and West. We shall here describe their habits in New England.

In the spring and early summer may be heard that remarkable sound called "drumming." Whoever is fortunate enough to approach closely an old cock in the act of drumming, will be well rewarded for the trouble that he may have taken in so doing. Generally on a log or broad stump, or in a cleared spot, the bird will be seen, puffed like a turkey to twice his natural size, with his crest erect, his ruffs extended (as in the cut, fig. 20), and his tail spread, strutting about, lowering or twisting his neck and head, and then suddenly beating violently with his wings his inflated body. This causes a sound, which on a favorable day may be heard for a mile or two, and which is often repeated at intervals for some time. One can appreciate the muscular vitality of the wings and the rapidity of their motion, by endeavoring to imitate the sound on a cushion (or other surface) with the hand. It will be found impossible to equal or even to approach the rapidity of the repeated strokes.

The eggs, deposited from day to day, are generally laid before the first of June, and mature in about eighteen days. The young leave the nest immediately, and find the greater part of their own food, though the hen sometimes offers them a few morsels. At this time, the latter part of June, and indeed through the rest of the summer, the young broods commonly frequent low, moist grounds in thick coverts, where food is abundant and water at hand, and there they are sure to be met with in a search for summer Woodcock. Should a brood be disturbed, while still with the hen, the latter feigns lameness, and decoys the intruder away, suffering him to put his hand almost upon her, uttering a clucking of anxiety, until she thinks him at a safe distance from her young, when she darts off on the wing, her chicks having meantime hidden, and leaves the deluded victim of this pretty ruse to wonder alone. Sometimes, she even bristles up and attacks the offender, as well as she can, and much like a brooding hen.

If the first nest be destroyed, a second hatching is often entered upon. The young increase rapidly in size, and by the first of September are two-thirds grown. Until then they remain more or less together in a covey, and, if undisturbed, even do so until the following spring. While young, they suffer severely from exposure to unusual weather, especially to cold and heavy rains, which are very destructive. Moreover, a species of wood-tick attacks them in summer, inserting its triangular head beneath the skin. It is said to be especially dangerous, when it attaches itself to the bird's head or neck, but, at all events, many birds suffer from it. They are also often infested with lice, and are occasionally troubled by a kind of bott-worm, which resembles a large maggot, and which must be fatal, since it reaches the flesh.

In the first part of the shooting-season, whether it be September or October, tolerable sport may be had with the birds over a gun, if they have not been disturbed previously, and if they are abundant and in passable woods, though in the wilderness or rough forest they can only be shot while stationary, as the woods are usually too thick and encumbered to allow of shooting at them on the wing. In such places, or wherever the birds are not suspicious of man, they often take to a tree, if pursued by a yelping cur or spaniel, and, apparently in a state of stupid wonder, allow the sportsman to walk up and shoot them. Except in the wilderness, however, it has never been my good fortune to have a covey wait, while, beginning with the lowest on the tree, I might shoot them one by one. This undoubtedly is and can be done, if the birds are wholly unsophisticated, but I caution young sportsmen against too firm a belief and too high hopes founded on such reports. Even with the very best of dogs, the newest kind of breechloader, the very acme of skill, and an abundance of birds, it is very rarely the case that a good bag is made. The birds seldom lie well to a dog, but steal away so rapidly on foot, that, if the dog is slow and staunch, they get away altogether, or, if the dog follows at an equal pace, it is generally impossible, owing to the thickness of the cover, for you to follow at the same rate. Again, half of the birds, when startled, get into a tree, and one can see them neither in the tree nor when they leave it. So on with one vexation after another throughout the early season. As the leaves drop, the birds become more shy and wary, getting up, often silently, instead of with their usual whirr, at long distances, and often flying with immense rapidity. Yet it is a pleasure to kill them. They fall with a satisfactory thud, they fill up one's bag, and are a very good addition to the larder. A few lucky chances at these seductive birds often inveigle the old and sagacious sportsman into trying them once more, though they all declare that the "Partridges" ought not to be ranked among game-birds. Sometimes, after a fall of light snow, the sportsman may pursue them successfully without a dog. He may also occasionally have good luck with a dog, on an exceptionally cold autumn morning, when the birds are more sluggish than usual.

The Ruffed Grouse feed throughout the summer on various small fruits and berries, and upon such insects as come in their way. They eat also small acorns, blackberries, grapes, and beech-nuts. On the arrival of snow, they begin to feed on the buds of various trees and shrubs; among others upon one or more kinds, which often render their flesh unwholesome and poisonous. As spring opens, they often eat the buds of appletrees and birches, of both of which they are particularly fond. They are able to endure an excessive degree of cold, and, so long as they can find sufficient food, they do not apparently suffer from severe winters; but some perish, like the Quail, from being caught beneath the crust of the snow, under which, as it falls, they frequently lie, contrary to their habit of roosting in trees.

The flight of the Ruffed Grouse, when well under way, is very rapid, and undoubtedly these birds sometimes accomplish even the first forty yards of their flight in a second. They usually rise rather slowly, especially in thick woods, and at first afford an easy mark, unless late in the season, when, with a clear path, they go off with great speed. Having reached the level of the tree-tops, a few yards suffice for headway, and the latter part of their flight, extended sometimes to several hundred yards, is usually made with very little motion of the wings.

(*d*). The ordinary note of the "Partridges" are a *chuck* or clucking, and the whining call of the hen to her young.

§ 31. Perdicidæ. Partridges. (See § 29.)

I. ORTYX

(A) VIRGINIANUS. *Quail. Partridge.* "*Bob White.*"

(In south-eastern New England, a common resident.)

(*a*). About nine inches long. ♂, with the crown-feathers somewhat erectile. Chief tint, reddish or chestnut-brown, somewhat restricted on the head, wanting on the tail and middle of the under parts, but becoming chestnut-red on the sides. Head, with much black, but with the throat, forehead, superciliary line, and edging of the lower feathers, white. Upper parts marked with black, gray, and tawny. Tail gray, scarcely marked; quills browner, slightly mottled with tawny. Breast, etc., waved or barred with black; belly, chiefly white, and less marked. ♀, with tints less bright, etc.; the throat, etc., buff.

(*b*). The nest is not unlike that of the Ruffed Grouse, but it is more neatly constructed, being frequently lined with strips of bark, and is often built in more open or bushy places. The eggs average about 1·20 × 1·00 of an inch, are somewhat pointed, and are white (often slightly stained but not strictly spotted). They are laid in the latter part of May, and there are sometimes, according to Wilson, twenty-four in the same nest, in which case two or three females probably contribute to the laying.

(c). The Quail are abundant in the three Southern States of New England, except in the colder and more hilly portions. They are not found much to the north or east of Boston, in the neighborhood of which, however, they are resident throughout the year. Our observations on them naturally begin at that season of the year when they relinquish their habits of extreme cunning and vigilance for those of confidence in man's respect for domestic life, that is in the early part of summer. Though among the hardiest and most active of feathered creatures, they are prudent in spring, and do not commit themselves to the risks of incubation until they have received full assurance of fitting weather. In this respect they differ from the feebler but more venturesome Woodcock, whose premature endeavors, founded upon the first deceptive smile of spring, to raise a family, are often defeated by an unexpected snow-storm. The Quail do not begin until May, when they announce the fact to all their neighbors within half a mile by their loud, frank, and cheery whistle, which is generally translated into

Fig. 21. Quail (⅓).

our uncouth language as "Bob White." The male is not now constrained by fear, and, instead of any false pride, he has a proper sense of his own comely appearance. He knows that he is attending adequately to his department in the great business of nature, and is entirely willing that any one should see him. He has no fear of man, but he keeps an eye to the hawks, cats, and those other predatory enemies, who respect neither time, place, nor season. He is willing to take any amount of the family responsibility; Nature cannot ask too much of him; he will whistle to two or three wives if necessary; and he will even accept the law of Moses, and assume the part of husband towards his brother's widow. Should his wife propose a family of fifteen instead of nine, he does not complain; and, moreover, having escorted his young family about for a short time, he is ready to go through this once or even twice more. In fact, he carries his amiability and industry so far as often to introduce a half-grown family to the rigors of winter, so that it is not uncommon to find a covey of these little "cheepers," when hardly able to fly, even in November. A successful pair of Quail often turn out twenty-five young in a season. During the period of incubation, the Quail often appear on our lawns, or on the walls and fences by the roadside. Though their bills are especially adapted to crushing, and their crops to dissolving small grains and seeds, they are also fond of grubs, worms, and other insects, and are thus useful in destroying the farmer's pests.

When the armistice granted by law and custom is over, the male, with his family, seeks securer spots, becoming restless and active. From this time forward, he seeks safety in concealment and silence, and only betrays his presence by the plaintive call which his social instincts compel him to utter when separated from his companions, or by the treacherous scent of his body, which he cannot retain. Besides being very uncertain in his daily wanderings, especially to those who are unfamiliar with the locality, he is to a certain extent migratory; but his migrations, unlike those of the true Quail of Europe, are always performed on foot, so far as possible. We believe that this is not much the case in New England; though, from the accidental appearance of a covey in the Berkshire hills, and in those of New Hampshire beyond the isothermal lines which mark the northern range of these birds, it may be inferred that they are very vagrant in their disposition. In Delaware and Maryland, however, coveys of Quail often appear, who are distinctively called by the sportsmen there "runners." On the western side of the Chesapeake, an old sportsman assured me that covey after covey passed through the country, where food and shelter were abundant, crossing the peninsula on foot, but often perishing by the wholesale in attempting to pass the wider inlets, and he added in proof of this that he had taken as many as forty at a time from the middle of the river near his house.

To return to their habits here:—At night, for at least many days in succession, the Quail select the same spot to sleep in, more usually in low ground, where the long grass affords shelter and warmth. There they encamp, not huddled together promiscuously and unadvisedly, but shoulder to shoulder in a circle, with their heads out, so that in the event of a sudden surprise they escape rapidly, and in every direction, without difficulty. Such roosting-places may very often be found self-attesting, from the arrangement and accumulation of hard, round fæces. Though they rarely take to wing except when surprised, they almost invariably do so on leaving their roost in the morning, which they do at an early hour. Let us suppose ourselves to be accompanying Quail on a day's ramble. They first fly from the swamp, perhaps four or five hundred yards, to some copse adjoining a stubble-field. After a little toilet and a few sips of dew, they breakfast on the edge of the grainfield, keeping somewhat together, though each seeks for himself, making an occasional demand for halves upon the lucky finder of some luscious morsel. Half an hour after sunrise, the birds have passed through the long field more rapidly than usual, since the dew is not heavy, owing to a breeze in the night. Otherwise, they might have skirted the field to avoid getting wet, which they much dislike. Having reached a fal-low field, the old cock suddenly squats; then, with wonderful rapidity and steps nearly eighteen inches long, he runs across this land, the others following. He passes through a dry oakwood, halts a moment for the stragglers, takes breath, and then flies silently from the crest of the hill across the little valley below. These hurried movements are due to a lad with a gun and an old dog. The latter of these new comers stops suddenly as if paralyzed, and then steps along slowly and stealthily to that part of the stubble-field where the birds left it, stopping from time to time for his master to come up. Puzzled, he now returns more rapidly, but circumspectly, to the point of the birds' entrance on the field, and there he is again puzzled. His master, after obliging him to go all through the stubble, after tramping himself all over this, as well as the adjoining woods, shoulders his gun and goes off. Meanwhile, our former companions have wandered half a mile further, and, after drinking in a lively little brook, have again taken a short flight. They are now sitting half asleep in the sunshine on a dry, sandy bank, though some are dusting themselves in little hollows which they have scratched out, just as hens do. In the latter part of the afternoon they return, perhaps by very much the same route, and reach the old stubble-field; but, just when they are in the middle of this, a hawk appears, and the whole covey instantly squat. Should the marauder detect them, notwithstanding the assimilation of their coloring to that of the mould and dead vegetation, one must perish. The danger is soon past, however, and the birds are feeding again; but they squat a second time, because our friend with the gun has reappeared. His dog soon ascertains their position and stops again, while the lad advances beyond him. The birds suddenly spring up with a startling *whirr*, which is immediately followed by the *bang, bang*, of two gun-barrels, which prove harmless. The old cock and one or two more go to a patch of scrub-oaks, the old hen and three others to a grove of maples; no, they have gone into a nasty swamp. The others have flown straight to a pine-grove. The old cock and his companions race over the dry leaves through the scrub oaks, at the rate of a hundred and fifty yards in a minute, so that one must trot to go as fast. The young do the same over the smooth, dry carpet of pine-needles. They pass along so rapidly, and the ground is so free from grass and undergrowth, that no scent is left behind. Two or three birds are in the pines, sitting close to the trunks or along the boughs. Two others have dropped into a bunch of briars, and the rest into bushes near by. Our friend has now passed through the intervening copse; he has reached the swamp, and has hunted over it thoroughly but without success. His fine-haired pointer has refused to go among the briars. Had our friend waited half an hour until the scent of the birds had become stronger through gradual dissemination, his dog would have found them easily. Tired and disappointed, he sits down to consider, when suddenly two of the Quail whirr almost at his feet. Meanwhile, the young birds have run half a mile, leaving no scent, and those who were in the trees have silently flown on to join their companions. Bye and bye you may be surprised to hear them calling each other together near the old field, and apparently on the very ground which our friend has searched so carefully. At last they will be back again at their roosting-place safe and sound, even if pursued until after dark. Now the lad also returns home, and explains his ill luck by an extraordinary theory, read of in books, and verified by his own experience, that our Quail have a wonderful power of retaining their scent. The only sound argument to prove this statement is that our game-birds, when very young, by a thoughtful provision of nature, emit little or no scent.[3]

Though the Quail are very hardy, and can probably endure very severe cold, they often perish in the snow. In winter, they lie on the ground as usual, always allowing the snow to

---

[3] Among the very numerous writers on this subject, none, so far as we have observed, have claimed to possess that scientific and exact knowledge of the Quail's physiological structure and functions, without which it is idle to argue the question. When game-birds drop suddenly to the ground and remain motionless, the dog does not perceive them. Quail most frequently alight in this way, but, as soon as they begin to move, the effluvia escapes and is disseminated.

accumulate, until morning, when they free themselves by united effort. Should a crust be formed, they frequently find it impossible to escape, and so perish.

The haunts and habits of our Quail of course vary much in different localities. In the South and West they are accounted easy to shoot, but, being very abundant there, they are less often followed into the "thick." In the wooded parts of New England, on the other hand, a good bag of Quail is the best test of a sportsman's skill. A successful pursuit of them requires the utmost vigilance and activity, a sure hand, strong nerves, and great quickness together with nice observation. Their flight, late in the season, is much more rapid than that of the Woodcock or Snipe. They are, moreover, exceedingly tenacious of life. Their habits of capricious wandering, of rapid running, of dropping suddenly like stones, of resorting to trees, and of seeking covers which are thick or rendered impenetrable by briars, necessitate vigor, a certain aim, and a familiarity with their habits.

(*d*). The principal notes of the Quail, which we have already spoken of, are both whistles. One (which is somewhat like the whistle of the Great Crested Flycatcher) is a single call-note, uttered as if the breath were drawn in at the latter part, and is employed at all times of the year. The other is heard in spring and summer, and consists of two or three loud notes, of which each is higher than the preceding. This latter is very well known, and is familiar to nearly all persons who live in the country. The Quail have also a few low twitterings, not audible at any great distance, and a *chuck*.

§ 32. Scolopacidæ. Snipe, etc. (See § 29.)

I. PHILOHELA

(A) MINOR.[4] (*American*) *Woodcock*.

---

[4] The larger European Woodcock (*Scolopax rusticola*) is said to have occurred in New England as a straggler. In this species, only the outer wing-feather (or first primary) is attenuate, i. e. extremely narrow. In the American species, three of the primaries present this appearance.

(In New England, most abundant as a migrant, but locally common as a summer-resident.)

Fig. 22. Woodcock (⅓).

(*a*). About eleven inches long. Beneath, varying from (very) pale reddish buff to ruddy chestnut, darkest on the sides, whitening on the chin and cheeks. Above, varied with the same tint, with black, and with grayish. Forehead scarcely marked, but bordered by a dark, irregular (and often indistinct) line from the bill to the eye. Immature specimens are paler and grayer above, and have several white markings.

(*b*). The eggs average about 1·50 × 1·20 of an inch, though variable in size and shape, and are creamy, brownish, or clay-color, spotted and blotched with lilac and rather dull or indistinct browns. In Massachusetts, a set of four is usually laid about the middle of April. The places chosen are swampy groves, especially of alders or birches, and sometimes pastures or clearings. There is but little or no nest.

(*c*). A "game-bird," though exceptions may be taken to almost any definition of this term, is generally understood to be a bird that lies to a dog, and that can be shot only when on the wing. This definition, however, excludes, and we think rightly, the "Partridge" or Ruffed Grouse, who will not lie to a dog, but who on the contrary often takes to a tree, thus causing to the scientific sportsman constant annoyance. But the Woodcock is *par excellence* a game-bird, and, though he may play in a game of life and death to him, he adheres as scrupulously to rules of honor as any Knight-Errant of old. He may have his cunning devices, but he does not sneak or hide in trees. This conduct, however, finds no corresponding sentiment in his rapacious and improvident pursuer, to whose reckless cravings for sport or gain, we in New England are indebted for the present scarcity of the luscious Woodcock. Unless the laws, and general feelings on the subject, are greatly modified, comparatively few more years will suffice to nearly exterminate them.

The Woodcock are almost universally distributed over North America, both as residents and birds of passage. We shall speak here of their habits in New England only. Though a friend once showed the writer a record of one or more Woodcock killed in Massachusetts during every month of the year, these birds are migratory, and, though apparently often solitary in their flights, find their way, by an admirable instinct, through "the illimitable waste of air," at least as far as from Labrador to Maryland. Many breed in the Southern States, even as far South as the Gulf, while others breed to the northward of Canada; but all pass the winter in the South, their northern range at that season being, it is believed, Maryland. They reach the neighborhood of Boston as early as March, and then, or more often early in April, they may be found on those dry hillsides, which were their last resorts in autumn. Almost immediately after their arrival, they begin to mate, and they may be observed in the dusk of evening to mount high in the air, going through a variety of eccentric motions, and from time to time darting suddenly down with great velocity. The eggs are laid early in April, sometimes on a warm knoll, sometimes on a high, bare hillside. After incubation has begun, it

27

is extremely difficult to find the birds; a few days later the sportsman may easily find three or four broods of young with one or both parents, where he may before have hunted by inches without flushing a bird. Should he, however, patiently search with his dog the dry grounds, he may find them, perhaps ten yards, perhaps half a mile, from the wet swale which he knows to be their favorite feeding-ground. The same is the case in August; also in winter (in districts of the South, where in many localities which the writer has visited the birds may be found in the ratio of ten to a township). In no part of the country are there Woodcock enough to occupy the whole of it; they may resort to any part of the many thousand acres outside of the particular spot to which at particular times they resort. While the young are feeble on the wing and their parents are with them, twelve birds may be found in summer in a swale of two acres, but later they may be dispersed over many hundred times that space. Their "borings" (small, clean-cut holes made in soft earth by their bills) may still, however, be seen in the same swale; moreover, by patient watching at evening, their shadowy forms may be detected, as they pass to the swamp, or cross the roadway, and, by patient search, the same twelve birds may be picked up one by one in odd places. This fact the author has verified by experience, when the temporary laws forbade the killing of the birds before August fifteenth. Will any one who cannot gainsay these facts still uphold the absurd old theory that Woodcock migrate in summer? Since this so-called disappearance is a notorious fact from Canada to the far South and West, we venture to ask to what place the birds migrate? To this there is no answer.

The period of incubation is supposed to be sixteen days, but it may be longer. As soon as the young are hatched, it becomes convenient and necessary that the whole family should be in the immediate vicinity of a feeding-ground, and it is asserted that the old birds frequently carry their young thither in their bills. Their food now consists of various earth-worms, which they obtain by probing the ground with their bills, evidence of which may often be found, usually in soft, black ground. Their borings are certain signs, which are eagerly looked for by the sportsman. They also glean among decaying leaves and logs, and in low, moist, vegetable growth; but from a peculiarity of structure or habit, their soft animal food is so compressed and macerated in the swallowing that the species eaten becomes indistinguishable, even when the bird is shot just after eating. Rich, soft earth, running water, and abundant shelter, are the most usual and certain conditions for a summer cover.

The young birds mature very rapidly, but are usually only two-thirds grown in July. From the fact that often neither parents, or at most only one of them, are to be found with the young in their summer cover, and that birds only half grown are frequently shot in September or late in October, it may be inferred that two broods are raised in a season. It is certain that a second set of eggs is laid, when those of the first nest are destroyed, either by accident or by the common vicissitudes of our climate, such as early snows, or long continued wet and cold. There are great differences in the productiveness of different seasons. The writer recalls one within a few years when there was a heavy snow-storm in the middle of April, and afterwards floods caused by northeasterly rains; the same extensive grounds, over which he had been accustomed to get three or four dozen birds in the course of July, contained that year just seven *old* birds, while a large portion of the few Woodcock found in September were mere fledglings. Others made similar observations during the same year.

By the first of August a majority of the Woodcock desert the low, wet grounds, and scatter themselves all over the country, generally choosing, however, some dry spot, protected by a dense second growth. The sportsman may chance to find them, however, in the long grass of a meadow, and in a variety of such places as corn-fields, pine-groves, bunches of dry alders, knolls of cedar, hillsides of birch, woods of chestnuts, thickets of briars, etc. They are now moulting and half-naked, and they can no longer make that peculiar whistle which at all other times warns the sportsman. Though they sometimes labor with their wings, as they heavily flutter up, they as often fly off silently like an owl, stealing along close to the ground. They are usually found too upon very dry land holding no scent, where they come merely to rest, and upon which they have dropped without running about. If disturbed, however, they occasionally steal away from the dog on foot, running over the parched ground, and thus elude him altogether, or get up out of shot or unperceived. On this account, a pursuit of them at this time is unsatisfactory, requiring for a good bag hard fagging, thorough knowledge of the ground, great observation and vigilance.

In September, the Woodcock are again in better condition. They are now less capricious, and are more easily found, frequenting, for the most part, drier grounds. In October, the birds are not only in prime condition, but they afford to sportsmen the most enjoyable and eagerly sought-for shooting. They are found again in localities which may easily be ascertained. The sportsman may always hope for the abundant sport which follows a flight, for it is in October that those remarkable movements of the birds occur. There is in flight-time an uncertainty as to when and where the birds may be found, which gives in the highest degree that element of chance, without which the sportsman's life would lose half its charm. Every one must form his own theories from his own experience and knowledge of the grounds, but certain it is that sometimes the lucky or sagacious sportsman may reach a spot in which the birds are almost literally swarming. Suddenly and inexplicably the cover becomes full of them; then as mysteriously it becomes vacant. One would suppose that birds apparently so feeble on the wing must perform these long journeys by short stages; but, though the Woodcock undoubtedly travel about much more actively than is commonly supposed from one part of a district to another, so that there are often local flights, yet it is well known that they very often appear simultaneously over wide areas. The writer himself has seen one in the gray of morning, a mile or two from land on the open ocean, flying in as if from sea. This bird was solitary, but in the afternoon of the same day we found six or eight birds in a bit of wood where we had never seen Woodcock before, and no doubt the morning's bird was among them.

It is quite evident that Woodcock do not fly in flocks, like plover or wild fowl, compactly and under the direction of a leader, but that each travels independently, coming in contact with his companions through their common tastes. Yet it is said to be wise to leave a bird or two in every cover as "tollers." Twice when the writer has met a flight, both occasions being late in the afternoon, he has gone through the cover once, thought it shot out, returned over the same ground as it was growing dark, found half as many more, and still, as he has stood after dark on the edge of the cover and has walked away, he has perceived the birds dropping in one by one. The next day scarcely a bird could be found there.

The Woodcock pretty generally disappear (near Boston) by the twenty-fifth of October, though it is not uncommon to have good shooting a fortnight later. It seems that the old birds sometimes precede the young in their flights, as is the case with the Sea Coot and Golden Plover. The writer once weighed eighteen, shot on the second of October, whose average weight was seven ounces. This may have been owing to some extraordinary combination of accidents; but every sportsman is familiar with those very small, wiry, compactly feathered, weather-tanned birds, who appear in October, and who are called, perhaps locally, "Labrador twisters."

The influence of weather upon the birds is an interesting but puzzling study. A heavy rain or frost causes them to shift their quarters from swamps to hillsides or *vice versa;* a drought or heavy flood drives them away altogether. In autumn, just before a northeast storm, birds that have been on a ground the whole season sometimes seem very nervous and restless, jumping up wildly and flying far; in the same cover, after the storm, no birds can be found.

The flight of the Woodcock, when first flushed, is short and very slow. In summer, the same bird may often be shot at eight or ten times, by persistent and thorough searching. He lies with his head dropped on his shoulders, and on rising makes one or two sharp whistles with his wings. It often happens, however, especially if the bird goes on to dry ground or into long grass, or if he drops, as he often does, like a stone, without running, that the best dog cannot find him by scent. Many and many a time in summer the bird may be marked down accurately, and may be found only by actually kicking him up. A little study shows this to be quite accidental, depending upon the condition of the ground, upon the kind of cover, and upon whether the bird runs or not. It is a fact which has some bearing on the vexed question whether or not the Quail voluntarily withhold their scent.

The structure of Woodcock's eyes is very peculiar, being adapted to their habits of moving and feeding at night; and the birds not unfrequently run against telegraph-wires in the day-time, and are thus killed. Our species differs radically from the European. The general appearance and markings of the latter are wholly different, especially in his being waved beneath. He is a third larger, two-thirds less luscious, much more indolent, and wholly silent on the wing. He may be described generally as a cross between a curlew and an owl. Our Woodcock is not a warbler, and does not alight on trees, the assertions of our farmers to the contrary notwithstanding.

(*d*). His notes are few and unmusical. In spring, at the time of his antics in the air, he utters a series of peculiar, and rather harsh but not very loud notes. Wilson speaks of his "sudden *quack*," and says that "when uttering his common note on the ground, he seems to do it with difficulty, throwing his head towards the earth and frequently jetting up his tail." The young have a feeble "peep."

II. GALLINAGO

(A) WILSONI. (*American*) *Snipe. Wilson's Snipe.*
(A common migrant through Massachusetts.)

(*a*). Average length, ten inches. Bill essentially like that of the Woodcock, and about as long. Head much less stout, and tail longer, than the corresponding parts of that bird.

Crown, dark, with a light median stripe. Back, etc., varied with black, brown, and a tint varying from chestnut to whitish. Belly, etc., white; generally unmarked, but with the sides darkly barred. Breast, etc., somewhat tawny, and streaked or mottled with brown.

(*b*). The eggs have about the same measurements as those of the Woodcock, but are much more pointed or "pyriform." They are drab, often tinged with olive, and are blotched with brown. "The loosely constructed nest is built on the ground in various wet places."

(*c*). The Snipe, more particularly designated as Wilson's Snipe or the "English" Snipe, differ so slightly from the latter as to be substantially the same, if not wholly so. In New England, they are birds of passage, breeding here but rarely. Near Boston, they appear from the South as soon as the frost is well out of the lowlands, where they feed, and where they may be looked for as soon as the Blue Bird enters seriously upon her preparations for summer housekeeping, or when the shad-bush is in bloom. Though they do not regulate their movements by the calendar, the sportsman will find that in a series of years the most favorable season for spring snipe-shooting is that between April tenth and twenty-fifth. Stragglers and small "wisps" may be found sometimes in March, often in May, and occasionally in early June. But at this time of year they are uncertain and capricious in their habits, appearing and perhaps in a few hours disappearing so suddenly and mysteriously, as to cause the formation of very different theories and speculations, as to what are the favorable conditions for a "flight," and to make it impossible for any person not living in the immediate vicinity of the grounds, to count surely upon finding birds. As to the flights, some say "clear warm weather with light westerly winds," others "thick weather and southerly winds;" some look for snipe after, and some before, a northeast rain-storm; and so on. Some say that thick weather makes them stop here, others that clear weather helps them to get here. Each theorist rejoices in his own wisdom, and there is not only this uncertainty as to the time of arrival, but also an equally trying one as to the locality in which the birds may be found.

Like Woodcock, the Snipe use their long and sensitive bills for probing the mud or soft earth, and the perforations which they make are often tantalizing evidences of their recent occupation of the grounds; but, unlike them, they are usually, though not invariably, found and shot in the "open." Like Woodcock, again, they are nocturnal birds, though the modified arrangement and structure of their eyes enable them to show greater observation and vigilance, to make long flights, and to feed, as they frequently do, by daylight.

It is during the season of mating in spring that the actions of the male birds are so remarkable and interesting. Rising in the air to a great height, they dart and twist about with wonderful agility, dropping plumb down from time to time in the midst of these eccentric gyrations, and producing, as they descend, a thrumming noise, possibly caused by forming the wing into a sort of Æolian harp. The sound is peculiar and unmistakable, resembling somewhat that made by throwing a nail held crosswise in the hand, but it is much louder and more full. It is said that at such times they will sometimes alight temporarily on a tree or fence, but this observation the author has never had the good fortune to verify, though he once saw one alight upon a fence-post for a moment, not, however, during an "exhibition."

The Snipe breed in the far North, and return to us in autumn, when they will, if permitted, remain on that ground which is to their liking for several weeks. But though they have been found and shot as early as August, and as late as December, the most favorable time is between September 10th and October 25th, and of this period the last fortnight is the best portion.

In all the accounts of these birds which are accessible to him, the author finds the ancient, time-honored tradition, that the Snipe always begin their flights by rapid zigzags, so that it behooves the shooter either to fire at the instant when the birds attain the height of their first spring, or to wait till they have completed their zigzags and begin their steady flight. The beginner, deeply impressed by these statements, his mind filled with the idea that the flight of the Snipe is much like that of a tortuous lightning flash through a cloud, sets out, and, adopting one or the other of these absurd rules, is sure to miss. Inasmuch as the Snipe, five times out of six, in most weather does not *spring* at all, to fire at the height of the first spring means to the beginner to fire as soon as he can, that is as much as possible *before he gets his aim*. On the other hand, to wait until the bird is *done* with zigzagging necessitates waiting until he has *begun* zigzagging, and, as he generally does not zigzag at all, this involves waiting some time. From the expression, " zigzag flight," would not the natural impression be that the bird kept darting rapidly with sharp, quick, short turns from side to side? That such is the Snipe's usual flight is certainly not true, though it is undoubtedly often rapid and sometimes eccentric. The author's experience is for these days of rapid travel limited, but after shooting snipe at different seasons in the British Provinces, in Maine, Massachusetts, Rhode Island, Maryland, Delaware, Virginia, and North Carolina, he ventures to assert that they almost never "zigzag" in their flight.

Unless there is a high wind, or the birds have been very much persecuted, they fly off, four times out of five, more or less rapidly in a direct line, and near the ground. On a bright, warm, quiet day, with a gentle breeze, they afford the sportsman more easy shots in succession than any other game-bird of New England, and, indeed, frequently flutter off so indolently that to shoot them is a mere bagatelle even for the most indifferent shot. Snipe usually start up the wind, and, if the wind is high, often dart away fifteen or twenty yards, gradually ascending, and then either fall away gradually before the wind till they cross it with a circumlinear flight, or, by throwing up one wing, make a sharp angle in the direction of their motion. But the abrupt change of direction is not common, and a rapid repetition of it rare. Sometimes, again, they go off up wind, bearing first more strongly on one wing than on the other, thus producing a sinuous motion in regular curves, varying a few feet on either side from a right line, and crossing it, perhaps, every thirty or forty feet. Sometimes, again, they start by a rapid and almost perpendicular ascent, and then sag away from the wind. The mode of flight depends of course on certain conditions: the state of the atmosphere, the force of the wind, the nature of the ground, the season, the bird's condition of body, etc. Snipe almost invariably fly into the wind; if a bunch of high reeds, a fence, or a line of trees, is in the way, or if for any other reason they ascend rapidly, they must afterward either fall off, flying across or down the wind, or else tack up into it to get headway. Since no bird can with rapidity start from a stationary position in the air against a strong wind, the more nearly stationary that a bird is, so is his difficulty the greater. If, on the contrary, there are no obstructions, and the birds jump at once from the ground into the teeth of the wind, taking a nearly horizontal line, there is less likelihood of their tacking or falling away, for it is not so necessary. In spring, the shooting is often more difficult, for the birds are light weights, and in great training when they reach us. They are both migrating and mating, and often seem to be in a state of restless activity and nervous excitement, which makes it very difficult to kill or even to approach them. So it is also in autumn, when the birds first appear; they are frequently wild and active, so much so as to make the pursuit of them a series of vexations; and yet, two days afterwards, the very same birds, having got fat and a little more lazy, afford delightful sport.

After hearing the accepted rules condemned, the reader may well ask for some substitute, but such rules are like rules of grammar; a man may shoot well, and speak grammatically, knowing no rules; he may know all rules and yet be able to do neither. Yet to know what others have learned is often useful. The success of sportsmen is more often due to their manner of getting shots than to their manner of making them. The chief difficulty in Snipe-shooting is the sudden and unexpected way in which the birds often jump, on either side or behind; but they may usually be marked down with accuracy, as they throw up their wings to alight, and they should then, as always, be approached down wind, no matter how great a detour is necessary. By a study of their habits the sportsman will soon find upon what days and in what places they may be most easily and successfully shot. More may generally be killed by a vigorous walker without a dog than with one, if one prefers birds to pleasure. As to the shooting, as in all shooting on the wing, you cannot shoot too quickly or too deliberately; when to fire quickly and when deliberately is to be learned by practice only. As for a precise rule, an old friend used to say: "Pull, as soon as the gun touches the shoulder, *if not sooner.*" There is humor in all wisdom, but perhaps an undue proportion in this advice for practical use. All that can be said is: "Shoot as soon as you know that the gun is right; the sooner, the better." After blowing a few birds to pieces, you will learn how far to modify this rule. Many birds will be missed by being undershot, and many by not being shot at well ahead. Some sportsman use number 8 shot; some number 12 and intermediate sizes. Number nine does very well.

Autumn is the proper season for Snipe-shooting, both because the birds are then more certainly found and because they are then very delicious morsels for the table. With us, when they arrive in spring, they are lean, dry, and sinewy, from long and hard exercise; the period of breeding has already begun, and well-developed eggs may often be found in the females. There is as much difference between the rich, tender, and juicy meat of the well-fed, lazy, autumn bird, and the meagre, dry, and sinewy flesh of the spring traveler, as between that of a stall-fed ox and that of a dray-horse. Yet there are many to whose coarse palates no difference appears. No doubt, it is hard to relinquish all field-sports in the spring; without such relief the period of inaction is long and tedious; one's fingers itch for the trigger. Yet spring Snipe-shooting is a sorry pastime, and a wasteful one, unworthy of the true sportsman.

(*d*). The notes of the Snipe are not susceptible of satisfactory description; their common note being a peculiar squeak, while their extraordinary love-note is usually called "bleating."

APPENDIX.

A. *Ornithological Calendar for Eastern Massachusetts.*

(Notes on the *Insessores*, or land-birds, only, excluding game-birds, shore-birds, and waders.)

§ I. JANUARY. Visitants and residents (those in brackets being always very rare, those italicized being (rare or) absent during many winters, and those marked with an asterisk (*) spending the winter, for the most part, more to the southward). [Black Hawks], Blue Jays,* "Butcher-birds," Cedar-birds,* "Chickadees," *Crossbills*, Crows, Downy Woodpeckers, Golden-crowned "Wrens," Golden-winged Woodpeckers,* Goldfinches, Goshawks,[1] [Great Gray Owls], Great Horned Owls, Hairy Woodpeckers,[1] [Hawk Owls], hawks (several, which are summer-residents), [Ipswich Sparrows]? [Jerfalcons], Kingfishers,*? Lapland Longspurs,[1] Meadow Larks,* nuthatches, owls (several, which are summer-residents), *Pine Finches, Pine Grosbeaks*, Purple Finches,*? Red-bellied Nuthatches,* *Red Crossbills, Red-polls*, Red-tailed Hawks, Robins,* [Rough-legged Hawks], Ruby-crowned Wrens,* Shore Larks, (G.N.) Shrikes, Snow-birds, Snow Buntings, Song Sparrows,* [Three-toed Woodpeckers], Tree Sparrows, White-bellied Nuthatches,* *White-winged Crossbills*, Wild Pigeons,* woodpeckers (see above), Winter Wrens,*? and various sea-birds, etc.

NOTE. The Black-throated Blue and Yellow-rumped Warblers, and also the Red-winged Blackbirds, have been known exceptionally to pass the winter here, and the Blue Birds are said to have been seen here in January.

§ II. FEBRUARY. The same birds may be found here in February as in January. In the latter part of this month, the Blue Birds, or even the Red-winged Blackbirds, sometimes come; and the Great Horned Owls sometimes lay their eggs.

§ III. MARCH.
1st–15th. The Song Sparrows and Snow-birds sing. The Blue Birds and Blackbirds usually arrive from the South; the Song Sparrows, and Robins (?), become more abundant.

---

[1] Rare.

15th–31st. The Robins, Cedar-birds, Meadow Larks, (and Golden-winged Woodpeckers) become more abundant. The Rusty Blackbirds, Fox Sparrows (20-25), Bay-winged Buntings? (25-31), Cow-birds (25-31, ?) and Pewees? (25-31), appear. Many winter-birds move to the northward.

§ IV. APRIL.

During this month, the Screech Owls and others lay their eggs, as do the Duck Hawks. The [Titlarks], Yellow-bellied Woodpeckers, Winter Wrens, Night "Hawks," [Wild Pigeons], *Carolina Doves, Crow Blackbirds*, and [Purple Finches] appear; but with great irregularity. Those inclosed in brackets are said often to pass the winter here; those italicized to often arrive in March, but the Night "Hawks" frequently do not come until May. Many winter-birds move to the northward in April, and other birds come from the South with more or less regularity at about the following dates.

1st. (Pine Warblers, usually later), Bay-winged Buntings, Cow-birds, Kingfishers, and Pewees.

10th (or earlier). White-breasted Swallows and Swamp Sparrows.

15th. Chipping Sparrows and Field Sparrows (usually not until the 20th), also Hermit Thrushes, Pine Warblers, Red-poll Warblers, Ruby-crowned "Wrens," Savannah Sparrows (Seaside and Sharp-tailed Finches?). The Crows, Red-tailed and Red-shouldered Hawks, sometimes lay their eggs.

20th. Chipping, Field, (and Savannah?) Sparrows usually arrive.

In the latter part of this month, the Crows, and many birds of prey, may lay their eggs. The following birds may arrive at this time, though often not until May, viz.:—Barn Swallows, Black and White "Creepers," Brown Thrushes, Least Flycatchers, Purple Martins, Solitary Vireos, Towhee Buntings, White-throated Sparrows (sometimes on the 20th), and "Yellow-rump" Warblers.

NOTE. The dates of arrival can only be approximately given, and it is to be remembered then the males of many birds arrive before the females.

§ V. MAY. *About the*

1st, the Barn Swallows, Black and White "Creepers," Brown Thrushes, Cliff (or Eave) Swallows, Least Flycatchers, Night "Hawks," Purple Martins, Solitary Vireos, Towhee Buntings, White-throated Sparrows, "Yellow-rump" Warblers, and Yellow-winged Sparrows often arrive, though sometimes earlier or later.

5th, the Baltimore Orioles (?), *Black and White Creepers*, Black-throated Green Warblers,[2] *Brown Thrushes*, Cat-birds, Chimney Swifts, *Towhee Buntings*, (Wilson's Thrushes, Yellow Warblers, usually about the 8th), and "*Yellow-rump" Warblers* arrive, those italicized (at least the B. T. and T. B.) generally coming earlier.

10th, the loitering Fox Sparrows, and various winter-birds, such as the Golden-crowned "Wrens," Snow-birds, and Tree Sparrows, finally disappear; the Blue Birds, Robins, Song Sparrows, Bay-winged Buntings or Grass Finches, Kingfishers, and Pewees often lay their eggs, chiefly the first three; and the Baltimore Orioles, Blackburnian Warblers, "Black-cap" Warblers, Black-throated Blue Warblers, Blue Yellow-backed Warblers, Bobolinks, Chestnut-sided Warblers, Connecticut Warblers, Golden-crowned "Thrushes" (or "Oven-birds"), Golden-winged Warblers, House Wrens, Hummingbirds, King-birds, Maryland "Yellow-throats," Nashville Warblers, Red-starts, Rose-breasted Grosbeaks, Warbling Vireos, Water "Thrushes," Wilson's Thrushes (usually earlier), Wood Thrushes, Yellow Warblers, and Yellow-throated Vireos arrive. (See 15th *ad fin.*)

15th, the Pine Warblers and Swamp Sparrows lay their eggs (the former usually later); the Bank Swallows, Black and Yellow Warblers, Black-billed Cuckoos, Cape May Warblers, Great Crested Flycatchers, Indigo Birds, Prairie Warblers, Red-eyed Vireos, Scarlet Tanagers, Swainson's Thrushes, Whippoor-wills, White-eyed Vireos, and Yellow-billed Cuckoos arrive. At this time, or more often earlier, Cooper's Hawks, Marsh Hawks, Sharp-shinned Hawks, and Sparrow Hawks lay their eggs. Swainson's Thrushes often come earlier.

20th, the Bay-breasted, and B and Y, Warblers, "Black-polls," Canada "Flycatchers," Mourning Warblers, Olive-sided Flycatchers, Orchard Orioles, Tennessee Warblers, Traill's Flycatchers (and White-crowned Sparrows[2]?) arrive. About this time (earlier or later), the (Red-winged) Blackbirds, Blue Jays, Pewees, Field and Savannah Sparrows, Downy and Golden-winged Woodpeckers, lay their eggs.

25th, the Canada "Flycatchers" or Warblers, Wood Pewees, and Yellow-bellied Flycatchers usually arrive. The Wood Thrushes (sometimes,— also the Wilson's Thrushes?), the

---

[2] These birds sometimes appear in April.

Barn Swallows, Brown Thrushes, Chickadees, Cliff Swallows, Crow Blackbirds, Meadow Larks, Pine Warblers, Towhee Buntings, and White-breasted Swallows lay their eggs.

§ VI. JUNE. *About the*

1st, the last migrants are seen, such as the "Black-polls" and Canada "Flycatchers;" and at this time (or later, particularly in the case of the flycatchers, except the Pewee, the Hummingbirds, vireos, Bank Swallows, and many warblers), the Baltimore Orioles, Black-billed Cuckoos, Bobolinks, Cat-birds, Chimney Swifts, Chipping Sparrows, Golden-crowned "Thrushes," (or "Oven-birds"), Indigo Birds, (Marsh Wrens ?), Night "Hawks," Purple Finches, Rose-breasted Grosbeaks, Whippoorwills, Wilson's Thrushes, Wood Thrushes, Yellow-billed Cuckoos, Yellow-winged Sparrows, the flycatchers (except the Common Pewee), the vireos, Tanagers, Hummingbirds, and most of the warblers, lay their eggs. The Cedar-birds, Goldfinches, Orchard Orioles, Wood Pewees, and perhaps other birds (inclusive of the Marsh Wrens ?) rarely lay their eggs before the middle of the month, the first two sometimes not until July.

NOTE. The above dates, given for the neighborhood of Boston, bear no reference to second broods. The names of several birds have been purposely omitted, chiefly from difficulty in satisfactorily stating or approximating the dates.

§ VII. JULY. The following (insessorian) birds are summer-residents of Massachusetts, who have been known to breed here since 1870. Acadian Owls,[3] Baltimore Orioles, Bank Swallows, Barn Swallows, Barred Owls, Bay-winged Buntings, Black and White "Creepers," Black-billed Cuckoos, Blackburnian Warblers,[3] Black-throated Blue Warblers[3]?, Black-throated Buntings,[4] Black-throated Green Warblers, Blue Birds, Blue Jays, Blue Yellow-backed Warblers,[3] Bobolinks, Broad-winged Hawks,[3] Brown Creepers, Brown Thrushes, Canada "Flycatchers," Carolina Doves, Cat-birds, Chestnut-sided Warblers, Chickadees, Chimney Swifts, Chipping Sparrows, Cliff Swallows, Cooper's Hawks, Cow-birds, Crows, Crow Blackbirds, Downy Woodpeckers, *Duck Hawks,* Field Sparrows, *Fish Hawks,* Golden-crowned "Thrushes," Golden-winged Warblers, Golden-winged Woodpeckers, Goldfinches, Gos-

---

[3] (Very) rare in summer so far to the southward.
[4] Very much more common to the southward of New England.

hawks,³ Great-Crested Flycatchers, Great Carolina Wrens? (just discovered), Great Horned Owls, Hairy Woodpeckers,³ Henslow's Buntings,⁴ Hermit Thrushes?,³ House Wrens, Hummingbirds, Indigo Birds, King-birds, Kingfishers, Least Pewees, *Lincoln's Sparrows*, Long-billed Marsh Wrens, Long-eared Owls, Marsh Hawks, Maryland " Yellow-throats," Meadow Larks, Nashville Warblers,³ Night " Hawks," Olive-sided Flycatchers,³ Orchard Orioles,⁴ Pewees, Pigeon Hawks,³ Pine Warblers, Prairie Warblers, Purple Finches, Purple Martins, Red-bellied Nuthatches?,³ Red-eyed Vireos, Red-shouldered Hawks, Redstarts, Red-tailed Hawks, Red-winged Blackbirds, Robins, Rose-breasted Grosbeaks, Savannah Sparrows, Scarlet Tanagers, Screech Owls, Sea-side Finches,⁴ Sharp-shinned Hawks, Sharp-tailed Finches,⁴ Short-billed Marsh Wrens, Short-eared Owls, Snow-birds,³ Solitary Vireos,³ Song Sparrows, Sparrow Hawks, Swamp Sparrows, Towhee Buntings, Traill's Flycatchers,³ Warbling Vireos, Water " Thrushes,"³ Whippoor-wills, White-bellied Nuthatches, White-breasted Swallows, White-eyed Vireos, *Wild Pigeons*, Wood Pewees, Wood Thrushes, *Yellow-bellied Flycatchers?*, Yellow-bellied Woodpeckers,⁵ Yellow-billed Cuckoos, Yellow-breasted Chats?,⁴ Yellow-throated Vireos, Yellow Warblers, and Yellow-winged Sparrows (108). The following other birds (of whom the list is probably incomplete) also breed here:—Arctic Terns, Bitterns, Black (or Dusky) Ducks, Carolina Rails, Coot⁴ (*Fulica Americana*), Great Blue Herons, Green Herons, "Killdeer" Plover, Laughing Gulls,˙ Least Bitterns,⁴ Least Terns, Little Blue Herons?,⁴ Loons,⁵ Night Herons, Pinnated Grouse⁶ (or Prairie Hens), Piping Plover, Quail, Ruffed Grouse (or " Partridges " of N. E.), Roseate Terns, Solitary Sandpipers,³ Spotted Sandpipers, Summer (or Wood) Ducks, Summer " Yellow-legs," Teal?,⁵ Upland Plover, Virginia Rails, " Willets," Wilson's Terns, and Woodcock (28). (Those italicized are very rare, at least as summer-residents.)

NOTE. The eggs of all the above birds form a nearly or quite complete collection of the birds' eggs of Massachusetts. The Pine Finches and Snow Buntings have been known to breed (altogether exceptionally) at Cambridge and near Springfield respectively; several birds, such as the Bald Eagles and Pileated Woodpeckers, have been so far driven from the State, as probably to breed here no longer. In regard to the dates

---

⁵ Confined in summer to Western Massachusetts.
⁶ See p. 387.

already given, there is apparently evidence that our summer-residents may have formerly arrived and laid their eggs somewhat earlier than they do now.

In July, singing is much less constant than in May or June, decreasing as summer advances, though occasionally heard in autumn (chiefly from the finches), and rarely in winter (from the Song and Tree Sparrows).

§ VIII. August.

During this month, many birds leave their summer-haunts, and even become gregarious, and some journey to the southward, as is occasionally observable even in the latter part of July. The Goldfinches, however, sometimes lay their first set of eggs after July, during which month many other birds have their second or even third broods.

§ IX. September.

During this month, the (smaller) hawks are often abundant, many migrating, but the migrations of our birds of prey cannot be easily determined as regards the dates. The Baltimore Orioles, Bobolinks, Chimney Swifts, cuckoos, flycatchers (except the Pewees and occasionally the Great Crested Flycatchers), Henslow's Buntings, House Wrens, Hummingbirds, Indigo Birds, Rose-breasted Grosbeaks, swallows (of whom some go in August), Tanagers, vireos, warblers (or most of them: see October), Wilson's Thrushes, and Yellow-winged Sparrows finally disappear, many occurring as migrants. Some are to be seen only in the first week, but others may occur up to late dates, as the Black-throated Blue Warblers (30th), Golden-crowned "Thrushes" (26th), Hummingbirds (23rd), and White-bellied Swallows (28th). The Red-winged Blackbirds generally leave the meadows, and associate in the grain and stubble-fields, etc.; the Wild Pigeons appear in large flocks; and a majority of birds are gregarious, particularly the White-bellied Swallows, who, previous to their departure, often gather "upon the salt marshes" "literally by millions." Even hawks occasionally travel in companies. In September, White-throated Sparrows and other birds appear from the North.

Note. It has generally been in autumn that accidental stragglers, whose usual habitat is more than a thousand miles away, have occurred in Massachusetts.

§ X. October.

During this month, the "Black-poll" Warblers, Brown Creepers, Golden-crowned "Wrens," nuthatches, Ruby-crowned

"Wrens," Rusty Blackbirds, Titlarks, Winter Wrens, and "Yellow-rump" Warblers, are generally abundant; and many winter-birds arrive from the North. In the latter part, the Sharp-tailed Finches and many Song Sparrows finally disappear, and the Fox Sparrows come from the North. *About the* 1st, the Brown Thrushes, Red-eyed Vireos (latest date, Oct. 3rd), and Towhee Buntings disappear, the Olive-backed Thrushes arrive from the North, and the Crow Blackbirds (as well as the variety of Bronzed Blackbirds) wander about in large flocks.

5th, the last Black-throated Green Warblers depart.

10th, the last Pine Warblers (latest date, however, Oct. 16th) and Cat-birds depart.

15th, the "Chippers," Field Sparrows, Pewees (latest date, Oct. 16th), Wood Thrushes, and most of the Blue Birds, Cowbirds, Meadow Larks, Purple Finches, Red-winged Blackbirds, and Robins disappear.

§ XI. NOVEMBER.

During this month, many winter-birds usually come from the North, and, as in spring, "bird-waves" may occur; Fox Sparrows are common, and Hermit Thrushes finally disappear. In the early part of November, the last Bay-winged Buntings, Blackbirds, Blue Birds, Savannah Sparrows, and Swamp Sparrows, move to the southward. I have seen Great-crested Flycatchers so late as Nov. 1st, and White-throated Sparrows on the 14th.

§ XII. DECEMBER.

I have seen Fox Sparrows, the last loiterers among our fall-migrants, so late as the 9th of December. During this month, additional winter-birds may arrive from the North; and the same birds generally occur here as in January (§ I).

B. *Distribution of the Birds of New England.*

A list of the birds of New England, confined in the breeding-season principally or wholly to the district of the Alleghanian Fauna (southward of the 44th parallel of latitude), or Southern New England. Wood Thrush, (Mocking-bird), Cat-bird (?), Brown Thrush, Long-billed Marsh Wren, Short-billed Marsh Wren, Golden-winged Warbler, Prairie Warbler, (Yellow-breasted Chat), Yellow-throated Vireo, White-eyed Vireo,

(Summer Red Bird), Scarlet Tanager, Henslow's Bunting, Yellow-winged Sparrow, (Sea-side Finch), Sharp-tailed Finch, Field Sparrow, Lincoln's Sparrow, Black-throated Bunting, Rose-breasted Grosbeak, (Cardinal Grosbeak), Towhee Bunting, Meadow Lark, Baltimore Oriole, Orchard Oriole, Purple Grakle (?), Black-billed Cuckoo, Yellow-billed Cuckoo, (Red-headed Woodpecker), (Barn Owl), Carolina Dove, (Prairie Hen), and Quail (also several water-birds, etc.).

A list of the birds of New England, confined in the breeding-season principally or wholly to the district of the Canadian Fauna (northward of the 44th parallel of latitude), or Northern New England. Hermit Thrush, Swainson's Thrush, Water "Thrush," Golden-crowned "Wren," Brown Creeper, Red-bellied Nuthatch, Winter Wren, "Blue Yellow-back," Mourning Warbler, Nashville Warbler (?), Tennessee Warbler, "Black-throated Blue," "Yellow-rump," Bay-breasted Warbler, Blackburnian Warbler, "Black-poll,"[1] Black and Yellow Warbler, Cape May Warbler, ("Black-cap"), Canada "Flycatcher," Solitary Vireo, Great Northern Shrike,[1] (Common Crossbill), (White-winged Crossbill), White-throated Sparrow, Snow-bird, Rusty Blackbird, (Bronzed Grakle), Canada Jay,[1] Traill's Flycatcher, Yellow-bellied Flycatcher, Hairy Woodpecker, Yellow-bellied Woodpecker, "Log-cock," Black-backed Three-toed Woodpecker, Banded Three-toed Woodpecker, (Acadian Owl), Golden Eagle, Bald Eagle, Fish Hawk, Goshawk, (Pigeon Hawk), Broad-winged Hawk, Wild Pigeon, and Spruce Partridge; also several water-birds, etc.

A list of the birds hitherto known in New England, only as migrants or winter-visitants (the latter in brackets). Gray-cheeked Thrush, Ruby-crowned "Wren" (?), Titlark,[2] Connecticut Warbler, Red-poll Warbler, White-crowned Sparrow, and Fox Sparrow. [Also (Varied Thrush), Hudsonian Titmouse (?), (Bohemian Waxwing), Butcher-bird (?), Pine Grosbeak, Red-poll, Snow Bunting,[3] Lapland Longspur, Ipswich Sparrow, Tree Sparrow, Shore Lark, Great Gray Owl, Snowy Owl, Hawk Owl, Richardson's Owl, Gyrfalcon, Rough-legged Hawk, and Black Hawk.] To the above list are to be added the names of many water-birds, shore-birds, etc.

---

[1] These birds scarcely breed except in the most northern and eastern portions.
[2] A few may sometimes winter.
[3] With one extraordinary exception. See p. 185.

C. D. *The Use of the Keys.*

It is impossible, so far as is known, positively to identify many eggs, without some knowledge of the nest and parent-birds. In the following "*Key to the Eggs of Massachusetts*" (C), the position, and sometimes the structure, of the nest is the chief point dwelt upon; the colors of the parent-birds being mentioned, only when the best means of identification. On observing a bird for the purposes of this Key, note the general coloration (as in the Downy Woodpecker, black and white), particularly above, the color of the breast, *whether streaked* (*spotted*) *or not*, the color of the crown and throat, or of the entire head, and the color of the tail, *whether the outer feathers are white or not* (best observed as the bird flies). Observe any prominent markings, and, in large hawks, the coloration of the tail beneath. Eggs plainly colored belong to § I; eggs which are marked (not stained) to § II. In the former, the uniform color (as white) leads to the sections lettered A, B, C. In the latter, the ground-color leads to similar divisions. The subsections, (a) etc., are arranged according to the position of the nest. Under each subsection, the list-numbers run continuously. Glance down the column of the next figures (the extreme length and breadth of the eggs expressed in hundredths of an inch), until you find a size apparently corresponding to that of the egg in hand. If there are several eggs together in the Key of nearly the same size, read across the page until the right description is reached. You will often find some characteristic or means of distinction in the names of the birds. The figures at the end refer to the main work. List-numbers (to the extreme left) in parenthesis indicate rarity of the corresponding nest in Massachusetts, or at least rarity under the circumstances mentioned. $>$ means *more than;* $<$ means *less than*. Before two numbers connected by a cross ($\times$), these signs affect both. ♂ means *male;* ♀ means *female*. Occasionally, as is the case with the Bald Eagles, birds breed before attaining their full dress.

The "*Key to the Land-birds of New England*" (D) has been arranged as much by the *coloration* of birds as possible, but it cannot be used without having the bird in question at hand.

On the first page, follow the lines of the table, and also the divisions (beginning at the right), until a reference is reached. These references are to sections of the main work, unless stated to be to those of the Key. The former are in Arabic, the other in Roman, numerals. On reaching the Key-section referred to, find (if it is divided) the right division marked with a capital letter, or even the subdivision, if any, which is marked by a small letter. Glance down the column at the left (not ruled off), which gives the *chief* color, the most conspicuous, or the one best characterizing the species, until you find the color which applies to the bird in hand. (This column is in many places wanting, or mentions some other characteristic than the chief color.) Work to the right until a satisfactory name or reference is reached. A glance at the size-column, giving the length in inches, will often be an assistance, or one at the list of birds, in whose names you may find expressed some characteristic. To measure a bird, refer to § V of the Introduction. Any characteristic written on a line is supposed to be also written on all the lower lines, so far as empty directly beneath, until a line is reached containing words to the *left* of that space. Observe carefully all foot-notes, and refer to § T of the Introduction for any descriptive terms not understood. ♂ means *male;* ♀ means *female.* > means *more than;* < means *less than.* Other abbreviations or abbreviated expressions will be easily understood (as *yg.* for young, *wh.* for white, *head-sides* for sides of the head). ———— frequently is employed to mean *ditto.* The general plan is one of reduction to a limited choice by the use of various divisions, of working from the beginning toward the end, of following certain alternations, and of working from left to right.

C. A KEY TO THE EGGS OF MASSACHUSETTS.

This list, limited to the eggs previously described in this volume, is not wholly reliable, since several birds, not yet known to have actually bred in Massachusetts, may do so occasionally, and since eggs vary greatly, often presenting abnormal forms, or forms like those of other kinds.

§ I. **Eggs Unmarked.**
A. Color, white.[1]
(a). Laid in holes of trees (or posts and stumps).
1. $> 1\cdot25 \times 1\cdot00$. *Screech Owl.* § 26, V.
(2). Av. $1\cdot00 \times \cdot90$. Bird entirely brown and white. *Acadian Owl.* § 26, IV.
3. $> 1\cdot00 \times \cdot80$, $< 1\cdot25 \times 1\cdot00$. Bird not red-headed. *Pigeon Woodpecker.* § 25, I.
(4). $> 1\cdot00 \times \cdot80$, $< 1\cdot25 \times 1\cdot00$. Bird red-headed. *Red-headed Woodpecker.* § 25, II.
(5). Av. $\cdot95 \times \cdot80$. Bird; crown scarlet, upper breast black. *Yellow-bellied Woodpecker.* § 25, III.
(6). Generally $> \cdot80 \times \cdot65$. Bird $>$ 9 in., (chiefly) black and white. *Hairy Woodpecker.* § 25, V, A.
7. Generally $< \cdot80 \times \cdot65$. Bird $<$ 7 in., (chiefly) black and white. *Downy Woodpecker.* § 25, V, B.
(8). Av. $\cdot75 \times \cdot55$. Bird metallic green above. *White-bellied Swallow.*[2] § 12, III.
(9). Av. $\cdot80 \times \cdot60$, usually blue. Bird with chestnut breast. *Blue Bird.*[2] § 2, I.
[The Martins and Chimney Swifts no longer (?) build in stumps (etc.), in N. E.]

(b). Nests built in trees (or bushes), but not in holes.
(1). $> 2\cdot75 \times 2\cdot25$. White, very impure or dirty. *Bald Eagle.* § 27, VIII.
2. $2\cdot25$ long (or more). Not often pure white. *Great Horned Owl.*[3] § 26, VI.
3. $2\cdot00$ long or less; subspherical. *Barred Owl.* § 26, III, B.
4. Av. $1\cdot90 \times 1\cdot50$. Not spherical. Generally bluish; often marked. *Cooper's Hawk.* § 27, III, B.
5. Av. $1\cdot60 \times 1\cdot35$. Nearly spherical. *Long-eared Owl.* § 26, II, A.
6. Av. $1\cdot45 \times 1\cdot20$. Generally marked. *Sharp-shinned Hawk.* § 27, III, A.
7. Av. $1\cdot50 \times 1\cdot10$; elliptical. Nest loose and frail. *Wild Pigeon.* § 29, I.
8. Av. $1\cdot10 \times \cdot80$. Nest loose and frail. *Carolina Dove.* § 29, II.
9. Av. $\cdot75 \times \cdot55$, often bluish. Nest in bush or shrubbery. *Indigo Bird.* § 15, XX.
10. Av. $\cdot63 \times \cdot50$, bluish. Nest in bush or shade-tree. *Goldfinch.* § 15, IV, A.
(11). Av. $\cdot70 \times \cdot55$. Pure wh. Nest in woods (?). *Yellow-bellied Flycatcher.* § 19, V, C.
12. Av. $\cdot62 \times \cdot50$. Nest in (woods) orchard or shade-tree. Bird olive-gray above. *Least Pewee.* § 19, V, B.

---

[1] Many water-birds lay *large* white eggs, some in hollow trees, but these are all tinged with blue, green, or buff. Some of the petrels, however, lay a *single* small pure white egg, but none do so here.
[2] The nests of these birds are usually well lined, the Blue Bird's generally most warmly; those of the woodpeckers are rarely so.
[3] See B, (a), (1).

13. (<) ·50 long. *Hummingbird.* § 22, I.

[The eggs of the buzzard-hawks and of Traill's Flycatcher may sometimes be white. See § II, A, d.]

(c). Nest on the ground, or very near it.
1. Av. 1·80×1·35. Occasionally marked. *Marsh Hawk.* § 27, I.
2. Av. 1·50×1·30. Normally, almost spherical. *Short-eared Owl.* § 26, II, B.
(3). Av. 1·20×·90. Blue-tinged, and nearly elliptical. *Least Bittern.*
4. Av. 1·20×1·00. White, often stained, and almost pointed at one end. *Quail.* § 31.
5. Av. ·70×·55, usually marked. Nest built near water. *Yellow Throat.* § 9, II, A.

(d). Nest about buildings (2, 3, 6, usually in bird-boxes, 4 in chimneys).
(1). > 1·50×1·25. Impure white. *Barn Owl.* § 26, I.
2. > ·85×·65. *Purple Martin.* § 12, V.
3. < ·80×·60. *White-bellied Swallow.* § 12, III.
4. Av. ·70×·40. *Chimney Swift.* § 21, I.
5. Av. ·75×·57. Nest built on beam, or under eaves. *Pewee.* § 19, III.
(6). Av. ·60×·60, usually blue. Bird with chestnut breast. *Blue Bird.* § 2, I.

(e). Eggs laid in a burrow in a bank of sand or sometimes gravel.
1. > 1·25×1·00. *Kingfisher.* § 23, I.
2. < 1·00×·75. *Bank Swallow.* § 12, IV.

(f). Nest built among reeds, or in tall meadow-grass.
1. Eggs small and brittle. *Short-billed Marsh Wren.* § 7, II, A.

(g). Nest very bulky, and built of sticks on cliffs.
(1). > 3·00×2·25. Impure white; usually marked. *Golden Eagle.* § 27, VII.

B. Color, blue, bluish-green, or greenish-blue, dark in "5" only.
(a). Nest made in trees (or bushes).
(1). 2·25×1·75 or more. Extremely light. Occasionally marked. *Goshawk.* § 27, IV.
2. Av. 1·15×·85. Bird with reddish or dun breast, unmarked. *Robin.* § 1, I, F.
3. 1·00×·70 or more. Bird's breast thickly spotted. Tail, dusky-olive. *Wood Thrush.* § 1, I, A.
4. Av. ·85×·60. Bird, soft reddish-brown above, slightly spotted beneath. *Wilson's Thrush.* § 1, I, B. (Nest generally on the ground.)
5. Av. ·90×·65. Dark emerald green. Nest often in thicket. *Cat-bird.* § 1, II, B.
(6). ·95×·65, light blue. ♂, dark blue; ♀, warm brown and flaxen. *Blue Grosbeak.* § 15, XXI.
7. 1·15×·87, usually dull. } Nest loose and frail. } *Black* { -billed } § 24, I, B.
8. Av. 1·25×·87, rather light. { Eggs long or elliptical. } *Yellow* { *Cuckoo.* } § 24, I, A.

(b). Eggs laid in a hollow tree or post, or in a bird-box.
1. Av. ·80×·60. *Blue Bird.* § 2, I.

(c). Nest made on the ground.
(1). Av. < ·75×·55? Nest made in dry fields. *Black-throated Bunting.* § 15, XIX.
2. > ·75×·55. Nest made in wet woods, etc. *Wilson's Thrush.* § 1, I, B.

(d). Nest about buildings.
1. Av. 1·15×·85. *Robin.* § 1, I, F.

[NOTE. There are many herons' eggs of the above color, but they are all > 1·25 long. There are also many white eggs, tinged with blue (or green), and perhaps among them should be included those of the Goshawk and Cooper's Hawk. Many ducks' eggs are strongly tinged with blue, green, drab, or yellowish. Most of them are laid on the ground or in hollow trees, but all are more than an inch and three-fourths long. The only ducks commonly breeding in Massachusetts are the Dusky Ducks, who build on the ground, and the Wood Ducks, who build in hollow trees.]

C. Color, brown, drab, or buff.

(a). On the ground, except the last, and sometimes "3."

1. Av. 1·65×1·25, pale drab buff to rich reddish buff.[*] *Partridge.* § 30, III.
(2). Av. 1·65×1·35, brownish drab or paler.[*] Nest where dry. *Prairie Hen.* § 30, II.
3. Av. 1·90×1·50, drab. Birds usually colonial in swamps. *Bittern.*
4. < ·75×·55; usually marked. Nest among reeds. *L-b Marsh Wren.* § 7, 11, B.

(b). In the holes of trees, or rarely in a nest made in a fork.

1. About 2·00×1·50. Yellowish-white, or very pale drab. *Summer Duck.*

---

[*] Often somewhat marked.

For § II of this Key, see the next page.

§II. EGGS NOT PLAIN, BUT MARKED.

ABBREVIATIONS.— hen = beneath, e = color, ch = chiefly, cn = crown or about crown, g = generally, o = often, r = rarely, s = sometimes, w = with. Bl = blotched, cl = clouded, sc = scratched or scrawled, sp = spotted, spk = speckled, spl = splashed, spr = sprinkled, st = streaked, v = vermiculated. Bn = brown, gm = green, li = lilac, lth = reddish, yh = yellowish, wh = white. & = and. : = or; coarsely = not finely.

A. Ground color white (often tinged).
(a.) Nest made in a cavity, such as a hole in a tree or post.

NO.	SIZE.	TINGED.	COLOR OF MARKINGS.	EGGS, HOW MARKED.	FURTHER DISTINCTIONS.	NAME OF THE BIRD.
1.	> 1·25×1·00	....	Reddish-bn.	Spotted or speckled.	Nest never (?) in a horizontal limb.	*Sparrow Hawk.*
2.	Av. ·63×·50	....	Reddish-bn.	Spotted or speckled.	Nest often in a horizontal limb.	*Chickadee.*
(3.)	Av. ·63×·50	....	Reddish-bn. & purph.	....	....	*Red-bellied Nuthatch.*
4.	> ·70×·55	....	Reddish-bn.	....	....	*White-bellied Nuthatch.*
(5.)	·60×·45	Often w. gray	Reddish-bn.	Finely, all over, and thickly.	Bird streaked above, unlike 2, 3, 4.	*Brown Creeper.*
6.	Av. ·60×·48	O. w. flesh-c.	Reddish, fleshy brown, or chocolate.		Bird brown and waved beneath.	*House Wren.*
(7.)	Av. ·70×·55	O w "cream" Gr't Carolina	Brown, or reddish. Wrens have been lately known to breed in		Bird entirely blk. & wh, unlike the above. Massachusetts. See p. 74.	*Black and White Creeper*

NOTE.— The Gr't Carolina Wrens have been lately known to breed in Massachusetts. See p. 74.

(b.) Eggs laid in the nests of other birds.

| 1. | Av. ·90×·65 | Often w. gray | brown. | Thickly sprinkled. | .... | *Cow-bird.* |

(c.) Nest built up on the ground (1, 6, 10, 12, 25, and 26, sometimes only very near it). If necessary, see 11, B, (a), 4, etc.

1.	> 1·30×1·25	Often w. blue	Chiefly lilac, etc.	Little, or not at all.	Eggs two, elliptical, laid in dry places ("⁎" often on rocks), with no nest.	*Marsh Hawk.*
2.	Av. 1·25×·85	W. cream.	Ch. dark-bn. or slate.	Not thickly.		*Whippoorwill.*
3.	Av. 1·25×·85	W. gray or lm	Reddish-bn. and lilac.	Finely and thickly.	Bird yellow-breasted, with black patch.	*Night "Hawk."*
4.	Av. 1·10×·85	O. w. cream.	Feather light sandy bn.	Not generally finely.	Bird bright reddish-brown above.	*Meadow, or Field Lark.*
5.	Av. 1·05×·75	W gray or gn	Rn. and perhaps lilac.	Thickly and finely.	Bird with outer tail-feathers chiefly white.	*Brown Thrush.*
6.	Av. 1·00×·73	O w bn or Fy	Ch. dark or redh-bn.	G finely, o. like 5.	Bird entirely black and white.	*"Towhee" Bunting.*
7.	Av. ·70×·55	....	Brown and lilac.	Generally finely.	Bird with breast yellow, black-marked.	*Black and White Creeper*
(8.)	Av. ·68×·50	....	Reddish-bn. (& lilac ?)	Most about crown.	Bird with crown yellow, throat black.	*Canada "Flycatcher."*
(9.)?	Av. ·63×·50	....	Redh-bn. & often lilac.	....	Bird with breast yellow, unmarked.	*Golden-winged Warbler.*
10.	Av. ·70×·55	....	Lilac, or lt-bn. or both.	....	Nest not in swampy places, like 8, 9, 10.	*Maryland Yellow-throat.*
11.	Av. ·63×·50	....	Brown and often lilac; one absent	....	Nest in swampy woods. Bird brown.	*Nashville Warbler.*
(12.)	Av. ·90×·70	....		....	Nest usually in dry woods. Bird not bn.	*Water "Thrush."*
13.	Av. ·80×·70	....	Reddish-bn. and lilac.	Chiefly bl. all over.	Bird's outer tail-feathers white. Nest In	*Golden-crowned Thrush.*
14.	Av. ·83×·60	....	Reddish-bn. and lilac.	Chiefly bl. about en.	Bird buff beneath, unstreaked. field or	*Red-ringed Bunting.*
15.	Av. ·75×·55	....	Reddish-bn. and lilac.	Chiefly bl. about en.	Bird streaked beneath (as 14). pasture.	*Yellow-winged Sparrow.*
(16.)	Av. ·80×·60	....	Reddish-bn. and lilac.			*Henslow's Sparrow.*

#						
17. Av. .75×.55	With grayish.	Very faint brown.	Spr. rather evenly.	Bird not buff ben., but st. Outer tail-feathers not wh. Bird st. beneath. See 14.	Nests in fields and in pastures.	Savannah Sparrow.[2]
18. Av. .75×.55	W. greenish.	Dark brown.	Blotched finely.			Bay-winged Bunting.
19. Av. .80×.60	impurely or lively.		With a *few* dark spots or scr and v.			Field Sparrow.
20. Av. .68×.50	Faintly.	Light fleshy-brown.	Evenly, often thinly.	Beneath pale brownish, unst.		Swamp Sparrow.
21. Av. .80×.60	W. gray or gn	Bn. (with some lilac?).	Blotched & splashed	Nest in swamps. Bird gray-breasted.		Lincoln's Finch.[3]
(22.) Av. .75×.55	With green.	Purp.-bn. or ferrug. browns (and lilac?).	Chiefly bl., c. finely.	Bird with brownish yellow breast, st. Bird streaked beneath.		Song Sparrow.[3]
23. Av. .90×.60	Variously.		Much, g. clearly.			Bobolink.
24. Av. .90×.70	W. gy. or bn.	Dark, usually dull bn.	Clouded or spl, s. bl.	Nest in long-grassed fields or meadows.		Sharp-tailed Finch.
25. Av. .80×.55	W. gy. or bn.	Brown, not bright.	Much, g. evenly, and not coarsely.	Bird markedly streaked. es: sea-shore.	Bird scarcely streaked.	Sea-side Finch.
(26.) Av. .85×.55	W. gy. or bn.	Brown, not bright.				
(d.) Nest built in trees, etc.				thickets ("d" occasionally in hedges).		Fish Hawk.[4]
(1.) Av. 2.40×1.70	W c'm or buff	Rich dk. bn. (reddish?)	es, shrubbery, and Thickly, chiefly bl. Boldly.	Nest extremely bulky, placed in a tall tree, near water.		Fish Hawk.[4]
(2.) Av. 2.25×1.85		Umber (rare form).		Bird with r banded silvery-white, unmarked.		Red-shouldered Hawk.
3. Av. 2.20×1.70	Impurely O w yh or rh	Various browns, rarely purplish.	S. little, s. much. Rarely finely, g. bl.	tail beneath, bird finely black and white.		Red-tailed Hawk.
4. Av. 2.20×1.70	Blue or green	Brown.	Little, or not at all.			Goshawk.
(5.) Av. 2.25×1.75	O. impurely.	Usually purplish-bn.	Chiefly bl., r. thickly.	Bird below, finely black and white.		Broad-winged Hawk.
(6.) Av. 2.20×1.70	G. w. blue.	Brown, usually light.	G. little and clearly.	Nest usually neater, smaller than 3, 4.		Cooper's Hawk.
7. Av. 1.90×1.50		Brown, usually umber.	Chiefly bl. coarsely.	Bird with no black marks on head, as 9.		Sharp-shinned Hawk.
8. Av. 1.15×1.20		Bn., usually Vandyke or rusty.	G. finely, thickly.	Eggs usually laid in holes of trees.		Sparrow Hawk.
(9.) Av. 1.40×1.15						
(10.) Av. 1.50×1.20	W. buff or rh.	Dark reddish-brown.	Thickly cl. and bl.	Eggs much like 1's or Duck Hawk's.		Pigeon Hawk.
11. Av. .90×.60	Faintly.	Ch. dark bn., or black.	Scraw's. s. spotted.	Nest usually >4 inches deep.		Baltimore Oriole.
(12.) Av. .80×.60	Faintly.	Bn. or blk. & purplish.	Scraw's & g. spotted.	Nest usually <4 inches deep.		Orchard Oriole.
(13.) Av. .77×.58		Usually reddish-bn.	Speckled about cn.			Solitary Vireo.
14. Av. .80×.60		Blk. & purph. or bnh.	Sp. ab., cn. s. thickly.	Nest much ornamented (?)	Nest pensile, 12, 3-8 in. deep.	Yellow-throated Vireo.
15. Av. .81×.62		Brownish-black.	Sp. about crown.			Red-eyed Vireo.
16. Av. .77×.58		"Reddish-blk.," or bn.	O, even coarsely.	Nest high, in elms, etc.		Warbling Vireo.
17. Av. .80×.55		Brownish-black?	" " " "	Nest low, often in briars, etc.		White-eyed Vireo.
(18.) Av. .62×.48		Reddish-bn., and lilac.	Sp. & bl., ch. cn.	Nest globular, of hanging moss.		"Blue Yellow-back."
19. Av. .67×.55		Brown, *and purplish*.	Clear & delicate, or coarse & obscure.	Nests *usually* >15 feet from ground.		"Black-throated Green."
20. Av. .67×.52			Ch. cn.; so in "19."	Nest *usually* <15 feet from ground.		Pine Warbler.[5]
21. Av. .65×.50		"Purph. or lilac. & bn.	Thickly about cn.			Redstart.
(22.) Av. .70×.50	With green.	"Light rusty-brown."		Bird much streaked.		Pine Linnet.
23. Av. 1.00×.75	With cream.	Umber, r. light, & lilac.	Sp. coarsely, r. spl.	Nest in orchard trees, bushes, etc.; latter in woods also.		King-bird.
24. Av. .85×.65	With c'm or buff.	Reddish-bn., or umber and lilac.	(G. sp. coarsely. Chiefly about cn.			Olive-sided Flycatcher.
25. Av. .70×.55				Nest saddled to limb in the woods.		Wood Pewee.
(26.) Av. .63×.50	With buff?	Rth-bn. "Purplish-bn."	G. finely, chiefly on.	Nest never "saddled" (?) but in a fork.		Traill's Flycatcher.
27. Av. 1.05×.75	W gray or gn	Light sandy brown.	Thickly and finely.	Bird dark-streaked beneath.		Brown Thrush.
(28.) Av. 1.00×.80		Reddish-bn. and lilac.	S. much; bn. s. gone.	Bird yellow-breasted, unmarked.		Yellow-breasted Chat.

NO.	SIZE.	TINGED.	COLOR OF MARKINGS,	EGGS, HOW MARKED.	FURTHER DISTINCTIONS.	NAME OF THE BIRD.
29.	Av. ·63×·48	....	Lilac and un. (umber?)	Bird yellow beneath, sparsely black-st.	Nest often semi-pensile, lined with hairs.	*Prairie Warbler.*
30.	Av. ·68×·50	R. w. buff.	Brown and purplish.	As in 29, 31. ch. w bn.	Bird white ben.; side-patches chestnut.	*Chestnut-sided Warbler.*
31.	Av. ·67×·50	O w greenish -gray.	Various browns (sometimes sandy) & lilac.	Bird yellow ben., st. faintly w orange-bn	Nest usually lined with plant-down.	*Yellow Warbler.*
32.	Av. ·80×·55	....	U'sn. brownish-black.	Sp. about crown.	Nest pensile.	*White-eyed Vireo.*
33.	Av. ·70×·60	W gray or gn	Bn. (and some lilac?).	Blotched & splashed	Nest in wet places only.	*Swamp Sparrow.*
34.	Av. ·80×·60	Variously.	Various bns. (& lilac?).	G. thickly, r. coarse.	Bird (unlike "33") dark-streaked below.	*Song Sparrow.*
35.	Av. ·70×·50	Faintly.	Light fleshy-brown.	Evenly, often thinly.	....	*Field Sparrow.*
(36.)	Av. ·70×·55	....	Reddish-brown.	Little, or not at all.	Nest in woods.	*Yellow-bellied Flycatcher.*
(e.)		Nest built in or about buildings.				
1.	Av. ·75×·50	....	Brown and faint lilac.	Evenly sprinkled.	Nests generally on beams and rafters.	*Barn Swallow.*
2.	Av. ·80×·55	....	Brown and faint lilac.	Evenly sprinkled.	Nests generally under eaves, *outside*.	*Cliff Swallow.*
(f.)		Nest built on cliffs & high rocks.				
(1.)	>3·00×2·25		Brown.	....	....	*Golden Eagle.*
(2.)	<2·50×1·75	W. buff or rh.	Brown, strongly rh.	Thickly, partly bl.	....	*Duck Hawk.*
B.			Ground-color bluish-green or greenish-blue, etc.	(See for egg, 70 × 50, or near the ground,	light green, marked with rusty-brown, (8?) 9 and 11, often in hedges.	A, d, 22.)
(a.)		Nest in trees, 4, 5, 9, 10, 11- generally in bushes				
1.	>1·50×1·00	....	Brown, or dusky, etc.	Rarely very thickly.	Nest of sticks, twigs, roots, etc.	*Common Crow.*
2.	>1·00×·75	....	Bn., etc., never bright.	Generally scrawled.	Nest composed partly of mud?	*Blue Jay.*
3.	Av. 1·25×·90	....	Black, brown, etc.	Generally scrawled.	Nest generally on or near the ground.	*Crow Blackbird.*
4.	Av. 1·00×·75	....	Black, brown, etc.	Sp. and bl. as 6, 7.	Birds chiefly gray.	*Red-winged Blackbird.*
(5.)	Av. 1·00×·75	(Grd. pale.)	Brown and lilac.	Rarely very thickly.	♂, scarlet, black; ♀, olive-green, yellow.	*Mocking Bird.*
6.	Av. ·90×·65	....	Purplish-bn. or bright umber.			*Scarlet Tanager.*
7.	Av. 1·00×·75	O. w. olive.	Rather dull reddish or purplish umber.	Generally thickly.	♂, black, white, carmine; ♀ plain, st.	*Rose-breasted Grosbeak.*
8.	Av. ·78×·60	....	Blackish and lilac.	Sp. finely, sometimes bl. or scr.	♂, chiefly carmine; ♀, plain, streaked.	*Purple Finch.*
9.	Av. ·63×·50	....	Blackish.	Chiefly bl. and spl.	Bird gray-breasted, unstreaked below.	*Chipping Sparrow.*
10.	Av. ·80×·60	ground {nev. bright o.	Brown and lilac.	Sp. or bl., s. both.	Bird unstreaked below, nest in swamps.	*Swamp Sparrow.*
11.	Av. ·80×·55		Browns (and lilac).	Finely, thinly.	Bird streaked below.	*Song Sparrow.*
(12.)	Av. <·70×·55		Reddish-brown.			*Blue-gray Gnatcatcher.*
13.	Av. ·65×·60	With clay.	Black, purplish, etc.	Evenly sp., r. scr.	Ground-color whitish and dull.	*Cedar-bird.*
(b.)		Nest on the ground, as often as of ten or generally is the case with (a), 4, (9, very rarely) 10, and 11.				
1.	Like (a), 7.					*Bobolink.*
C.		Ground-color *decided* gray, brown, buff, or rusty.[6]				

NO.	SIZE.	GRD.-COLOR.	COLOR OF MARKINGS.	EGGS, HOW MARKED.	SITUATION OF THE NEST.	NAME OF THE BIRD.
(1.)	Av. 2·10×1·70	Reddish, buff, etc.	Rich dark reddish-brown, etc.	Thickly clouded, blotched, etc.	In trees, near water.	*Fish Hawk.*
(2.)	Av. 2·20×1·70				On high rocks and cliffs.	*Duck Hawk.*
(3.)	Av. 1·50×1·20	Rh. buff, etc.	Rich dark rh.-bn., etc.	Thickly clouded, bl.	In trees.	*Pigeon Hawk.*
4.	Av. 1·40×1·15	O. buff, etc.	Ch. Vandyke or rusty.	G. fine, r. coarse.	Almost invariably in holes of trees.	*Sparrow Hawk.*
5.	Av. 1·25×·90	Brown.	Black, brown, etc.	Generally scrawled.	Nest (composed partly of mud?) in trees.	*Crow Blackbird.*
6.	Av. 1·05×·75	In. or buff.	Brown, etc.	Spotted, etc.	Nest (with no mud) in trees.	*Blue Jay.*
7.	Av. 1·00×·75	Brown.	Brown, etc.	Spotted, etc.	Nest on the ground, in meadows, etc.	*Bobolink.*
8.	Av. 1·00×·75	Buff or cream.	Bn., purplish, & lilac. (Red) umber, & lilac.	Scratched, st., etc.	Nest in the holes of trees.	*Great-crested Flycatcher.*
9.	Av. ·70×·55			Coarsely, chiefly on.	Nest saddled to moss-covered limb.	*Wood Pewee.[7]*
10.	Av. ·85×·60	Dull faint bluish-clay	Black, purplish, etc.	Evenly sp., r. se.	Nest in trees.	*Cedar-bird.*
11.	< ·70×·55	Mahogany or chocolate.	Chocolate, reddish, or the like.	Thickly & very finely	Nest suspended among reeds.	*Long-billed Marsh Wren.*
12.	< ·70×·55	Fleshy or Rh.	Peculiar reddish-b-bn.	Thickly & very finely	Nest in some hole.	*House Wren.*

[1] Other allied species may occasionally breed here.

[2] Great caution must be used in distinguishing certain eggs of these two species.

[3] Of exceptional occurrence in Massachusetts.

[4] To be found chiefly in northern New England.

[5] Other tree-nesting warblers occasionally breed in Massachusetts. The "Black-throated Green" generally have more or less black on the throat, but no yellow breast as in "20."

[6] For eggs strongly tinged merely with these colors, see § II. A. Among them are exceptions which perhaps belong to this section. See particularly § I, C, (a), 1, 2, and § II, A, (d), 30. Plover's eggs, etc., etc., are here omitted.

[7] See A, (d), 21, 25, 26.

D. A KEY TO THE LAND-BIRDS OF NEW ENGLAND.

This Key contains only the land-birds (*Insessores*), with the exclusion of the well-known pigeons (§ 29), the recently discovered White-throated Golden-winged Warbler (§ 9, VI, BB), and two or three species, such as the Varied Thrush, which have occurred in Massachusetts but once, having wandered more than a thousand miles from their usual *habitat*. It must not be too much relied on, as birds new to our *fauna* may occur here. *It has no reference to young birds or albinos.* For the former, see E.

---

[1] See § T of the introduction. The cere is concealed in the well-known owls by feathers.
[2] By the nearly complete union of the outer and middle front-toes.
[3] Here, inclusive of the Hummingbirds, Swifts, Whippoorwills, and Night "Hawks," the only *Insessores* (with no *cere*) having *ten* tail-feathers, except the *Scansores*, but even the Woodpeckers have twelve, counting a spurious pair.
[4] In all other birds lateral.
[5] The distinctions between these two subfamilies are not (outwardly) obvious, being of a technical character (unless the *tarsi* are characteristic, as Dr. Coues has described them to be). The *Clamatores* of North America include the flycatchers only.
[6] If with the head largely naked, *Cathartidæ*, or vultures. See § 28.
[NOTE. Some old groups have been here retained, in limited forms, for convenience merely.]

APPENDIX. 431

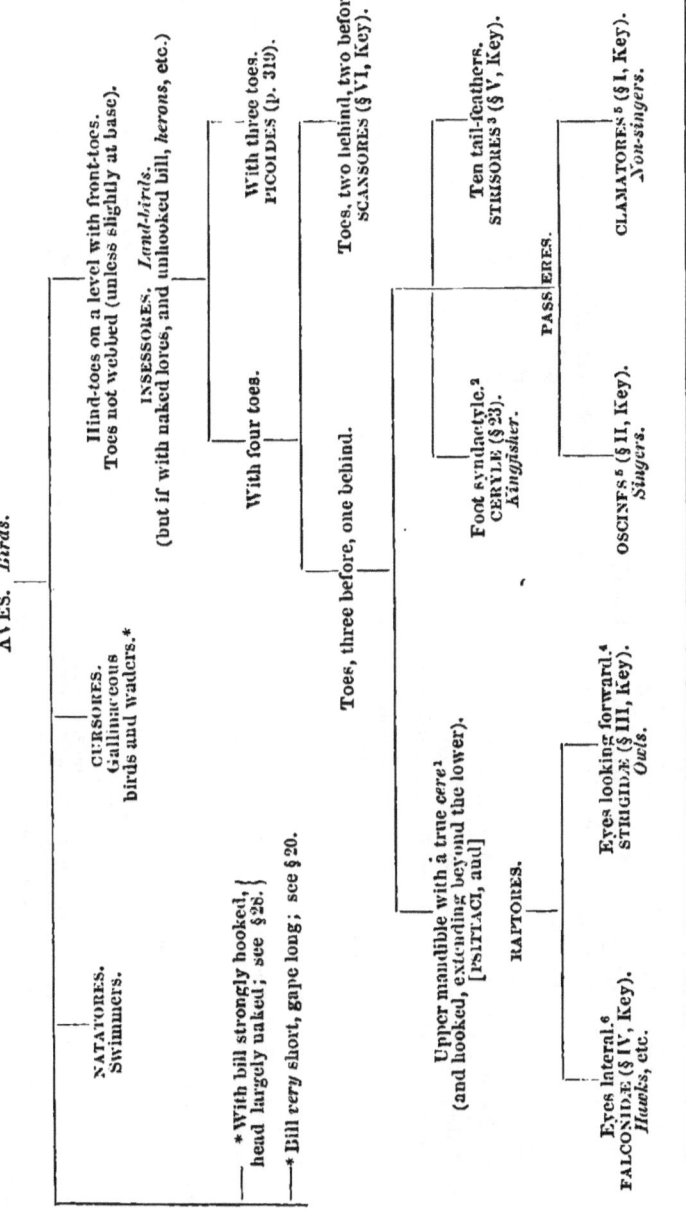

APPENDIX.

§I. CLAMATORES (flycatchers).

1. About 8 in. long. Tail black, broadly white-tipped. No black eye-bar. (Erectile crown-feathers touched with orange or the like.) King-bird (§ 19, I).

2. >8 in. Throat and upper breast gray; under parts otherwise bright yellow. *Great Crested Flycatcher* (§19, II).

The six or seven smaller flycatchers (<8 in.) cannot easily be identified except by detailed descriptions, though the species of the genus Empidonax (§ 19, V) may be distinguished from the others by their unforked tails. They are all slightly crested, or have erectile crown-feathers, have a slightly hooked bill, which is rather equilaterally triangular as seen from above, and are olive-green above, often tinged strongly with brown, gray, or dusky, and beneath white, more or less tinged with yellow or the colors of their upper parts. See §19, III, IV, V.

§II. OSCINES.

A. *Birds wholly unstreaked and unspotted* (including those obsoletely but not distinctly streaked, those with a few side-streaks from patches above, etc. For birds waved or finely barred, see E).

NO.	COLOR.[1]	SIZE.[2]	NAME OF BIRD.	SECTION.
	Black, (if confined to the crown and throat, see A, 86; if to the throat, see *passim,* especially 27, 28, G2.)			
1.	lustrous,	24	Raven........	§ 18, I, NOTE
2.	"throat-feathers {acute, lengthened, dis-connected"........	20	*Crow.* (See note to..)	§ 18, I.
3.	iridescent........{oval and blended"........	7¾	♂ *Cow-bird*........	§ 17, III.
4.	very highly {chiefly purple, violet, blue.		♂ *Crow Blackbird*,[3]	§ 17, VII.
5.	Iridescent with {metallic bronze, olive, etc...	12½	♂ *Bronzed Blackbird*,[3]	§ 17, VII.
6.	glossy. Often with green reflections or brown skirting	9	♂ *Rusty Blackbird*.....	§ 17, VI.
7.	lustrous; (approaching?) steel-blue........	7	♂ *Purple Martin*,[3]	§ 12, V.
8.	————; with scarlet wing-patch........	9	♂ *Swamp Blackbird*.....	§ 17, IV.

APPENDIX. 433

(For very small birds with bright crown-patch, see 47–53, and 57, 59). For line 9, see 20, 21, etc.

10.	*Vermilion;* bill yellowish...	♂ *Summer Red Bird*......... §10, I, B.
11.	———— reddish, face black; bird crested.......................	♂ *Cardinal Grosbeak*.³.... §15, XVIII.
12.	———— approaching flame-color, and much confined to patches......	♂ *Redstart*.................. §9, XII.
13.	*Scarlet;* wings and tail black (see 8.)..............................	♂ *Scarlet Tanager*........... §10, I, A.
14.	*Crimson*, or the like...	♂ *Purple Finch*............. §15, III.
15.	usually carmine, confined to the breast (etc.).....................	♂ *Pine Grosbeak*............ §15, XVII.
16.	*Red*, bricky. } *Mandibles crossed*. } and white-barred............	♂ *Rose-breasted Grosbeak*... §15, I, A.
17.	rosy. } *Wings* dark, ...	♂ *Red Crossbill*............. §15, I, B.
18.	or chestnut, whole breast, etc. Otherwise black...................	♂ *White-winged Crossbill*... §17, V, B.
19.	on sides only. Otherwise black and white..........................	♂ *Orchard Oriole*............ §9, XVIII.
20.		♂ *Towhe Bunting*¹........... §1, II, B.
21.	*Slate*, under tail-coverts *chestnut-red*...........................	*Cat-bird*................... §15, XVII.
22.	lower breast, etc., white (or brown-tinged?).......................	*Snow-bird*,⁴................ §1, II, A.
23.	*Ash*,³ grayish. Wings with white bars or patch....................	*Mocking Bird*............... §18, III.
24.	dark; (if with any rusty or brownish yellow, see 1), b, 5)).......	*Canada Jay*................ §11, I, B.
25.	———— "slaty." (?) } Broad bar through }	*Great Northern Shrike*...... §9, N, G.
26.		*Loggerhead Shrike*.......... §9, N, H.
26a.	*Blue*,⁵ light, bluish. } the eye black.	♀ + "*Black-throated Blue*." §9, VI, B.
27.	greenish. Beneath yellowish. No throat-patch......................	*Golden-winged Warbler*...... §3, II.
28.	slaty. Throat black...	"*Blue Yellow-back*"......... §5, I, A.
29.	———— crown yellow...	*Blue-gray Gnatcatcher*....... §15, XXI.
30.	———— yellow..	*White-bellied Nuthatch*...... §5, I, B.
31.	graylish. Throat white...	*Red-bellied Nuthatch*........ §15, XXI.
32.	ashy. } Beneath with more or less }	♂ *Blue Grosbeak*............ §15, I.
33.	rusty. ♀, with crown black. } Eye-stripe black or dusky...........	♂ *Indigo Bird*.............. §12, II.
34.	indigo. With chestnut on the wings................................	*Blue Jay*.................. §12, II.
35.	With green reflections...	*Blue Bird*.³............... §12, III.
36.	bright. Breast chestnut. Forehead blue.............................	*Cliff Swallow*.............. §9, II, C.
37.	purplish. With black collar.......................................	*Barn Swallow*.............. §9, II, H.
38.	steely. Throat chestnut...	*White-breasted Swallow*..... §9, II, G.
39.	(See A, 7.) } rump rufous.......................................	*Yellow-breasted Chat*....... §9, XIII.
40.	*Steel-green*.⁵ (See A, 6; etc., if not) < 6 inches long...........	*Maryland Yellow-throat*.⁶... §9, II, A.
41.	*Olive-green* } Decided yel- } on fore-.........................	*Pine Warbler*............. §3, XI.
42.	or olive⁵ (See I.) low beneath, } parts only. } Under tail-coverts yellow...	*Yellow-throated Vireo*....... §3, III, B.
43.	with white } wing-bars, } black-wared, or black.	*Mourning Warbler*........... §9, II, B.
44.	etc., only. } Throat } ashy or } brown. *Eye-ring white*	*Connecticut Warbler*......... §3, II.
45.	only on the sides, crissum, etc....................................	*White-eyed Vireo*........... §13, F.
46.	crown yellow..	*Prothonotary Warbler*........ §9, VI, A.
47.	} yellow, eye-stripe black...	*Blue-winged Yellow Warbler*.. §9, VI, C.
48.		chestnut.? } Nape ashy [in ♂], below...	*Nashville Warbler*........... §9, VI, B.
49.	orange.? "Yellow, greenish" below................................	*Orange-crowned Warbler*..... §9, XI, B.
50.	black (in ♀ obscure)...	*Wilson's "Black-cap"*........ §3, III, NOTE.
51.	plain. } Throat black-bordered.....................................	*Kentucky Warbler*........... §9, XI, B.
52.	} "*Black-cap*." see §9, 50.......................................	
53.	plain. Whole side of head yellow.................................	♂ *Scarlet Tanager*........... §10, I, A.
54.	Yellow less clear } greenish......................................	♂ + *Summer Red Bird*......... §10, I, B.
55.	} than in 40–53? except 50. Tints } brownish.....................	

29

NO.	COLOR.[1]	SIZE.[2]	NAME OF BIRD.	SECTION.
56.	buff beneath. Head the same, with four dark stripes............	5¼	*Worm-eating Warbler*......	§ 9, IV.
57.	beneath white or yellowish. V, 70–1. } with bright crown-patch, } red (*sometimes wanting?*)....	4¼	*Ruby-crowned "Wren."*.....	§ 3, I, A.
58.	yellow, black-bordered.....	4¼	*Golden-crowned "Wren"*....	§ 3, I, B.
59.	centre flame-colored	4¼	♂ *Golden-crowned "Wren."*...	§ 3, I, B.
60.	Upper part of head dark (blue-) gray........	5½	*Solitary Vireo*............	§ 13, I, A.
61.	With pronounced white wing-bars. } *Conspicuous* wh. eye-ring	5¼	*Solitary Vireo*............	§ 13, I, A.
62.	Throat black............	5	♂ *"Black-throated Green."*....	§ 9, X, I.
63.	Head-sides rich yellow..	5	*"Black-throated Green."*....	§ 9, X, I.
64.	White on < 6 t-feathers..	> 5¼	♀ *Pine Warbler*................	§ 9, X, J.
65.	Crown and eye-stripe dark..................	6	*Red-eyed Vireo*.............	§ 13, I. C.
66.	Base of tail above largely yellow...........	5¼	♀ *Redstart*....................	§ 9, XII.
67.	With a white spot on the edge of wing.......	5	♀ *"Black-throated Blue."*.....	§ 9, X, H.
68.	Never >2 wh. tail-spots. No ash unless on hd	< 5	*Tennessee Warbler*..........	§ 9, VI, E.
69.	Bill slightly hooked (never in 67 or 68).......	5	*Warbling Vireo*............	§ 13, I, D.
70.	*Olivaceous* or *olive-yellow*,[3] } Not *bright* yellow beneath. Back brown-tinged	> 6½	♀ *Orchard Oriole*............	§ 17, V, B.
71.	Not *bright* yellow beneath. Bill conical. See Pl., fig. 12....	< 5	♀ *Goldfinch*..................	§ 15, IV, A.
72.	*Yellow*, (bright). Crown black. (See 47, 48.)......................	5	♂ *Goldfinch* (April–Sept.)....	§ 15, IV, A.
	Confined to head and outer edge of wing. See D, *a*	....		
73.	(orange). Usually with black, olive-skirted or glossed......	> 7	♀ *Baltimore Oriole*...........	§ 17, V, A.
74.	*Orange*, with large areas of black (with white on wings)............	7½	♂ *Baltimore Oriole*...........	§ 17, V, A.
	Brown, (if with outer tail-feathers largely or wholly white, but throat	dark,	see A, 20, 22). See D. *a*, 9..	§ 15, IX, A.
75.	orange-tinted. Under tail-coverts chestnut.................	7¼	*Bohemian Waxwing*.........	§ 11, I, B.
76.	*tail yellow-tipped* (as 75). Under tail-coverts whitish.........	6¾	*Cedar-bird*.................	§ 11, I, A.
77.	paler below, but without pure white..........................	5½	♀ *Indigo Bird* (see 86).........	§ 15, XX.
78.	With whitish wing-bars..........................	6½	♀ *Blue Grosbeak* (see 86)......	§ 15, XXI.
79.	Without wing-bars. >6¼ long..................	7	♀ *Cow-bird*...................	§ 17, III.
80.	below dark, often with rusty intermixed......................	9	♀ *Rusty Blackbird*...........	§ 17, VI.
81.	usually with bright reflections, } chiefly purple, violet, blue.............	....	♀ *Crow Blackbird*...........	§ 17, VII, A.
82.	chiefly metallic bronze, olive, etc..........	....	♀ *Bronzed Blackbird*..........	§ 17, VII, B.
83.	ashy-brown, or the like, above. Crown and throat, black...	5	*"Chickadee."*...............	§ 4. I, A.
84.	or olive-brown above; "pale;" "throat brownish-black"...	5	*Hudsonian Titmouse*........	§ 4. I, B.
85.	or olive-bn. above. Rump bright yw. Side-streaks beneath?	5½	*"Yellow-rump" W.*........	§ 9, X, L.
86.	or olive bn. (or flaxen) above. With white (-ish ?) wing-bars	5	♂ *Goldfinch* (in winter)........	§ 15, IV, A.
87.	dull, or even *gray*. Under parts, except breast, white.......	< 5	*Bank Swallow*..............	§ 12, IV.
88.	*White*, (with black markings, and (in winter) brown patches).......	7	*Snow Bunting*..............	§ 15, VII, A.
B.	*Birds streaked or spotted beneath, but not above* (including those spotted above when young, or streaked on the back, etc., obsoletely but not distinctly, and excluding those with a few side-streaks from throat-patches or the like. NOTE.—"6" has, however, usually a speckled crown, "5 a" few dorsal spots, and the ♀ of "4" is usually spotted or streaked above).			
	If with yellow, only from bill to eye, and on outer edge of wings..........	....	*Sea-side Finch*..............	§ 15, IX, A.
1.	On the throat only (or perhaps behind also)........................	10	*Robin*........................	§ 1, I, F.
2.	Beneath bright yellow, streaked } with orange-brown. Crown yellow..................	5¼	*Yellow Warbler*.............	§ 9, X, A.
3.	with reddish-brown. ——— "chestnut"............	5¼	*"Red-poll" Warbler*.........	§ 9, X, K.
4.	with black. Rump bright yellow........................	5	*Black and Yellow Warbler*..	§ 9, X, M.
5.	Back with red spots..................	< 5?	*Prairie Warbler*............	§ 9, X, B.
6.	Without above marks................	> 5?	*Canada "Flycatcher."*......	§ 9, XI, A.

APPENDIX. 435

7.	Beneath white (or) olive-green. Crown orange (-brown)	6	Golden-crowned "Thrush."	9, I, C.
8.	tinged). Above } soft dusky olive (if without buff on head, §1, I, E)	7¼	Olive-backed Thrush	5, I, D.
9.	Rump and tail rufous	7	Hermit Thrush	1, I, C.
10.	reddish-brown, soft. Tail, etc., strongly olive	7¼	Wilson's Thrush	1, I, A.
11.	bright. With white wing-bars	11	Wood Thrush	1, III.
12.	dark brown. } pale yellow. Streaked sharply (14 not)	<6?	Brown Thrush	2, I, A.
13.	Beneath tinged with } buff (behind). Streaked, not on throat	6	Water "Thrush."	9, I, A.
14.	See, if necessary, 1b, a, 4; A, 80; A, 77.		Large-billed Water "T."	
C.	Birds distinctly streaked (or the like) above only (including those streaked below, solely on the sides, or behind, or obsoletely, or streaked below when young, and excluding those obsoletely streaked above, and B, 5, with brick-red marks on the back). If with a blue crown, see.			
1.	With distinct } Crown carmine; ♂ rosy-breasted	5½	Red-poll "Linnet."	9, M, G.
1a.	side-streaks below. } Throat white, (if crown is yellow, see 9).	5½	"Black-poll" Warbler	15, X, E.
2.	orange	5½	"Black-poll" Warbler	9, X, E.
3.	bright yellow	5½	Black and White "Creeper."	9, X, F.
4.	Black crescent on breast	5	Blackburnian Warbler	9, X, F.
5.	brownish-yellow. Tail-feathers extremely acute	5½	Blackburnian Warbler	9, X, F.
6.	Beneath white } often brown-tinged behind (see 21)	10	Meadow Lark.⁹	17, L.
7.	(see below; } throat, etc., chestnut (-red); also crown (♂ only?)	5½	Bobolink	17, L.
8.	sides only chestnut (-red); crown yellow	5½	Brown Creeper	6, X. D.
9.	Crimson, or the like. Edgings on wings white	5½	Bay-breasted Warbler	9, X. C.
10.	reddish	8	Chestnut-sided Warbler	9, X.
11.	or the like. Edgings on wings white	6	Pine Grosbeak	15, III.
12.	Beneath yellow, } breast, etc., only. Throat-patch black	7	Purple Finch	15, XIX.
13.	(or yellowish) on } throat and chin only. Breast-patch black?	7	Black-throated Bunting	16, L.
14.	Beneath black (on throat, 12?; on breast, 13?;) entirely	7	Shore Lark	17, II.
15.	on the throat only (see §15, XXIV and XXV)	6½	Bobolink (May.-Aug. inc.).	♂♂
16.	Beneath (light) } Crown blk (-ish). Median } Latter yw. from bill to eye	7	White-throated Sparrow.	15, XV, A.
17.	warm gray ("ash"), } and superciliary lines wh. } needing behind	7	White-crowned Sparrow	15, XV, B.
18.	Throat white (-ish). } Without wh. wing-bars, differing from 16, 17, 19, 20, etc.	5½	Swamp Sparrow	15, XIII. C.
19.	Wing-bars } narrow. Forehead usually black	6	Chipping Sparrow	15, XIV, A.
20.	white and } conspicuous. Breast with dusky central spot	5?	Tree Sparrow	15, XIV, B.
21.	Beneath buffy } on sides etc. } Streaked with } on interscapulars only	7	Long-billed } Marsh	7, II. B.
22.	or brownish } on breast, etc. } black and wh. } on back, rump, and nape.	4½	Short-billed } Wren	7, II. A.
23.	Throat chestnut (-red). Bill not conical	6	Bay-breasted Warbler	15, X. D.
24.	With white } No spot on breast. Bill reddish	5½	See } Field Sparrow	15, XIV, C.
25.	on the wings } conspicuous. "Bill bl'k above, yel. below"	6	"23." } Tree Sparrow.	15, XIV, B.
26.	Without wh. } Distinct patch on the wing yellowish	5	Yellow-ringed Sparrow	15, X. A.
27.	wing-bars. } Beneath, often grayish. Crown chestnut	6	English (House) Sparrow	15, XXIV - V.
28.	Beneath ashy, grayish, or the like. Crown with ("rusty"?) yellow	8	Pine Grosbeak	15, H.

NO.	COLOR.[1]	SIZE.[2]	NAME OF BIRD.	SECTION.
D.	*Birds distinctly* (not obsoletely) *streaked both above and below* (excluding those waved, E, those with only *side*-streaks, etc., beneath, and those with ground-color of *throat and breast bright* yellow, except the Cape May Warbler, *b*, 7, with orange-brown ear-patch).			
a.	*Without yellow* (unless only on superciliary stripe and outer edge of wing, or unless decidedly brownish), and without *blue, carmine, or pink.* (If with the mandibles of bill crossed see *b*, 3 and 4.) See *b*, 8.			
1.	*Black and white only*	5	*Black and White Creeper*	§ 9, VII.
2.	*Streaked* above and below *with bright rusty* or fox-red	7	*Fox-colored Sparrow*	§ 15, XVI.
3.	*Outermost tail-feathers white,* wholly (?). Wing-patch (lesser coverts) chestnut	6	*Bay-winged Bunting*	§ 15, XII.
4.	Bill slender, commissure straight	6¼	*Titlark*	§ 8, I.
5.	partly. Throat black	6	♂ *Lapland Longspur*	§ 15, VII, B.
6.	(yellowish ?), on terminal half of outer web	6¼	*Ipswich Sparrow*	§ 15, XI, A.
	if on edge only, see below.			
	Breast buff or brownish-yellow, > 7 inches long, see 12 and 13.			
7.	without yellow on the outer edge of wing	5¼	*Lincoln's Sparrow*	§ 15, XIII, B.
8.	supercil- (prolonged), buff or *orange-brown*[10]	5¼	*Sharp-tailed Finch*	§ 15, IX, B.
9.	iary line bright yellow from bill to eye[10]	6	*Sea-side Finch*	§ 15, IX, A.
10.	but faint. Streaks beneath, if black, brown-edged	5¼	*Savannah Sparrow*	§ 15, XI, B.
11.	always distinct. Superciliary line not yellow	5	*Henslow's Sparrow*	§ 15, X, B.
12.	*Breast white* (-ish), > 7 inches long. Under wing-coverts saffron-yellow	8	♀ *Rose-breasted Grosbeak*	§ 15, XXII.
13.	Bill not deep (uncurved above). See Pl., fig. 18	7¼	♀ *Red-winged Blackbird*	§ 17, IV.
	with yellow on the outer edge of wings; 9 or 10.			
14.	streaked with (olivaceous-) brown. *No* reddish-brown above	6	♀ *Purple Finch*	§ 15, III.
15.	streaked with black (sparsely ?). Hind-claw very long	6	♀ *Lapland Longspur*	§ 15, VII, B.
16.	wings reaching only to the base of the *rounded* tail	6	*Song Sparrow*	§ 15, XIII, A.
b.				
1.	*Carmine* crown (♂ with a rosy breast)	5¼	"*Red-poll.*"	§ 15, V.
2.	*Blue* above	5	♂ *Cærulean Warbler*	§ 9, X, G.
3.	*Saffron* -yellow on rump, etc.	6	♀ *Red Crossbill*	§ 15, I, A.
4.	*Mandibles crossed.* Wing-bars white	6	♀ *White-winged Crossbill*	§ 15, I, B.
5.	*Rusty* (?)-yellow (marks) on head (and rump)	8	♀ *Pine Grosbeak*	§ 15, II.
6.	*Pure yellow* on rump and crown	5¾	"*Yellow-rump*" *W.*	§ 9, X, L.
7.	on rump and breast, etc. (latter streaked)	5¼	*Cape May Warbler*	§ 9, IX.
8.	as edging only, unless generally suffused (May–Aug.)	< 5?	*Pine Linnet*	§ 15, IV, B.
9.	(pale); on the black-streaked breast, etc.; none on rump	6¼	♀ *Black-throated Bunting*	§ 15, XIX.
E.	*Birds waved or finely barred.*			
1.	*Above and beneath.* With several whitish markings. Tail short	4	*Winter Wren*	§ 7, I, A.
2.	With little whitish, or none (wing-coverts white-spotted ?)	> 4¼	*House Wren*	§ 7, I, B.
3.	*Beneath only.* (See A, 25, 26)	> 7¼	*Shrike*	§ 14.
4.	On the wings, tail (and under tail-coverts ?). Breast buffy	5¼	*Great Carolina Wren*	§ 7, I, A. NOTE.

APPENDIX. 437

§ III. STRIGIDÆ. Owls.
A. *Barred and streaked beneath in contrasted areas.*
1. Throat only streaked... 16 *Hawk Owl*............ § 26, VIII.
2. Breast streaked (if bird is <20 in. long, see D)....................... 27 *Great Gray Owl*... § 26, III, A.
3. Breast barred.. 18 *Barred Owl*.......... § 26, III, B.

B. *Entirely (chocolate-) brown and white above.*
1. .... 10¾ *Richardson's Owl*.. § 26, IV, A.
2. .... 7½ *Acadian Owl*........ § 26, IV, B.

C. *Large owls, 21-24 inches long.*
1. White all over (with blackish markings)................................. 24 *Snowy Owl*.......... § 26, VII.
2. conspicuous as a throat-patch only....................................... 23 *Great Horned Owl* § 26, VI.

D. *10 inches or less long.*
1. Beneath, white or fulvous, usually black-speckled................. 9 *Screech Owl*......... § 26, V.
2. Eyes *completely* surrounded with black................................ 16 *Barn Owl*............. § 26, I.
3. Without the characteristics of 1, 2, or 3. Belly finely barred?. 15 *Short-eared Owl*... § 26, II, A.
4. .... 15 *Long-eared Owl*... § 26, II, B.

§ IV. FALCONIDÆ. Eagles, hawks, etc.
A. *30-40 inches long.*
1. Tarsus } thickly feathered... 35 *Golden Eagle*....... § 27, VII.
2. or "leg" } chiefly naked. Head and tail white (not in young).. 33 *"Bald" Eagle*........ § 27, VIII.

B. *<14 inches long.*
1. Tail dark, with several white (-ish) bands............................... 12 *Pigeon Hawk*....... § 27, II, C.
2. Tail chestnut (-red), with black (and white) markings............ 11 *Sparrow Hawk*..... § 27, II, D.
3. Tail gray (or brown), dark-banded (and white-tipped?)......... 12 *Sharp-shinned Hawk* § 27, III, A.

C. Tarsus (or "leg") thickly feathered } Bird nearly uniform blackish. 24 *Rough-legged Hawk* § 27, VI.
1. in front to the toes.. 24 *Black Hawk*......... § 27, VI.
2. *White* } and below *conspicuously*, with dark markings........ 21 *Gyrfalcon*............. § 27, II, A.
3. *above* } on the tail-coverts only.. 18 *Marsh Hawk*........ § 27, I.
4. bird otherwise brown.. 18 *Marsh Hawk* (♀ or young) § 27, I.
5. on part of crown. Throat white. Eye-stripe dark.................... 20 *Fish Hawk*........... § 27, IX.
6. (paler-waved or barred). Cheeks black.................................. 17 *Duck Hawk*......... § 27, II, B.
7. *Above gray,* } beneath slaty-barred, black (-ish)-streaked..... 21 *Goshawk*............. § 27, IV.
8. *ash, or slate;* } Without above marks or dark stripe behind the eye 19 *Cooper's Hawk*.... § 27, III, B.
9. *Brown* } Tail chestnut-red, terminally black, white-tipped..... 22 *Red-tailed Hawk*.. § 27, V, A.
10. *above.* } Tail dark (black?) } Bend of wing orange-brown ("rufous") 21 *Red-shouldered Hawk* § 27, V, B.
11. white-banded. } Bend of wing not orange-brown................ 18 *Broad-winged Hawk* § 27, V, C.
12. Tail dark, whitish-barred, etc. Bands >5?........................... 19 *Red-shouldered Hawk* (yg.) § 27, V, B.
13. Tail brownish, } Without the characteristics of 15 or 16..... 19 *Cooper's Hawk*[11] § 27, III, B.
14. dark-banded. } Irregular dark abdominal zone................... 20-4 *Red-tailed Hawk*[12] § 27, V, A.

438 APPENDIX.

NO.	COLOR.[1]	SIZE.[2]	NAME OF BIRD.[12]	SECTION.
16.	Conspicuous broad dark line bordering throat.	17	Broad-winged Hawk.[12]	§ 27, V, C.
17.	No broad dark line bordering the throat. Tarsi not scutellate behind. See § T, Intro.	18 or >	Red-shouldered Hawk.[12]	§ 27, V, B.
	V. "STRISORES."			
1.	Chiefly variegated. Tail forked	9¼	Night "Hawk."	§ 20, II.
2.	Chiefly variegated. Tail rounded	8¼	Whippoorwill	§ 20, I.
3.	Chiefly sooty-brown	5	Chimney Swift	§ 22, I.
4.	Golden-green above; tail marked with black and white	3¼	♀ { Ruby-throated	§ 22, I.
5.	throat glittering ruby-red	3¼	♂ { Hummingbird	§ 22, I.
	VI. "SCANSORES." (Parrots), cuckoos, woodpeckers			
A.	Beneath white, (tinged?) but wholly unmarked	(See,	for 3-toed woodpeckers,	§ 25, IV.)
1.	Eye-ring red	11	Black-billed Cuckoo	§ 22, I. B.
B.	Middle pair only of tail-feathers drab or brown	11	Yellow-billed Cuckoo	§ 22, I. A.
1.	> 15 inches long. With scarlet crest (in ♀ half black)	17	Pileated Woodpecker	§ 25, VI.
2.	Whole head crimson	9	Red-headed Woodpecker	§ 25, III.
3.	Crown crimson; throat-patch in ♂ crimson, in ♀ white. (for variety of "3" with nape scarlet, see § 25, III, A, ad finem. For	8¼	Yellow-bellied Woodpecker; see { § 25, II. A. foot-note.	
4.	Black and white	9¼	Hairy Woodpecker	§ 25, V, A.
5.	(bill-feathers yellowish)	6½	Downy Woodpecker	§ 25, V, B.
6.	With scarlet nuchal patch,	9¼	Hairy Woodpecker	§ 25, V, A.
7.	i.e. on hind-head or nape.	6½	♂ Downy Woodpecker	§ 25, V, B.
8.	Black crescent on breast. Rump white in contrast to back and tail	12	Pigeon Woodpecker	§ 25, I.

[1] The principal color, or the most conspicuous, or the one best characterizing the species, or often the brightest.
[2] Approximate or average length in inches.
[3] ♀, less bright, or with much duller coloring.
[4] In ♀ of 20 (and ⚹ 2?), and many winter-specimens of 22, the slate is replaced by warm brown.
[5] The chief color above only, except in 33, 34.
[6] ♀ with less and paler yellow. ♂ with forehead and eye-bars black.
[7] These patches are more or less concealed, or even wanting (chiefly in ♀).
[8] This species is tinged with mouse-color above. It does not differ from the *Philadelphia Vireo* (§ 13, 1, E) in coloration. The characteristic of "6" is borrowed from Dr. Coues.
[9] This bird has the breast otherwise bright yellow. See, if necessary, 13.
[10] These birds have acute, "stiffened" tail-feathers, and rather slender bills. Their wings, as also 11's, do not reach to the middle of the tail, as 10's. "8" has an "olive-gray" ear-patch (or auriculars), and "9" is not sharply or even distinctly (?) streaked.
[11] Much less stout than "16" (whose maxillary patch bordering the throat may be wanting). Tail slightly rounded. Moreover, tarsi not scutellate behind (see § T, Introduction). •For a characteristic of "16," see § 27, V, C, a, *ad fin.*
[12] Young.

E. *Coloration peculiar to young birds, or to mature birds in the winter-season.*

Young birds are so called from the time of first being fully feathered until the acquirement of all the characteristics of maturity. They are for the most part more or less distinct from their parents in general appearance, though often closely alike among themselves in different species. But, since they are known on attaining their full growth, but before attaining their full coloration, often to be larger than their parents (owing to their long feathers), they in some cases, particularly among the hawks, seem mature before being so.

Young birds may be classified in three divisions.

(1). Those with the male-parents strikingly different from the females, as in the Scarlet Tanagers, or Orchard Orioles. These at first resemble the females, but afterwards, if males, assume gradually, but often slowly, the characteristic coloration of their sex, and in this way sometimes pass through confusing changes.

(2). Those differing from their parents, who are essentially alike, as in the Robins.

(3). Those who essentially resemble both their parents, as in the Crows.

Young birds do not generally differ from their parents, except in size and coloration, but those *of all species with " booted" tarsi*, are said to *have scutellate tarsi*. (See § T of the Introduction, etc.) The following is a synopsis of the Insessorian families.

Turdidæ or *thrushes* (§ 1). Young easily recognized, but often more or less abnormally[1] spotted.

Saxicolidæ or *bluebirds* (§ 2). Young essentially like the female; when very young, spotted.

Regulinæ, "*wrens*," or "*kinglets*" (§ 3). Young essentially like the female.[2]

Paridæ or *titmice* (§ 4). Class third.

Sittidæ or *nuthatches* (§ 5). Young like the females or less distinctly marked.

Certhiidæ or *creepers* (§ 6). Class third.

Troglodytidæ or *wrens* (§ 7). Class third.

Anthinæ or *titlarks* (§ 8). Class third.

---

[1] i. e. Abnormally in respect to maturity.

[2] Young *satrapa*, if without crown-markings, may be known by the "presence of a tiny bristly feather overlying the nostrils; this is wanting in *calendulus*." (Coues.)

Sylvicolidæ or *warblers* (§ 9). Young students will find the young of this family very confusing, from their frequent similarity one to another, and their abundance during the fall-migrations. It is best to study warblers in the spring, and to avoid immature birds until the differences between their parents are mastered. The young of those species, not further mentioned, either resemble the females or the males also, or are characterized by indistinct markings and impure colors, such as greenish-blue, yellowish-white, etc. *Helminthophaga celata* is "often difficult to distinguish in immature plumage; but a general *oliveness* and *yellowness*, compared with the ashy of some parts of *ruficapilla*, and the different color of the crown-patch in the two species, will usually be diagnostic." (Coues.) The young male of the "Black-throated Blue" (*Dendrœca cœrulescens*) resembles the adult male, but the colors are impure, and the black restricted. The immature "Yellow-rumps" (*D. coronata*) are common during both migrations. Their coloration varies from an imperfect full dress to the following extreme. Beneath, white or whitish, with slender streaks; above, chiefly brown, with more or less yellow, especially on the rump (which is concealed by the wings when closed). The other young *Dendrœcæ* with yellow rumps are *maculosa* (Black and Yellow Warbler) and *tigrina*[3] (Cape May Warbler). The former have more or less distinct (and pure ?) yellow beneath, "*small* tail-spots near the *middle* of all the feathers except the central;" and are rather gray above. The latter are greenish above. The young Yellow "Red-poll" (*D. palmarum*), with a yellowish rump, has the "tailspots *at very end* of inner webs of two outer pairs of tail feathers only, and *cut squarely off*— a peculiarity distinguishing the species in any plumage." (Coues.) Of the Bay-breasted Warbler (*D. castanea*) the young "so closely resemble young *striata* ["Black-poll"], that it is sometimes impossible to distinguish them with certainty. The upper parts, in fact, are of precisely the same greenish-olive, with black streaks; but there is *generally* a difference below — *castanea* being there tinged with buffy or ochrey, instead of the clearer pale yellowish of *striata;* this shade is particularly observable on the belly, flanks and under tail coverts, just where *striata* is whitest; and moreover, *castanea* is usually not streaked on the sides at all." (Coues.) The young Blackburnian Warbler is not unlike these, though sufficiently like the female to be distinguishable. The other species require no notice, unless

---

[3] Properly *Perissoglossa tigrina.*

the young Mourning Warblers (*Geothlypis Philadelphia*), who have no gray (?) or black, though recognizable from their shape and proportions, unless confused with the "Yellow-throats."

Tanagridæ or *tanagers* (§ 10). Class first.

Ampelidæ or *waxwings* (§ 11). ⎫ The young of these fami-
Hirundinidæ or *swallows* (§ 12). ⎬ lies are recognizable from
Vireonidæ or *vireos* (§ 13).   ⎥ their likeness to their pa-
Laniidæ or *shrikes* (§ 14).   ⎭ rents.

Fringillidæ or *finches* (§ 15). The young Pine Finch (*Chrysomitris pinus*) often resembles the young "Red-polls" (*Ægiothi*), but these species, unless very young, show respectively more or less yellow or carmine. Our sparrows are separable into two groups, with the wings decidedly longer than the tail (genera *Ammodromus*, *Coturniculus*, *Passerculus*, and *Pooecetes*), and with the wing equal to or shorter than the tail (genera *Melospiza*, *Spizella*, and *Zonotrichia*). The young Yellow-winged Sparrow (*C. passerinus*) is spotted, but never streaked, beneath. In the second group, the *Spizellæ* are characterized by their *forked* tails. The young of *pusilla* may be told from that of *socialis* by the reddish bill, and (faint) streaks on the crown, instead of on the rump (?). Young *monticola* has the "breast, *throat, and crown, streaked*." Young *Melospiza palustris* (or Swamp Sparrow) is also streaked beneath. Other young finches are more easily recognized. In the Towhee Bunting (*Pipilo erythropthalmus*) "*very* young birds are streaked brown and dusky above, below whitish tinged with brown and streaked with dusky; but this plumage, corresponding to the very early speckled condition of thrushes and warblers, is of brief duration; sexual distinctions may be noted in birds just from the nest, and they rapidly become much like the adults." (Coues.)

Alaudidæ or *larks* (§ 16). Young easily recognized.

Icteridæ or *starlings* (§ 17). Young like the females, but, in the Cow-bird, streaked.

Corvidæ, or *crows* and *jays* (§ 18). Class third (?). In the Canada Jay (*Perisoreus Canadensis*), the young are said to be quite distinct, being much darker, duller, and browner. *Tyrannidæ* or *flycatchers* (§ 19). In many species, the young have rufous or ochrey edgings, especially on the wings.

The young of all our picarian birds (§ § 20-25) are easily identified, except those of certain woodpeckers (*Picidæ*, § 25). In our species of *Picus*, "young with the crown mostly red or bronzy, or even yellowish." (Coues.) Young *Sphyrapici* have at first no distinct *markings*, but are easily recognized. The crown shows black, and then scarlet, very early. In *Melanerpes erythrocephalus* (Red-headed Woodpecker), at first "young without any red, the head and neck being grayish streaked with dusky; breast with an ashy tinge, and streaked sparsely with dusky; secondaries with two or three bands of black; dorsal region clouded with grayish." (B. B. and R.)

The owls (*Strigidæ*, § 26) belong more or less distinctly to the third class. The young of *Nyctale* are described as more or less brown beneath, where they are unmarked. Descriptions of the young hawks who are much unlike their parents (*Falconidæ*, § 27) may be found with those of the adults. The young of our two pigeons (*Columbidæ*, § 28) resemble at first the females.

The *adult birds* of many species change their dress for the *autumn and winter*, so that the coloration is materially altered.

During the winter-*season* (only), the males resemble the females in the Blue Birds (*Sialia sialis*), a majority of our warblers (several of whom lose an *ashiness* or *grayness*, observable above in spring), the tanagers (?), many of the finches (even several plainly-colored kinds), and some of the starlings, notably the Bobolinks (*Dolichonyx oryzivorus*). The male "Yellow-rump" (*Dendrœca coronata*) and Goldfinches (*Chrysomitris tristis*) become in autumn more or less *brown*, and remain so throughout the winter.

I have now detailed the most important seasonal changes observable in the (insessorian) birds of New England. I have often quoted Dr. Coues, on account of his rank as an authority, and the frequent terseness of his descriptions.

F. *Additions and Corrections.*

Add to the list of books given in foot-notes to the Preface, "Studer's Ornithology," "the Birds of North America, drawn, engraved, and colored from life by Theodore Jasper, A.M., M.D." This is to be published (by subscription, at one dollar for each number) in about forty parts, many of which have already been issued. Each part contains one uncolored, and three colored lithographic plates, in which the figures of the larger birds are often admirable, while those of the smaller kinds are generally very much less successful. The letter-press consists of short biographical sketches, and synopses of classification.

Add to § 8 of the Introduction, on the study of birds' habits, the following: It will be found very advantageous to make observations continuously from day to day, as one will not only see many birds who otherwise would escape him, but will acquire an invaluable familiarity with their little characteristics (which one may often think insignificant) and so an intimacy with the birds themselves, which will enable him, for instance, to detect the presence of the Brown Creepers by their shrill and slightly tremulous *tsip*, where another person might require more certain indications, or more impressive evidence. Moreover, one will find that intimacy suffers from interruption, and that knowledge is easily lost, however thoroughly gained. Therefore, one may chance to find a familiar song no longer associated with any bird. On the other hand, those who in studying nature are obliged to do so at intervals will be surprised at the amount of pleasurable acquaintance which they can form with her at odd moments. There are few places where birds cannot be studied to advantage, not excluding the hearts of our cities, where may be found creepers, nuthatches, titmice, warblers, vireos, flycatchers, shrikes, etc., sometimes even hawks. Finally, it is to be remembered that birds are frequently erratic, and that observations on their abnormal habits are, as a rule, interesting observations rather than important discoveries.

The Hermit Thrushes are said occasionally to catch flies in the manner of Swainson's Thrushes, who perhaps are more common migrants through southern New England than I have indicated in my biography of those birds.

The Hudsonian Titmice probably breed in several parts of northern New England, and in the Adirondacks. They wander in winter so far to the southward as Connecticut, and more than one has been obtained in Massachusetts. The Crested Tomtit (*Lopophanes bicolor*), is said to have occurred in New England.

To the accounts of the warblers, it may be added that several Orange-crowned Warblers have now been obtained in Massachusetts (for which information I am chiefly indebted to Mr. H. A. Purdie); that the Blackburnian Warblers are considered by a friend, rather to the contrary of my own observations, to be very expert flycatchers, and that I have seen them near Boston on the tenth of October; that the Prairie Warblers sometimes feed upon the ground, and, moreover, have been found exceptionally among the White Mountains, at Bethlehem; that the Hooded Warbler has been definitely reported from Connecticut; and that the Yellow-breasted Chats are reported to be common summer-residents at Oyster Bay, Long Island, where Blue Birds winter, and where Cedar-birds have been seen in autumn in flocks of more than a hundred.

Mr. Ridgway has suggested that the anecdote quoted from the "Naturalist," pp. 141, 142, of this book, is probably referable to the Rough-winged Swallow, a bird closely resembling the Bank Swallow, and common in that section of the country, where the circumstance quoted is reconcilable to the usual habits of this species.

On p. 257, it should have been mentioned that the Adirondacks belong to the Canadian faunal district.

To my biography of the *Hummingbird* I will here add that one fluttered about the artificial flowers on the hat of a young lady sitting out of doors, and that another, having become entangled in cobwebs, so that he could not see, remained on the twig of a piazza-vine, the twig having been cut off by scissors, while carried through the house, and until his plumage was cleared of the web, and his sight restored, when he at once became active.

By my description of the Fish Hawk's notes, I did not wish to imply that those notes were ever musical, but merely that they were not always harsh or piercing.

The coloration of the Ruffed Grouse is variable, the tints varying from reddish to grayish. So in the Quail, the chestnut is often restricted, particularly in the females. In reference to the first line of p. 390, it is to be remarked that the Scotch Capercailzie is called the "Wood Grouse."

The specimen, from which the figure of the Winter Wren was drawn (p. 71), had an unusually short tail, in consequence of which the figure must be considered inaccurate in regard to that feature.

p. 56, 5th line, for *bird* read *birds*.

pp. 71 and 75, for *œdon* read *aëdon*.

p. 181, foot-note, for *wilder* read *milder*.

I take the last opportunity offered to record an observation which I have just made (Nov. 19th, 1876), that of a Black-throated Blue Warbler busied in catching insects among weeds, and also in some trees, where were several Chickadees. From other observations made near Boston, I am inclined to believe that this species is always a rather late migrant in fall, and that individuals may occasionally pass the winter in New England.

The reference to *Psittaci*, given in the opening table of the Key to birds, is owing to their bill, which has a true cere. The reference is improper, inasmuch as the parrots have their toes in pairs.

I have just learned, from the fourth number of the Nuttall Ornithological Club Bulletin, that the nests of our kinglets had been found previously to my discovery.

G. ABSTRACT OF THE GAME-LAWS OF MASSACHUSETTS.

Extract from Chap. 304, Statutes of 1870, as amended.

Whoever takes, kills, sells, buys, has in possession, or offers for sale any WOOD COCK, from January 1st till July 4th, any PARTRIDGES, from January 1st till September 1st, any QUAIL, from December 15th till October 15th, shall forfeit for every such Bird TWENTY-FIVE DOLLARS.

Whoever takes or kills ANY WILD BIRD, AT ANY SEASON OF THE YEAR, or wilfully disturbs or destroys their nests and eggs, shall forfeit for each offence Ten Dollars.

The following are exceptions: Marsh, Shore, and Beach Birds, such as Plover and Sandpipers, may be killed after 15th of July; Black Duck, Summer Duck, Teal and Wild Pigeons after September first; other fresh water Ducks, Geese, all Sea Ducks, Birds of Prey, Crow Blackbirds, Crows, Herons, Bitterns, Wilson's Snipe, Black Breast and Red Breast Plover at any time of year.

Possession, by any person, of Birds mentioned as protected in this Act shall be prima facie evidence to convict under the same, and one half of all forfeitures shall be paid to the informant or prosecutor.

The attention of the public is respectfully invited to these laws, which will be enforced. Their co-operation is requested by the SOCIETY FOR PROTECTION OF USEFUL BIRDS.

INDEX TO ENGLISH NAMES.

(For the terms used in descriptions, see § T of the Introduction. No references are here made to works consisting of a single volume. In other cases, the volume only is indicated, unless a species is referred to under different names. The first number after each name usually refers to a page of this work. A stands for Audubon's "Ornithological Biography," AA for Audubon's "Birds of America," B for Bonaparte's "American Ornithology," BB for Messrs. Baird, Brewer, and Ridgway's "Birds of North America," N for Nuttall's "Manual of the Ornithology of the United States and Canada," W for Wilson's "American Ornithology," C for Dr. Coues' "Check List,"[1] and S for " Smithsonian Catalogue,"[1] first 8vo edition.)

(1) *Acadian Flycatcher.* 289; A, 2; AA, 1; BB, 2; N, 1; W, 2; C, 256; S, 143.
(2) *Acadian Owl.* 331; A, 2; AA, 1; BB, 3; N, 1; W, 4, p. 66; C, 328; S, 57.
(3) *Alice's* (or *Arctic*) *Thrush.* 39; BB, 1; C, 5a; S, 154.
(4) *American Barn Owl,* or the like. See Barn Owl, etc.
(5) *Autumnal Warbler.* N, 1; W, 3. See young of the Bay-breasted (or "Black poll"?) Warbler.
(6) *Bald Eagle.* 369; A, 1; AA, 1; BB, 3; N, 1; W, 4, and 7, p. 16; C, 362; S, 43.
(7) *Baltimore Oriole.* 252; A, 1; AA, 4; BB, 2; N, 1; W, 1, and ♀, 6; C, 216; S, 415.
(8) *Banded Three-toed Woodpecker.* 320; A, 5; AA, 4; BB, 2; N, 1 (2d ed.); C, 301; S, 83.
(9) *Bank Swallow.* 148; A, 4; AA, 1; BB, 1; N, 1; W, 5; C, 115; S, 220.
(10) *Barn Owl.* 328; A, 2; AA, 1; BB, 3; N, 1; W, 6; C, 316; S, 47.
(11) *Barn Swallow.* 142; A, 2; AA, 1; BB, 1; N, 1; W, 5; C, 111; S, 225.
(12) *Barred Owl.* 332; A, 1; AA, 1; BB, 3; N, 1; W, 4; C, 323; S, 54.
(13) *Bay-breasted Warbler.* 108; A, 1; AA, 2; BB, 1; N, 1; W, 2; C, 82; S, 197.
(14) *Bay-winged Bunting.* 200; A, 1; AA, 3; BB, 1; N, 1; W, 4; C, 161; S, 337.
(15) *Bee " Martin."* 273. See (158).
(16) *Belted Kingfisher.* 305; A, 1; AA, 4; BB, 2; N, 1; W, 3; C, 286; S, 117.
(17) *Birds of prey.* Chap. III, p. 326; AA, 1; BB, 3; N, 1; C, 316–366; S, 1–62.
(18) *Black Hawk.* 366; BB, 3; W, 6. C, =356; S, 31.
(19) *Black " Log-cock "* (or *Woodpecker*). 324. See (224).
(20) *Black and White " Creeper."* 97; A, 1; AA, 2; BB, 1; N, 1; W, 3; C, 57; S, 167.
(21) *Black and Yellow Warbler.* 126; A, 1; AA, 2; BB, 1; N, 1; W, 3; C, 84; S, 204.
(22) *Black-backed Woodpecker.* 319; A, 2; AA, 4; B, 1; BB, 2; N, 1 (2d ed.); C, 300; S, 82.
(23) *Black-billed Cuckoo.* 309; A, 1; AA, 4; BB, 2; N, 1; W, 4; C, 290; S, 70.
(24) *Blackbirds.* § 17, VI. VII, etc.; AA, 4; BB, 2; N, 1.
(25) *Blackburnian Warbler.* 112; A, 1; AA, 2; BB, 1; N, 1; W, 3; C, 80; S, 196.
(26) *Black-capped Chickadee.* 59. See (68).

---

[1] The author has carefully revised these numbers, so that they may be taken from the Index *without hesitation.*

(27) "*Black-cap*" (Warbler, or "Flycatcher"). 120; A, 2; AA, 2; BB, 1; N, 1; W, 3; C, 102; S, 213.
(28) "*Black-poll*" *Warbler*. 110; A, 2; AA, 2; BB, 1; N, 1; W, 4 (and 6, p. 101); C, 81; S, 202.
(29) *Black-throated Blue Warbler*. 115; A, 2 (and p. 279); AA, 2; BB, 1; N, 1 (and p. 406); W, 2 (and 5, p. 100); C, 76; S, 193.
(30) *Black-throated Bunting*. 228; AA, 3; BB, 2; N, 1; W, 3; C, 191; S, 378.
(31) *Black-throated Green Warbler*. 117; A, 4; AA, 2; BB, 1; N, 1, W, 2; C, 71; S, 189.
(32) *Blue Bird*. 50; A, 2; AA, 2; BB, 1; N, 1; W, 1; C, 16; S, 158.
(33) *Blue Grosbeak*. 231; A, 2; AA, 3; BB, 2; N, 1; W, 3; C, 195; S, 382.
(34) *Blue Jay*. 266; A, 2; AA, 4; BB, 2; N, 1; W, 1; C, 234; S, 434.
(35) "*Blue*" *Snow-bird*. 223; A, 1; AA, 3; BB, 1; N, 1; W, 2; C, 174; S, 354.
(36) *Blue Warbler*. 114 (G); A, 1, pp. 255 and 258; AA, 2; B, ♀, 2; BB, 1; N, 1; W, 2 (p. 141, and 3, p. 119); C, 77; S, 201.
(37) *Blue Yellow-backed Warbler*. 99; A, 1; AA, 2; BB, 1; N, 1; W, 4; C, 58; S, 168.
(38) *Blue-eyed Yellow Warbler*. 103. See (350).
(39) *Blue-gray Gnatcatcher*. 58; A, 1; AA, 1; BB, 1; N, 1; W, 2; C, 23; S, 282.
(40) *Blue-headed Vireo*. 152. See (287).
(41) *Blue-winged Yellow Warbler*. 91; A, 1; AA, 2; BB, 1; N, 1; W, 2; C, 62; S, 180.
(42) *Bobolink*. 243; A, 1; AA, 4; BB, 2; N, 1; W, 2; C, 210; S, 399.
(43) *Bohemian Waxwing*. 139; A, 4; AA, 4; B, 3; BB, 1; N, 1; C, 118; S, 232.
(44) *Brewster's Linnet*. 185; BB, 1; C, 147; S, ——.
(45) *Broad-winged Hawk*. 365. A, 1; AA, 1; BB, 3; N, 1; W, 6; C, 355; S, 27.
(46) *Bronzed Blackbird*. 261; BB, 2; C, ——; S, ——.
(47) *Brown Creeper*. 68; A, 5; AA, 2; BB, 1; N, 1; W, 1; C, 42; S, 275.
(48) *Brown Thrush*. 48; A, 2; AA, 2; BB, 1; N, 1; W, 2; C, 10; S, 261.
(49) *Buntings*. §§ 15, 17, passim.
(49a) *Burrowing Owl*. 343; A, 5; AA, 1; B, 1; BB, 3; N, 1; C, 332; S, 58.
(50) *Butcher-bird*. 161. See (126).
(51) *Buzzards*. § 27, V, VI. AA, 1; BB, 3; N, 1; W, 6. See (318). For "*American Buzzard*" (see (251).
(52) *Cerulean Warbler*. 114. See (36).
(53) *Canada* "*Flycatcher.*" 127; A, 2; AA, 2; BB, 1; N, I; W, 3; C, 103; S, 214.
(54) *Canada Grouse*. 386; A, 2; AA, 5; B, 3; BB, 3; N, 1; C, 380; S, 460.
(55) *Canada Jay*. 268; A, 2; AA, 4; BB, 2; N, 1; W, 3; C, 239; S, 443.
(56) *Canada* "*Robin.*" 137. See (60).
(57) *Cape May Warbler*. 102; A, 5; AA, 2; B, ♀, 1; BB, 1; N, 1; W, 6; C, 85; S, 206.
(58) *Cardinal Grosbeak*. 234; A, 2; AA, 3; BB, 2; N, 1; W, 2; C, 203; S, 390.
(59) *Carolina Dove*. 384; A, 1; AA, 5; BB, 3; N, 1; W, 5; C, 371; S, 451. For *C. Wren*, (§ 7, I, NOTE), see (123).
(60) *Carrion* "*Crow.*" 375; A, 2; AA, 1; BB, 3; N, 1; W, 9; C, 366; S, 3.
(61) *Cat-bird*. 46; A, 2; AA, 2; BB, 1; N, 1; W, 2; C, 9; S, 254.
(62) *Cedar-bird*. 137; A, 1; AA, 4; BB, 1; N, 1; W, 1; C, 119; S, 233.
(63) *Chat*. 132; A, 2; AA, 4; BB, 1; N, 1; W, 1; C, 100; S, 176.
(64) "*Chatterers.*" § 11; AA, 4; BB, 1; N, 1; C, 118-121; S, 232-235.
(65) *Cherry-bird*. 137. See (62).
(66) *Chestnut-sided Warbler*. 106; A, 1; AA, 2; BB, 1; N, 1; W, 2; C, 83; S, 200.
(67) "*Chewink.*" 226; A, 1; AA, 3; BB, 2; N, 1; W, 2 C, 204; S, 391.
(68) *Chickadee*.[2] 59; A, 4; AA, 2; BB, 1; N, 1; W, 1; C, 31; S, 290.
(69) "*Chicken Hawk.*" 357; etc. See (75).

---

[2] Other allied titmice are called "Chickadees," but always with a prefix.

(70) *Chimney* ("*Swallow*" or) *Swift*. 290; A, 2; AA, 1; BB, 2; N, 1; W, 5; C, 271; S, 109.
(71) "*Chipper*" or *Chipping Sparrow*. 210; A, 2; AA, 3; BB, 2; N, 1; W, 2; C, 178; S, 359.
(72) *Cliff Swallow*. 144; A, 1; AA, 1; B, 1; BB, 1; N, 1; C, 114; S, 226.
(73) *Common Crow*, or the like. See Crow, etc.
(74) *Connecticut Warbler*. 88; A, 2; AA, 2; BB, 1; N, 1; W, 5; C, 95; S, 174.
(75) *Cooper's Hawk*. 357; A, 1; AA, 1; B, 2; BB, 3; N, 1; C, 339; S, 15.
(76) *Cow-bird*. 216; A, 2; AA, 4; BB, 2; N, 1; W, 2; C, 211; S, 400.
(77) *Creepers*. § 6. See (47), and, if necessary, (20).
(78) *Crossbills*. § 15, I; AA, 3; BB, 1; N, 1; W, 4; C, 142-143a; S, 318-319.
(79) *Crow*. 262; A, 2; AA, 4; BB, 2; N, 1; W, 4; C, 228; S, 426.
(80) *Crows*. § 18, 1; AA, 4; BB, 2; N, 1; C, 226-231; S, 423-431 (?).
(81) *Crow Blackbird*. 258; A, 1; AA, 4; B, ♀, 1; BB, 2; N, 1; W, 3; C, 225; S, 421.
(82) *Cuckoos*. § 24. A, 1; AA, 4; BB, 2; N, 1; W, 4; C, 288-292; S, 67-71.
(83) *Cuvier's Kinglet*. 57; AA, 2; BB, 1; N, 1; C ——; S, 163.
(84) *Day Owl*. 312. See (110).
(85) *Doves*. § 29, 11; AA, 5; BB, 3; N, 1; C. 371-377; S, 449-455.
(86) *Downy Woodpecker*. 322; A, 2; AA, 4; BB, 2; N, 1; W, 1; C, 299; S, 76.
(87) *Duck Hawk*. 318; A, 1; AA, 1; BB, 3; N, 1; W, 9; C, 313; S, 5.
(88) *Eagles*. § 27, VII, VIII; AA, 1; BB, 3; N, 1; C, 361-362 (and 363 ?); S, 39-43.
(89) *Eastern Blue Bird*, or the like. See Blue Bird, etc.
(90) *Eave Swallow*. 144. See (72).
(91) "*English*" *Snipe*. 406. See (335).
(92) "*English Sparrow*." 235; C, 187.
(93) *English Tree Sparrow*, etc. 236, and *note*.
(94) *Falcons*. § 27. 11; AA, 1; BB, 3; N, 1; C, 311-317; S, 5-13.
(95) *Ferruginous Thrush*. 48. See (48).
(96) *Field Lark*. 211; A, 2; AA, 4; BB, 2; N, 1; W, 3; C, 214; S, 406.
(97) *Field Sparrow*. 215; A, 2; AA, 3; BB, 2; N, 1; W, 2; C, 179; S, 358.
(98) *Finches*. § 15; AA, 3; BB, 1 and 2; N, 1; C, 136-209; S, 303-398.
(99) *Fire-bird*. 252. See (7).
(100) *Fish Crow*. 262. NOTE; A, 2; AA, 4; BB, 2; N, 1; W, 5; C, 229; S, 429.
(101) *Fish Hawk*. 373; A, 1; AA, 1; BB, 3; N, 1; W, 5; C, 360; S, 44.
(102) "*Flicker*." 312. See (117).
(103) *Flycatchers*. § 19; AA, 1 and 7; BB, 2; N, 1; W, 2; C, 240-263; S, 120-147.
(104) "*Flycatchers*." § 13. Also § 9, XI.
(105) *Flycatching warblers*. § 9, XI and XII; AA, 2; BB, 1; N, 1; C, 101-105; S, 211-219.
(106) *Fox Sparrow*. 221; A, 2; AA, 3; BB, 2; N, 1; W, 3; C, 188; S, 374.
(107) *Game-birds*. Chap. V., p. 386; AA, chiefly 5; W, chiefly 6.
(108) *Gerfalcon*. See *Gyrfalcon*.
(109) *Gnatcatchers*. § 3, II; C, 23-25; S, 283-284. See (39).
(110) "*Goatsuckers*." § 20; AA, 1; BB, 2; N, 1; C, 264-268; S, 111-116a.
(111) *Golden Eagle*. 367; A, 2; AA, 1; BB, 3; N, 1; W, 7; p. 13; C, 361; S, 39.
(112) *Golden* "*Robin*." 252. See (7).
(113) *Golden Warbler*. 103. See (350).
(114) *Golden-crowned* "*Thrush*." 84; A, 3; AA, 2; BB, 1; N, 1; W, 2; C, 92; S, 186.
(115) *Golden-crowned* "*Wren*" or *Kinglet*. 55; A, 2; AA, 2; B, ♀, 1; BB, 1; N, 1; W, 1; C, 22; S, 162.
(116) *Golden-winged Warbler*. 91; A, 5; AA, 2; B, ♀, 1; BB, 1; N, 1; W, 2; C, 63; S, 181.
(117) *Golden-winged Woodpecker*. 312; A, 1; AA, 1; BB, 2; N, 1; W, 1; C, 312; S, 97.
(118) *Goldfinch*. 176; A, 1; AA, 3; B, ♀, 1; BB, 1; N, 1; W, 1; C, 149; S, 313.

(119) *Goshawk.* 358; A, 2; AA, 1; BB, 3; N, 1; W, 6, p. 80; C, 340; S, 14.
(120) *Grass Finch.* 200. See (14).
(121) *Gray-cheeked Thrush.* 39; BB, 1; C, 5a; S, 154.
(122) *Gray King-bird.* 273, (a), *note;* AA, 1; BB, 2; C, 243; S, 125.
(123) *Great Carolina Wren.* 74; A, 1; AA, 2; BB, 1; N, 1; W, 2; C, 47; S, 265.
(124) *Great Crested Flycatcher.* 275; A, 2; AA, 1; BB, 2; N, 1; W, 2; C, 217; S, 130.
(124a) *Great (Cinereous* or) *Gray Owl.* 331; A, 4; AA, 1; BB, 3; N, 1; C, 322; S, 53.
(125) *Great Horned Owl.* 339; A, 1; AA, 1; BB, 3; N, 1; W, 6; C, 317; S, 48.
(126) *Great Northern Shrike.* 161; A, 2; AA, 4; BB, 1; N, 1; W, 1; C, 134; S, 236.
(127) *Green Black-capped " Flycatcher."* 129. See (28).
(128) *Green-crested Flycatcher.* See (1).
(129) *" Greenlets "* = *vireos,* § 13.
(130) *Grosbeaks.* §§ 15, XXI, XXII, and XXIII.
(131) *" Ground Robin."* 226. See (67).
(132) *" Ground Sparrow."* § 15, *passim* (especially XIII, A).
(133) *Grouse.* § 30; AA, 5; BB, 3; N, 1; C, 380–388; S, 459-470.
(134) *Gyrfalcon.* 317; A, 2 and 4; AA, 1; BB, 3; C, 341 & 341a; S, 11 and 12. See § 27. II. (A).
(135) *" Hair-bird."* 210. See (71).
(136) *Hairy Woodpecker.* 321; A, 5; AA, 4; BB, 2; N, 1; W, 1; C, 298; S, 74.
(137) *" Hang-nest."* 252. See (7).
(138) *Harriers.* § 27, I. See (179).
(139) *Hawks.* § 27, (especially III and IV); AA, 1; BB, 3; N, 1; C, 333–363; S, 5–46.
(140) *Hawk Owl.* 342; A, 4; AA, 1; BB, 3; N, 1; W, 6; C, 326; S, 62.
(141) *Hemlock Warbler.* 112; AA, 2; N, 1; W, 5. See (26).
(142) *Hen Hawks.* § 27, especially V, (A) and (B); AA, 1; BB, 3; N, 1; W, 6.
(143) *Henslow's Bunting* (or *Sparrow*). 193; A, 1; AA, 3; BB, 1; N, 1 (2d ed.); C, 163; S, 339.
(144) *Hermit Thrush.* 34; A, 1; AA, 3; BB, 1; N, 1; W, 5;[3] C, 4; S, 149.
(145) *" High-hole."* etc. 312. See (117).
(146) *Hooded "Flycatcher"* (or *Warbler*). 129, NOTE; A, 2; AA, 2; BB, 1; N, 1; W, 3; C, 101; S, 211.
(147) *Horned Lark.* 237. See (274).
(148) *Horned Owl.* 339. See (125).
(149) *House Sparrow.* 235; C, 187.
(150) *House Wren.* 75. A, 1; AA, 2; BB, 1; N, 1; W, 1; C. 49; S, 270.
(151) *Hummingbird.* 302. See (261).
(152) *Hummingbirds.* § 22; AA, 4; BB, 2; N, 1; C, 273–283; S, 100–106.
(153) *Indigo Bird.* 229; A, 1; AA, 3; BB, ♀, 2; BB, 2; N, 1; W, 1; C, 199; S, 387.
(154) *Ipswich Sparrow.* 195; BB, 1; C, 158; S, ——.
(155) *Jays.* § 18, II and III; AA, 4; BB, 2; N, 1; C, 232–239; S, 432–444.
(156) *Jerfalcon.* 317. See (134).
(157) *Kentucky Warbler.* 88, NOTE; A, 1; AA, 2; BB, 1; N, 1; W, 3; C. 96; S, 175.
(158) *King-bird.* 273; A, 1; AA, 1; BB, 2; N, 1; W, 2, p. 66; C, 212; S, 124.
(159) *Kingfisher.* 305; A, 1; AA, 4; BB, 2; N, 1; W, 3; C, 286; S, 117.
(160) *Kingfishers.* § 23; AA, 4; BB, 2; N, 1; C, 286–297; S, 117–118.
(161) *" Kinglets."* § 3, I; A, 2; AA, 2; BB, 1; N, 1; W, 1; C, 21–22; S, 161–163.
(162) *Lapland Longspur.* 188; A, 4; AA, 3; B, 2; BB, 1; N, 1; C, 153; S, 326.
(163) *Large-billed Water " Thrush."* 83; A, 1; AA, 3; BB, 1; N, 1; W, 3, pl. 23; C, 94; S, 188.

---

[3] I am inclined to decide that fig. 2 of pl. 45 is that of the Hermit Thrush, whereas confusion with the Olive-backed Thrush occurs in the text.

(164) *Lark Finch.* 189; A. 5; AA, 3; B, 1; BB, 1; N. 1; C, 186; S, 344.
(165) *Larks.* § 16 (also § 17, I, and § 8).
(166) *Least Flycatcher* (or *L. "Pewee."*) 286; AA, (1 ?*) 7; BB, 2; N. 1; C, 258; S, 142.
(167) *Lesser " Red-poll."* 182; A, 4; AA, 3; BB, 1; N, 1; W, 4; C. 146; S. 320.
(168) *Lincoln's Finch.* 207; A. 2; AA, 3; BB, 2; N. 1 (2d ed.); C, 167; S, 368.
(169) *Linné's Hummingbird.* 302, NOTE; C, 283; S, ———.
(170) *" Linnet."* 174. (Also, § 15, IV, B, and V.) See (234).
(171) *" Log-cock."* 324. See (224).
(172) *Loggerhead Shrike.* 165; A, 1; AA, 4; BB. 1; N. 1; W, 3; C, 135; S, 237.
(173) *Long-billed Marsh Wren.* 78; A. 1; AA. 2; BB, 1; N, 1; W, 2; C. 51; S, 268.
(174) *Long-eared Owl.* 329; A, 4; AA, 1; BB, 3; N, 1; W, 6; C, 320; S, 51.
(175) *Longspur.* 188. See (162).
(176) *Louisiana " Thrush."* 83. See (163).
(177) *Magnolia Warbler.* 126. See (21).
(178) *Marsh Blackbird.* 249. See (252).
(179) *Marsh Hawk.* 346; AA, 1; B, 2, p. 30; BB, 3; N, 1; W, 6; C, 333; S, 38.
(180) *Marsh Owl.* 330. See (276).
(181) *" Marsh Robin."* 226. See (67).
(182) *Marsh wrens.* § 7, II, especially (B); AA, 2; BB, 1; N, 1; C, 51-52; S, 268-269.
(183) *Martins.* § 12, V. See (236).
(184) *Maryland " Yellow throat."* 85; A, 1; AA, 2; BB, 1; N, 1; W, 1, and ♀, 2; C, 97; S, 170.
(185) *Maynard's Sparrow.* 195. See (154).
(186) *Meadow Lark.* 241; A, 2; AA, 4; BB, 2; N, 1; W, 3; C, 214; S, 406.
(187) *Meadow Wren.* 77. See (275).
(188) *Mealy " Red-poll."* 182. V, (a), NOTE; A, 5; AA, 3; BB, 1; C, 146b; S, 321.
(189) *Migratory Thrush* = *Robin.* See (257).
(190) *Mocking Bird.* 45; A. 1; AA. 2; BB, 1; N. 1; W, 2; C, 8; S, 253.
(191) *Mocking thrushes.* § 1, II (and III ?); AA, 2; BB, 1; N, 1; W, 2; C, 7-14; S, 253-281a.
(192) *Mottled Owl.* 335; A, 1; AA. 1; BB, 3; N. 1; W, 3; C, 318; S, 49.
(193) *Mourning Warbler.* 87; A, 5; AA, 2; BB, 1; N, 1; W, 2; C, 98; S, 172.
(194) *" Mouse Hawk."* 346. See (179).
(195) *" Myrtle-bird."* 124. See (356).
(196) *Nashville Warbler.* 94; A, 1; AA. 2; BB, 1; N, 1; W, 3; C, 67; S, 183.
(197) *New York " Thrush."* 83. See (163).
(198) *Night " Hawk."* 297; AA, 1; BB, 2; N, 1; W, 5: C, 267; S, 114.
(199) *" Nightingale."* A name applied to several American birds, as (344), (350), etc.
(200) *" Night-jar."* 295. See (336).
(201) *Nuchal Woodpecker.* 318 at bottom; BB, 2; C, 302a; S, 86.
(202) *Nuthatches.* § 5; A, 2; AA, 4; BB, 1; N. 1; C, 38–41; S, 277-281.
(203) *Olive-backed Thrush.* 36; AA, "III, pl. cxlvii; not the text"; BB, 1; W, 5, pl. 45. fig. 2 (?); C, 5; S, 153.
(204) *Olive-sided Flycatcher.* 280; A, 2; AA, 1; BB, 2; N, 1; C, 253; S, 137.
(205) *Orange-crowned Warbler.* 95; A, 2; AA, 2; B, 1; BB, 1; N, 1; C, 68; S, 184.
(206) *Orchard Oriole.* 255; A, 1, AA. 4; BB, 2; N, 1; W, 1; C, 215; S, 414.
(207) *Orioles.* § 17, V; A. 1; AA, 4; BB, 2; N, 1; W, 1; C, 215-220; S, 408-416.
(208) *Osprey.* 373. See (101).
(209) *" Oven-bird."* 84. See (114).

---

* The *Muscicapa pusilla* of Swainson is either this species or a variety of Traill's Flycatcher.

(210) *Owls.* § 26; AA, 1; BB, 3; N, 1; C, 310–332; S, 47–62.
(211) *Pallas' Thrush.* 34. See (144).
(212) *Palm Warbler.* 122; B, 2. See (248).
(213) "*Partridge*" = Quail, p. 393, and Ruffed Grouse, p. 388. See (237) and (262).
(214) *Passenger Pigeon.* See (346).
(215) "*Peabody-bird.*" 217. See (344).
(216) *Peregrine Falcon.* 348. See (87).
(217) *Pewee* (or "*Phœbe.*") 277; A, 2; AA, 1; BB, 2; N, 1; W, 2; C, 252; S, 135.
(218) "*Pheasant.*" 388. See (262).
(219) *Philadelphia Vireo.* 159; BB, 1; C, 124; S, 241.
(220) *Pigeons.* Chap. IV; AA, 4 and 5; BB, 3; N, 1; C, 367–370; S, 445–448; inc. doves, C—377; S—455.
(221) *Pigeon Hawk.* 351; A, 1; AA, 1; BB, 3; N, 1; W, 2; C, 344; S, 7.
(222) "*Pigeon Hawk.*" 355. See (272).
(223) *Pigeon Woodpecker.* 312. See (117).
(224) *Pileated Woodpecker.* 324; A, 2; AA, 4; BB, 2; N, 1; W, 4; C, 294; S, 90.
(225) *Pine Finch* (or *P. Linnet*). 180; A, 2; AA, 3; BB, 1; N, 1; W, 2; C, 148; S, 317.
(226) *Pine (Bullfinch* or) *Grosbeak.* 172; A, 4; AA, 3; B, ♀, 3; BB, 1; N, 1; W, 1; C, 137; S, 304.
(227) *Pine Warbler.* 120; A, 2; AA, 2; BB, 1; N, 1; W, 3; C, 91; S, 198.
(228) *Pinnated Grouse.* 387; A, 2; AA, 5; BB, 3; N, 1; W, 3; C, 384; S, 464.
(229) "*Pipit.*" 79. See (312).
(230) "*Politician.*" 160. See (328).
(231) *Prairie Warbler.* 105; A, 1; AA, 2; BB, 1; N, 1; W, 3; C, 86; S, 210.
(232) "*Prairie Hen*" (or "*Prairie Chicken*"). 387. See (228).
(233) *Prothonotary Warbler.* 90; A, 1; AA, 2; BB, 1; N, 1; W, 3; C, 59; S, 169.
(234) *Purple Finch.* 174; A, 1; AA, 3; BB, 1; N, 1; W, 1 (and yg. 5); C, 139; S, 305.
(235) *Purple Grakle.* 258. See (81).
(236) *Purple Martin.* 150; A, 1; AA, 1; BB, 1; N, 1; W, 5; C, 117; S, 231.
(237) *Quail.* 393; A, 1; AA, 5; BB, 3; N, 1; W, 6; C, 380; S, 471.
(238) *Raven.* 262. NOTE; A, 2; AA, 4; BB, 2; N, 1; W, 9; C, 226; S, 423.
(239) *Red Crossbill.* 168; A, 2; AA, 3; BB, 1; N, 1; W, 4; C, 143; S, 318.
(240) *Red Owl.* 335; W, 5. See (192).
(241) *Red-bellied Nuthatch.* 66; A, 2; AA, 4; BB, 1; N, 1; W, 1; C, 39; S, 279.
(242) *Red-bellied Woodpecker.* 315, NOTE; A, 5; AA, 4; BB, 2; N, 1; W, 1; C, 306; S, 91.
(243) *Red Bird* = Summer Red Bird; 136; = Cardinal Grosbeak, 234.
(244) *Red-eyed Vireo.* 155; A, 2; AA, 4; BB, 1; N, 1; W, 2; C, 122; S, 240.
(245) *Red-headed Woodpecker.* 315; A, 1; AA, 4; BB, 2; N, 1; W, 1; C, 309; S, 94.
(246) *Red-naped (or Red-throated) Woodpecker.* 318 at bottom; BB, 2. See (201).
(247) "*Red-polls.*" § 15, V, p. 182; AA, 3; BB, 1; N, 1. See (167).
(248) "*Red-poll*" *Warbler.* 122; A, 2; AA, 2; B, 2, p. 12; BB, 1; N, 1; W, 4; C, 90; S, 208.
(249) *Red-shouldered Hawk.* 361; A, 1; AA, 1; BB, 3; N, 1; W, 6, and 4, p. 73; C, 352; S, 25.
(250) *Redstart.* 130; A, 1; AA, 2; BB, 1; N, 1; W, 1 and 5; C, 104; S, 217.
(251) *Red-tailed Hawk.* 360; A, 1; AA, 1; BB, 3; N, 1; W, 6 (pl. 52, fig. 1, 2); C, 351; S, 23.
(252) *Red-winged Blackbird.* 249; A, 1; AA, 4; BB, 2; N, 1; W, 4; C, 212; S, 401.
(253) *Reed-bird* (or *Rice-bird*). 213. See (42).
(254) "*Republican*" *Swallow.* 144. See (72).
(255) *Richardson's Owl.* 333; A, 4, p. 559; AA, 1, p. 122; BB, 3; C, 327; S, 55.
(256) *Ring-tailed Eagle* = *Golden Eagle.* 367. See (111).
(257) *Robin.* 41; A, 2; AA, 3; BB, 1; N, 1; W, 1; C, 1; S, 155.

(258) *Rose-breasted Grosbeak.* 232; A, 2; AA, 3; B, ♀, 2; BB, 2; N, 1; W, 2; C, 193; S, 330.
(259) *Rough-legged Hawk.* 366; A, 2; AA, 1; BB, 3; N, 1, pp. 97, 98; W, 4; C, 356; S, 30. See (18).
(260) *Ruby-crowned " Wren"* (or *Kinglet*). 53; A, 2; AA, 2; BB, 1; N, 1; W, 1; C, 21; S, 161.
(261) *Ruby-throated Hummingbird.* 302; A, 1; AA, 4; BB, 2; N, 1; W, 2; C, 275; S, 101.
(262) *Ruffed Grouse.* 388; A, 1; AA, 5; BB, 3; N, 1; W, 6; C, 385; S, 465.
(263) *Rusty Blackbird* (or *Grakle*). 256; A, 2; AA, 4; BB, 2; N, 1; W, 3; C, 221; S, 417.
(264) *Sand " Martin."* 148. See (9).
(265) *" Sapsucker."* § 25, *passim.*
(266) *Savannah Sparrow.* 197; A, 2; AA, 3; BB, 1; N, 1; W, 3 and 4; C, 159; S, 332.
(267) *" Saw-whet" Owl.* 334. See (2).
(268) *Scarlet Tanager.* 134; A, 4; AA, 3; BB, 1; N, 1; W, 2; C, 107; S, 220.
(269) *Screech Owl.* 335. See (192) and (240).
(270) *Sea-side Finch.* 190; A, 1; AA, 3, pp. 103, 106; BB, 1; N, 1; W, 4; C, 165; S, 342.
(271) *Serin Finch.* 236, NOTE.
(272) *Sharp-shinned Hawk.* 355; A, 4; AA, 1; BB, 3; N, 1; W, 5, and 6, p. 13; C, 338; S, 17.
(273) *Sharp-tailed Finch.* 191; A, 2; AA, 3; BB, 1; N, 1; W, 4; C, 166; S, 341.
(274) *Shore Lark.* 237; A, 2; AA, 3; BB, 1; N, 1; W, 1; C, 53; S, 302.
(275) *Short-billed Marsh Wren.* 77; A, 2; AA, 2; BB, 1; N, 1; C, 52; S, 269.
(276) *Short-eared Owl.* 330; A, 5; AA, 1; BB, 3; N, 1; W, 4; C, 321; S, 52.
(277) *Shrikes.* § 14; AA, 4; BB, 1; N, 1; C, 134-135a; S, 236-239.
(278) *Siskin.* 180. See (225).
(279) *Sky Lark.* 237, and note *ad fin.* of § 16; BB, 1. See (274).
(280) *Slate-colored Hawk* (of Wilson). 355; N, 1; W, 6. See (272).
(281) *Small-headed Flycatcher.* 129, NOTE; AA, 1; BB, 1; N, 1; W, 6; C,——; S, 212.
(282) *Snipe.* 406; AA, 5 and 6; BB, 4; N, 2. See (349).
(283) *Snow-bird.* 223; A, 1; AA, 3; BB, 1; N, 1; W, 2; C, 174; S, 354.
(284) *Snow Bunting* (or *" Snow-flake"*). 185; A, 2; AA, 3; BB, 1; N, 1; W, 3; C, 152; S, 325.
(285) *Snowy Owl.* 341; A, 2; AA, 1; BB, 3; N, 1; W, 4; C, 325; S, 61.
(286) *Social Sparrow.* 210. See (71).
(287) *Solitary Vireo.* 152; A, 1; AA, 4; BB, 1; N, 1; W, 2; C, 127; S, 250.
(288) *Song Sparrow.* 202; A, 1; AA, 3; BB, 1; N, 1; W, 2; C, 169; S, 363.
(289) *Song Thrush.* 48; also 29; See (48) and (341).
(290) *Sparrows.* § 15, IX-XV (English, XXIV, XXV); AA, 3; BB, 1 and 2; N, 1; C, 157-189a; S, 331-370a.
(291) *Sparrow Hawk.* 353; A, 2; AA, 1; BB, 3; N, 1; W, ♀, 2, and ♂, 4; C, 346; S, 13.
(292) *Sparrow Owl.* 333. See (255).
(293) *Spotted Grouse* (or *" Spruce Partridge"*). 386. See (54).
(294) *Starlings.* § 17; AA, 4; BB, 2; N, 1; C, 210-225a; S, 399-422.
(295) *Summer Red Bird.* 136; A, 1; AA, 3; BB, 1; N, 1; W, 1; C, 108; S, 221.
(296) *Summer Warbler* (or *Yellow Bird*). 103. See (364).
(297) *Swainson's Thrush.* 36. See (203).
(298) *Swallows.* § 12; AA, 1; BB, 1; N, 1; W, 5; C, 111-117; S, 225-231a.
(299) *Swamp " Robin."* 226; also § 1, I, (C) (and D?). See (67) and (144).
(300) *Swamp Sparrow.* 208; A, 1; AA, 3; BB, 2; N, 1; W, 3; C, 168; S, 369.
(301) *Swamp Thrush.* 34. See (144).
(302) *Swifts.* § 21, A, 2; AA, 1; BB, 2; N, 1; W, 5 (p. 48); C, 269-272; S, 107-110.
(303) *Tanagers.* § 10; AA, 3; BB, 1; N, 1; C, 107-110; S, 220-224.
(304) *Tawny Thrush.* 32; W, 5. See (350).

(305) *Tengmalm's Owl.* A European owl, of which Richardson's Owl is a variety.
(306) *Tennessee Warbler.* 96; A, 2; AA, 2; BB, 1; N, 1; W, 3; C, 69; S, 185.
(307) "*Thistle-Lird.*" 176. See (118).
(308) "*Thrasher.*" 48. See (48).
(309) *Three-toed woodpeckers.* § 25, IV, p. 319; AA, 4; BB, 2; N, 1; C, 300–301a; S, 82-84.
(310) *Thrushes.* § 1; AA, 3 (mocking thrushes, 2); BB, 1; N, 1; C, 1-14; S, 148-156 and 253-261a.
(311) "*Thrushes.*" § 9, I; AA, 2; BB, 1; N, 1; C, 92-94; S, 186-188.
(312) *Titlark.* 79; A, 1; AA, 3; BB, 1; N, 1; W, 5; C, 55; S, 165.
(313) *Titmice.* § 4;. AA, 2; BB, 1; N, 1; C, 27-37; S, 285-300.
(314) "*Towhee.*" 226; A, 1; AA, 3; BB, 2; N, 1; W, 2; C, 204; S, 391.
(315) *Traill's Flycatcher.* 284; A, 1; AA, 1; BB, 2; N, 1; C, 257; S, 140.
(316) *Tree Sparrow.* 212; A, 2; AA, 3; BB, 2; N, 1; W, 2; C, 177; S, 357.
(317) *Turtle Dove.* 384. See (59).
(318) "*Turkey Buzzard.*" 375; A, 2; AA, 1; BB, 3; N, 1; W, 9; C, 365; S, 1.
(319) *Tyrant Flycatcher.* 273; W, 2. See (158).
(320) *Varied Thrush.* 44; A, 4; AA, 3; BB, 1; C, 2; S, 156.
(321) "*Veery.*" 32. See (350).
(322) *Vesper Sparrow.* 200. See (14).
(323) *Vireos.* § 13; AA, 4; BB, 1; N, 1; C, 122-133; S, 240-252.
(324) *Virginian "Nightingale."* 234. See (58).
(325) *Virginia Partridge.* 393. See (237).
(326) *Wagtails.* § 8; BB, 1; N, 1; C, 54-56; S, 164-166.
(327) "*Wagtails.*" § 9, I. See (311).
(328) *Warblers.* § 9; AA, 2; BB, 1; N, 1; C, 57-105; S, 167-219.
(329) *Warbling Vireo.* 157; A, 2; AA, 4; BB, 1; N, 1; W, 5; C, 125; S, 245.
,330) *Washington Eagle = Bald Eagle* (?). 369; A, 1; AA, 1; S, 41.
(331) *Water "Thrush."* 81; A, 5; AA, 3;[5] BB, 1; N, 1 (W, 3?); C, 93; S, 187.
(332) *Water "thrushes"* § 9, I, (A) and (B); AA, 3; BB, 1; N, 1; C, 93-94; S, 187-188.
(333) *Water "Wagtail."* 81. See (331).
(334) *Water Warbler.* 83. See (163).
(335) *Waxwings.* § 11; AA, 4; BB, 1; N, 1; C, 118-119; S, 232-233.
(336) *Whippoorwill.* 295; A, 1; AA, 1; BB, 2; N, 1; W, 5; C, 265; S, 112.
(337) "*Whiskey-Jack.*" 268. See (55).
(338) *White Owl.* 311. See (285).
(339) *White-bellied* or } *Nuthatch.* 63; A, 2; AA, 4; BB, 1; N, 1; W, 1; C, 38; S, 277.
(340) *White-breasted* } *Swallow.* 116; A, 1; AA, 1; BB, 1; N, 1; W, 5; C, 112; S, 227.
(341) *White-crowned Sparrow.* 220; A, 2; AA, 3; BB, 1; N, 1; W, 4; C, 183; S, 315.
(342) *White-eyed Vireo.* 160; A, 1; AA, 4; BB, 1; N, 1; W, 2; C, 129; S, 248.
(343) *White-headed Eagle.* 369. See (6).
(344) *White-throated Sparrow.* 217; A, 1; AA, 3; BB, 1; N, 1; W, 3; C, 182; S, 349.
(344a) *White-throated Warbler.* 92.
(345) *White-winged Crossbill.* 170; A, 4; AA, 3; B, ♀, 2; BB,♂1; N, 1; W, 4; C, 142; S, 319.
(346) *Wild Pigeon.* 378; A, 1; AA, 5; BB, 3; N, 1; W, 5; C, 370; S, 448.
(347) *Willow Warbler.* 124. See (356).
(348) *Wilson's "Black-cap."* 129. See (28).
(349) *Wilson's Snipe.* 406; A, 3; AA, 5; BB, 4;[6] N, 1; W, 6, p. 18; C, 414; S, 523.

---

[5] In Audubon's "Birds of America" considered identical with the Louisiana Water "Thrush."

[6] This volume has not yet been published, Nov. 1876.

INDEX. 453

(350) *Wilson's Thrush.* 32; A, 2; AA, 3; BB, 1; N, 1; W, 5, p. 98; C, 6; S, 151.
(351) *Winter Falcon* (of Wilson). 361; W, 4.
(352) *Winter Wren.* 71; A, 4; AA, 2; BB, 1; N, 1; W, 1; C, 50; S, 273.
(353) *Woodcock.* 399; A, 3; AA, 6; BB, 4; N, 1; W, 6; C, 412, (English) 413; S, 522.
(354) *Wood Pewee.* 281; A, 2; AA, 1; BB, 2; N, 1; W, 2; C, 255; S, 139.
(355) *Wood Thrush.* 29; A, 1; AA, 3; BB, 1; N, 1; W, 1; C, 3; S, 148. *Wood thrushes*, § 1, I, (A-E).
(356) *Wood Wren* = Winter Wren, 71; = House Wren; A, 2; AA, 2; S, 272.
(357) *Woodpeckers.* § 25; AA, 4; BB, 2; N, 1; C, 293-314; S, 72-99.
(358) *Worm-eating Warbler.* 89; A, 1; AA, 2; BB, 1; N, 1; W, 3; C, 60; S, 178.
(359) *Worm-eating warblers.* § 9, IV, V, VI; AA, 2; BB, 1; N, 1; C, 59-69; S, 178-185.
(360) *Wrens.* § 7; AA, 2; BB, 1; N, 1; C, 43-52; S, 262-273.
(361) " *Wrens.*" § 3, 1; A, 2; AA, 2; BB, 1; N, 1; W, 1; C, 21-22; S, 161-163.
(362) " *Yellow Hammer.*" 312. See (117).
(363) *Yellow Red-polled Warbler.* 122. See (248).
(364) *Yellow Warbler.* 103; A, 1; AA, 2, pp. 50 and 53; BB, 1; N, 1, pp. 364 and 370; W, 2; C, 70; S, 203.
(365) *Yellow-bellied Flycatcher.* 288; AA, 7; BB, 2; C, 259; S, 144.
(366) *Yellow-bellied Woodpecker.* 317; A, 2; AA, 4; B, yg., 1; BB, 2; N, 1; W, 1; C, 302; S, 85.
(367) *Yellow-billed Cuckoo.* 307; A, 1; AA, 4; BB, 2; N, 1; W, 4; C, 291; S, 69.
(368) *Yellow Bird* = Yellow Warbler, 103; = Goldfinch, 176.
(369) *Yellow-breasted Chat.* 132; A, 2; AA, 4; BB, 1; N, 1; W, 1; C, 100; S, 176.
(370) (*Yellow-crowned* or) " *Yellow-rump*" *Warbler.* 124; A, 2; AA, 2; BB, 1; N, 1; W, 2, and yg., 5; C, 78; S, 194.
(370a) *Yellow-headed Blackbird.* 252, NOTE.
(371) *Yellow-shafted Woodpecker.* 312. See (117).
(372) " *Yellow-throat.*" 85. See (184).
(373) *Yellow-throated Vireo.* 153; A, 2; AA, 4; BB, 1; N, 1; W, 1; C, 126; S, 252.
(374) *Yellow-winged Sparrow.* 192; A, 2; AA, 3; BB, 1; N, 1; W, 3; C, 162; S, 338.
(375) " *Yucker.*" 312. See (117).

INDEX TO SCIENTIFIC NAMES.

(When several species belong to one *genus*, they have been here given in the same order in which they are lettered. The Arabic figures refer to pages, unless preceded by a section-mark, when they refer to the families, as numbered in this volume. The letters in parenthesis stand for authorities, or originators of the scientific names; A for *Audubon*, BD for *Baird*, B for *Boie*, BP for *Bonaparte*, C for *Cabanis*, CU for *Cuvier*, G for *Gray*, L for *Linnæus*, S for *Swainson*, V for *Vieillot*, and W for *Wilson*. Names occurring less often are given in full. When one name is authority for both genus and species, it is given but once. When there are two authorities, the latter is usually given in ordinary mention of the bird; i.e. *Ampelis cedrorum*, BAIRD. It may be observed that most of the scientific names in the index will not be found in other than modern works, and often not in all of those. The sign ′ marks the accent.)

Acci'piter (BRISSON) *fuscus* (BP). 355.
    Coope'ri (BP). 357.
Ægio'thus lina'rius (C). 182.
    var. *fuces'cens* (COUES). } 182,
    var. *exi'lipes* (COUES). } NOTE.
Agelæ'us phœni'ceus (V). 249.
Alau'didæ. § 16.
Alau'da (auctorum) *arven'sis*. 240.
Alcedi'nidæ. § 23.
Ammo'dromus mari'timus (S). 190.
    caudacu'tus (S). 191.
Am'pelis (L) *cedro'rum* (BD). 137.
    gar'rulus (L). 139.
Ampe'lidæ,[1] *Ampelinæ.* § 11.
Antros'tomus (GOULD) *voci'ferus* (BP). 295.
A'quila (auctorum) *chrysa'ëtus* (L). 307.
Archibu'teo (BREHM) *la'gopus* (G), var. *Sanc'-ti-Johan'nis* (RIDGWAY). 306.
As'tur (LACEPEDE) *atricapil'lus* (BP). 358.
Aves aë'reæ. § 1-29.
Aves terres'tres. § 30-32.

Bona'sa umbel'lus (STEPHENS). 388.
Bu'bo (CU) *Virginia'nus* (BP). 339.
Bu'teo (CU) *borea'lis* (V). 360.
    linea'tus (JARDINE). 361.
    Pennsylva'nicus (BP). 365.

Calandritinæ. § 16.
Caprimul'gidæ, Caprimulginæ. § 20.
Cardina'lis Virginia'nus (BP). 234.
Carpo'dacus (KAUP) *purpu'reus* (G). 174.
Cathar'tes au'ra (ILLIGER). 375.
    atra'tus (LESSING). 375.
Cathar'tidæ. § 28.
Centu'rus (S) *Caroli'nus* (BP). 315, NOTE.

Cer'thia familia'ris (L). 68.
Certhi'idæ, Certhiinæ. § 6.
Cer'yle Al'cyon (B). 305.
Chætu'ra pela'gica (STEPHENS). 299.
Chondes'tes (S) *gramma'ca* (BP). 189.
Chorde'iles (S) *Virginia'nus* (BP). 297.
Chrysomi'tris (B) *tris'tis* (BP). 176.
    pi'nus (BP). 180.
Cir'cus cya'neus (LACEPEDE).
    var. *Hudso'nius* (COUES). 346.
Clamato'res. § 19.
Coccy'gus (V) *America'nus* (BP). 307.
    erythropthal'mus (BD). 309.
Coccyginæ. § 24.
Colap'tes aura'tus (S). 312.
Collu'rio (VIGORS) *borea'lis* (BD). 161.
    Ludovicia'nus (BD). 165.
Colum'bæ, Colum'bidæ, Columbinæ. § 29.
Con'topus (C) *borea'lis* (BD). 280.
    virens (C). 281.
Cor'vus (L) *America'nus* (A). 262.
    co'rax (L). 262, NOTE.
    ossi'fragus (W). 262, NOTE.
Cor'vidæ, § 18; *Corvinæ*, § 18, 1.
Coturni'culus passeri'nus (BP). 192.
    Henslow'i (BP). 193.
Co'tyle ripa'ria (B). 148.
Cucu'lidæ. § 24.
Cupido'nia (REICHENBACH) *cupi'do* (BD). 387.
Curso'res. § 30, etc.
Curviros'tra (SCOPOLI) * * *, var. *America'na* (COUES). 168.
Curriros'tra leucop'tera (W). 170.
Cyanospi'za cya'nea (BD). 220.
Cyanu'rus crista'tus (S). 266.
Cypse'lidæ. § 21.

---

[1] An accented vowel is often short, as in *Ampelidæ*.

Dendrœ'ca (G) *œsti'va* (BD). 103.
    dis'color (BD). 105.
    Pennsylva'nica (BD). 106.
    casta'nea (BD). 108.
    stria'ta (BD). 110.
    Blackbur'niœ (BD). 112.
    cœru'lea (BD). 114.
    cœrules'cens (BD) 115.
    vi'rens (BD). 117.
    pi'nus (BD). 120.
    palma'rum (BD). 122.
    corona'ta (G). 124.
    maculo'sa (BD). 126.
Doli'chonyx oryzi'vorus (S). 243.

Ectopis'tes migrato'rius (S). 378.
Empido'nax (C) *Trail'li* (BD). 284.
    mi'nimus (BD). 286.
    flaviven'tris (BD). 288.
    Aca'dicus (BD). 289.
    [*pygmœ'us*.] 290.
Eremo'phila alpes'tris (B). 237.
Euspi'za America'na (BP). 228.

Fal'co (L) *gyrfal'co*. 347.
    commu'nis, var. *ana'tum* (BP). 348.
    columba'rius (L). 351.
    sparve'rius (L). 353.
Falco'nidœ. § 27.
Fringil'lidœ. § 15.

Gallina'go (LEACH) *Wilso'ni*. 406.
Galli'nœ. §§ 30, 31.
Garrulinœ. § 18, II and III.
Geothlypis tri'chas (C). 85.
    Philadel'phia (BD). 87.
Goniaphea (BOWDITCH) *cœru'lea*. 231.
Grallato'res. § 32, etc.

Halia ëtus leucoce'phalus (SAVIGNY). 369.
Harporhyn'chus ru'fus (C). 48.
Helmintho'phaga (C) *pi'nus* (BD). 91.
    chrysop'tera (BD). 91.
    leu'cobronchia'lis. 92.
    ruficapil'la (BD). 94.
    cela'ta (BD). 95.
    peregri'na (C). 96.
Helminthopha'ginœ. § 9, IV - VI.
Helmi'therus (RAFINESQUE) *vermi'vorus* (BP). 89.
Hirun'do (L) *horreo'rum* (BARTON). 142.
Hirundi'nidœ. § 12.
Hydeme'les (BD) ? *Ludovicia'na* (L.). 232.
Hylo'tomus pilea'tus (BD). 324.

Icte'ria (V) *vi'rens* (BD). 132.
Icterinœ. § 9, XII.
Ic'terus (BRISSON) *Baltimo're* (BAUDIN). 252.
    spu'rius (BP). 255.
Icte'ridœ. § 17.
Icterinœ. § 17, V.

Jun'co (WAGLER) *hyema'lis* (SCLATER). 223.

Lani'idœ, Laniinœ. § 14.
Lino'ta Brewsteri. 185.

Melaner'pes erythroce'phalus (S). 315.
Melospi'za melo'dia (BD). 202.
    Lincol'ni (BD). 207.
    palus'tris (BD). 208.
Mi'mus polyglot'tus (B). 45.
    Carolinen'sis (G). 46.
Miminœ. § 1, II and III.
Mniotil'ta va'ria (V). 97.
Molo'thrus pe'coris (S). 246.
Motacil'lidœ. § 8.
Myiar'chus crini'tus (C). 275.
Myiodioc'tes Canaden'sis (A). 127.
    pusil'lus (BP). 129.
    mitra'tus (A). 129, NOTE.
    minu'tus (BD). 129, NOTE.

Nisus. See *Accipiter*.
Nycta'le (BREHM) *Tengmal'mi*.
    var. *Richardso'ni* (BP). 333.
    Aca'dica (BP). 334.
Nyc'tea (STEPHENS) *ni'vea* (G). 339.

Oporor'nis a'gilis (BD). 88.
    formo'sus (BD). 88, NOTE.
Or'tyx (STEPHENS) *Virginia'nus* (BP). 393.
Os'cines. §§ 1 - 18.
O'tus (CU) *vulga'ris* (L).
    var. *Wilsonia'nus* (ALLEN). 329.
    brachyo'tus. 330.

Pan'dion halia'ëtus (SAVIGNY),
    var. *Carolinen'sis* (BP). 373.
Pa'rula America'na (BP). 99.
Pa'rus atricapil'lus (L). 59.
    Hudso'nicus (FORSTER). 63.
Pa'ridœ, Parinœ. § 4.
Pas'ser domes'ticus (L). 235.
Passer'culus (BP) *prin'ceps* (MAYNARD). 195.
    savan'na (BP). 197.
Passerel'la ilia'ca (S). 221.
Pas'seres. § 1 - 19.

Perissoglos'sa tigri'na (BD). 102.
Periso'reus Canaden'sis (BP). 268.
Petrocheli'don lu'nifrons (C). 144.
Philohe'la mi'nor (G). 399.
Pica'rice. §§ 20-25.
Pico'ides (LACEPEDE) *arc'ticus* (G). 319.
                America'nus (BREHM). 320.
Pi'cus villo'sus (L). 321.
     pubes'cens (L). 322.
Pi'cidæ. § 25.
Pini'cola enuclea'tor (V). 172.
Pi'pilo erythropthal'mus. 226.
Plectropha'nes niva'lis (MEYER). 185.
        Lappo'nicus (SELBY). 188.
Poliop'tila cœru'lea (SCLATER). 58.
Pooece'tes grami'neus (BD). 200.
Prog'ne purpu'rea (B). 150.
Protonota'ria citræ'a (BD). 90.
Pyran'ga ru'bra (V). 134.
     æsti'va (V). 136.
Pyr'gita monta'na ( ). 286.

Quis'colus(V)*purpu'reus*(LICHTENSTEIN).258.
     and var. *æ'neus* (BD). 261.
Quiscalinæ. § 17, VI and VII.

Rapto'res. Chap. III.
Re'gulus (CU) *calen'dula* (LICHTENSTEIN). 53.
     satra'pa (LICHTENSTEIN). 55.
     Cuvie'ri (AUD). 57, NOTE.
Regulinæ. § 3, I.

Saxicol'idæ. § II.
Sayor'nis (BP) *fus'cus* (BD). 277.
Scoleco'phagus ferrugi'neus (S). 255.
Scolopa'cidæ. § 32.
Scops (SAVIGNY) *a'sio* (BP). 335.
Sciu'rus (S) *noveboracen'sis* (NUTTALL). 81.
     Ludovicia'nus (BP). 83.
     aurocapil'lus (S). 84.
Seto'phaga ruticil'la (S). 130.
Setophaginæ. § 9, XI and XII.
Sia'lia (S) *sialis* (BD²). 50.
Sit'ta (L) *Carolinen'sis* (GMELIN). 63.
     Canaden'sis (L). 66.
Sit'tidæ. § 5.
Spheo'tyto (GLOGER) *cunicula'ria.*
     var. *hypogæ'a* (CASSIN) 343.
Sphyrapi'cus va'rius (BD).
     var. *nucha'lis* (ALLEN). 318.

Spizel'la socia'lis (BP). 210.
     monti'cola (BD). 212.
     pusil'la (BP). 215.
Sturnel'la (V) *mag'na* (S). 241.
Strix flam'mea (L), *America'na* (A). 328.
Stri'gidæ. § 26.
Sur'nia (DUMERIL) *u'lula* (BP).
     var. *Hudso'nica* (RIDGWAY). 342.
Sylvico'lidæ. § 9; *Sylvicolinæ*, § 9, I-X.
Sylvi'idæ. § 3.
Syr'nium (SAVIGNY) *Lappo'nicum* (L).
     var. *cine'reum* (RIDGWAY). 331.
     nebulo'sum (G). 332.

Tachycine'ta (C) *bi'color* (CASSIN). 146.
Te'trao Canaden'sis (L). 386.
Tetrao'nidæ, Tetraoninæ. § 30.
Thryo'thorus (V) *Ludovicia'nus* (BP). 74.
Tro'chilus co'lubris (L). 302.
Trochi'lidæ, Trochilinæ. § 22.
Troglo'dytes hyema'lis (V). 71.
     æ'don (V). 75.
Troglody'tidæ. § 7.
Tur'dus (L) *musteli'nus* (GMELIN). 29.
     fusces'cens (STEPHENS). 32.
     Palla'si (C). 34.
     Swainso'ni (C). 36.
     Ali'ciæ (CASSIN). 39.
     migrato'rius (L). 41.
     næ'vius (GMELIN). 44.
Tur'didæ. § 1; *Turdinæ*, § 1, I.
Tyran'nus (CU) *Carolinen'sis* (BD). 273.
     Dominicen'sis (RICH). 273, (a), NOTE.
Tyran'nidæ, Tyranninæ. § 19.

Vi'reo solita'rius (V). 152.
     fla'vifrons (V). 153.
     oliva'ceus (V). 155.
     gil'vus (BP). 157.
     Philadel'phicus (CASSIN). 159.
     noveboracen'sis (BP). 160.
Vireo'nidæ. § 13.

Xanthoce'phalus icteroce'phalus (BD). 252, NOTE.

Zenædu'ra Carolinen'sis (BP). 384.
Zonotri'chia (S) *albicol'lis* (BP). 217.
     leu'cophrys (S). 220.

---

² In Dr. Coues' Check List, *Haldeman.*

www.ingramcontent.com/pod-product-compliance
Lightning Source LLC
Chambersburg PA
CBHW022104300426
44117CB00007B/584